DATE DUE C/R 2005

THE
DEMOCRACY
ADVANTAGE

THE
DEMOCRACY
ADVANTAGE

HOW DEMOCRACIES PROMOTE
PROSPERITY AND PEACE

MORTON H. HALPERIN
JOSEPH T. SIEGLE
MICHAEL M. WEINSTEIN

A COUNCIL ON FOREIGN RELATIONS BOOK

Routledge
New York • London

Published in 2005 by
Routledge
270 Madison Avenue
New York, NY 10016
www.routledge-ny.com

Published in Great Britain by
Routledge
2 Park Square
Milton Park, Abingdon,
Oxon OX14 4RN U.K.
www.routledge.co.uk

Founded in 1921, the Council on Foreign Relations is an independent, national membership organization and a nonpartisan center for scholars dedicated to producing and disseminating ideas so that individual and corporate members, as well as policymakers, journalists, students, and interested citizens in the United States and other countries, can better understand the world and the foreign policy choices facing the United States and other governments. The Council does this by convening meetings; conducting a wide-ranging Studies program; publishing Foreign Affairs, the preeminent journal covering international affairs and U.S. foreign policy; maintaining a diverse membership; sponsoring Independent Task Forces; and providing up-to-date information about the world and U.S. foreign policy on the Council's website, www.cfr.org.

The Council takes no institutional position on policy issues and has no affiliation with the U.S. Government. All statements of fact and expressions of opinion contained in its publications are the sole responsiblity of the author or authors.

Routledge is an imprint of the Taylor and Francis Group.

Printed in the United Stated of America on acid-free paper.

10 9 8 7 6 5 4 3 2 1

Library of Congress Cataloging-in-Publication Data

Halperin, Morton H.
The democracy advantage : how democracies promote prosperity and peace/by Morton H. Halperin, Joseph T. Siegle, and Michael M. Weinstein.
p. cm.
Includes bibliographical references and index.

ISBN 0-415-95052-X (hb : alk. paper)

1. Democracy. 2. Economic development—Political aspects. I. Siegle, Joseph T., 1961- II. Weinstein, Michael M. III. Title.
JC423.H3734 2004
321.8—dc22
2004009571

in memory of Carol Pitchersky

Table of Contents

Acknowledgments

From the initial discussions that were the genesis of this book through the research, critical feedback, and physical production that have gone into its publication, we have benefited enormously from the intellect, expertise, encouragement, and hard work of numerous individuals whose help made this book possible and to whom we are deeply grateful.

Les Gelb and Larry Korb were early and unwavering enthusiasts for this project and the imperative of better understanding the complex interrelationships between democracy and development so as to guide policy during this exceptional era of political and economic transition. We also thank the Council on Foreign Relations for its comprehensive support to this project throughout its lifetime. It has served as a superb institutional home to this effort. We owe a debt of gratitude to Hank Greenberg, in particular, for his vision to spur the Council to devote more attention to the intersection between politics and economics.

The project benefited intellectually from some of the world's sharpest minds on the political and economic challenges to development. These contributions came in various forms. We would first like to acknowledge attendees to the White Oak workshop, which served as a kick-off to the project in its most unformulated stage: Nancy Birdsall, Larry Diamond, David Dollar, Stephen Heintz, Robert Herman, Terry Karl, Allan Meltzer, Joshua Muravchik, Joan Nelson, Minxin Pei, Theodore Piccone, Joseph Stiglitz, Nicolas van de Walle, Mark Weisbrot, Jennifer Windsor, and David Yang. We also profited from several subsequent study group sessions that aided in the evolution of our thinking. Additional participants to these meetings included: Jonathan Berman, Gail Buyske, Carolyn Campbell, John Cavanagh, Natasha Despotovich, Nadia Diuk, Eleanor Fox, Carol Graham, Wendy Luers, Barry Metzger, Sakiko Fukuda-Parr, Kilaparti

Ramakrishna, Amity Shlaes, and Samuel Smoots. Feedback from participants in several additional seminars further deepened our understanding of common perceptions in the foreign policy community on the relationship between democracy and development. We appreciate their engagement and contributions.

A number of individuals gave generously of their time in one-on-one sessions. Their expertise and perspective generated an enormous amount of constructive feedback in particular subject areas. We are thus grateful to Daniel Adams, Thomas Carothers, Carl Eicher, David Hamburg, Gary Hufbauer, Bruce Klatsky, Monty Marshall, Johanna Mendelson-Forman, Barry Metzger, and Adam Przeworski.

Detailed comments on draft versions of the manuscript by James Lindsay and an anonymous reviewer also contributed valuably to the final product.

We are perhaps most indebted to the research assistance of Kristin Gosselin and Cheryl Igiri whose talents, creativity, enthusiasm, attention to detail, and tireless commitment have left their mark on every page of this book. Owing to the broadness of the subject matter as well as the quantitative and narrative analysis involved, this project presented a particularly robust series of research challenges. Nonetheless, these two young scholars were indefatigable in tracking down relevant information in whichever dimension of the undertaking they were working.

Essential research and administrative support was also graciously provided by Rene Bartholomew, Michelle Baute, Ian Bournland, Olivia Carballo, Mirna Galic, Bridget Grage, Julanar Green, Lilita Gusts, Oakley Johnson, Raena Khorram, Jonathan Kirschner, Michael McCarthy, Elizabeth Packard, Elli Parsa, Christine Quinn, Courtney Rusin, Garnett Russell, Christie Seefried, Marcia Sprules, Connie Stagnaro, and Tom Wasiak.

We are furthermore grateful to Trish Dorff and David Kellogg who shared extensively of their expertise and time to streamline the manuscript style— and ensure early drafts found their way into the hands of the right publisher. Their efforts led us to Routledge, who in the person of Rob Tempio has demonstrated all the intellectual vibrancy, enthusiasm, and openness that we could have hoped for in an editor.

Finally, we wish to thank the Hewlett Foundation, the Open Society Institute, and BP for their commitment to and interest in the unfolding questions of how democracy influences economic development. Their financial support to this project has been highly valued. The views and positions taken in the book, naturally, are solely those of the authors.

Foreword

Over the years many have claimed that some kind of dictatorship is needed to get economic development going in poor countries. Dictatorships are more capable of maintaining stability, holding wages down, and forcing high savings rates that lead to economic development. Economic growth under autocratic regimes eventually leads to democracy. We are invariably reminded of these perceived truths during economic or political crises in poor countries. And poor countries — with their grinding material privation, corruption, propensity for conflict, and instability — are no strangers to crisis.

The Democracy Advantage: How Democracies Promote Prosperity and Peace provides a cogent, well-documented refutation of the dictator-is-best nostrum. Moving past the anecdotes that have perpetuated the myth of authoritarian superiority, this book painstakingly examines the social and economic track record of all developing countries over the past 40 years. In the process, it exposes the fact that the development performance of the typical authoritarian government has been abysmal. By contrast, developing countries that adopt democratic institutions have posted consistently stronger economic results — providing more ample supplies of basic goods like health, education, and food production that shape the lives of the vast majority of people in poor countries.

Recognition of a democratic advantage should reshape the West's strategies to reduce poverty, enhance economic development, and stoke opportunity in the two-thirds of the world that remains mired in poverty. Yet forces within the current global system that might push individual countries in a democratic direction are missing. International banks and multinational corporations often feel more comfortable with a strong, if autocratic, regime. Development strategies typically ignore how aid recipients are governed. Such direct or implicit support for autocratic leadership reflects a more fundamental reality — many people living in industrialized democracies do not believe in democracy as a universal principle.

Economic progress in the modern world requires people to discuss ideas candidly and imaginatively. This is far more likely in open societies. Though at times slow to make decisions and quick to generate disagreement, democracies offer unmatched economic and political strength. They embrace participation, competition of ideas, and access to information — all of which leads to more responsible politics, checks on the hegemony of an ideology, and self-corrective mechanisms to mitigate disaster. Good governance and sustained strong economies feed on each other.

We must also take the right lessons from history and not be stampeded into sacrificing the fruits of democracy in the face of pressing security arguments. Fascism and communism ensnared large segments of the global population in their ideological vise — populations who otherwise may well have chosen the path of freedom. Protagonists on both sides of the Cold War perpetuated authoritarian systems so as to advance their ambitions. Today, the war on terrorism threatens to do the same, once again making the promotion of democracy subservient to demolishing this latest evil. Yet although democracies are not immune from terrorism, they are far less likely to be complicit of coddling terrorist networks or proliferating weapons of mass destruction. Many policy thinkers argue that we face a choice between security and democracy. *The Democracy Advantage* proves this to be a false choice. Only by enthusiastically supporting democracies and democratizing countries can the industrialized powers buttress a stable, secure, and prosperous world. We bypass democracy promotion at this juncture of history at our own peril.

This book offers bold, practical policy recommendations of what should be done to knock down the historical and bureaucratic barriers that constrain the West's support of democracy in poor countries. It makes a compelling case that an agenda to promote economic progress should start with a focus on poor countries that are taking the difficult steps to democratize. The creation by the United States of the Millennium Challenge Account, which rewards countries that rule justly, is a hopeful development in this direction.

This is an important work addressing some of the most fundamental challenges of our time. Everyone who has an interest in the economic development of poor countries, democratization, or international security can learn from this shrewd analysis.

George Soros

Prologue

Debate over the relationship between democracy and development has long been controversial. Although Western nations have embraced liberal, pluralistic political traditions and enjoyed widespread prosperity, there have been persistent doubts in diplomatic and academic circles over whether democracy is right for other, less prosperous parts of the world. For most of the post-World War II era, the prevailing view has been that economic development should precede democracy. The urbanization, expanded literacy, and broadened middle class that this economic growth could be expected to bring would pave the way for the political power sharing, compromise, and common identity required for a democracy to succeed. By implication, this view holds that autocratic governments are better able to generate development at the early stages of a country's development. Poor countries have been seen as particularly ill suited for democracy. The absence of a literate, middle-class society made them susceptible to manipulation by elites. Self-governance in predominantly poor societies would also lead to demands for immediate redress from their many problems. The state would be forced to take fiscally irresponsible and unsustainable policies. The ensuing macroeconomic instability would undercut prospects for growth. Everyone would be worse off. Holding elections in the already fractious ethnic settings that characterize many low-income societies was likely to be polarizing. Civil strife would be the inevitable outcome. Compounding these concerns has been the belief that the cultural values in certain societies—be they Asian, African, Eastern European, the former Soviet republics, or Arab—were inherently incompatible with democracy.

Despite these views, since the late 1970s and particularly the end of the Cold War, a steady stream of poor countries has taken substantive steps toward democracy. Is this a good thing? Should the international community more vigorously support the emergence of democracy? Or should stability be the primary goal? What are the implications for economic development and international security?

Nearly 15 years after the collapse of communism, we felt it was time to take stock of what we now know about the relationship between democracy and development—and in the process attempt to provide answers to these questions. Thus, this book. Our collective experience in the foreign policy, development, journalistic, and academic worlds suggested to us that the recent democratizing trend was indeed positive for alleviating poverty and advancing economic development. Rather than there being a trade-off between democracy and development, we saw the two as compatible and complementary. In fact, given the propensity of many Third World authoritarian governments to monopolize political *and* economic power, thereby stymieing broad-based progress, in our view, only after some degree of popular political participation were established could most poor societies realize economic advancement.

We realize our position cuts across the grain of much conventional thinking on this subject. Popularized in 1959 by Seymour Martin Lipset, the revered former political sociologist at Harvard and Stanford, and frequently repeated since then in scholarly journals, textbooks, newspaper columns, and foreign policy lectures, the economic superiority of authoritarian governments over democracies at the early stages of development comes close to dogma within foreign policy circles. This view had particularly deep resonance during the Cold War when the prospects for any sudden shifts to democracy appeared remote and the West was supporting numerous autocrats in its life-and-death struggle against communism. Rather than fading away since the demise of the Soviet Union, however, the conventional view has instead been revitalized by a new generation of writers and continues to be taught as doctrine to graduate students in international relations programs at leading universities.[1] The belief in an "authoritarian advantage" remains widespread among many economists, national security experts, ambassadors to Third World countries, aid officials, heads of United Nations (UN) missions, and other individuals who shape the policies of the international community toward the developing world.

More is at stake in this debate than reducing poverty and spurring economic growth around the world, pressing as these goals are. Countries facing stagnant economic development are more vulnerable to political instability and violent upheavals. Once civil conflicts begin, they tend to persist and eventually to spill over into neighboring countries. Similarly, to the extent that autocracy and underdevelopment contribute to the viability of international terrorist organizations, *realpolitik* calculations to support certain authoritarian governments may, in fact, be undermining international security.

Our research shows that democracies have compelling advantages over their authoritarian counterparts in fostering social and economic development. We will present the evidence. But our purpose goes beyond an examination of the track record. Recognizing the economic and security virtues of democracy in poor countries fundamentally alters strategies for augmenting international development and security in the early twenty-first century. Making such changes will be a considerable undertaking. With this book we aim to advance this process by laying out a series of far-reaching recommendations for United States and international policymakers to consider as the global community grapples with some of the most pressing challenges of our time.

CHAPTER 1
Exposing a 50-Year-Old Myth

Dictatorship is like a big proud ship—steaming away across the ocean with a great hulk and powerful engines driving it. It's going fast and strong and looks like nothing could stop it. What happens? Your fine ship strikes something—under the surface. Maybe it's a mine or a reef, maybe it's a torpedo or an iceberg. And your wonderful ship sinks! Now take democracy. It's like riding on a raft, a rickety raft that was put together in a hurry. We get tossed about on the waves, it's bad going, and our feet are always wet. But that raft doesn't sink . . . It's the raft that will get to the shore at last.[1]

A Yankee Businesman in New Hampshire

This book makes the case that democracy does a better job raising living standards in poor countries than does authoritarian government. At first, you might think the claim sounds a bit trite—What decent person would argue otherwise? The truth is that for the past half-century or so, the bulk of academic literature, United States policymakers, and Third World leaders have done so. While America's support for selected dictators across Latin America, sub-Saharan Africa, and Asia has been primarily based on Cold War calculations, this has been further justified by the conviction that democracy in poor countries breeds economic stagnation and civil unrest.

Today, it is politically incorrect to extol publicly the virtues of autocracies—countries where leaders are not popularly elected nor subject to meaningful checks and balances. Nonetheless, the view that these governments do a better job of promoting economic growth and stability among poor countries remains firmly entrenched in the minds of many world

1

leaders, economists, national security advisors, business executives, political scientists, and international civil servants. According to this perspective, promoting democracy in poor countries is naïve and potentially dangerous.

Which side wins this debate matters, a lot. Acknowledging a democratic advantage for development—that is, a nation's social and economic progress—opens the door to a major rethinking of political and economic policy toward the developing world. The case for the United States and other industrialized democracies to back unstintingly democratization throughout the Third World becomes overwhelming. This would mark a sharp turnaround from current, tentative measures, where meaningful support for the emergence of democracy often falls short of the rhetoric lofted in its name.

Many readers are no doubt wondering at this point, "What about China?" China's rapid growth over the past 25 years makes it the contemporary poster child of authoritarian-led economic development. Doesn't it pose a major obstacle to our claim about the superiority of the democratic over the authoritarian model? Although a complex and still unfolding phenomenon, we will argue that, paradoxically, China's stunning economic performance helps make our case by highlighting the exceptional and fragile nature of economic growth in autocratic systems. First, however, let's take a look at the contours of China's economic boom.

Starting with market reforms in 1978 giving peasants incentives to boost agricultural productivity, China has experienced a nearly uninterrupted expansion of its economy. Income per person, adjusted for inflation, has risen more than six-fold over the past 25 years, to $940 from $151. In just the past decade, China has grown to the sixth from the eleventh largest economy in the world, with a gross domestic product (GDP) of $1.2 trillion.

Like other East Asian countries, China rode an export-led development strategy to economic stardom. Trade makes up 50 percent of its economy and 5 percent of world exports. Lured by cheap labor and the prospect of gaining access to a market of 1.3 billion people, international investors have flocked to China, pouring some $40 billion a year into its economy in recent years, or about 5 percent of GDP. Building on one of the highest savings rates in the world—40 percent of GDP—China has upgraded its communications technology and modernized its roads, ports, bridges, dams, and irrigation systems. In a single generation, farmers have switched from using donkeys to tractors. Television now reaches almost all city dwellers and the Internet connects with more than 12 percent of them.[2] To facilitate its transition to a market economy, China established experimental capitalist enclaves known as Special Economic Zones that were free of many of the legal and bureaucratic restrictions that were typical of China's command economy and that hindered trade, foreign investment, and technology transfers.

As China's economy has grown, the quality of life of its people has improved. More than 90 percent of children attend primary school and 50 percent make it through high school. Life expectancy has reached more than 70 years, comparable to that of the United States and Europe. Malnutrition rates plummeted by nearly 50 percent in the 1990s, and untold millions of people have risen above the poverty line. In short, China has become an economic dynamo.

The Argument for Authoritarian Rule

China's experience is refueling the long-running debate about which type of political system is better able to boost economic development. Doesn't China's performance validate the conventional assertion that autocratic governments are better at mobilizing economic growth in poor countries? Is our instinctive desire to see democracy flourish in the developing world simply a projection of Western values? If we were genuinely honest with ourselves, wouldn't we acknowledge that there really is a "cruel choice" between democracy and development?[3] If so, shouldn't we be pragmatic and support authoritarian governments in the world's poorest countries in order to reduce the misery of their citizens? Then, after material needs were addressed, as part of some Maslowian hierarchy of priorities, we could focus on the more ethereal issues of freedom and self-governance.

In other words, after taking a good, hard look at China, shouldn't we adopt the view that has prevailed among foreign policy experts almost since the end of World War II? Popularized by Seymour Martin Lipset, this perspective holds that democracies can flourish only if they are grounded in a literate and urbanized middle class. In poorer societies, its adherents argue, democracies can be manipulated by opportunistic leaders who will make populist promises to get elected but pursue their selfish priorities once in office. Unrestrained by adequate counterweights, these unscrupulous politicians are likely to abuse their power and rig the system to maximize their interests. The economy stagnates. Social conditions deteriorate. Alas, the disciples of Lipset argue, while democracy is a desirable goal, it is one that can best be achieved after a sequence of economic development and social maturation occurs. Democracy should be seen as the crowning achievement of a long process of modernization.

To spur development in poor nations, they assert, authoritarian[4] governments are better able to marshal the limited resources available and direct them toward productive activities that will increase economic output. Because of the superior organizational abilities inherent in their hierarchal structures, only authoritarian governments can match resources to the urgent tasks besetting them of increasing savings and investing them in public works like highways and dams, building up a disciplined military, enforcing the rule of law, and creating a functional educational system. Authoritarian governments can undertake all of these things more efficiently than can lumbering democracies. And, as the labor force becomes more skilled, more sophisticated technology can be employed and productive capacity further improved.

It was with this reasoning that Samuel Huntington, in his still influential 1968 classic *Political Order in Changing Societies*, touted the advantages of one-party states for low-income countries. Dominant political parties, particularly those backed by the military, were seen as unifying institutions.

The efficiency of authoritarian systems also supposedly lies in their perceived longer-term planning horizon. Spared of the arbitrary deadlines imposed by elections, they can identify long-range objectives, decide on the best policies for achieving them and implement these policies without deviating from the master plan. And there is no need to waste time and energy in endless negotiations with special interest groups, as democratic governments must do. These groups can be safely ignored, and unhappy though they might be at their impotence at first, they will ultimately realize they also benefit from the modernization efforts of a benign dictatorship.

In other words, by banishing politics from its economic policymaking, an authoritarian government is able to focus on the bigger picture. And it will seek to find solutions that benefit the society as a whole, rather than this or that favored group.

By dint of the same freedom from competing interest groups, the reasoning goes, authoritarian governments are more capable of instituting a fair, consistent rule of law, better able to establish and protect the property rights that form the basis for investment and asset accumulation, and in a stronger position to enforce contracts—thus assuring firms that enter into agreements that they will be paid.

The appeal of this perspective extended beyond the Cold War mindset in the West that the ideological battle against communism necessitated supporting friendly authoritarian governments. The orthodoxy of this view was captured in the World Bank's 1993 report *The East Asian Miracle*[5] in which the global development bank endorsed the notion that authoritarian governments were better able to generate economic growth in the early stages of their development. Indeed, it was the meteoric growth of the East Asian Tigers (South Korea and Taiwan) that seamlessly bridged the Cold War moorings of the authoritarian advantage thesis to its persistent post-Cold War resonance. Although the East Asian financial crisis of the late 1990s caused the buoyancy of this view to lag somewhat, the underpinnings of the mentality remain strong. This is reflected in a 2002 report to the Asian Development Bank that concludes, " . . . whereas democracies have been slow in grappling with poverty, the authoritarian regimes in the miracle economies achieved spectacular success . . . In a democracy with a thriving civil society, the process of policy consultation, adoption, and execution is much more time-consuming and involves many more procedural formalities than under an authoritarian regime."[6]

A 2003 best seller by Fareed Zakaria, *The Future of Freedom: Illiberal Democracy at Home and Abroad,* picks up these themes in a contemporary repostulation of the Lipset–Huntington argument. Coupling the perceived superiority of the authoritarian growth record among poor countries and the notion that democracies have never regressed to authoritarianism once they've surpassed per capita income levels of $6,000, Zakaria argues that the goal should be to support "liberal autocracies" in the developing world.

Authoritarian governments in poor countries supposedly have another huge advantage over democracies. They are insulated from the demands of the poor. In a system of one person, one vote, democratic governments in developing countries are pressured to respond to the population's desire for costly entitlements like free schools, decent health care, minimum wage laws, labor rights, and generous pension plans.[7] Not only would caving into these demands break the national budget, it would also discourage savings and investment. What foreign business would want to pour serious money into a country with so many extra costs attached, when it could move it instead to low-wage countries like China and Vietnam? Democracy's everlooming electoral cycle puts great pressure on politicians to extend fiscal commitments to particular constituencies that undermine a nation's longterm economic health.

The argument further claims that the firm hand of an authoritarian government is required to maintain order and stability in backward nations in which tribal loyalties, economic disparities, social tensions, and regional conflicts are rife. Just look at Africa, Asia, the Middle East, and parts of Latin America, especially the former colonies. Too often, the people living there lack a real sense of national identity. In such places, only a strong national government can provide the security needed for people to go about their daily lives and safeguard the highways, bridges, and dams from insurgents. In other words, only a monopoly of power in the early stages of a country's economic development can prevent anarchy.

This is the recurrent theme in Robert Kaplan's widely read articles on democratization in the post-Cold War era.[8] An unabashed Huntington revivalist, Kaplan challenges the West's liberal instincts to promote democracy in the developing world. Lacking the Western traditions of tolerance and multiculturalism, efforts to encourage democratization in other regions of the world are likely to be highly destabilizing. Rather than advancing democracy, civil conflict and the emergence of neo-autocrats is the more likely result. A realist-based strategy of supporting authoritarian governments that can consolidate the authority of the state is what is needed.

According to this school of thought, democracies in ethnically diverse societies are highly vulnerable to social fragmentation. Each tribe or clan will be reluctant to cede any authority or share power with rival groups, leading to hair-trigger tensions and the constant threat of civil conflict. State policymakers are left wringing their hands at the near impossibility of coordinated action to alleviate national ills. More ominously, weak politicians will have obvious incentives to stir up ethnic divisions in order to cast themselves as defenders of their own cultures against the machinations of rival groups. Such a stance might win them public office, but it can also unleash violent passions. In fact, it is argued, the very act of staging democratic elections in the diverse societies of much of the developing world can trigger conflict.[9] Single-party rule, by contrast, can channel a profusion of interests into a central political apparatus that can minimize ethnic divisions and clamp down on troublemakers who would attempt to exploit them.

In another best-selling book from 2003, Amy Chua, in *World on Fire: How Exporting Free Market Democracy Breeds Ethnic Hatred and Global Instability*, argues that the global spread of "free-market democracy" has been a principal cause of ethnic instability and violence throughout the world. Her concern is that by increasing the political voice and power of the majority, democratization has fostered the emergence of demagogues who opportunistically whip up mass hatred against the wealthy minority elite found in most societies. The result has been ethnic confiscation, authoritarian backlash, and mass killing.[10]

In short, the tenets of the authoritarian advantage doctrine continue to resonate in contemporary debates over prosperity and peace. This directly factors into policy over what international actors should do in regions of the world facing political or economic transition: the Arab world, the former Soviet Union, Africa, Asia, and Latin America. The bottom-line policy question remains—should the international community promote democratization in poor countries?

The experts who favor authoritarian rule for poor nations, to be clear, are not disavowing the goals of freedom and democracy. They are no friends of tyranny. Rather, they say, they are realists and their pragmatism is a surer path to economic prosperity and democracy than the principled, though idealist notions of democracy proponents.

In their view, the key is timing. Once a society has reached some middle-income level of development, a transition to democracy becomes viable. Education and literacy levels will have risen to a point that political charlatans can less easily dupe the general population. With economic development comes urbanization, a precondition for the formation of genuine political parties with broad popular support.

A country that has achieved a middle-income level of development is also more likely to have an established middle class that by its nature is a moderating political force. If poor people are forced by necessity to strive for short term gain, the middle class is concerned about economic stability and the prospects for steadily improving their lot. The middle class has more incentives to work within the political system than against it, and greater fondness for pragmatic politicians than for fiery radicals.

As an economy develops, the attitudes of a nation's elites also mature. They will find common interest with the middle class on many issues. And with the threat by populist politicians to their wealth and status receding, they will become more amenable to sharing power. Little by little, they will come to accept the concept of political equality, even to the point of giving the poor a voice in the nation's affairs.

This whole process arguably characterizes the transition to democracy by the southern European dictatorships of Spain and Portugal and certain of the East Asian Tigers (South Korea and Taiwan).[11] In all those countries, political participation was restricted to a single party for decades after World War II. Sound economic policies were pursued that facilitated rapid and stable economic development. Though Franco's Spain and Salazar's Portugal had fascist features, none of these states was totalitarian, enabling a private sector to develop and flourish. Some independent civic and associational life was allowed, fostering a degree of popular participation, provided it was not politically oriented. Over time and with varying degrees of political turmoil, transitions to more pluralistic political systems were successfully undertaken once these countries reached a fairly comfortable range of middle-income development. For Portugal and South Korea, this was a per capita income of roughly $6,500.[12] The level was $10,500 for Spain and Taiwan.

Democratic Disappointment in Latin America

The "development first" school also invokes Latin America to buttress its position. Latin America began its democratization process in the late 1970s and 1980s. Virtually every country in the region took steps away from military rule, eventually establishing competitive multi-party political systems. The average per capita income in Latin America was roughly $1,800, ranging from around $650 in countries like Honduras, Nicaragua, and Guyana to just under $7,000 for Argentina when it moved to civilian rule in 1983. The late 1980s and early 1990s were subsequently a period of robust, rapid growth for Latin America, raising hopes that democratization and prosperity could grow hand-in-hand.

However, the results in a number of Latin countries have been much more subdued since then, with growth slowing and poverty rates on the rise.[13] The region's notorious economic disparities appear to be as acute as ever, and corruption is widespread. Nine of the 20 countries in the region were ranked in the bottom 30 percent of countries around the world by Transparency International, a leading nonprofit advocacy group, in its 2003 corruption perception survey. It is little surprise therefore, that political tensions have been boiling over. In 2003 and 2004, Venezuela, Ecuador, Bolivia, Paraguay, Argentina, and Peru have all had political protests resulting in violence and deaths.

Perhaps nowhere are these tensions more evident than in Venezuela. The economy has been steadily contracting there since 1980, with per capita incomes shrinking from $4,400 to $3,300. Railing against the sharp income disparities within Venezuelan society, populist Hugo Chavez, a former junior army officer who had led a failed coup attempt in 1992, was elected in 1999, promising to improve the lives of the country's poor. Chavez has undertaken high-profile programs to address poverty such as Plan Bolivar. This mobilized military personnel to construct various infrastructure projects including highways, schools, and hospitals as well as to provide various social services. Conditions have only seemed to worsen, however.

Concurrently, Chavez took actions that weakened Venezuela's long-established democratic institutions, including amending the constitution so as to centralize power in the presidency,[14] stacking the courts with his allies, politicizing Venezuela's armed forces, removing civilian checks on the military, attacking the credibility of the country's political institutions, and bypassing the legislature through referendums. Despite the controversy created by such actions, Chavez maintains widespread support among the 30 percent of the population living under the poverty line, keeping him in power. Thumbing his nose at his political opponents who have not been able to displace him at the polls, he boasts of his revolutionary ideology and intention to stay in power until 2021.[15]

A short-lived coup against Chavez in April 2002 vividly demonstrated the strains between social classes in Venezuelan society. While many from the middle and upper echelons of society and even important elements of organized labor backed it, the poor rose up in Chavez's defense. Clashes resulted in the deaths of at least 12 people. This resistance, the ineptitude of the coup leaders, the uneasiness of the general population with the autocratic nature of the coup plotters, and widespread condemnation by the international community resulted in a sudden evaporation of support for the coup. Chavez was returned to power within two days. A subsequent three-month strike in late 2002 and early 2003 again brought the country to a standstill and exposed the depth of Venezuela's division. To their credit, both the government and the strikers sought to curb violence. However, once the strike was broken, Chavez had a number of the strike leaders, led by executives from the state oil company, arrested.[16] In 2004, a referendum to recall Chavez failed—perpetuating Venezuela's political impasse.

All of this turmoil hurt the economy. Venezuela experienced a contraction in real GDP per capita of 27 percent between 1998 and 2003. The social, political, and economic cleavages of Venezuelan society appear destined to pull the country into still deeper malaise. It thus represents the worst of both scenarios—deteriorating economic performance and hardening dictatorial rule. It is the prospect of such a democratic reversal that many fear will engulf the entire region.[17]

The divergent experiences of China and Venezuela compel us to ask, as the conventional school would have us do: Is supporting democracy the right thing to do in the developing world? Doesn't it actually hinder economic development? In the process, are we ultimately undermining the likelihood that these countries can establish sustainable democracies?

Defying the Predictions, Democracy Works
We answer these questions emphatically: supporting democracy in developing countries is the right thing to do. It does not hurt their pursuit of prosperity and peace. It helps it.

Before proceeding further, let's take a moment to clarify what we mean by democracy since this gets to the heart of the debate. When we refer to democracy we mean those governance systems in which national leaders are selected through free and fair elections, there are institutions that foster a shared distribution of power, and citizens have extensive opportunities to participate in political life.[18] This explicitly requires a high degree of basic political freedoms, civil liberties, and political rights. Countries that hold flawed elections or technically fair elections where opposition political parties cannot campaign freely or an independent press does not exist are not democracies. The notion of an "illiberal democracy," which some writers have propounded, is an oxymoron that only muddies the waters.[19] Clearly, a state does not become a democracy overnight but rather reaches this threshold only after a period of political evolution. As such, a wide spectrum of governance systems, from the most oppressive authoritarian to the most liberal democracy, exists. However, when we refer to democracies, we include only those countries that have been determined to meet the robust criteria of democratic governance (see Appendices A and B for lists). Others that may not have reached this threshold, though are making progress along the spectrum are considered democratizers. Those in the lower tier of this governance spectrum are categorized as autocracies. With that said, let's take a look at the evidence.

Defying the predictions of the "development first" perspective, some 70 low-income countries have made marked advancements toward democracy over the past two decades. More than half of these countries, 43 in all, had fully authoritarian governments before they started their transition. According to the conventional theory, this shouldn't have happened. Poor countries were not supposed to be able to undertake, much less sustain, democratic reforms. Yet, the quest for freedom and citizens' desire to gain greater control over their destiny has been unrelenting. In Africa, Asia, Eastern Europe, Latin America, and the former Soviet Union—all regions long considered resistant to democratic governance—societies have demonstrated the universality of this aspiration.

Not only were these low-income countries supposed to be unable to democratize, however, they were expected to stagnate economically. And yet the opposite happened. As we examine in detail in Chapter 2, low-income democracies and democratizing countries have outperformed their authoritarian counterparts on a full range of development indicators. Whether we consider life expectancy, literacy, access to clean drinking water, agricultural productivity, or infant mortality, democracies at all income levels have typically achieved results that are 20 percent to 40 percent superior to those of autocracies. Moreover, contrary to the concerns of some economists, they accomplished this without generating larger fiscal deficits than nonrepresentative governments. These differences in development performance, based on data for the past 40 years, have grown wider over recent decades.

Here, then, is the crux of our argument: Despite the enduring theoretical underpinnings to the authoritarian-advantage thesis, the evidence for it has always been weak. Not only can poor countries democratize, poor democracies can develop quite effectively. As a leading scholar in this field, Adam Przeworski, and his colleagues have succinctly put it, "There was never any solid evidence that democracies were somehow inferior in generating growth—certainly not enough to justify supporting or even condoning dictatorships."[20]

Notice that we are not saying that all democracies enjoy sterling development experiences. In fact, some democracies have struggled in their economic performance. Indeed the movement of more poor countries toward democracy has sharpened the relevance and the stakes of the democracy and development debate. Nor are we saying that certain autocratic governments haven't realized rapid economic growth. As the experience of China shows, in some cases they have. What we are saying is that when one looks at the experience of developing countries as a whole, those with more representative and pluralistic political systems have typically developed significantly more rapidly, broadly, and consistently than those with closed systems. This record is persistent and striking, even for the least developed countries. In percentage terms, two-thirds of developing country democracies exceed the growth medians for their regions over the past 20 years.

It is the experience of this solid majority, rather than the exceptional cases, that should guide our understanding of democracy's role in sustaining development. This is what is most relevant for policy guidance. The handful of instances where authoritarian governments have overseen spectacular growth hold important lessons. But to attempt to generalize these cases to the entire developing world is a mistake.

Low-income democracies exhibit another feature that runs counter to the conventional theory about how they ought to behave: resiliency. Even in the face of economic setbacks and social unrest, the majority of countries on the path to democracies has not backtracked into authoritarianism, but has held onto its newfound freedoms (a phenomenon we review in Chapter 3). And as they have stayed the course, their numbers have swelled. This momentum continues to the present. There are more low-income democracies and democratizing countries today than there were five or 10 years ago.

The change has been momentous. As recently as 1988, two-thirds of the world's states were nondemocratic. By 2002, the proportion had reversed. Some two-thirds of all nations, accounting for 70 percent of the world's population, were on the democratic path.[21] Indeed, the trend marks a turning point in human history. Starting in the 1990s, for the first time a

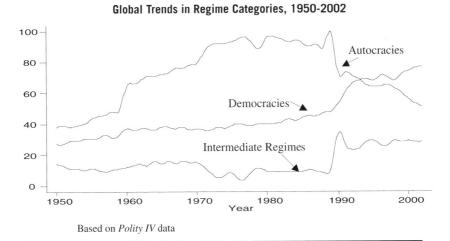

Global Trends in Regime Categories, 1950-2002

Based on *Polity IV* data

Figure 1.1 There has been a dramatic shift toward democracy since the mid-1980s, transforming global governance patterns.

majority of the world's people were living under some form of self-government (see Figure 1.1).[22]

"Democratic Peace"

That might sound like a positive development, but is it? Some experts remain skeptical. After all, poor democracies are weak democracies, inherently unstable and fertile ground for conflict. Luckily for the world, that truism turns out to be not so true, either (something we discuss in Chapter 4). Low-income countries undergoing political pluralization are no more likely to be engaged in conflict than other low-income countries. And contrary to the claims that democratization increases fragmentation in ethnically diverse societies, the record shows that democracies do a better job of developing broad social coalitions and balancing multiple, competing interests in diverse cultures. In other words, global security hasn't been thrown into disarray since substantial numbers of new democracies have been created. Rather, in the early years of the twenty-first century, the gravest threat to international security is global terrorism. And the terrorist networks undertaking these nefarious acts are virtually all based in politically closed societies.

Counter to the expectations of the prevailing school, a great deal of research in the 1990s on the political dimension of conflict has revealed a powerful pattern of a "democratic peace." Democracies rarely, if ever, go to war with each other. This pattern has held from the establishment of the first modern democracies in the nineteenth century to the present. As an ever-greater share of the world's states become democratic, the implications for global peace are profound. Indeed, as the number of democracies has been increasing, major conflicts around the world (including civil wars) have declined sharply. Since 1992, they have fallen by two-thirds,[23] numbering just 13 as of 2003.

Why Democracies Do a Better Job

What explains the consistently superior development outcomes of democracies? We outline the conceptual underpinnings of democracy's superior developmental performance in Chapter 2. The reasons are many and varied, but boil down to three core characteristics of representative government: shared power, openness, and adaptability.

Although holding free elections is what commonly defines democracy, what makes it work is the way it disperses power. Consequently, in contrast to most autocratic governments, a broader range of interests are considered on a more regular basis. This increases the likelihood that the priorities of the general public will be weighed. Indeed, the argument that authoritarian governments can ignore special interest groups and therefore make deci-sions that are for the overall good of the society is based on a series of highly dubious assumptions. One is that the unelected leaders in these systems ac-tually have the interest of the public at heart. The behavior of Fidel Castro in Cuba, Kim Jung-Il in North Korea, Alexander Lukashenko in Belarus, and Hassan Ahmad al-Bashir in Sudan, to say nothing of former Iraqi dic-tator, Saddam Hussein, would strongly suggest otherwise.

Another assumption is that authoritarian governments don't have to satisfy their own special-interest constituencies. In fact, most authoritarian systems are built on the foundations of extensive patronage networks upon which they rely to stay in power. Although typically shielded from public view, these networks have enormous impacts on economic opportunity and development. The separation of powers inherent in a democracy acts as a constant reminder to the public that the central government's powers are limited. Thus, it encourages the expansion—and the independence—of the private sector. This, in turn, fosters a climate of innovation and entre-preneurship, the engines of economic growth.

The multiplicity of influences on the decision-making process in democracies also leads to more moderate and nuanced policies. This mod-erating influence contributes to one of the most distinctive qualities of democratic development—its steadiness. The ups and downs of economic growth in low-income countries are smaller in democracies. Rather than experiencing alternating bouts of boom and bust, economies in democra-cies are more likely to undergo a stable pattern of moderate gains and small declines. For poor democracies, that quality of steadiness is exceedingly important, for it means that they are more able than countries run by dic-tators to avoid economic and humanitarian catastrophes. For broad seg-ments of their populations, this is the difference between life and death.

Consider this remarkable statistic: 95 percent of the worst economic performances over the past 40 years were overseen by nondemocratic gov-ernments. Similarly, virtually all contemporary refugee crises have been wrought by autocratic governments. Although shared decision-making is frequently slower, this process is more likely to weigh risks, thereby avoid-ing calamitous policies. When something is going wrong, leaders hear about it and are forced to take action.

Interest groups in democratic societies not only have greater influence over decision-making, they are also better informed for the simple reason that democracies generally guarantee basic civil liberties like freedom of speech and association. The resulting free flow of information, including as-sessing and disseminating ideas from abroad, discourages insular thinking and stimulates vigorous debate. That in turn increases the likelihood that a broader range of options and concerns will be taken into consideration than would occur in a more narrow political structure. Rather than being concealed, society's shortcomings are exposed and the seeds of a solution to them are sown. The end result is better and more informed decisions. Freewheeling discussion of a society's problems also acts as a curb on corruption, both public and private. Finally, it promotes efficiency, not only by preventing the misuse of resources, but also by facilitating a more informed allocation of investment and by deepening confidence in market systems.

Democracies also realize superior developmental performances because they tend to be more adaptable. Our catch phrase to characterize this is "democracies are learning organizations." That is, people who live in them are continually engaged in gathering more information, making adjustments to their positions, and reassessing progress. The mindset is: If something isn't working, you change it, and if something is working, you do more of it. Thus, through trial and error, democracies find the most suitable route forward. Typically, the policy adopted is a nuanced, middle-of-the-road one, reflecting numerous, and sometimes conflicting, points of view. The right course will vary from country to country, depending on its economic, political, and cultural circumstances. In other words, democracy does not guarantee that you will get the policy decision right. However, it does guarantee you the right to change it when you've got it wrong. Structurally, democracies' "horizontal networking"—that is, the flow of ideas back and forth between the public, private, and civic sectors—allows for greater versatility, timeliness, and capacity for adjustment in the adoption and implementation of a policy than the hierarchal structures typical of authoritarian systems.

Finally, democracies' adaptability allows them to get rid of corrupt or ineffective leaders. This reduces the amount of long-term damage they can inflict. It also provides a process of perpetual renewal. New actors with different ideas and priorities can come into power. Problems can be approached from fresh perspectives. In such a climate, innovation flourishes and deadwood—whether in people or systems—that builds up in public bureaucracies shrivels.

That a process for removing leaders is built into the structure of democracy provides a systematic mechanism for succession that minimizes political crises. This feature of democratic politics lessens the likelihood of civil conflict stemming from challenges to political legitimacy. Thus, the disruptions of war are avoided and the energies that would be spent in conflict are preserved for economic development. The resulting political stability in democracies, esteemed economist Mancur Olson observed, contributes to greater investor confidence, facilitating economic continuity and incentives for long-term asset accumulation.[24]

Our point is that the type of political system a country has in place affects its rate and type of economic development. To many readers this may seem like common sense. However, international development agencies have been designed to ignore a country's political orientation when making funding decisions. The rationale is that this would detract from making these allocations on hardheaded, technical economic criteria. By overlooking democracy's developmental contributions, however, the effectiveness of many internationally funded development initiatives is muted. Worse yet, ignoring the political dimension can at times cause international development efforts to inadvertently undermine nascent democratization efforts—a subject we focus on in Chapter 5.

Accounting for Democracy's Shortcomings

None of this is to say that the mere establishment of a democracy is going to solve all of a nation's problems—far from it. The process of democratization is rarely smooth and straightforward. And even in the established democracies, there are competing and conflicting interests. A number of low-income democracies maintain growth rates that are below the median for their regions. Often, the slower pace is a legacy of their authoritarian pasts. For instance, after inheriting societies torn by acute inequality and corruption, a number of new democracies in Latin America have struggled to find the right path forward. Similarly, while elections have been held throughout Africa over the past decade, in far too many cases strongman regimes are reemerging with no accountability to the people. In parts of the former Soviet Union, democracy has been stillborn. In others, elected leaders have used the powers of the state to suffocate free speech or any public criticism of their rule. Whatever the cause, slow growth is demoralizing for citizens of an emerging democracy who had pinned their hopes for a better life on their new freedoms.

These are all serious problems and require concerted attention. Meeting the material aspirations of newly democratic societies is crucial to consolidating democratic gains across the world—the achievement of which remains uncertain. It is important to place the struggles of these newly democratic regions in context, however. Economic growth in both Latin America and Africa in the 1990s exceeded their respective performances during the 1980s, when most still had autocratic governments. Similarly, the median proportion of Latin American populations living on less than $1 a day (in inflation-adjusted terms) has declined steadily under democratic governance (dropping to 11 percent in 2001).[25] And the increased attention given to corruption in these regions does not necessarily indicate that corruption has become more prevalent. More likely, it reflects the increased willingness of people in these societies to talk about it. And despite the economic and political struggles in a number of Latin American and African countries, public support for democracy remains robust.[26]

We contend, therefore, that shortcomings in a country's economic development are often explained by too narrow, rather than too much democracy. And yes, there are degrees of democracy, because democracy is about more than elections. As we have already pointed out, democracy's contribution to economic development comes through its creation of structures of shared power. Putting checks on the power of the chief executive, separating the party from state decision-making, establishing a merit-based civil service, fostering an independent private sector, facilitating the free flow of ideas, and creating expectations that a country's leadership will adhere to the rule of law—all of these are hallmarks of a democratic political structure that augments the prospects for social and economic development. Democracies at every income level that have established stronger mechanisms of checks and balances grow more rapidly than those that have not. To address the shortcomings of economically struggling democracies, therefore, requires broadening these structures of shared power.

It is possible, of course, for dictatorships to create checks on power. A number of the East Asian dynamos did so. Fearing the emergence of communist insurgencies like those that ultimately seized power in China, North Korea, and Vietnam, they certainly had a powerful incentive to spur broad-based economic development.[27] They also began their drive to develop with relatively egalitarian societies, diminishing the pitched social battles encountered in other regions. And they did a good job of it, reinvesting the assets created from their initial economic gains in education, health care, and job training. But the fact remains that, unlike democracies, dictatorships have no built-in inclination to create a system of restraints on government.

The Flaws of the Authoritarian Growth Model

The two overarching views we have described—authoritarian advantage versus democratic development—portend dramatically divergent visions of the way forward for low-income countries. We have already discussed some of the risks if the democratic-development position is misguided. Indeed, concerns over the anticipated political instability that would accompany "premature democratization" have been folded into the development-first argument. But let's examine the downside implications if the authoritarian-led development theory is off the mark.

They assert that the chances for poor countries to make the transition to democracy improve once they reach some middle level of development. Until then, they say, authoritarian governments are best suited to lift up these countries' economies. But why is this? A strong case can be made that they are the worst suited. Since they are narrowly based, the economic growth that is realized is likely to be confined to a sliver of the population. Lacking transparency, autocratic governments tend to encourage patronage and corruption. Their repressive nature also makes them susceptible to internal conflict. Far from nudging their economies to that magical middle-income threshold, autocratic government may actually impede the process. We believe that a policy strategy dependent on autocratic-led economic development is thus perpetually caught in a vicious circle. Since these societies rarely develop, they are never considered "ready" for democracy.

It is a sort of "catch-22" of economic development: A poor society can't go democratic until it becomes relatively prosperous, but it can't become relatively prosperous until it goes democratic. The contradiction highlights another conspicuous flaw in the authoritarian thesis first noted by political scientist Guillermo O'Donnell: It does not specify at just what level of economic development an autocracy becomes ready to make the big leap to democracy.[28] In fact, we see that among the handful of authoritarian governments that have grown steadily over an extended period of time (such as Singapore, China, Soeharto's Indonesia, Tunisia, and Egypt), most have been no more willing to share power after decades of growth than they were at early stages of development.

Furthermore, this transition theory does not take into consideration the social and cultural dimensions involved. As one observer noted, it treats political systems like coats. It assumes that a society can just take an autocratic system off and put a democracy on.[29] The reality, of course, is that political systems affect the culture, values, incentive structure, and economy of a society. Nations that have lived with authoritarian rule undergo a persistent deterioration of societal values and cohesion.[30] The breakdown in order following the toppling of Saddam Hussein in Iraq and the lawlessness and perceived moral vacuum in Russia after decades of communism are contemporary manifestations of the decay that builds up under the shell of autocratic stability. The further down an autocratic path a society has gone, the longer and bumpier is the road to democracy.

And the greater is the risk, by far, of human misery, even catastrophe. Over the past 40 years, autocracies have been twice as likely to experience economic collapse as democracies.[31] When that happens, the danger of mass starvation looms. In contrast, Nobel laureate Amartya Sen has observed, there has never been a democracy with a free press that has experienced a famine.[32] Autocracies are also more prone to conflict. Eighty percent of all interstate conflicts are instigated by autocracies.[33] Furthermore, they are more vulnerable to civil wars. And since civil wars have a 30 percent chance of spilling over into neighboring countries, the consequences of this instability must be considered in the context of the broader region.[34] In short, a development strategy based on supporting autocracy is akin to picking one's way through a minefield.

A review of the weak empirical support for an authoritarian growth advantage, coupled with the high probability of risk, prompts us to revisit the question of why this conceptual framework has had such resonance. The fact that this thesis gained currency during the Cold War certainly had some bearing on the outcome. The West was obsessed with the communist threat. Cooperation from anticommunist authoritarian allies was highly valued. Moreover, at the time the groundwork for this theory was laid in the 1950s and 1960s, there weren't many low-income democracies in existence; 70 percent of the world's states were nondemocratic. Most of the new states of this era were rightly seen as possessing limited levels of human, financial, and infrastructure capacity. Concerns over how they could be held together shaped an acceptance of the need for hierarchal political structures. Moreover, the superpower alliances that divided the world and propped up many of these authoritarian governments seemed highly durable. Therefore, for scholars writing during this period to imagine successful democratic transitions, much less a wholesale shift toward democratic governance, would have required exceptional vision. Finally, development thinking at this juncture was still dominated by the belief that purely technocratic solutions could address poverty and stimulate economic growth around the world. Many of the prevailing theories (for example, industrialization, investment to fill the finance gap, forced savings, and import-substitution) focused on top-down approaches. These strategies were well suited to hierarchal political structures. The belief was that if the correct technocratic development formula could be found and adopted by the leadership in the developing world, then rapid development would result. In other words, the appeal of the authoritarian-led approach has always had at least something to do with its expediency, in comparison to the messy and time-consuming procedures typical of democracy.

It is really no surprise, then, that the authoritarian advantage thesis enjoyed such support in the decades following World War II. However, revivalist supporters of this view in the post-Cold War era—when the numbers of democracies around the world have been increasing—are in a much more awkward position. From our perspective, they have seized on specific cases of supposed economic successes in dictatorships, compared these to selected democratic failures, and used them to justify the original theory. To sustain this view, they have had to rely on idealized versions of autocratic success. Over the last 20 years, there have only been a handful of cases of sustained growth under authoritarian regimes: Bhutan, China,

Egypt, South Korea, Singapore, Taiwan, Tunisia, and Vietnam.[35] However, to hold these up as a model for other developing countries requires ignoring the 60 or so other dictatorships that had sustained sub-par growth during this period. In other words, seven times as many authoritarian regimes had poor growth as had superlative growth. Moreover, 43 had at least one episode of a disastrous economic experience—which we define as an annual contraction per capita GDP of 10 percent or more—during this time. To cling to the notion that autocratic government is required for development among poor countries requires an exceptional degree of selective thinking.

Succinctly put, the autocratic growth model is terribly narrow. The number of countries that have followed it with success is few. Those that have gone on to become democracies are even fewer. Proponents of this model, therefore, are hinging their claims on a few exceptional cases: South Korea, Taiwan, Portugal, and Spain (all of which did move into the democratic camp). How valid are these cases as a template for today's developing countries in Latin America, Africa, Asia, and the former Soviet Union? The political cultures in these regions are generally characterized as personalistic, elitist, and patronage-based—traits that are inimical to promoting economic development. Yet these are the very characteristics that an authoritarian growth model reinforces. Furthermore, the deepening monopolization of political and economic power typical of autocratic government makes the proposition that they are better suited to improving and sustaining living conditions in developing countries even less credible.

For historical perspective, let's consider some of the one-party states of the 1960s touted by Huntington and others as models for development: the Soviet Union, Yugoslavia, Mexico, North Korea, and North Vietnam. Several enjoyed periods of rapid growth over an extended period. In some years, they set the pace for growth globally. However, in none was the early growth sustained into subsequent decades. On the contrary, they all went through disastrous economic ordeals between growth spurts. This volatility is characteristic of growth in authoritarian economies. To repeat an important point: While a small number of countries with closed governments post the most rapid growth rates in the world, a much larger group of them clogs the ranks of the worst performers. In many cases the same country can occupy both positions in a period of a few years. The poor track record of even the historically star performers of the autocratic-growth thesis reveals the sandy ground upon which this model is built.

China vs. India

This brings us back to China. Will it continue on its torrid pace of growth and make a smooth transition to democracy? Or will it begin to shudder and eventually endure economic collapse as so many other autocratic governments have before it? In other words, is China more likely to be the next South Korea or the next Indonesia? We are hoping for the former. This would be in the best interests of the Chinese people and the world at large. However, economists point to economic flaws—ranging from insolvent banks, environmental destruction, and soaring unemployment to swooning returns on foreign investments—that could undermine China's future performance.

Whatever the strengths and weaknesses of China's economy, we rivet on two points. First, China's rapid growth began only after it adopted market-based reforms—economic performance flowed from economic policies rather than its form of government. In the previous three decades under an authoritarian government and a planned economy, the economy stagnated. Clearly, authoritarian rule paved no road to prosperity. To the contrary, prosperity came as the dictatorship, copying the example of Japan and the East Asian Tigers, moved away from micromanaging the economy and toward a market system. Second, China faces profound challenges in the years ahead, not the least of which is the task of absorbing workers rendered unemployed by the closure of moribund state-controlled enterprises.

As the Communist Party moves away from its ideological roots, it increasingly becomes primarily a mechanism to maintain power. Its rural base has dwindled, suggesting that its social base is narrowing sharply. While some have applauded the move to accept entrepreneurs into the party as a means of broadening this base, in fact, this is really an elaborate means of consolidating patronage relationships.[36] Rather than creating an independent middle class that will serve as a counterweight to the party, the party is co-opting the wealthy entrepreneurs to ensure that it remains the sole power center in society. Entrepreneurs that join the party have privileged access to public contracts and bank loans. Unsurprisingly, levels of corruption are on the rise.[37]

Even if the Chinese economy continues to grow, it faces daunting challenges. Will the Communist Party allow for a genuine transition to democracy? Or is it racing toward the edge of an economic cliff like so many other autocratic countries in the past that had seemed to be performing economic miracles? The latter is an unsettling—and real—possibility. For Beijing's only claim to political legitimacy today is its ability to deliver economic growth. If it is no longer able to do so, its governance structure will be exposed not only as closed and inflexible but unworkable—and will crumble under its own weight. Should that happen, the consequences for the Chinese people will be severe and foreign investors will be left with the sad realization that their dreams of a big payout blinded them to the economic realities of an opaque system built on a weak adherence to a rule of law.

Whatever happens, China faces a period of great transition in the years ahead. Despite the successful transfer of power to new leadership in the sixteenth Party Congress in late 2002, the lack of a legitimizing process leaves its political structures unstable. The Communist Party's narrowing political base, which now represents a scant 5 percent of the population, only magnifies its alienation from the population. Indeed, a survey of migrant laborers indicates that the prevailing image of the party is that of a self-serving elite.[38] Ultimately, therefore, Chinese authorities retain power by their capacity for repression. As Minxin Pei has noted, "the preservation of a one-party state and the implementation of the rule of law are fundamentally incompatible."[39] In short, China must establish a legitimate, stable political structure. Until it does, the sustainability of its economic progress remains uncertain.

The performance of democratic India, the other Asian behemoth, has frequently been compared to China's as a barometer of the superiority of authoritarian governance to that of democracy. By most measures, over the last two decades, China has dominated. For while India's achievement has been impressive, its doubling of per capital incomes from $239 to $496 between 1982 and 2002 falls far short of China's quadrupling of incomes from $189 to $940 in the same period.[40]

And yet, the comparison is not as clear-cut as it might seem. While both China and India established their political structures in the aftermath of World War II, it was arguably China that first adopted a capitalist economy. Starting with its economic reforms in the late 1970s, it pursued more liberalized pricing, labor, export, and capital policies than India (at least until 1993 when India seriously undertook economic reforms). In contrast, India borrowed heavily from the Soviet economic model. Consequently, it maintained a significant degree of central planning in its economy into the 1990s (the over-regulated legacy of which, many argue, remains a problem today). India's public sector share of GDP growth increased to 26 percent in the 1980s from 10 percent in 1960.[41] Furthermore, drawing on the development theories that prevailed from the 1950s well into the 1970s, India largely adhered to the import-substitution and industrialization models of development even as China was embracing market-based reform. But as India has adopted a more liberal economic posture, its growth too has accelerated, averaging annual per capita gains of more than five percent in the 1990s.

In short, the China–India economic rivalry is still playing out. And already, India is exhibiting the corrective traits of democratic governance. Its growth is robust, though not exceptional. Nonetheless, it has avoided economic crises and humanitarian catastrophes, something China has not.[42] India has been more willing to reduce subsidies to state-owned enterprises and allow foreign ownership.[43] Moreover, India has demonstrated an ability to innovate—as seen by the originality of the high-technology products that have been generated in Bangalore—products that China cannot match, despite the massive state subsidies it lavishes on its technology sector.

As it has moved into an era of competitive party politics, the Indian ship of state is also benefiting from a long-overdue "scraping of the barnacles" —the breaking up of some of the entrenched formal and informal patronage networks that had come to characterize Indian economic life. China, while enjoying the exhilaration of rapid growth—as have other authoritarian systems before it—still has some treacherous shoals to navigate. The encrustation of its one-party monopoly is increasingly burdensome, as seen by the growing levels of corruption. Public outrage and violence against state officials have been on the rise, especially in rural areas. Most seriously, China must yet address how it will negotiate a transition to a more representative form of government, something India has already done. Until then, China's economic gains are inherently unstable.

The Way Forward

We've put forth the argument that democracies perform consistently better on a range of social and economic development indicators than authoritarian governments do. They respond more readily to people's needs, they are adaptable, and they create checks and balances on government power that discourage reckless policies.

Why is it important to delve into this debate? Because ideas matter—they have consequences. If the "development first" view holds, the international community will pursue one set of policies to spur economic development in poor countries. If instead democracy's developmental and security advantages are recognized, major shifts in policy would be required. Highlighting some of these changes is the focus of Chapters 6 and 7.

Indeed, frustrated with a long string of development failures, the World Bank, the United Nations Development Program (UNDP), and other development organizations began to focus more explicitly on governance issues starting in the 1990s. Poor governance and its draining by-product, corruption, were identified as root causes to chronic underdevelopment. This led to many new projects aimed at enhancing governance effectiveness by strengthening the capacity of the civil service, judiciary, and anticorruption agencies. Similar efforts were undertaken to establish and implement more consistent property rights and contract enforcement legislation to make emerging market economies more attractive to private investment. In parallel to these changes, many bilateral donors, led by the

United States Agency for International Development (USAID), established democracy promotion units that focused on a wide range of activities including electoral and constitutional reform, capacity-building for legislators, encouraging civil society, and promoting norms for civil-military relations. Despite this increased attention, the focus on "good governance" has, by and large, not translated into linking development assistance to democracy. Low-income autocracies continue to receive the same level of official development assistance, on average, as democracies. Reorienting United States and other industrialized democracies' development policies, therefore, would at the very least require gauging how far down the path of democracy a given country has gone before allocating development assistance to it. That may sound like a simple exercise, but in fact it would require major changes in the way countries and multinational organizations divide up the economic-aid pie. At present, certain agencies are legally required to ignore political characteristics of a government to which funding is provided. If a democracy-led development thesis gains acceptance, that mandate would have to be revised.

Policy adjustments in timing and approach are also in order. To accept the role of democracy in triggering economic development compels recognition of the role of coalition building in democratic societies. There are, of course, the broad social compacts between labor and management, rich and poor, rural and urban that establish the norms and parameters that guide a democratic society's politics. However, democracies also thrive on engaged citizens acting through private associations. They provide an active brake on repressive government, forcing authorities to take proper heed of legitimate interests. Think of the essential role in the West played by coalitions of consumers, small businesses, tax opponents, labor, and human rights groups. Such coalitions take time to build—a process that varies by country. If international donors try to force poor countries into a standardized prescription of economic reforms without taking this into account, they could undercut incipient democratization efforts.

Changes in U.S. national security policy are also required. National security concerns have regularly been invoked to trump democracy considerations in U.S. foreign policy decisions. This Cold War tendency has persisted long after the fall of the Berlin Wall. As American foreign policy leaders come to recognize the nexus between autocracy, poverty, and conflict, they will be obliged to revisit the wisdom of this approach. The long-term downside costs are frequently greater than is recognized when these relationships are initiated. Indeed, the expanding threat of international terrorism is in certain respects a direct outgrowth of earlier instances of U.S.-supported autocratic governance.

The tensions between the short-term goal of gaining the support of strategically important authoritarian governments and the long-term damage to American policy that such a policy might have are likely to intensify in the coming years. Viewing the issue in this way is a departure in strategic thinking from the often-accepted formula that giving military assistance to dictatorships is a tradeoff between our partiality for democracy and our need for security. In fact, the United States' experience since World War II, made vivid by the September 11, 2001 terrorist attacks, has shown that America's vital foreign-policy interests of promoting democracy and safeguarding national security are not only compatible, they are complementary.

For the past half-century, the United States and much of the industrialized world have supported a strategy of relations with low-income countries built on a mix of false assumptions. In this book, we will hold those suppositions up to the light. In the process, we demonstrate the superiority of democracy over dictatorship in spurring economic development and preserving social stability. We invite readers to walk with us as we review the record and to contemplate the policy dimensions of a democracy-centered foreign policy. Such an approach, we believe, greatly improves the prospects for a safer and more prosperous world.

CHAPTER 2

Setting the Record Right

I believe what a country needs to develop is discipline more than
democracy. The exuberance of democracy leads to indiscipline and
disorderly conduct, which are inimical to development.

Lee Kuan Yew
former President of Singapore

Democracy is the answer. Not because democracy is perfect. It is precisely because it is imperfect. We are not looking for another utopia; we
are looking for an optimal solution based on the systems available to us.
By that standard, there is no contest . . . and there is no justification for
further delay. For decades after independence, many of our populist
regimes told us that democracy had to be suspended until "national lib-
eration;" until Palestine had been liberated; until we have economic development; until we have true social justice; and so on. As it turns out
now, after 50 years of depriving ourselves of democracy, we find ourselves with none of these things! And we're no closer to democracy.

Saad Eddin Ibrahim
Egyptian Democracy Activist

The belief that authoritarian[1] government is better suited to propel economic growth in low-income societies draws on a storied intellectual tradition. Aristotle believed that only in a wealthy society in which assets were
equitably distributed could ordinary citizens develop the self-restraint to
participate in politics without succumbing to the irresponsible appeals of

demagogues. This idea built on the view of his mentor, Plato, that matters of state were so serious and complex that only a specially trained technocratic elite was equipped to manage the day-to-day responsibilities of governance.

In the twentieth century, the notion of an authoritarian advantage among low-income countries was popularized by the work of Seymour Lipset, who contended that only with elevated levels of income, education, and urbanization could political pluralism take hold.[2] Conceived at the height of the Cold War when there were relatively few democracies, Lipset's thesis viewed democracy as the crowning achievement of a country's development.[3] At early stages of development, by extension, authoritarian governments were considered more capable catalysts of economic progress. That development, in turn, would create the conditions—industrialization, literacy, and a substantial middle class—that would eventually lead to stable democracy.

There were social, political, economic, and security dimensions to this argument. Higher incomes helped the poor to develop longer time horizons and a more gradualist view of politics. Meanwhile, widespread attainment of basic material needs and literacy made the concept of power sharing with commoners more conceivable to the wealthy. In contrast, if democracy were attempted prematurely in a society still mired in poverty, illiteracy, and weak social institutions, the likely result would be irresponsible government leading to social instability or domination by an elite class that was unaccountable to the general public.

The validity of this theory was widely accepted in academic and policy circles.[4] The reasoning was that in a society with limited resources and capacity, the iron fist of an authoritarian regime was better suited to mobilizing the nation's limited financial and human resources. The evidence seemed to support this logic: communist Soviet Union, Yugoslavia, and Romania were among the fastest growing economies in the world in the 1950s and 1960s. In his 1968 classic, *Political Order in Changing Societies*, Samuel Huntington touted the invaluable organizing role that a strong single political party could bring to a poor society: "The great utility and the great appeal of the single-party system in modernizing countries is that it is an institution that, in large measure, promotes both concentration (and hence innovation) and also expansion (and hence group assimilation)." "In various ways the established one-party systems in Mexico, Tunisia, North Korea, and North Vietnam have all demonstrated both these capacities." Liberal, pluralistic, democratic governments lacked the political power to bring about fundamental change.[5]

Authoritarian governments were also assumed to be better equipped than democracies to overcome cultural and legal obstacles to development and plunge into the nation-building tasks of educating the masses, creating a national transportation system, and exploiting natural resources. And, crucial to reducing disparities in wealth and income, they had the where-withal to force through land reform, as South Korea, Taiwan, Japan,[6] Mexico, Turkey, Egypt, Pakistan, Syria, and numerous systems had all amply demonstrated.[7] Huntington and Nelson neatly summed up the harsh necessity: "Political participation must be held down, at least tem-porarily, in order to promote economic development."[8] It was a view that gave moral support to the West's Cold War policy of supporting authori-tarian governments that disavowed communism.

Even with the end of the Cold War and the movement toward democ-racy by numerous developing countries, the notion of an authoritarian ad-vantage remains embedded in the worldviews of many international actors. Some have cited the need to face a "cruel choice" between democracy and development[9] and the destabilizing effects arising from unmet expectations created by simultaneously supporting both.[10] In its 1993 report, *The East Asian Miracle: Economic Growth and Public Policy*, the World Bank en-dorsed the technocratic and efficiency-enhancing advantages of authori-tarian systems for generating development—a view echoed in 2002 by the Asian Development Bank.[11] Some leading growth economists continue to warn against the dangers democracy poses to economic growth. Robert Barro, for example, has urged Western policymakers to support efficient authoritarian regimes that provide political stability and improve eco-nomic conditions in poor countries.[12] Although rarely voicing open sup-port for this view, many diplomats and multilateral agency representatives quietly endorse it.[13] The attractions for them are more than intellectual. Dealing with one individual or a small number of powerful bureaucrats in an authoritarian system is a lot easier for diplomats than maintaining a broad network of relations in a democracy.

It goes without saying that authoritarian leaders are big fans of the au-thoritarian advantage theory.[14] At a private presentation of the path-breaking *Arab Human Development Report* to Arab League foreign ministers in August 2002, all but two of the 19 ministers in attendance were reported to have dis-missed the report's recommendation to address the region's "freedom deficit." Their ostensible rationale was that this would hurt prospects for de-velopment in the region.

Proponents of authoritarian-led development also based their position on the perceived weaknesses that democracies bring to the task. Democratic leaders, they say, are too quick to cave into the demands of the masses for budget-busting welfare programs, too willing to cater to special interests, too indecisive to take the bold steps necessary to build strong state institutions, and just plain too weak to stave off political instability.

The first of these major failings is "macroeconomic populism," the inevitable surrender by democratic leaders to the electorate's demands for higher wages and social service entitlements that will satisfy poor people's short-term needs but breed long-term macroeconomic instability.[15] Invariably, taxes will go up, public-sector deficits will widen, private entrepreneurs will be starved of capital, innovation will be stifled, and productivity will decline.

A second often-stated drawback of democracy in spurring economic development is the vulnerability of politicians to the influences of wealthy individuals, resource-rich monopolies, or powerful labor unions that can mobilize funding, publicity, and popular support on their behalf. As a result, policies are skewed to benefit these special interests at the expense of the general public and worsen rather than alleviate economic inefficiencies. By contrast, dictators can resist such pressures and forge policies that will serve the nation's long-term interests.

A third perceived deficiency of democracies, deriving from their need to placate competing coalitions of power, is their inherent messiness and slowness to act. Stalemates are common, and when compromises are reached, they often have little practical effect. Furthermore, decisions are never final.[16] Rather, they are regularly open to review, renegotiation, and reversal, particularly if a new leadership comes to power. Even in the prosperous and politically mature United States, this dynamic can be seen at work in the never-ending debates and legislative maneuvering over abortion, campaign finance reform, and affirmative action. Elections, from this perspective, are a perpetual source of uncertainty and, therefore, a disincentive to investment. Consider the case of a major international energy firm that in the late 1990s invested several billion dollars in a number of emerging democracies in Latin America that had adopted free-market systems. The understanding of the firm was that electricity would be supplied on a cost basis, allowing it to recoup its investment over a designated period. The flow of revenue in turn would provide the company with an incentive to sustain and expand its services. Alas, before long, populist candidates in some of those countries were declaring that essentials like electricity should be provided to the public for free, or at least at reduced cost. The proposals threw the company's planning into disarray and discouraged further investment, not just by the energy provider but any foreign company. Advocates of authoritarian governments as the surest route to economic development say they offer greater security to outside investors because a smaller number of people in power reach decisions more quickly and more certainly.

A fourth disadvantage cited by critics of democracies is their tendency to precipitate political instability.[17] This view holds that elections in poor countries populated by fractious ethnic, regional, religious, and economic groupings have a polarizing effect.[18] In such a context, there is a great temptation for politicians to fan factional conflicts to gain the support of this group or that. This is particularly the case in winner-take-all societies that lack established checks on public authority, a tradition of professional journalism, norms of compromise, and transparency. Low-income countries are considered particularly susceptible because their very poverty limits the potential for economic trade-offs that can lead to compromise among the competing factions. Authoritarian governments can avoid that trap by using their power to keep factional rivalries in check.

Empirical Experience

However many scholars have studied the relationship between democracy and development, they have been hard put to find a causal relationship between them.[19] There is always the possibility that none exists. But assuming one does, it is difficult to measure. So many factors come into play both in a country's political evolution and in its economic progression that separating them all out, quantifying and analyzing them and the connections among them are practically impossible. Seemingly straightforward matters, like defining democracy, can be daunting. For example, does a country merit the name just because it holds elections? It depends on how the elections are held, of course. But then, how do you evaluate that process? For clarity's sake, when we say democracy we mean political systems characterized by popular participation, genuine competition for executive office, and institutional checks on power. This is operationalized using the Polity IV democracy index, which assigns a 0 to 10 democracy rating annually for every country with populations greater than 500,000.[20] (For a list of countries and their democracy scores, see appendices A & B.) We set a high bar in our designation of democracies so as to avoid introducing bias from countries that may demonstrate certain trappings of self-governance, though eschew meaningful mechanisms of shared power.

Similarly, economic growth is a crude measure of development—it doesn't capture distributional questions or the extent to which citizens are meeting basic needs. Furthermore, economic data, particularly among poorer countries, are often missing. Compounding the complexity, many analyses have drawn heavily from the Cold War era when relatively few low-income democracies existed and much development aid was used to solidify superpower alliances rather than address poverty.

Given all those difficulties, we have approached the empirical questions surrounding democracy and development differently. Rather than looking for a causal link between them, we aim to study the extent to which they coexist in low-income countries—in other words, whether they are compatible with each other. This, after all, is the central issue to the overarching policy question to this debate: Should the international community support democratization in developing countries? The common wisdom asserts that democracy hinders economic progress in the early stages of development. If, however, it can be shown that the two phenomena occur simultaneously, then the empirical basis for the authoritarian-led development model largely dissolves.

Toward that end, we examine as large a sample of countries as possible—covering the period from 1960 to 2001—the most inclusive and recent years for which reliable cross-country data is available. Recognizing that there is a spectrum of governance types, we compare countries that qualify as democracies versus autocracies (i.e., at the top and bottom tiers of the Polity IV democracy ratings). This allows for the sharpest comparison of how governance type may affect development outcomes—and is most directly relevant to the question of whether or not an authoritarian advantage exists for developing countries.

We find that despite the wide acceptance of the prevailing wisdom, democracies have, on average,[21] out-performed autocracies on virtually every aspect of development considered. When a full sample of countries is considered, democracies have realized consistently higher levels of economic growth than autocracies during the past four decades (Figure 2.1). This translates into a 30 percent advantage in annual per capita economic growth rates (2.3 percent versus 1.6 percent).[22] Since these figures include countries that are better off, this difference in itself is not startling. It has long been recognized by all sides that most prosperous states in the world are well-established democracies. These democracies have an impressive record of improving productivity, asset creation, and superior economic growth.[23] The real debate, therefore, is whether low-income democracies[24] are capable of growing at a clip comparable to low-income authoritarian governments. (We categorize countries with per capita incomes below $2,000 as low-income.) In other words, can countries such as the Dominican Republic, Bulgaria, India, and the Philippines keep up? The disagreement is not on the goal (prosperous democracies) but on the path and the timing to get there.

Limiting our review to low-income countries, we find little discernible difference in per capita growth rates between democracies and autocracies from 1960 to 2001 (see Figure 2.2). The median growth levels for each decade considered are very comparable. The clear-cut democratic dominance seen in the full sample does not hold among low-income countries. Nevertheless, we do not see any evidence of an authoritarian advantage— as long argued by the conventional wisdom—even during the early decades of this period when this thesis was first put forward. For the entire 40-year

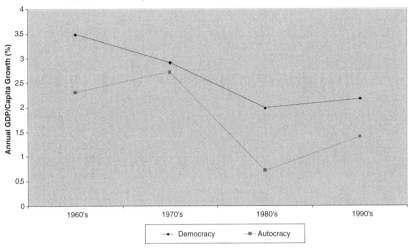

Based on data from *World Development Indicators 2003; Polity IV.*

Figure 2.1 Over the decades democracies have consistently outpaced autocracies in their rates of economic growth.

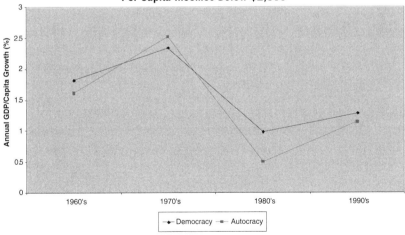

Based on data derived from *World Development Indicators 2003; Polity IV.*

Figure 2.2 Low-income democracies have grown just as rapidly as low-income autocracies over the four decades since 1960.

period, the median growth rate among low-income countries is roughly equivalent: 1.5 percent for democracies versus 1.3 percent for autocracies. There is more to this story, however. The phenomenal growth experience of the East Asian Tigers skews the overall growth rate of authoritarian countries. When East Asia is removed from the low-income sample, the median authoritarian rate drops markedly while the democratic rate holds steady (see Figure 2.3). This reveals a pattern of democratic growth rates 50 percent superior to that of autocracies for the rest of the world over the 40-year sample period. The differential since 1970 has widened with low-income democracies outside of East Asia outpacing their autocratic counterparts in their average rates of growth by 1.6 percent versus 0.9 percent. Even stronger 40-year divergences emerge for countries with per capita incomes below $1,000 (1.75 percent versus 0.75 percent) and $500 per year (1.6 percent versus 0.6 percent). Some of the faster growing low-income democracies that are reflected in these results include Botswana, Costa Rica, Dominican Republic, India, Lithuania, Mauritius, Nicaragua, and Trinidad and Tobago.

This gap in growth rates between democracies and autocracies might be larger except for a simple, though frequently overlooked, recording problem:

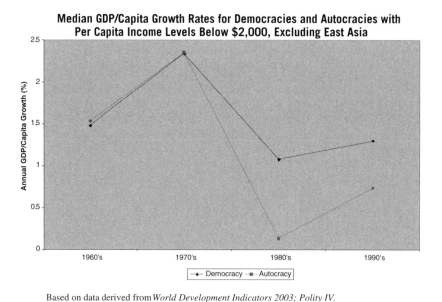

Median GDP/Capita Growth Rates for Democracies and Autocracies with Per Capita Income Levels Below $2,000, Excluding East Asia

Based on data derived from *World Development Indicators 2003; Polity IV.*

Figure 2.3 Outside of East Asia, low-income democracies have dramatically outpaced low-income autocracies in their rate of economic growth—a divergence that widened since 1970.

many authoritarian governments do not make their economic statistics publicly available. Consequently, these data points are not included in the comparative growth rates we examine. If they were, the level of autocratic growth would likely be even lower than what we document. Specifically, from 1960 to 2001, a full one-fourth of economic growth data for autocratic countries is missing. For the same period, just under five percent of the data from democracies are missing.[25] Thus, growth data for 38 authoritarian countries during parts or all of this period are not considered. This includes states such as Afghanistan, Cambodia, Cuba, Djibouti, Iraq, North Korea, Somalia, and numerous Middle Eastern and Eastern Bloc states. In contrast, only five democratic countries have missing data. The availability of data does improve in the 1990s but sharp differences between the two categories of countries remain evident. Eleven percent of authoritarian developing-country growth data points are missing compared with 1 percent for democracies. To fill in some of these data gaps, the creators of the World Bank's World Development Indicators, considered the most comprehensive dataset available, have estimated the per capita GDP growth rates for certain autocratic countries even when they do not have a credible base level of income from which to gauge growth. Although these figures are included in our comparisons, the compilers of the indicators acknowledge that these estimates do not have the same degree of reliability as other growth figures that are listed.[26] In short, a distinguishing feature of regime types—degree of openness—directly affects even our ability to conduct reliable economic comparisons.

Another distinguishing characteristic of democratic growth is its relative stability. Even among low-income countries, democracies have demonstrated less volatility in their growth rates than autocracies (a pattern reflected in Figures 2.1 to 2.3). Therefore, the strength of democracies' economic performance is as much their ability to maintain steady growth over time as it is to achieve relatively rapid progress.[27]

To a large extent, this reflects democracies' tendency to avoid disastrous economic outcomes. If we consider the 20 worst per capita economic-growth rates for each of the past four decades, we find that only five of these 80 "worst performers" have been democracies—Mauritius in 1968, Bangladesh in 1972, Nigeria in 1981, and Latvia and Lithuania in 1992. The same pattern holds up in proportionate terms. The probability of any country experiencing an "economic disaster" (defined as a 10 percent decline in annual per capita GDP) during the 1960 to 2001 period is 3.4 percent. For democracies, it is less than 1 percent. As might be expected, the tendency for disastrous decline is greater among less wealthy countries. Countries with per capita GDP's below $4,000 had a 3.7 percent probability of experiencing a 10 percent contraction. The rate for democracies in this income category was 2.3 percent.[28] In short, democracies, regardless of income level, rarely allow the bottom to fall out of their economies. These figures are particularly noteworthy in that the 1990s were a period of great economic volatility among democracies. Of the 15 instances since 1960 in which a democracy experienced a contraction of more than 10 percent of GDP, 11 occurred in the 1990s. Ten of these 11—all but Thailand in 1998— were transitioning from a communist economic system. Nonetheless, even during the 1990s among countries with per capita GDP's under $4,000, democracies experienced economic disasters at roughly half the rate of states below the democratic threshold (3 percent versus 6 percent).

Volatility can also be measured by looking at the coefficient of variation.[29] This is simply a statistical measure of variance. Larger coefficients of variation represent more volatility. By assessing the coefficients of variation, we can gauge the level of stability associated with the respective rates of growth. A review of the 1980 to 2001 period reinforces the assessment that growth in democracies is markedly more consistent than autocratic governance systems (see Table 2.1). At every income level, the coefficient of variation is smaller for democracies than autocracies.[30] As would be expected, the volatility in growth rates generally declines as income levels increase. This is particularly the case among the prosperous democracies, whose growth rates tend to hover within a relatively narrow band.

In sum, the experience of the last four decades of the twentieth century shows that democracies, even low-income democracies, outperform autocracies in economic growth, in part because that growth is steadier and less prone to sudden, sharp dips. Their superior track record spares the poor much suffering, both present and future, for the poor have no choice in times of economic emergency but to sell what few assets they have to stay alive. Reacquiring these assets afterwards typically costs them anywhere from 50 percent to 300 percent of the price they got for them.[31] Thus, democracies' ability to mitigate against disaster—whether economic or humanitarian—provides protection against catastrophic material loss, which in turn facilitates the acquisition and maintenance of assets over time. This

Table 2.1 Coefficient of Variation for Democracies and Autocracies 1980 to 2001

GDP per Capita	Democracy	Autocracy
$0–$500	3.49	23.1
$500–$1,000	5.24	24.2
$1–$2,000	4.29	8.93
$2–$5,000	3.69	5.37
$5,000+	1.21	10.6

Based on data from *World Development Indicators 2003; Polity IV.*

is consistent with the observation by economist Mancur Olson that only established democracies have been able to consistently create assets over multiple generations.[32]

Although economic growth is the most commonly cited way to compare one country's economic development against another's, it is in many ways an inadequate indicator of socio-economic progress. Taken alone, it does not reveal the extent to which economic output is shared among households or concentrated in a few sectors like oil or minerals. It does not necessarily take account of gains or declines in productivity. It does not capture improvements in living conditions like health care and education. Although levels of well being generally mirror improvements in national income, this is not always the case. A number of Middle Eastern countries enjoy substantial wealth but have lagged in their level of social welfare.[33] Similarly, there is considerable variation between countries with comparable income levels. For example, the Republic of Congo and Sri Lanka had comparable levels of per capita GDP in 2000 ($841 versus $860, respectively), but exhibited a gap of more than 20 years in life expectancy (51 years versus 73 years).

In other words, in addition to GDP, one must look at how well an economy satisfies people's basic needs, like access to food and clean drinking water. These social-welfare indicators are an important gauge of how efficiently the benefits of a growing economy are distributed to the general population. Whatever the size of GDP, equally important measures of national welfare lay in statistics like death rates, school enrollment, and cereal yields.

And comparisons of social welfare by regime type do reveal distinct differences. Citizens of democracies live longer, healthier, and more productive lives, on average, than those in autocracies. Moreover, they have done so consistently for the past four decades—a gap that grew wider in the 1980s and 1990s (see Figure 2.4a to Figure 2.4d). Specifically, people in low-income[34] democracies have had life expectancies that are eight to 12 years longer than those in autocracies, on average (see Figure 2.4a). To cite a few examples, Ghanaians born in the 1990s were expected to live a decade longer than their West African counterparts in Guinea—even though they have comparable levels of per capita income. Similarly, the 63-year life expectancy in India is seven years longer than that found in Burma, despite the latter having double the per capita income. Although there are numerous country-specific factors that can help explain these differences, like resource availability, regional location, and colonial history, on average low-income democracies distinguish themselves by posting consistently superior levels of social welfare across various measures of development progress. Consider secondary school enrollment (Figure 2.4b); low-income

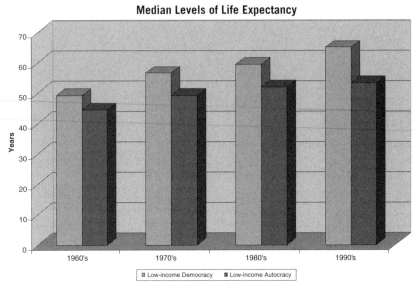

Based on data from *World Development Indicators 2002; Polity IV.*

Figure 2.4a Citizens in low-income democracies live up to a decade longer than individuals in low-income autocracies.

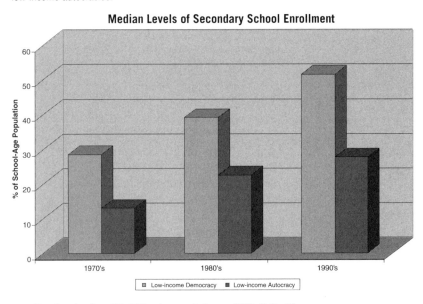

Based on data from *World Development Indicators 2002; Polity IV.*

Figure 2.4b Secondary school attendance levels in low-income democracies are nearly double those of autocracies.

democracies have typically realized enrollment levels nearly double to those of autocracies. To give a conservative illustration, in 2000, 77 percent of school-aged Filipino children were attending secondary school, compared with the 57 percent enrollment rate in (until recently) autocratic Indonesia—despite having nearly identical levels of per capita income.

Agricultural productivity is a vital measure of social well being in many low-income societies in which the vast majority of people live off the land. Higher yields mean not only more food but increased employment. Indeed, the assets generated from improved agricultural productivity were the principal source of capital for savings and investment for many of today's industrialized countries at the early stages of their development. Figure 2.4c shows how democracies have been consistently better able to generate superior yields. For example, from 1995 to 2001, both pluralistic Malawi and autocratic Cameroon averaged agricultural yields of 1,450 kilograms per hectare. This was the case even though Malawi had less than one-third of the per capita wealth of Cameroon, ($165 versus $650) and possessed significantly fewer natural resources.

Figure 2.4d measures the progress made on levels of childhood mortality. This chart demonstrates the dramatic advances that have been made in reducing the rate of childhood deaths over the past four decades—approximately a

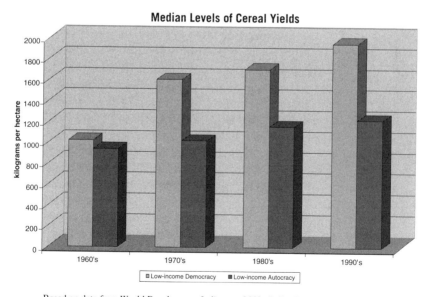

Median Levels of Cereal Yields

kilograms per hectare

| 1960's | 1970's | 1980's | 1990's |

☐ Low-income Democracy ■ Low-income Autocracy

Based on data from *World Development Indicators 2002; Polity IV.*

Figure 2.4c Cereal yields in low-income democracies are typically a third higher than in low-income autocracies.

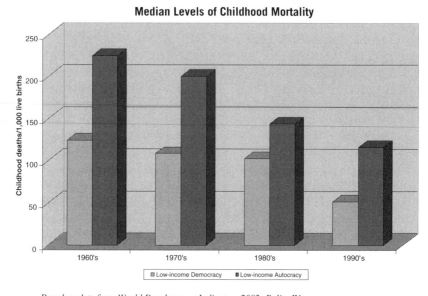

Median Levels of Childhood Mortality

Based on data from World Development Indicators 2002; Polity IV.

Figure 2.4d The global decline in levels of childhood mortality has been characterized by low-income democracies posting child mortality rates that are typically nearly half those of low-income autocracies.

two-thirds decline from the 1960s. But, decade after decade the mortality rate of democracies was roughly half that in autocracies. Illustrative of this is the contrasting experiences of autocratic Belarus and its democratic neighbor, Lithuania. At the break up of the Soviet Union, Lithuania had a slightly higher incidence of child mortality—20 as opposed to 16 deaths per 1,000 live births. By 2001, reflecting their divergent political trajectories, Belarus' rate had increased to 20 whereas Lithuania had cut its levels in half—to nine. Similarly, while authoritarian Bhutan had a per capita GDP 30 percent larger than pluralistic Bangladesh ($550 as opposed to $400), Bangladesh had a lower child mortality rate, 77 per 1,000 births versus 95.

Many development experts believe a nation's infant mortality rate is the most reliable barometer of its overall economic and social health because it embraces such a multitude of social and economic conditions, from access to food, health care, and housing to the availability of schooling for girls. So they pay particular heed to it.[35] Again, as shown in Table 2.2, democracies attain consistently superior results across income levels. For example, democracies with per capita incomes below $500 have averaged 104 infant deaths per 1,000 live births. This compares to a rate of 117 for autocracies. In the lower-middle income category (those with per capita incomes

Table 2.2 Median Levels of Various Social Welfare Indices by Political Category (1960-2001)

GDP/Capita	Infant Mortality Rate (deaths/1000 births)		Childhood Mortality Rate (deaths/1000 births)		Life Expectancy (years)	
	Democracy	Autocracy	Democracy	Autocracy	Democracy	Autocracy
$0-$500	104	117	107	172	53	47
$0-$1,000[1]	93	112	102	159	55	49
$1,000-$2,000	39	64	40	51	67	64
$2,000-$5,000	27	39	23	39	70	67
$5,000+	10	24	9	18	75	71

GDP/Capita	Primary School Enrollment (%)		Adult Illiteracy (%)		Female Youth (15-24) Illiteracy (%)	
	Democracy	Autocracy	Democracy	Autocracy	Democracy	Autocracy
$0-$500	77.2	56.1	56.5	60.7	51.5	56.7
$0-$1,000	77.2	60.5	47.3	55.3	41.5	49.5
$1,000-$2,000	92.0	85.9	14.5	36.3	6.0	21.6
$2,000-$5,000	91.2	92.6	11.0	12.9	3.8	6.0
$5,000+	97.3	78.2	4.8	25.0	0.5	9.1

(continued)

Table 2.2 (continued)

GDP/Capita	Female Sec. School Enrollment (%)		Access to Clean Water (%)		Births Attended by Health Staff (%)	
	Democracy	Autocracy	Democracy	Autocracy	Democracy	Autocracy
$0–$500	20.5	9.9	54	40	48	32
$0–$1,000	19.2	12.1	54	45	44	37
$1,000–$2,000	58.5	39.0	71	71	69	57
$2,000–$5,000	61.9	56.0	89	70	92	86
$5,000+	93.3	61.3	100	98	100	97

GDP/Capita	Cereal Yields (kg/ha)		Crude Death Rate (per 1,000 people)		Population Growth (Annual %)	
	Democracy	Autocracy	Democracy	Autocracy	Democracy	Autocracy
$0–$500	1,197	1,052	11.9	17.2	2.34	2.51
$0–$1,000	1,368	1,067	11.8	15.8	2.39	2.56
$1,000–$2,000	2,126	1,323	7.2	10.0	2.08	2.54
$2,000–$5,000	2,302	1,683	6.7	10.0	1.49	1.83
$5,000+	3,770	1,938	9.4	5.1	1.30	3.14

Democracy - Democracies (8–10 on Polity scores); Autocracy - Autocracies (0–3 on Polity scores)

Sources: World Bank, *World Development Indicators 2003*; *Polity IV Democracy Scores*; Observations based on country-year;

[1]As there are relatively few cases in the $500–$1,000 GDP/capita range, the $0–$1,000 category is included to represent this income iteration.

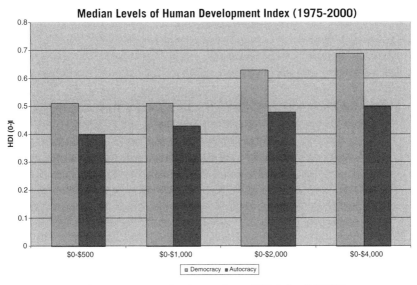

Based on data from *UNDP Human Development Report 2002; Polity; WDI 2002.*

Figure 2.5 Democracies score consistently higher on UNDP's Human Development Index for each income category considered.

between $1,000 and $2,000), democracies have experienced some 40 percent fewer infant deaths—39 versus 64—than autocracies.[36] Similarly, female youth illiteracy is closely monitored since women play such a critical role at the household level in promoting other aspects of development—from health and education to maintaining the environment and starting small businesses. Table 2.2 demonstrates a rapid decline in female youth illiteracy as per capita income levels rise in democracies. Among democracies at the $1,000 to $2,000 interval, typically only 6 percent of young women are illiterate. In autocracies, the female illiteracy rate remains at nearly 22 percent. Perhaps most importantly, Table 2.2 reveals the breadth of social-welfare differences that emerge along regime-type categorizations. Access to basic levels of health, education, and food production define living standards for many developing countries. In 57 of the 60 categories compared, democracies demonstrate an advantage over autoocracies—differences that are, for the most part, statistically significant. Meanwhile, mixed political systems, those governments with certain, though limited institutional checks on power, generate results that are typically in between those of the more distinctive democracy and autocracy categories.

In certain respects, these results are even more noteworthy since they cover a period when a number of communist autocracies (for example, the

Soviet Union, Cuba, China, and Mongolia) established commendable public health and education systems.

In an attempt to create an alternative to raw economic growth as a measure of national well being, the UNDP has published a Human Development Index annually since 1990 that covers three basic dimensions of human development: a long and healthy life, knowledge (as determined by adult literacy and by secondary and tertiary educational enrollment), and a decent standard of living (as measured by per capita GDP). A country's level of attainment on each of these dimensions is scaled on a 0 to 1 basis relative to the performance of other countries in a given year. The three scaled scores are then averaged to determine a country's overall rating for that year. Sweden and Norway have typically achieved the highest Human Development Index scores, roughly 0.94, whereas Sierra Leone and Niger have generated the lowest, 0.27. In 2003, scores for 175 countries were tabulated. Using this methodology, the UNDP has calculated index scores for all countries from which sufficient data are available for five-year intervals from 1975 to 2000. The results show a strong association between democracy and well being among developing countries (see Figure 2.5). At each income category considered, democracies generate higher median levels of the Human Development Index than autocracies.

A similar pattern is apparently evolving with regards to HIV and AIDS. Although the lack of reliable data makes firm comparisons premature, a snapshot of the spread of this disease suggests a continuation of the pattern of democratic responsiveness to human needs among developing countries (see Table 2.3). In every income category considered, democracies post substantially lower estimated percentages of adults who are HIV positive. Given the singular importance of public awareness for the slowing of this highly contagious virus, this result is not surprising. (And these figures do not factor in the presumed greater accuracy of reporting in democracies.) Although certain democracies have been seriously challenged by HIV/AIDS (for example, Botswana), the openness that is encouraged under democratic governments is a distinct advantage for public health efforts.

Table 2.3 Median Percentage of Adult Population with HIV/AIDS (2000/2001)

GDP per Capita	Democracies	Autocracies
$0–$500	0.20%	3.2%
$500–$1,000	0.15%	2.8%
$1,000–$2,000	0.20%	1.6%
$2,000–$4,000	0.45%	0.95%

Sources: World Health Organization; UNAIDS; *Polity IV.*

As a result of the poor quality of cross-national data on income inequality, we refrain from making any direct comparisons of this gap based on governance type. Nonetheless, as mentioned earlier, the extent to which a greater percentage of a population has access to basic services and opportunities for a healthy life implies such a relationship. Consistent with this observation, the percentage of a population living on $1 a day (according to UNDP figures) is larger in autocracies than in democracies for every income category considered. For example, in countries with per capita GDPs below $1,000 in the late 1990s (the latest period for which data are available), 26 percent of the population of the average democracy subsists on less than $1 a day, compared with 36 percent in autocracies. Therefore, while the difficulty of measuring income inequality in a manner reliable enough for cross-national comparisons limits generalities, indications suggest that the disparities in democracies are less acute.

In short, the historical record shows that low-income democracies have demonstrated a strikingly superior performance of democracies across a broad range of development indicators. The consistency of this pattern underlines the robustness of this association. Democratic governance matters for development. Of course, democracies, autocracies, and regimes that are somewhere in between all exhibit wide ranges in their development performances. Being a democracy does not ensure rapid development progress. Nonetheless, at every income level considered, democracies on the whole have consistently generated superior levels of social welfare. This pattern holds even at the lowest income category (below $500 per capita GDP), in which democracies outperform other governance types in all 12 measures considered in Table 2.2.

A Growing Differential in the Post-Cold War Period
Figures 2.4a through 2.4d also suggest a growing divergence in the standards of living between democracies and autocracies over the course of recent decades. There are many possible explanations for this. The quality and coverage of development data in developing countries has improved dramatically over the past 20 years. This has made measuring differences in development performance more reliable. Moreover, for a variety of reasons, the 1980s and 1990s were a time of great economic volatility for many developing countries. Autocratic governments have, by and large, fared particularly poorly during this period. The growing discrepancy in development performance may also reflect the curtailment of subsidies from both sides of the superpower rivalry that propped up autocratic governments. As this external revenue stream has dried up and with it the distorting effects on development have diminished, democracy's distinctive developmental advantages may be coming more sharply into focus. The

performance differentials may also reflect the decline in the number of autocratic governments that were communist (and that invested relatively more heavily in health and education than other authoritarian governments). There may be other global phenomena that are contributing to the growing gap in development performance. It may be that there is greater relative compatibility between democracies and the widespread adoption of market-based economic systems. With a growing reliance on trade to stimulate economic performance, democratic societies may be demonstrating a greater ability to absorb and adapt to new information in a way that enhances their competitiveness. Similarly, recent decades have seen a dramatic increase in the accessibility of telecommunications, transport, and air travel. Societies that are relatively more open are likely to benefit from these features of the emerging global economy. Regardless of cause, recent patterns of development performance suggest that these global trends are accentuating the relative developmental strengths of democracies.

Social Welfare Expenditures

Perhaps one reason that low-income democracies have achieved a development advantage is that they pour more money into social services than do autocracies. This is not true. Public spending on education differs relatively little between democracies and authoritarian systems over the 1960 to 2001 time period (see Table 2.4). Low-income countries, regardless of political type, have typically spent between 2.5 percent and 3.5 percent of their GDP

Table 2.4 Median Levels of Social Spending Among Low-Income Countries

Variable	Regime	1960s	1970s	1980s	1990s	Overall
Public Spending on	Democracies	2.27	2.75	3.15	3.22	**3.17**
Education	Autocracies	2.42	3.49	3.31	3.94	**3.47**
(% of GDP)						
Spend/Primary	Democracies	10.2	17.6	10.5	11.4	**11.0**
Student	Autocracies	12.5	12.7	11.7	12.5	**11.9**
(% of GDP per						
Capita)						
Public Spending	Democracies	—	—	—	2.39	**2.39**
on Health	Autocracies	—	—	—	1.90	**1.90**
(% of GDP)						

Based on data from *World Development Indicators 2003; Polity IV.*

on public education—with autocracies spending more overall—3.5 versus 3.2 percent. On a per-student basis, autocracies have spent nearly a full percentage point more of per capita GDP on primary school students than democracies over this four-decade period.

As extensive cross-national health expenditure data are only available for the 1990s, we are limited in our ability to generalize for this sector. As per the data available, low-income democracies did spend a slightly greater share on public health as a percentage of GDP than autocracies—2.4 percent versus 1.9 percent. This observation is matched by low-income democracies' relatively greater per capita health expenditures ($37 versus $18), though again this data is limited to the 1990s. Therefore, the superior health-related outcomes among democracies may be due to their relatively greater commitment of resources to the health sector.

To the extent that democracies are spending greater shares of their public resources on health activities, however, this does not translate into larger fiscal deficits. Both democracies and other governance systems have averaged deficits of between 3.0 percent and 4.5 percent of GDP in the years 1970 to 2001 (see Table 2.5). Differences in aggregate averages are negligible. Nor do low-income democratic governments exhibit disproportionate levels of government spending. The overall share of government expenditures as a part of the economy is comparable for low-income democracies and autocracies—12.7 percent versus 13.1 percent from 1960 to 2001. Consequently, given the breadth of democracies' superior developmental track record, factors other than lopsided funding of the social sector must be responsible.

In summary, the historical patterns of democratic development imply that even low-income democracies are better able to marshal the resources at their disposal into services that contribute to improved standards of living. That is, contrary to the conventional hypothesis, democracies are capable of creating administrative structures that are both efficient and effective. They typically generate higher levels of social welfare and (possibly)

Table 2.5 Median Levels of Public Expenditure Among Low-Income Countries

Variable	Regime	1960s	1970s	1980s	1990s	Overall
Gov't. Expenditures	Democracies	11.5	11.6	12.8	13.1	**12.7**
(% of GDP)	Autocracies	10.8	12.5	14.7	13.7	**13.1**
Budget Deficit	Democracies	n/a	3.20	4.41	3.02	**3.46**
(% of GDP)	Autocracies	n/a	2.70	4.76	2.27	**3.24**

Based on data from *World Development Indicators 2003; Polity IV.*

economic growth for a greater share of their populations than autocracies do. Considering the importance of human capital to improved economic productivity, the tendency of low-income democracies to more effectively build the health and education capacities of their societies suggests that democratic policies also indirectly contribute to long-term economic development.

Democratic Advantages

The track record of the past 40 years compels us to alter how we frame the debate about democratic or authoritarian advantage. The question is no longer whether authoritarian regimes have a development advantage. The evidence we've reviewed makes it clear they do not. Nor is the question whether low-income democracies are capable of developing at comparable levels to autocracies. They are. The pressing question becomes, how do low-income democracies spur development? Specifically, why do low-income democracies generate higher standards of living than autocracies? On an intuitive level, the superior development track record of democracies should come as little surprise. In instances where history has created recent "natural experiments" (pairs of countries with similar cultural, economic, and geographic origins), states that pursued relatively more open and democratic forms of government have developed much more rapidly. In East Germany versus West Germany, North Korea versus South Korea, Haiti versus the Dominican Republic, and China versus Hong Kong and Taiwan, the advantage of countries with more open governance structures has been self-evident. Robert Putnam observed a parallel pattern in his seminal work comparing southern and northern Italy.[37] Putnam argues in great detail that the stronger democratic and civic culture of northern Italy has fostered its relative prosperity compared to the south. Clearly multiple factors contribute to the divergences; nonetheless, these cases are instructive.

There are a lot of reasons why democracies are better suited than authoritarian forms of government to promote economic and social development. Some have to do with the way they are structured, others with the manner in which they operate. Below, we have organized those explanations around three core characteristics of democracy: shared power, openness, and adaptability.

Shared Power

1. *Vertical Accountability.* At its core, government is the mechanism created by societies to determine "the public interest" from among many competing alternatives. Through governments, priorities are

identified and resources allocated. The type of government in place is thus critical to the way these decisions are made. Democracies are designed so that this decision-making process is more representative. In an effort to gain the support of a majority of voters either directly or through governing coalitions, politicians in democracies have incentives to act in accordance with the political center of a society (that is, according to "the median voter"). In other words, by requiring the support of a broad segment of the population to earn their right to govern, democratic structures encourage public officials to serve the interests of ordinary citizens in government spending and policymaking. Structurally, this enhances the likelihood that a broader percentage of the population benefits from the public goods and services provided. Democracies are thus based on the premise that the electorate will hold leaders accountable for their actions (vertical accountability).

It isn't just the need to win elections that prods a democratic government to respond to the priorities of its citizens. Civic groups that champion ordinary people's interests also hold elected officials accountable for their actions. These groups, furthermore, foster the public participation that has long been the decisive factor in the effectiveness of development projects. A World Bank study examining levels of participation in Tanzania found that villages in which adults belonged to two or more civic associations had income levels that were 40 percent higher than comparable villages with less participation.[38] These qualities are also important at the national level. In a cross-national assessment of projects financed by the World Bank, the economic rate of return was 8 percent to 22 percent higher in countries with the strongest civil liberties than in countries with the weakest civil liberties.[39]

2. *Horizontal Accountability.* Democracies are conceived on the notion of shared power, especially the horizontal checks and balances stemming from multiple branches of government. This creates a self-reinforcing mechanism for curtailing abuses of power by any one individual or entity, notably the chief executive. The moderating influences of such a system avoid the devastating consequences of radical policy choices made by an exclusive set of individuals, thereby providing better protection from economic or political disasters. The debilitating outcomes resulting from unchecked autocratic rule are evident in the reckless actions of Kim Jong-Il in North Korea, Robert Mugabe in Zimbabwe, Alexander Lukashenko in Belarus, and former Iraqi leader Saddam Hussein, to note just a few. In the developing

world, the moderating influences frequently spell the difference between life and death. Amartya Sen recognizes this association with his observation that contemporary democracies with a free press have never experienced a major famine.[40] The "quiet" famine of the late 1990s in North Korea that is estimated to have killed 10 percent of the population is a horrific illustration of unchecked power.

3. *Greater Allocation of Opportunity.* Government power in democracies is not only separated among various branches and levels, it is also limited. And the recognition of the distinction between the public and private spheres fosters a separation between political authority and economic opportunity. That in turn underpins the creation of private property rights and government adherence to the rule of law, innovation, economic productivity and asset creation. In such a society, individuals are able to pursue prosperity without belonging to a dominant political party. Merit, not political allegiance, is the relatively more decisive factor in their access to education, jobs, business licenses, credit, and other opportunities for improving their lot.

In other words, democracy is more efficient than dictatorship at tapping people's talent and unleashing their energies to pursue their dreams. It would seem self-evident then, that breaking up the nexus of entrenched political and economic interests that thrive in dictatorships is often a prerequisite for economic development in poor countries.

In his pioneering work on this subject, Donald Wittman contends that the competitive nature of democratic political markets, as with economic markets, make them inherently efficient. The structures of both markets, he argues, are organized to promote wealth-maximizing outcomes. The parallels are striking. Politicians can be thought of as political entrepreneurs who, like their economic counterparts, are rewarded for efficient behavior. The populace is allowed to judge their accomplishments, just as the market judges products and services, and voters can reject them, just as consumers have the freedom to reject whatever is offered for sale. Rival politicians can profit by exposing their shortcomings, just as companies can publicize their competitors' flaws. Wittman writes: "(Only) a model that assumes that voters are constantly fooled and that there are no alternate political entrepreneurs to clear up their confusion will predict that the decision-making process leads to inefficient results . . . Theories of elite control of democratic politics tend to leave out the *democratic* part entirely: either policies are formed and conducted outside the democratic domain or the elites lull the mass of voters to sleep."[41]

Openness

4. *Information Access.* Many of democracy's development advantages revolve around its support for freedom of speech. In a freewheeling public debate, a greater range of ideas is considered than would otherwise be the case. Given the greater accessibility of information to the public, the quality of analysis is higher. Government officials contemplating a new policy must face a higher level of scrutiny that they would in a dictatorship. Journalists, scholars, and business and civic leaders will offer their opinions and counterproposals. In a democracy, policymakers will be compelled to take into account these views and any new information they provide. In contrast, the absence of this information, analysis, and dialogue in autocracies increases the likelihood that a new policy will fail because government officials won't have considered all the possible negative consequences.[42] In democracies, the deliberative decision-making process not only leads to more informed choices, it also generally results in greater public support for decisions once they are made.

Democracies' horizontal linkages allow them to better absorb and disseminate information throughout their bureaucratic structures and society at large than autocracies do, especially autocracies with hierarchal structures. Janus Kornai documented the deleterious effects of poor information flow in hierarchal organizations in his study of Eastern bloc state-owned enterprises.[43] Although authoritarian governments have succeeded in mobilizing production in large, repetitive-function sectors like manufacturing, energy, and mining, they have had a harder time sustaining those industries' economic performance because that requires improving efficiency through innovation and productivity gains. This inherent weakness isn't always apparent. Controlled economies can grow rapidly for years or even decades without developing the mechanisms necessary for improving efficiency.

Democracies' superior capacity for disseminating information and adapting to changing circumstances is especially crucial in today's fast-paced and highly competitive global economy. The free flow of information that characterizes democracies spurs innovation and productivity gains, reduces the risk and lowers the transaction costs of financial transactions, fosters investment, and improves economic efficiency.[44] In a similar vein, Joseph Schumpeter, writing at the end of World War II, recognized that the innovation central to the dynamism of capitalism lay in the creativity of the individual. He worried that as economic power became centralized in monopolies (and information flow was curtailed), individual initiative and thus innovation would be suffocated. It followed that maintaining the capacity for innovation in capitalism was contingent on maintaining competition.[45]

5. *Greater Transparency.* The relative openness of democracies also contributes to greater levels of transparency in the use of public resources. Although this is insufficient to prevent corruption, it does increase the probability that such illegal activity will be exposed. Democracies in the late 1990s are perceived, on average, to exhibit levels of corruption that are nearly half that of autocracies, according to annual surveys by Transparency International, a nonprofit organization that aims to raise awareness about and expose corruption. Its 2003 survey involved 133 countries. Similarly, data from the International Country Risk Guide (ICRG), a monthly survey produced since 1982 mainly for corporate investors by the for-profit firm Political Risk Services, finds that the level of corruption in democracies is typically 15 percent to 25 percent lower that that in autocracies, no matter how rich or how poor the country. The ICRG assessed 139 countries in 2003. A separate World Bank study of 4,000 firms in 22 East Bloc countries found an inverse relationship between the level of corruption[46] and the extent of civil liberties, regardless of the pace of economic reform. The study also showed that higher levels of corruption were accompanied by greater concentrations of political power, fewer checks and balances to counter that power, more restraints on political competition, and greater influence over the government by big corporations.

Along with fostering corruption, economic monopolies impede transparency and hamper economic development. In general, the more open the society and the freer the flow of information within it, the greater the likelihood that corporate-governance standards will emerge. Conventions such as accounting principles, external audits, standardized financial reporting, shareholder protections, external boards, and disclosures of conflict of interest are the preconditions of a healthy and competitive marketplace.

Adaptability

6. *Political Stability.* An established mechanism for replacing leaders augments democracies' political stability. The recognized legitimacy of this succession process serves as a deterrent to those who would contemplate unconstitutional seizures of power. Periodic elections allow for the peaceful replacement of ineffectual leaders,

limiting the damage they can do, mitigating the disastrous effects of their unchallenged policy assumptions and preventing the institutional sclerosis endemic to governments that remain in power for prolonged periods or are beholden to special interests. By contrast, in authoritarian systems, the very narrowness of their claim on power carries with it the ever-present risk that leaders in these systems will be deposed through unconstitutional means. As Mancur Olson noted, the stability of even durable autocrats is limited to a single lifetime.[47] Even if a leader isn't overthrown but dies or retires, the succession process must be reinvented every time. And the absence of a legal mechanism for a transition practically guarantees unscrupulous behavior on the part of potential successors.

7. *Democracies as "Learning Organizations."* Just as the process leading up to a decision in democracies is likely to be more open and deliberative, so too, is the post-decision period. Ineffective policies are apt to come under greater scrutiny and criticism, hastening adjustments. In fact, democracies are systems of constant self-surveillance and adaptation. They govern through a process of trial and error. When something is working, that approach is expanded. If a policy is ineffective, it is discarded. And a range of interests that are represented in the legislature, judiciary, press, and civil society act as early warning signals of such ineffectiveness. They thus help facilitate the adoption of a nuanced course forward in what are often uncharted waters. In short, while democratic governance does not guarantee coming up with the "right" policy, it does guarantee the option of changing a policy if it is "wrong."

The adaptive capacity of democracies was demonstrated in the aftermath of the East Asian financial crisis from which democracies rebounded more quickly than autocracies.[48] The comparative approaches of South Korea and Indonesia are particularly illustrative. South Korea was able to use elections in December 1997 to restore confidence in government and generate credibility for structural reforms. The reform-minded Kim Dae Jung administration came into office undertaking significant policy reforms that revitalized the economy. In Indonesia, meanwhile, the crisis exposed the structural weaknesses of the authoritarian system, ultimately leading to the collapse of the Soeharto regime.[49] Indonesia has yet to recover economically from this precipitous fall.

These structural and procedural features of democracies create conditions that are conducive to economic and social development. They may also partly explain the paradox that while private investors often express leeriness about democratization, in fact, foreign direct

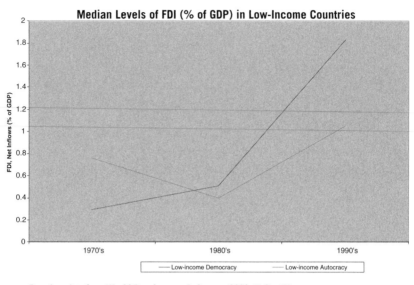

Based on data from *World Development Indicators 2003; Polity IV.*

Figure 2.6 Median levels of foreign direct investment in emerging markets have shifted toward democracies, as a percentage of GDP, since the mid-1980s.

investment has gravitated to low-income democracies to a greater extent than less representative governments since the mid-1980s (see Figure 2.6).[50] Notably, the accelerating swing in favor of investment in low-income democratic countries occurred during a period of rapidly increasing global economic integration and democratization. Indicative of this trend, India is ranked higher than China on the Economist Intelligence Unit survey of the best places in Asia to do business.[51]

What About East Asia?

Although the record of democratic development is compelling, the rapid economic growth of a number of East Asian authoritarian nations presents conceptual and empirical challenges to the notion of the developmental superiority of democracies. South Korea, Taiwan, Indonesia, Singapore, Vietnam, and China have all realized rapid rates of economic growth over extended periods under autocratic systems.

So too did Chile under Pinochet, many would say. In reality, though, this experience is more ambiguous. Pinochet took over a country with well-established democratic institutions that provided the civil, legal, and administrative structures on which subsequent economic development was built. Moreover, economic growth fluctuated wildly during his years in power, fitting the pattern of volatility that we have described for dictatorships. Seizing power from Allende in 1973 in the midst of an economic crisis in which the economy contracted by 6.5 percent, Pinochet oversaw per capita economic declines of 13 percent in 1975 and 17 percent in the years 1982 to 1983. Although Chile realized positive growth in 14 of Pinochet's 17 years of rule, it took until the mid 1980s for the country to surpass for good the $2,300 of per capita output it had in 1973. Unemployment remained in the double digits until 1986. For all these reasons, it must be said that Chile under Pinochet does not fit the autocratic growth model. This is not to dismiss the importance of certain economic policies adopted by the Pinochet regime. Pinochet pioneered the use of an export-oriented liberal economic model in Latin America at a time when import substitution was the norm. Moreover, his administration distinguished itself from other autocratic governments by refraining from predatory behavior and practicing fiscal discipline.

The rapid growth of the East Asian authoritarians demonstrates that democracy is not indispensable for development. The relationship between regime type and economic performance is not ironclad. Although the trend is clear, exceptions exist and overarching generalizations should be avoided. It works both ways: for all the talk of the East Asian Tigers,[52] there have been a number of cases of East Asian development disasters under authoritarian rule, notably the Philippines (under Marcos), Cambodia, Burma, and North Korea. Reflecting their exceptionalism, the East Asian authoritarian dynamos experienced growth rates in the years 1960 to 2001 that were on average triple those of other authoritarian-run nations. Yet they made up less than 5 percent of such regimes during this time period. Thus, their authoritarianism was not a decisive factor in their extraordinary economic performance. Other distinguishing characteristics have to be considered, including the following:

1. *Good Economic Policies.* The high-performance East Asian economies all made choices to pursue market-oriented economic systems at a time when central economic planning was still in vogue. They managed to uphold a system of property rights that created the foundation for a vibrant private sector. Moreover, government policies in these countries were distinguished by their macroeconomic stability. They typically posted fiscal surpluses, established a stable exchange rate, and maintained a disciplined monetary policy that held inflation in check. Building on their populations' tradition of saving, they were able to funnel domestic capital into a reliable engine for growth. At the early stages of their development, with between 60 percent and

90 percent of their populations engaged in agriculture, the East Asian Tigers also strategically invested in agricultural technology to increase the production of rubber, palm oil, silk, rice, and the like, improving their nations' competitiveness and increasing both their export income and jobs.[53]

2. *Chinese Businessmen.* The East Asian dynamos did not develop in a vacuum. Rather, they benefited from the synergy of the broader regional dynamism. A particularly important element of this regional network was the expertise and capital mobility of ethnic Chinese businessmen based in many of the key East Asian economies.[54] Working through these informal channels with established mechanisms for assessing credit worthiness and penalties for default, firms in the East Asian Tigers were able to expand relatively rapidly to take advantage of neighboring markets. This network of Chinese traders acted as a proxy for the contracting culture that Douglass North identified as integral for economic development.[55]

3. *Japanese Capital.* The East Asian dynamos also benefited from the ready availability of Japanese capital. Having become major international creditors by the 1970s, Japanese banks recognized the potential of the emerging East Asian economies and invested heavily in them. By the mid 1990s, roughly 40 percent of East Asia's asset liabilities were to Japanese banks.[56] There was a downside to this. During the East Asian crisis of 1997–1998, the Tigers' reliance on a single creditor contributed to a regional financial meltdown. Nonetheless, between the Japanese banks and the Chinese business networks, fledging firms were not constrained by lack of capital.

4. *Access to Markets.* Following Japan, the East Asian authoritarian growers pursued aggressive export-oriented growth strategies. They thus avoided the constraints to growth imposed by small domestic markets typically encountered by developing countries. The West's willingness to maintain large trade deficits with East Asia without pressing for an immediate reciprocal opening of markets was another fortunate, though historically exceptional, circumstance. Meanwhile, the East Asian dynamos benefited greatly from their close proximity to China as it became an economic force.

5. *Collective Interests.* Before their take-off, the high-performance East Asian economies exhibited a high degree of income equality compared with Latin America and the Middle East. In addition to removing a common source of friction, this characteristic contributed to a strong sense of national solidarity. This translated into relatively wide access to health services and educational opportunities as these countries grew economically. Improved human capital, in turn, has

contributed to higher levels of economic productivity and investment. Cultural norms[57] that placed a high value on equality may also partly explain why East Asian leaders, unlike other authoritarians, kept patronage and graft under control. Campos and Root also argue that leaders in East Asia had incentives to pursue strategies of shared growth lest they face communist insurgencies such as those that crippled China, Vietnam, North Korea, and Cambodia.[58] In a number of important cases (South Korea, Taiwan, and Hong Kong), the East Asian dynamos were also relatively ethnically homogeneous. This characteristic may have contributed to their political stability as authoritarian governments are particularly susceptible to conflict in ethnically divided societies.[59]

6. *Capital Mobilization.* As with most authoritarian growth historically, much of the East Asian "miracle" can be explained by high rates of investment, transfer of labor from agriculture to manufacturing, and higher labor participation rates.[60] However, the extent to which they have been able to make the transition to productivity-enhancing, sustained development has varied considerably. Notably, this transition is something democratic South Korea and Taiwan were able to make, whereas authoritarian Indonesia was not.

7. *External Influence.* The economic exceptionalism of East Asia has also dovetailed with geopolitical developments. During the Cold War, the United States was committed to providing support to countries resisting communism. This translated into the transfer of substantial political, economic, and military resources from the United States for each of the East Asian authoritarian growers. Moreover, the United States and the United Kingdom helped shape key legal and economic institutions in South Korea, Taiwan, Singapore, Hong Kong, Thailand, and Malaysia, and by extension their property rights laws, land reforms, business and accounting codes, and financial institutions. Similarly, many of the post-independence institutions that contributed to subsequent economic dynamism in Malaysia and to a lesser extent, Singapore and Indonesia, were established under democratic governments. Malaysia had a democratic government from 1957 to 1968 and Singapore for most of the 1959 to 1964 period. In Indonesia, a robust parliament capable of mediating political conflict, independent courts, a free press, and fair elections also existed before Sukarno seized power.[61] Therefore, while often overlooked, the East Asian dynamos have their own democratic imprints that have shaped their subsequent economic gains.

8. *Strong Institutions.* In addition to strong legal and economic institutions, the dynamic performers in East Asia have developed relatively

competent and efficient civil structures that provided public goods and services, enforcement of government regulations, revenue collection, and policy guidance. In comparison with other regions, notably Latin America, whose median GDP in 1960 was more than 50 percent higher, East Asia has had substantially lower corruption. This illustrates the high-performing East Asian's ability to restrain governments' predatory behavior with a measure of independent oversight.[62] Reflecting the comparative efficiency of the East Asian growers' public institutions, these advances in living conditions relative to Latin America have been realized without incurring correspondingly greater levels of government spending.

9. *Information Flow.* Finally, while not bastions of civil liberty, the fast-growing East Asian authoritarian nations allowed some scope for free expression. In South Korea, student protests were tolerated throughout the 1960s and 1970s. And the authoritarian governments of East Asia allowed press freedoms at levels comparable with the global median over the past three decades.[63] This permitted the flow of both information and technology, increasing the efficiency of financial transactions and spurring economic development.

China is the largest and most frequently cited contemporary authoritarian economic dynamo. Its experience parallels those of the earlier East Asian growers. It has maintained a strong macroeconomic environment of low inflation, fiscal prudence, and a strong savings rate—the second highest in the world in the 1990s.[64] Like the other East Asian dynamos, and contrary to pure liberal economic models, it has retained certain capital controls, including a nonconvertible currency, and limits to foreign ownership of its privatized enterprises. China started its economic development by lifting the constraints on its agricultural sector in the late 1970s.[65] This liberalization led to increases in food output, employment and personal income, and wealth that together acted as a springboard to modernization. China also has enjoyed ready access to capital from Taiwan, Hong Kong, and Japan, absorbing $1/3$ of all foreign direct investment in the developing world in the 1990s. It was able to sell its goods to western markets with few barriers, racking up massive trade surpluses with the United States. In addition, China began its economic growth spurt on a social foundation of general income equality. Healthcare services and educational opportunities were unusually extensive for a low-income country. Moreover, unlike the Soviet Union, communist China opted for a more decentralized administrative structure, including the retention of local taxes within respective jurisdictions for the provision of public services. This augmented the accountability demanded of local officials by the general population.[66] China has also gradually instituted certain political and legal reforms reducing the scope for arbitrary behavior on the part of government officials.[67] Simultaneously, China has eased access to certain types of media and information technology, facilitating economic growth. However, it retains tight control over content so as to stifle criticism of the government.

Although China's economic performance over the past 20 years has been phenomenal, certain qualifications apply. China was starting from a low base; its economy had been stagnating for decades, reaching per capita GDP of only $128 in 1970 (in 1995 U.S. dollars). The result was a huge, pent-up demand for goods and services. Meanwhile, systematic understatement of inflation by firms accounts for 2.5 percent of growth per year in China's nonagricultural economy from 1978 to 1998.[69] Some economists explain much of China's remaining growth as a result of one-time adjustments in the economy such as the reallocation of labor from rural to urban centers and rising participation of women in the workforce.[70] This would be the typical authoritarian phenomenon of capital mobilization. Others note that what productivity gains have been seen are among private firms (while productivity has been declining in state-owned enterprises).[71] Productivity differences are also observed by sector. Agriculture, transport, and telecommunications do seem to show improvements in efficiency. In contrast, growth in the manufacturing, construction, and service sectors relies on the increased mobilization of resources (rather than productivity increasing investment).[72] In other words, the sustainability of China's rapid growth remains in doubt.

In summary, the economic development of the East Asian autocratic growers has been highly exceptional. It has been closely linked to their pursuit of market economics, access to formal and informal capital markets, constraints against predatory leaders, relative social equality, and geopolitical factors, including the openness of Western markets to East Asia's goods and to the political, economic, and military support of Western governments eager to provide a bulwark against communism in the Cold War years. Therefore, while the East Asian experience demonstrates that democracy is not indispensable for development, the distinctiveness of the conditions that have fostered economic growth in its absence need to be recognized. This, in turn, tempers propositions that the East Asian experience can be easily replicated in other autocratic-led developing countries.

In the words of Nobel laureate Amartya Sen, the policies that led to growth in the East Asian authoritarian-run nations included "openness to competition, the use of international markets, a high level of literacy and education, successful land reforms and public provisions of incentives for investment, exporting, and industrialization . . . There is nothing whatsoever to indicate that any of these policies is inconsistent with greater democracy, that any one of them had to be sustained by the elements of authoritarianism. What is needed for generating faster economic growth is a friendlier economic climate rather than a harsher political system . . . To concentrate only on economic incentives (which the market provides) while ignoring political incentives (which democratic systems provide) is to opt for a deeply unbalanced set of ground rules."[73]

Institutions That Contribute to Development

Since the mid-1990s there has been a growing consensus among economists, political scientists, and international investors over the vital importance to development of strong social institutions.[74] Institutions are social values and norms that characterize how people in a society relate to one another. Some of these conventions may become formalized in a country's legal code, like freedom of the press or restrictions on the sale of alcohol, while others are not written down but are embedded in the nation's psychology, like respect for traffic laws, the extent to which police officers expect bribes, the inclination to resolve private disputes through litigation, the tolerance of sky-high pay packages for corporate executives, the willingness to question authority, and the readiness to participate in civic activities. Whether they take the form of law or custom, these institutions shape the behavior and interactions of public and private individuals and organizations and have a profound influence over the rate and manner in which a society develops.

The economist Douglass C. North has championed the focus on institutions. His view is that institutions, particularly those that contribute to more predictable behavior in the marketplace, explain much of the historical differences in levels of development around the world.[75] Consequently, though a number of Latin American countries may have adopted constitutions based on the U.S. model, the ways that they interpret and apply the rule of law can be starkly different from that in the United States. These institutional disparities go a long way toward explaining the divergence in incentives for investment, innovation, and asset accumulation. In fact, he contends that they are a more decisive force than technology in economic development. After all, once technology has been developed, it becomes readily accessible throughout the world, but societies vary widely in their openness to adopting it. North attributes this to the diversity of incentives created by a society's institutional structures.

Our analysis shows that democracies are better able to generate the institutions that foster efficient economic outcomes. Democratic institutions of shared power, adherence to the rule of law, and a free press, for example, contribute to more informed policy, greater transparency and financial analysis for investors, enhanced responsiveness of leaders to the interests of their constituents, and stronger incentives to expose special interests.

Institutions that promote a separation of political and economic authority in a society provide checks and balances that mitigate against a monopolization of power that lead to economic distortions. Other examples of institutions that serve to strengthen democracy and the economy include checks on the executive branch, an impartial legal system, apolitical access to the market and credit, a merit-based civil service, autonomous anticorruption bodies, a transparent and systematic budgeting and disbursement process, accounting and auditing standards, and campaign finance regulations buffering candidates from private sector capture.

Although economists and investors often speak of the importance of the rule of law for economic growth, there is a political dimension to ensuring that the rule of law is established, enforced, and amended when necessary. As Ibrahim Shihata, the longtime General Counsel of the World Bank, noted: "Laws are not self-enforcing."[76] How laws are enforced depends on who is enforcing them. Inevitably, then, the basis for a society's rule of law is its system for selecting its leaders. The more rules-based, participatory, and transparent this process, the greater legitimacy and incentives an executive branch will have to enforce regulations in a manner that is fair and in the public interest. The institutions that foster stronger democratic processes reinforce those that improve the application of the rule of law.

Most research on the institutional dimension of economic development has emphasized the importance of "economic rights" like contract enforcement, property rights, protection from expropriation, and capital mobility, all of which can be classified under the rubric of rule of law.[77] Such analysis indicates that these institutions account for as much as 47 percent of economic growth. This equates to a difference in growth of up to two percentage points per year of GDP.[78] Over 20 years, this difference results in income levels that are 50 percent superior to that of a country with a flat rate of growth. The establishment of these economic institutions has been identified as a distinguishing factor of the relatively few developing countries (for example, Botswana, Chile, Costa Rica, Mauritius, Singapore, South Korea, and Thailand) that have been able to narrow the prosperity gap with the industrialized world.[79]

Some researchers have expanded the analysis of institutions beyond a focus on economic rights to cover civil liberties, the autonomy of the civil service, the independence of the media, and constraints on the executive branch as part of a more comprehensive network of checks and balance that represent good governance. This research finds that each of these additional institutional categories is also an important explanatory factor for more rapid growth.[80] Moreover, in a study of contemporary democratizing countries, press freedom was the institutional factor most consistently associated with predicting higher levels of growth across all regions.[81] These findings demonstrate that more than just economic institutions are central to explaining developmental performance.

Understanding the importance of institutions also provides insight into why not all democracies attain superior development outcomes: democracies have dissimilar levels of institutional strength. On one 50-point scale of accountability institutions, democracies' scores range from 20 to 50.[82] Those that distinguished themselves by the strength of their accountability institutions have typically enjoyed relatively more rapid economic development (see Figure 2.7). From 1980 to 2000, low-income democracies with above median levels of accountability grew at an annual per capita GDP rate of 2.0 percent, compared with 1.3 percent for those with below average accountability scores. Similar growth-accountability distinctions emerge when considering a sample of autocracies or countries with mixed governance features. Autocracies with above-average levels of accountability institutions posted a median grow rate of 1.2 percent, compared with 0.9 percent for those with sub-par levels; for regimes with mixed features the difference was 1.5 percent versus 1.0 percent. In short, countries with stronger accountability institutions typically grew between 30 percent and 60 percent faster than politically similar countries that had relatively weaker institutions.

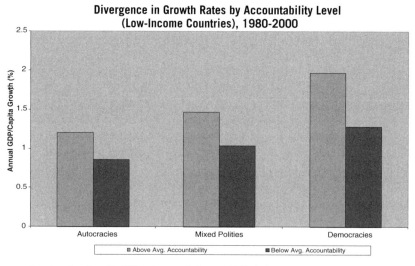

Based on data from *World Development Indicators 2002; Polity IV; Siegle, 2001.*

Figure 2.7 Within each governance category, countries that exhibited stronger machanisms of accountability tended to grow more rapidly than those with weaker institutions of accountability.

The importance of institutions[83] to economic growth helps explain why elections, in isolation, do not contribute to improved development. Nations that hold elections, yet have weak institutions, display significantly lower economic growth and social welfare than democracies with strong institutions. Given the regularity of sham elections, this is unsurprising. An election in Zimbabwe or Belarus is far less meaningful than one in Costa Rica, Senegal, or Estonia. This underlines the point that elections by themselves are poor mechanisms for defining democracy. However, even when legitimate, elections, in their most functional form, are simply mechanisms for selecting political leaders. They do not have direct economic or development linkages. Rather, democracies' development advantage is tied to their ability to establish institutional checks and balances. These mechanisms moderate the pursuit of radical policies, ensure greater accountability of leaders to the general population, create incentives for responsiveness, encourage transparency, and foster adherence to the rule of law.

Said another way, democracies embrace stronger institutions of accountability than do other systems of governance. This is so even among low-income countries—marked by their distinctively superior levels of accountability ratings over time (see Figure 2.8). Adoption of stronger accountability structures, in turn, has a strongly positive effect on development. Correspondingly, low-income democracies score 10 percent to 20 percent higher on the International Country Risk Guide's indices of rule of law, bureaucratic efficiency, and (anti)corruption than do autocracies over the 1982 to 2000 period. Similar patterns emerge when assessing Kaufmann et al.'s index of governance indicators, including measures of

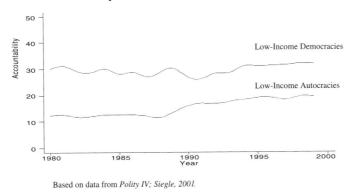

Accountability Levels of Low-Income Deocracies and Autocracies

Based on data from *Polity IV; Siegle, 2001.*

Figure 2.8 Low-income democracies have consistently exhibited stronger institutions of accountability compared to autocracies.

rule of law and government effectiveness. Whereas democracies typically rank demonstrably above the governance medians for low-income countries, autocracies consistently score below average. Advances in civil liberties, press freedom, and checks on executive power generally move in the same direction as improvements in the levels of rule of law, bureaucratic quality, and autonomy of the private sector.[84] Societies that enhance their institutional checks and balances in one area generally enhance them in others as well. Strengthening democratic structures enhances the accountability mechanisms that contribute to growth.

The East Asian Tigers have also distinguished themselves by the accountability structures that they have established. Although of a different nature and not as robust as democracies, these accountability structures are clearly more evident than those typical of autocratic governments (see Figure 2.9). Early on, this was largely realized by their superior standing in the areas of bureaucratic efficiency, rule of law, and space for the private sector. As several of the East Asian Tigers democratized—augmenting their institutional checks on the chief executive and civil liberties—accountability scores mirrored those of democracies.

Although often overlooked because of the global nature of the democracy and development debate, the importance of institutions to growth varies widely by country. There is no magic institutional bullet. Different combinations of institutional checks and balances appear to have been influential for different countries. All bring some value. In addition to the unique qualities that we have already discussed of the East Asian dynamos, other regional variations warrant notice. Take, for example, sub-Saharan Africa, where the relationship between levels of accountability and democc-

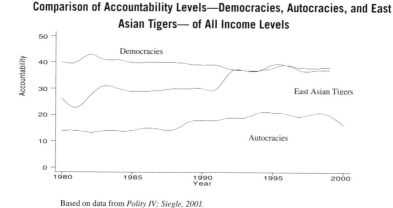

Comparison of Accountability Levels—Democracies, Autocracies, and East Asian Tigers— of All Income Levels

Based on data from *Polity IV; Siegle, 2001.*

Figure 2.9 The East Asian Tigers distinguished themselves from other autocracies by their relatively stronger accountability institutions.

racy is weaker than any other region—pointing to the shallowness of democratic processes on this continent. Those institutions most consistently linked to economic growth in Africa are a free press, rule of law, and a reliable civil service. In other words, it is the substance of creating systems of shared power rather than solely the holding of elections that matters for development. Stated bluntly, the neo-patrimonial structures that continue to characterize many African political systems are diametrically opposite to the institutions of accountability that are vital for development. In Latin America and central Europe, the move toward political pluralism has been closely associated with improved economic performance. Within these regions, however, countries that have demonstrated greater autonomy in their judiciary and private sectors have grown relatively more rapidly. South Asia is the region of the world with the least developed rule of law—posing a significant handicap to sustained economic growth. South Asian states that grew most rapidly established relatively autonomous private sectors, bureaucratic transparency, and a free press. In the Arab world, countries that have realized the most consistent economic performance have had comparatively greater levels of press freedom and executive constraints. In the former Soviet Union, the rule of law, a free press, and lower levels of corruption stood out as the institutional qualities that distinguished nations that realized the most growth during the 1990s.

Summary

Four decades of experience show that low-income democracies consistently outpace their autocratic counterparts on a wide range of development indicators. This can be attributed to democracies' relatively greater propensity for establishing institutions of shared power, information openness, and adaptability. Key to this performance, and critically important for developing countries, is democracies' ability to mitigate disaster. In addition to avoiding the human costs of such catastrophes, progress in democracies can be incrementally accumulated rather than constantly committed to making up lost ground. Economic concerns over supporting democratization in low-income countries—macroeconomic populism, inability to build human capacity, fractiousness, vulnerability to special interests, and so on—are not borne out in relative comparisons with autocracies or mixed systems.

Nonetheless, the relationship between regime type and economic performance is not universal. A select number of autocratic countries, particularly in East Asia, have grown rapidly. This group of strong performers, however, is highly exceptional on a number of fronts, especially in comparison to other autocratic states. Although held up as model, the robust economic performance of the East Asian Tigers is more than offset by the poor (and oftentimes catastrophic) economic experiences of other authoritarian governments. Given this, perhaps the most compelling feature of the strikingly positive democracy–development relationship is its breadth. It does not rely on a select group of super performers. Rather, it is when considered on aggregate terms that democracies' more rapid and consistent development performance relative to autocratic states shines through most clearly.

It is this consistently superior developmental performance of democracies that provides the surest basis for policy guidance. Contrary to well-entrenched views established by the development-first perspective, the track record clearly shows that development in low-income democracies is not only possible but also far more reliable.

CHAPTER 3
Sustaining New Democracies

Communism is dead but we must be careful not to let its still twitch-
ing corpse pull the infant democracy down into the grave with it.

Zhelyu Zhelev
former president of Bulgaria

Chapter 2 showed that democracies generally experience more rapid and
consistent improvements in the well being of their populations than do autocracies. Yet, some experts still caution against promoting democracy in
poor countries, arguing that embryonic democratic institutions in these
societies would be too fragile to survive an economic downturn. This fear
cannot be dismissed out of hand. From its inception in 2000, the 118-mem-
ber Community of Democracies has warned repeatedly about the political
consequences of economic stagnation. A slowing or declining economy in
a country that has just started down the road to participatory politics not
only undermines the popularity of political incumbents but also potentially tarnishes the appeal of democracy itself. Many new democracies inherit economies saddled with onerous debt servicing requirements,
corrupt and patronage-based civil services, huge gaps between rich and
poor, and widespread human suffering. Sluggish economic growth worsens
each of these legacies. This chapter sifts the evidence behind the threat that
economic adversity poses to fledgling democracies and examines the type
of development that preserves a country's commitment to democracy.

The promise of prosperity under democracy can flicker under economic
strains. For citizens in countries undertaking this transformation, the answer to the question, "Is democracy really worth it?" may not be obvious.

Conversely, the tantalizingly simple, if specious, economic solutions promised by authoritarian regimes can seem compelling.

Which Countries Qualify as Democratizers?

Part of the challenge of assessing the performance of countries on the path to democracy is categorizing them. We define democracies as societies in which political authority is derived from the citizenry—through their selection of chief executive, participation of competing political parties, adherence to institutions of shared power, and exercise of basic political rights and liberties (including freedom of thought, speech, press, and association). However, with "consent of the governed" emerging as the international standard for conferring legitimacy on a government, virtually every leader in the world has touted his or her government's democratic credentials, regardless of how dubious they might seem. For example, Presidents Hosni Mubarak of Egypt and Hu Jintao of the People's Republic of China each regularly extol their countries' commitment to democracy in public appearances. But if merely claiming to be a democracy is insufficient proof that a regime really is one, so is the classic litmus test of popular elections. Nearly every dictator in the world today holds them. This includes the reclusive regime of Kim Jung-Il of North Korea, whose candidates for the Supreme People's Assembly always get 100 percent of the votes.[1] Obviously, it is not whether elections are held but whether they are true contests for power that counts. In the attempt to meet the international democracy threshold without truly sharing power, numerous authoritarians have adapted certain trappings of democracy such as an ostensibly independent press, legislature, and civil society. In actuality, many of the key actors in these bodies are frequently government loyalists. To the extent that they are independent, these institutions are heavily circumscribed, leaving them impotent to serve as real checks on executive authority. This has compelled political scientists to invent such odd and contradictory-sounding terms as "illiberal democracies," "liberal authoritarians," "semi-authoritarians," and "pseudo-democracies" to describe phony democracies like Belarus, Egypt, Cameroon, Malaysia, and Zimbabwe. We prefer to avoid qualifying democracy. Instead, we categorize as democracies only those countries that have met the relatively high standards of having instituted genuine checks and balances on executive power and created mechanisms for popular participation in the political process.

Another frequent error is to assume that countries that are moving *away* from authoritarian rule are automatically moving *toward* democracy. Under this rule of thumb, all countries in the former Soviet Union would have to be considered democratizers, whereas in reality a number of them, like Belarus,

Turkmenistan, Uzbekistan, and Azerbaijan, have done little or nothing to build democratic institutions or processes. Escaping the tyranny of a totalitarian state is a positive development. However, reduced repression does not necessarily indicate increased democracy. Conflating the two trends risks creating an unjustifiably broad classification of democratizers (that is, countries on the path to democracy). This, in turn, makes identifying the distinguishing characteristics of genuine democratizers more difficult.

To minimize the spurious categorization of countries moving toward democracy, we again rely on the widely recognized Polity IV democracy index.[2] All countries that have made and sustained at least a 1-point advance on this 0-to-10 scale since 1977 are considered democratizers.[3] By this count, there are 87 democratizers (see Table 3.1).[4] This reflects the scope of this global transition towards democracy—nearly half of all countries in the world have made advances in their level of democracy over the past 25 years. This measure also reveals a continuously rising number of democratizers. Using 1977 as a base, there are more democratizers today than there were in 2000. There were more in 2000 than in 1995, and so on. The vast majority of these democratizers are poor countries, with a median annual per capita income of $950 in 2000. Sixty of them, or 71 percent, have annual per capita incomes below $2,000. In other words, contemporary democratization is largely a developing country phenomenon.

Democratization is a widespread movement. Every major region that does not already have established democracies is represented (see Figure 3.1). Notably, sub-Saharan Africa makes up one-third of all contemporary democratizers. But there is substantial regional variation. The median democracy score for democratizers in Central Europe is a nine. Democratizers in Latin America, East Asia, and the Baltics score in the upper tier of the scale, on average. In South Asia and Africa, democratizers typically score in the middle of the 11-point index. The relatively few democratizers in the Middle East are in the lowest tier of this spectrum.

Many of the contemporary democratizers have made notable gains in their democratic institutions during this period of transition. The median degree of change in democracy scores since 1977 is six. This would be the equivalent of democratic advances made by countries such as Bangladesh, Ecuador, Macedonia, and Malawi—that have moved from largely authoritarian systems to those that offer a fair degree of political participation and civil liberties, yet still fall short of the democratic threshold. Two-thirds of the democratizers scored in the top half of the 0-to-10 democracy scale. In contrast, only 10 democratizers have a democracy score of one.

These observed democratic advances reflect not just the arrival of newcomers to the democratic path but also the long slog toward democracy many countries in the group have experienced. Of the 87 democratizers, 45

Table 3.1 Categorization of Contemporary Democratizers by Polity Democracy Score in 2002[5]

1	2	3	4	5	6	7	8	9	10
Algeria	Burkina Faso	Cambodia	Comoros	Georgia	Armenia	Albania	Argentina	Bolivia	Czech Rep.
Angola	Jordan	Djibouti	Iran	Guinea Bissau	Bangladesh	Croatia	Brazil	Botswana	Hungary
Burundi	Tajikistan	Ethiopia	Niger	Ivory Coast	Benin	El Salvador	Dom. Rep.	Bulgaria	Lithuania
Cameroon		Liberia	Nigeria	Sierra Leone	C.A.R.	Estonia	Guatemala	Chile	Mongolia
Chad		Tanzania			E. Timor	Ghana	Indonesia	Macedonia	Slovenia
Guinea		Zambia			Ecuador	Honduras	Kenya	Panama	Uruguay
Haiti					Fiji	Madagascar	Latvia	Peru	
Kyrgyzstan					Guyana	Paraguay	Lesotho	Poland	
Nepal					Malawi	Russia	Mexico	S. Africa	
Togo					Mali	Sri Lanka	Moldova	Slovak Rep.	
Tunisia					Mozambique	Ukraine	Nicaragua	Taiwan	
Yemen					Namibia	Yugoslavia	Philippines	Thailand	
							Romania		
							S. Korea		
							Senegal		
							Turkey		

[5] Based on changes in democracy score since 1977 (or independence if more recent). Only countries with populations greater than 500,000 are considered. Otherwise, Antigua & Barbuda, Bahamas, Cape Verde, Dominica, Grenada, Kiribati, Malta, Samoa, Sao Tome & Principe, Seychelles, St. Kitts & Nevis, St. Lucia, and Suriname could be included. See also Notes.

Number of Democratizers and Median Democracy Score by Region (2002)

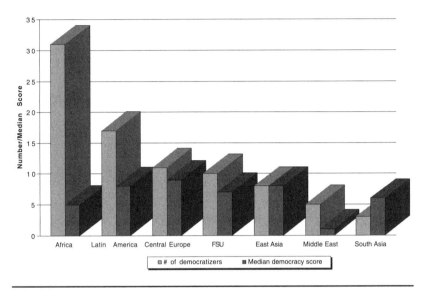

Figure 3.1 All developing regions are contributing to the global democratization trend even though the scale and depth vary widely.

have maintained the same democracy level over the past five years.[6] Of these, only 12 are in the lower third on the democracy scale—Algeria, Angola, Cameroon, Chad, Ethiopia, Guinea, Jordan, Kyrgyzstan, Togo, Tunisia, Yemen, and Zambia. In other words, nearly 33 democratizers have been sustaining their democratic institutions at a mid- to upper-level on the Polity democracy index. Although still a process in flux, the breadth and extent of change in regime type over the past 25 years have been a historically remarkable departure from the relatively static period in the decades preceding these democratic gains.

A quick glance at the list of democratizers would suggest that income levels are important in determining the extent to which a country is likely to establish democratic institutions (see Figure 3.2). For countries that scored in the bottom and middle third of the Polity democracy index, per capita incomes averaged $425. But democratizers who scored in the upper third enjoyed substantially higher incomes. In fact, all 11 democratizers with per capita incomes above $4,000 are in the top tier of the Polity democracy index—Argentina, Brazil, Chile, Czech Republic, Hungary, Poland, Slovak Republic, Slovenia, and South Korea, Taiwan, and Uruguay. This pattern might seem to support the conventional wisdom that only

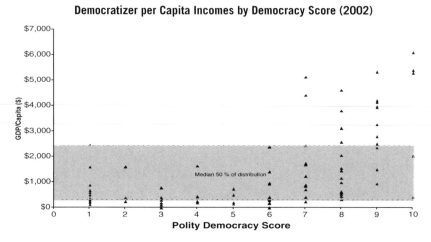

Data from *World Development Indicators 2003; Polity.*

Figure 3.2 Although wealthier democratizers appear to have established stronger democratic institutions, democratizers in the median 50% of the income sample are also well represented in the upper quadrant of the democracy spectrum.

relatively prosperous countries successfully democratize. However, two-thirds of the 34 countries in the top tier of the democracy scale have per capita incomes under $4,000—Bolivia, Botswana, Bulgaria, Dominican Republic, Guatemala, Indonesia, Kenya, Latvia, Lesotho, Lithuania, Macedonia, Mexico, Moldova, Mongolia, Nicaragua, Panama, Peru, Philippines, Romania, Senegal, South Africa, Thailand, and Turkey. The median per capita income for this geographically and economically diverse group is $1,558. Moreover, countries that fall in the middle two quartiles of the income distribution, that is those with per capita incomes between $350 and $2,600, are heavily represented in the upper quadrant of the democracy spectrum.

A closer look at the 11 richest countries in the group further diminishes the seemingly strong connection between per capita income and embrace of democracy. Half are former Soviet satellites whose transition to democracy was delayed by their subjugation to Moscow. Once they were freed, their swift adoption of democratic institutions was strongly influenced by their proximity and exposure to the prosperous democracies of Western Europe as well as the prospect of joining the European Union. The implied argument that half a century of authoritarian rule by the communists paved the way for their future democratization reveals the awkward circular reasoning the income threshold argument subsumes.

Our point is that income level-democratization patterns can be deceiving. Although the correlation between income and scores on the Polity democracy index is positive and should not be ignored, there is no precise cause and effect tie. In fact, when controlling for other factors, income level is not a significant explanatory factor for predicting democracy levels among democratizers. Economic vitality, dependence on natural resources, duration of the democratization process, and regional effects all exert stronger influences on the outcome.

Democratization is a complex and dynamic process, subject to many internal and external influences. Moreover, the global democratization patterns are still evolving. Therefore, a long-term perspective is required; democratic consolidation takes a generation, and moves along in fits and starts—a topic to which we now turn.

Democratic Backtracking

Although the global democratization trend is upward, democratizing countries often backtrack. The initiation of a multiparty system and the upsurge in political participation, for example, may suddenly face a backlash resulting in a curtailment of civil liberties. The about-face can be the result of political sabotage by remnants of a dying dictatorial regime desperately trying to cling to power, as happened in Belarus and Kazakhstan. Or backtracking can reflect the maneuvering of a wily autocrat who made concessions during a period of reformist fervor for appearances' sake but who, with the passing of time, reverts to his old ways, a pattern that can be detected in Cambodia, Egypt, Uzbekistan, Cameroon, and Burkina Faso to name a few. Sometimes the backpedaling accelerates and the one-time democratizer falls back into autocracy and political oppression, an outcome that has occurred in the Congo, Gambia, and Pakistan among others.

Countries are classified as backtrackers whenever, having once started down the democratization path, they experienced a decline of a point or more in their Polity-democracy score.[7] By this definition, 48 countries have backtracked at least once since 1977. This is nearly half of the 100 countries that were at one time or another democratizers during this period. Of these, 26 experienced a "democratic collapse" reverting to a score of zero on the democracy scale.

Not only is backtracking common, it can be sudden and severe. Of the 26 cases of democratic collapse just mentioned, 10 were in the upper half of the democracy scale in the year before they collapsed. Surprisingly, the annual probability of backtracking among democratizing nations that ranked in the top half of the democracy scale (4.7 percent) is double that of those on the lower end (2.4 percent).[8] The lesson is that countries on the road to democracy remain susceptible to the authoritarianism virus even though they may have seemingly made rapid and extensive progress. Even the seemingly best-designed democratic institutions will remain fragile until they become internalized into a society's political consciousness.

Not surprising, vulnerability to backtracking is greatest in the early years of democratization; on average, it happens in countries that started the process three years earlier. Similarly, the longer a society remains on a democratic path, the lower the likelihood it will slide back to its old ways. Only 4 of the 26 countries that reverted to dictatorship had been on the democratic path for more than 10 years. Gambia holds the record for longevity, with a 1994 coup ending its 28-year experiment with democratization, followed by Fiji, Guyana, and Pakistan, where democratization efforts collapsed after 16 years, 13 years, and 10 years, respectively.[9]

Notably, the duration of the democratization process appears to be a more significant factor in avoiding backtracking than income level, which is frequently cited as the critical consideration. The probability of backtracking in any given year once a democratization process has persisted for more than 10 years is 1 percent, substantially lower than the 2.5 percent norm for democratizers overall. In comparison, the probability of backtracking at income levels above a $2,000 per capita income is 2 percent. These patterns bolster the contention that countries need a long time, generally 25 to 30 years, to institutionalize democracy.

Economic Decline in Democratizers

There are many causes of democratic backtracking. Economic stagnation is one that preoccupies political leaders in democratizing societies because of the heightened social and political strains it creates. This concern is well placed. The experience of democratic backtracking over the past several decades confirms a strong linkage between economic decline and the propensity to backtrack. We find that 70 percent of the countries that have backtracked from their democratic path since 1977 experienced stagnant economic growth[10] in the years leading up to the backtracking (see Table 3.2). Similarly, three-fourths of democratic collapses were preceded by stagnant growth. A single year of economic malaise, although correlated with democratic backsliding, was not as injurious.

As mentioned earlier, there is a 2.5 percent probability that a democratizer will backtrack in a given year. However, if the preceding three-year

Table 3.2 Democratic Backtrackers During Stagnant Growth Since 1977

Country	Year of Backtracking	3 Yr. Avg. GDP Per Capita Growth Rate in Year of Backtrack	Years of Stagnant Growth Before Backtracking
Algeria	1992	−1.99	3
Argentina	1989	−3.76	5/6
Armenia	1995	0.53	5
Azerbaijan*	1995	−15.58	5
Belarus*	1995	−9.84	5
Burkina Faso	1980	0.61	2
Congo-Brazzaville	1997	−3.91	7
Comoros	1999	−0.11	10
Ecuador	2000	−3.38	6
Fiji*	1987	−2.62	5/6
Gambia*	1994	−0.32	9
Ghana	1981	−3.98	2
Guinea Bissau	1998	−5.39	1
Guyana	1980	−1.29	3
Haiti	1991	−0.24	2
Honduras	1985	−0.64	5
Madagascar	1998	0.12	8
Malawi	2001	−0.69	2
Niger	1996	−0.18	6
Nigeria	1984	−6.45	7
Pakistan	1999	−0.02	3
Paraguay	1998	−1.45	3
Peru	1992	−2.94	5
Russia	1993	−9.46	4
Sierra Leone	1997	−10.79	2
Slovak Republic	1993	−8.58	4
Sudan	1989	−0.96	5
Tajikistan	1992	−14.38	4
Turkey	1980	−2.10	2
Uganda	1985	−1.22	2
Venezuela*	1999	−1.86	2
Zambia	1996	−4.14	5
Zimbabwe*	1987	−3.80	4

Sources: *WDI 2003, Polity Index.*

*Countries that have experienced more than one episode of backtracking during economic stagnation.

average rate of per capita growth is less than 1 percent, this probability nearly doubles, to 4.3 percent, a statistically significant difference. If the preceding three-year period was characterized by economic decline, the probability of backtracking increases to 4.8 percent. Clearly, economic hardship has negative implications for democratization.

Analyzing another influence on the pace of a country's political evolution toward democracy, Adam Przeworski and his colleagues have found that parliamentary systems are a more durable institutional structure than presidential systems.[11] Our results corroborate this. Whereas democratizers with presidential systems were likely to backtrack at the median level for all democratizers (that is, 2.5 percent) in a given year, democratizers with parliamentary structures faced a backtracking probability of only 1.4 percent. Mixed presidential-parliamentary systems were most vulnerable—experiencing a 5.4 percent probability of backsliding. In times of economic distress, however, the parliamentary-presidential distinction disappears, though mixed systems had twice the failure rate.

Democratic Resilience

So far, we have been emphasizing the precariousness of the process. But there is another, equally important, angle to this story—that of democratic resiliency. Once a society has started down the democratic path, there is a tendency for it to demonstrate great tenacity in sustaining and expanding its freedoms. Of the 48 countries that have backtracked, 28 subsequently made a full or partial recovery in their level of democracy. It is as if once exposed to the possibilities of a participatory system, expectations of what is normal are indelibly changed. This is true even for countries that have experienced a democratic collapse. In 15 of the 26 such cases, the democratization process was revived, on average, after three years.[12] Importantly, then, a collapse is not necessarily the end of the democratization experience. Rather, it may just be another stage, albeit an unfortunate one, in a country's evolution toward political maturity. Furthermore, it may be one in which valuable lessons are learned by political leaders and a society at large, lessons that ultimately will strengthen their democratic resolve.

Similarly, although economic stagnation is hazardous to a democratizer's health, in more than 95 percent of the cases since 1977 in which countries on a democratic path experienced a three-year period of stalled growth, *no democratic backtracking occurred.*[13] A total of 49 countries are on this perseverance list, including Brazil, Bulgaria, Czech Republic, Dominican Republic, El Salvador, Estonia, Hungary, Jordan, Latvia, Mali, Mexico, Moldova, Mongolia, Nicaragua, Philippines, Romania, and Senegal. All clung to their emerging democratic institutions through extended periods of stagnant per capita income growth in the 1980s and

1990s. Even countries that ultimately did backtrack put up a good fight against the pull of retrenchment; of 33 that succumbed in times of economic distress, 26 held out for several years (four, on average) (see Table 3.2). These figures suggest that democracy puts down deeper roots than is generally recognized, enabling it to withstand economic storms that last for years, though not in all cases, and not forever.

Democratic Backtracking, Economic Stagnation, and Income Levels
Professor Adam Przeworski of New York University and his colleagues also identified $4,000 as something of a per capita income threshold above which reversions to authoritarianism are extremely rare.[14] Since the mid 1970s, Argentina has been the stark exception to this rule of thumb, backtracking at a per capita income level of $7,000 in 1976.[15] The only other two countries to lapse after surpassing the $4,000 level were Malaysia, after reaching $4,300, and Croatia, at $4,050, both in 1995. Aside from those unusual cases, the country with the highest per capita income to experience a democratic collapse at any time over the past quarter century was Fiji, at $2,700, in 2000. Once a democratizing country has reached a comfortable middle-income level of prosperity, regression is rare.

Indeed, proponents of the conventional wisdom have seized on this fact to argue that policymakers should hold off pushing democracy in the developing world until the country in question achieves a supposed "take-off" stage of prosperity. We think their conclusion is wrong. We have shown that poor democratizers are slightly more likely to backslide than prosperous democratizers.[16] We have also seen that countries experiencing stagnating development are significantly more likely to regress. Presumably, then, a poor country that was also economically stagnant would lapse back toward dictatorship more often than would wealthier countries that fall on hard times. But, in fact, that prediction is untrue. The rate of relapse in times of economic hardship is the same, about 4.5 percent. The rate of growth of an economy packs a stronger impact on the robustness of democratization than does its level of income. Controlling for other factors, income level does not emerge as a significant factor behind democratic reversals in countries experiencing economic pain. The rate of economic growth, inflation, the strength of the private sector, and the extent of dependence on natural resources, by contrast, do.

Figure 3.3 tells a similar story. The number of low-income backtrackers is large because the number of low-income democratizers is large. But the *proportion* of backtrackers that are economically stagnant remains stable at roughly 7 out of 10, regardless of income level. *The small number of democratic backtrackers at higher income levels reflects the small number of high-income democratizers*, rather than a marked advantage at avoiding

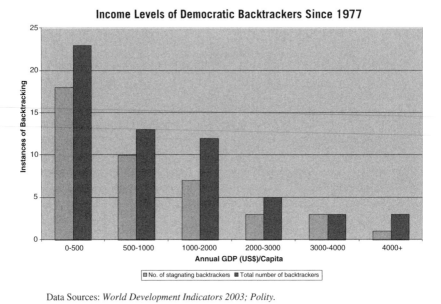

Income Levels of Democratic Backtrackers Since 1977

Data Sources: *World Development Indicators 2003; Polity.*

Figure 3.3 The proportionate number of democratic backtrackers in times of economic stress is generally consistent across income levels.

backtracking once the high-income democratizers suffer economic hard times.

Fareed Zakaria is perhaps the most prominent contemporary proponent of the development-first school. Building on the observation of an income threshold after which there have been no democratic backtrackers, Zakaria suggests that democratization should be deferred until countries have reached a per capita income level of $6,000. Yet, our review highlights the faultiness of this approach. Using this rationale, 83 of the 87 democratizers in Table 3.1 would not qualify—even though as a group, they are growing more rapidly than the norm for developing countries. For that matter, 80 percent of all nations in the world would be deemed insufficiently prepared for democracy.

Holding off on all democratization until there is absolute certainty that backtracking will not occur is akin to never getting into a car so as to avoid having an accident. You may achieve your objective but in the process, you are not going anywhere. One could caricature this view as accepting autocracy, so as to avoid the potential eventuality that a certain percentage of democratizers would stumble—and revert to autocracy. In the process, this proposal would condemn to (potentially perpetual) poverty and autocracy, those 80 percent of low-income democratizers that are successfully advancing toward democracy.

We also observe that democratizing countries that fall off the democratic wagon in hard economic times tend to be in economic distress more often than those who don't. From 1977 through 2001, for example, they were mired in economic stagnation for 60 percent of the time, compared with 49 percent for all other democratizers. In addition to giving substance to the much-talked-about "poverty trap" facing developing countries, these figures highlight the fact that long-term economically stagnant countries are the ones most likely to turn back from democracy. From this observation follows an important policy prescription. Prosperous democracies should proactively try to help democratizing countries gripped by economic stagnation to get back on a growth path and, at the same time, work closely with them to keep them on a positive political path.

Regional Distinctions

Geography is another distinguishing factor in identifying backtrackers. Backsliding under economic stress appears to be nearly entirely limited to certain parts of Africa, Latin America, and the former Soviet Union, which together represent 28 of the 33 affected countries (see Table 3.3). Forty-five percent of countries on a democratic course in the former Soviet Union have backtracked under stagnant economic conditions, as have 40 percent

Table 3.3 Countries Experiencing a Democratic Backtrack During Economic Decline Since 1977 by Region

Latin America	Sub-Saharan Africa	Former Soviet Union
Argentina	Burkina Faso	Armenia
Ecuador	Comoros	Azerbaijan
Guyana	Congo-Brazzaville	Belarus
Haiti	Gambia	Russia
Honduras	Ghana	Tajikistan
Paraguay	Guinea-Bissau	
Peru	Madagascar	
Venezuela	Malawi	
	Niger	
	Nigeria	
	Sierra Leone	
	Sudan	
	Uganda	
	Zambia	
	Zimbabwe	

in Latin America and 36 percent in Africa. In comparison, Western Europe, Central Europe, the Middle East/North Africa, South Asia, and East Asia each only have one country in this category.[17]

Within the three regions where backtracking under economic duress is most common, further concentration of backtrackers is evident. Of the 15 economically stagnant backtrackers in Africa listed in Table 3.3, eight are from West Africa. A possible contributing factor for countries in the region was the devaluation of the CFA, the common currency in former French colonies in West Africa, by 50 percent in 1994, effectively halving household asset values overnight. Another factor was the protracted and destabilizing civil conflicts that erupted in Liberia, Sierra Leone, and the Democratic Republic of Congo during the 1990s.

In Latin America, the countries that retreated from democracy following economic decline were Guyana, Venezuela, Ecuador, and Peru. If Colombia—a backtracker, though not associated with economic stagnation—is added to the list, a contiguous string of countries at the continent's northern rim emerges. The destabilizing influence brought about by the drug trafficking and insecurity of the ongoing civil conflict in Colombia are obvious contributing factors for this regional pattern.

The record of retrogression is more diffuse in the former Soviet Union, yet a geographical pattern is perceptible. The Baltic states have moved decisively toward democratization despite economic downturns. Democracy in Central Asia has been largely stillborn, while the experience of the new republics at the center of the old communist empire, including Russia, has varied. Consequently, it is the countries in the middle tier that account for nearly all of the cases of backsliding in rough economic times. In other words, in the former Soviet Union it appears that social and historical factors had the strongest influence on a country's experimentation with democracy. Economics became a tipping force in those middle-range countries where the direction of the democratization trajectory was in doubt.

The geographic concentration of countries that lapse from democracy in harsh economic weather holds important policy implications. Most of the discussion of the "neighborhood effects" of democratization has focused on the supposed propensity of countries to follow the example of democratic neighbors. However, the geographic clustering we have observed suggests that the process may also work in reverse, and that region-wide phenomena may be simultaneously stunting the political and economic transformations underway in several countries. An increasingly global economy raises the prospect of even greater synchronization of democratic backtracking in the future.

Economic Decline and the Erosion of Support for Democratization
Our review of the record confirms that economic stagnation is a serious threat to contemporary democratization efforts. Now, let's take a brief look at the processes by which a stagnant economy strains a new democracy.

Unmet Expectations
Expectations within newly democratizing societies are often very high. People expect prosperity to arrive soon after the removal of a repressive government. They commit the fallacy of assuming that because the West is democratic and the West is wealthy, then democracies are automatically bound to be wealthy. What they often fail to understand is the need to take substantive and often difficult steps to build the legal and institutional framework needed to create and sustain the conditions for this wealth. Consequently, once the euphoria of political freedom has worn off, they are ripe for disappointment at the lack of immediate improvement in material conditions.

As a result of bottled up demand for all kinds of goods and services, the leaders of new democracies are often subject to strong pressures to deliver tangible improvements—and quickly. To the extent these are not managed adroitly at the macroeconomic level, policy choices made by a democratizing government can quickly generate fiscal deficits and inflation. Paradoxically, inflation hits the poor and middle class disproportionately hard due to the loss in value of savings that cannot be readily transferred abroad and the increase in the cost of living.

A stagnant economy simultaneously reduces the capacity to build the institutional infrastructure needed to support a democracy, such as an accessible and independently supervised electoral process, an informed legislature, a well-paid and trained judiciary, and a professional civil service.

Governing Coalitions
A democratizing society depends on the support from a robust coalition of constituencies committed to democratic rules for sharing power. Typical coalitions include a combination of ideological, economic, regional, ethnic, and religious groups—all of which must see that their interests are better served by adherence to a transparent, participatory, and rule-based political system. Balancing these interests while maintaining the support from each constituency depends on the skill of a political leadership and the unique circumstances of that nation. In many poor countries, relatively narrow governing coalitions of political and economic elite have traditionally exercised political authority. Given the power and influence this entails,

such a ruling class has clear incentives to hold onto its privileged position. Broadening a governing coalition under such circumstances, therefore, will require assuring this group that its economic interests will not be threatened under a more representative government. Meanwhile, groups historically excluded from these coalitions (like wage earners, farmers, small businesses, and human rights groups) will need to learn to balance participation in the coalition with pressures for immediate improvements in living and working conditions.

A review of democratic transitions undertaken by Stephan Haggard and Robert Kaufman[18] in the mid 1990s identified "fragmented party systems" —defined as a multitude of competing political parties—that operate in new democracies as particularly ineffective. Specifically, fragmented party systems were more likely than other party systems to lead to demagogic populism of the sort that inflames the masses against the well to do. Such an occurrence can undermine coordinated action to deal with a stagnating economy. The Haggard–Kaufman analysis found that societies with a history of inequality were more likely to adopt fragmented political systems, reinforcing the inequality. Two-party or dominant-party systems were more likely to marshal the authority to implement redistributive and other policy responses. The policy compromises forged under such two-party or dominant-party arrangements were also more likely to avoid highly risky strategies that could exacerbate a fragile economic situation. Fewer but stronger political parties were also found to act as a greater restraint on attempts by the military to seize power.

Slow economic growth limits actions that government can take to build cohesive governing coalitions. Options for counter-cyclical fiscal or monetary policy are restricted by the crippling deficits inherited from a previous regime, pressures from international financial markets, and restrictions from multilateral lending organizations. Enthusiasm for a democratically elected government can run headlong into the immediate demands of meeting basic needs. Undertaking austerity measures in the midst of an economic downturn further sharpens this tension. Reformers who are insensitive to popular sentiment risk being voted out of office or toppled by nondemocratic means, with their successors empowered to reinstate the old elites and restore the old status quo. Economic decline can thus seriously jeopardize the political reform process. To the extent that changes are pushed from governments and institutions outside the country without regard for the political consequences, the effect may be the removal from office of the very individuals most committed to the reforms for which these international actors are calling.

Belarus is a case of a democratization process that lacked a strong supporting coalition. Opposition parties were established and gained considerable popular support in 1989 and 1990 under glasnost. A number of opposition party leaders were elected to the Belarusian Supreme Soviet, including Stanislav Shushkevich of the reformist Belarusian Popular Front, who was elected as First Deputy Chairman. Nonetheless, communist apparatchiks managed to retain control of key positions of authority. These were leaders who were able to use the power base they constructed during the communist era to ensure their places in the emerging representative system. After their failure to condemn the communist putsch in Moscow in August 1991, however, Belarus' communist leaders were forced to resign and the Belarusian Communist Party was suspended. Shushkevich was elected as president of the parliament in September 1991. He proceeded to expand political openness and civil liberties—raising prospects of a future mirroring the former Warsaw Pact countries. Economic reforms aimed at moving Belarus toward a market-oriented economy and greater global integration were also initiated.

Despite these gains, the path of democratic transition in Belarus was not a straight one. More than any other former Soviet republic, there was considerable ambivalence and anxiety over separating from Russia—owing significantly to Belarus' economic dependence. Consequently, the move towards an independent state was undertaken much more reluctantly than in the newly autonomous central European states. Belarus' transition towards democratic politics did not involve the sort of national dialogue and formulation of a broad social compact that are characteristic of democratic systems. Furthermore, Belarus' new political parties remained weak and democratic coalitions were less unified than in the Baltic or Central European states. Tellingly, the former communists retained a strong power base. By the end of 1993, the communist party was officially permitted to resume activity. On top of this, poorly designed and implemented economic liberalization and privatization schemes undertaken in collaboration with the International Monetary Fund (IMF) led to the rapid economic stratification of the population. The ratio of incomes for the top and bottom 10 percent of the population widened drastically in a very short time, from 3-to-1 to 10-to-1 between 1992 and 1994.[19] This was accompanied by major increases in property crime and larceny. An effect of the poorly conceived and implemented macroeconomic transition was hyperinflation averaging 1,600 percent in 1993 and 1994. Agitations by the pro-Russian parliament and (largely unfounded) accusations of government corruption led to Shushkevich's ouster as parliamentary chairman (and head of state) in January 1994.

The election of Alexander Lukashenko with 80 percent of the vote in June of 1994 was widely seen as a statement of protest resulting from loss of respect for government and perceptions of corruption among elected officials. Lukashenko proceeded to reinstitute certain price controls and re-nationalize some segments of the economy, particularly the financial sector, as part of his vision of a "socially oriented market economy." Lukashenko's rule quickly became dictatorial as he reinstated the secretive and imperious practices of the past. Certain independent newspapers were closed and the separation of powers between the president and the parliament and Central Bank were overridden. Lukashenko further augmented his unchecked authority by propagating the impression that an empowered legislature was the main cause of Belarusians' diminished quality of life. Today, Belarus retains the most unambiguously autocratic government in Europe. Eighty percent of all industry remains state-owned. Economic policy continues to be dominated by the strong rent-seeking special interests from the old structure of the economy.[20]

Crime and Corruption
Democracies are generally committed to upholding standards of individual, human, and labor rights. To succeed, they rely on attitudes of public-spiritedness and willingness to compromise. Where these are absent, democratizing societies must foster them and also develop the legal capacity to stipulate those rights and to enforce them. All this takes time and energy, especially in societies that lack a democratic tradition. A thriving economy provides breathing room for democratic leaders to inculcate those values.

Unfortunately, a social evil kept in check under dictatorial rule may burst forth when the old controls are replaced by a more open system reliant on individual responsibility—petty and violent crime. And to the extent that the new security systems are weak and social accountability is limited, organized crime frequently fills the void. In some cases, fear for personal security and a sense that events are spiraling out of control drive a population to nostalgia for the stability of a repressive regime.

Perceptions of corruption among democratizing leaders also corrode the public's support for new democratic institutions. In most democratizing societies, there is at least a modicum of understanding that there will be a challenging period of transition requiring sacrifice on the part of all. Based on this recognition and the freshness of the previous repressive system, citizens may be willing to undergo economic hardships for a sustained period of time. However, if the perception becomes widespread that common people are enduring a disproportionate share of the hardship while their leaders are reaping great personal profit, popular enthusiasm for democracy will quickly dim. Under such an atmosphere, the distinctions between democratic and authoritarian government may blur in the minds of the citizenry. And of course, opponents of democratic rule are always ready to foment the very rumors that will create this impression.

Opening to Authoritarians

The constraints precipitated by economic stagnation outlined above foster a climate of disillusionment within a society. Popular discord leads many citizens to conclude that "any change would be better than the present situation." Such an attitude, augmented by the perception that there is little difference between democratic and nondemocratic leaders, allows citizens to overlook the advantages of maintaining a system of democratic representation, accountability and succession. In other words, widespread disenchantment provides the fuel that can be ignited by authoritarian political or military leaders to torpedo budding democratic institutions.

Under such circumstances, a coup attempt is likely to be met with broad popular support. Coup leaders can claim they are implementing "the will of the people" and "acting in the best interests of the nation." Once in power, they frequently seize control of the media, close parliament, suspend the constitution, and remove other institutional checks and balances, giving them free rein to rule as they see fit. Having control over the main vehicles of communication, coup leaders are prone to amplify the extent of corruption, mismanagement, and other threats posed by a multiparty system. Short of claiming that their government is in fact a purer form of democracy, they are likely to promise elections and a return to representative government at some future date in order to pacify any lingering domestic or international concerns.[21] In a striking paradox, a majority of a citizenry may willingly (if impulsively) forego their political rights and civil liberties in the hopes of restoring social stability and economic vitality.

In other cases, a sitting democratically elected leader may use the charged climate of an economic crisis and social despair to claim the need to remain in office past his or her constitutionally specified limit in order to lead the nation through the difficult period. In the case of Zimbabwe, economic turmoil prompted Robert Mugabe to revive the longstanding issue of land distribution, to which he attributed the country's economic decline. The violence that ensued provided a rationale for the expanded use of coercive power by the government and suspension of long-held civil liberties. Mugabe subsequently claimed victory in a much-disputed March 2002 election. Thereafter, Zimbabwe's economy went into a free fall—averaging inflation of 400 percent in 2003–2004.

In summary, a democracy is consolidated only when all major political forces in a society are committed to democratic governance[22]—even though they may disagree on the specific policies the government should pursue. Until that point in the process of political maturity is reached, steady economic development is an important stabilizing force and vital source of resources by which governance systems can be established, political coalitions solidified, and democratic norms internalized. Economic contraction can strain the evolving political and social institutions of a democratizing society. Juxtaposed with the high expectations of a new political system, these pressures may precipitate strikes, riots, and an increase in violence. Such a context provides the opening for an authoritarian intervention "to correct the excesses of the democratic process."

Distinguishing Characteristics of Democratic Backtrackers

Economic vitality is clearly important to sustaining democratization. But how important might other economic, demographic, and social characteristics be? We explored this question by looking at a range of such factors that could distinguish democratizing countries prone to backtracking in harsh economic times. Surprisingly few clues emerged; such relapsing regimes have median levels of life expectancy, population growth, primary or secondary school enrollment, trade, government expenditure, financing from abroad, and so forth, that are quite comparable to democratizing nations that did not regress.

We then examined a host of social-welfare indicators, like infant mortality rates, immunization programs, malnutrition levels, population growth, literacy, and crude death rates that capture the breadth of well being in a society. We did so on the assumption that if democratizers did not expand their middle class in the process of developing, they would lose the popular support of this important constituency and thus be more likely to backtrack when the economic going got tough. After all, societies with a relatively large share of households with access to these basic services (and thus with lower levels of absolute poverty) are thought generally to be more equitable. Nonetheless, our analysis found that countries that backtracked in times of economic stagnation were, by and large, not distinguished by noticeably lower levels of overall well being. Within the three regions where recession-related backtracking was most common—Latin America, former Soviet Union, and Africa—the countries that were sidetracked from their democratic ways did not have greater poverty than neighbors that resisted the impulse. For example, infant mortality rates—considered by many development experts to be the best summary measure of social welfare—were nearly identical for the two categories of countries within each region during the 1990s (see Table 3.4). In sub-Saharan Africa, countries that backtracked in periods of economic stagnation had 96 infant deaths per 1,000 live births, whereas the median for democratizers overall was 97. The only

Table 3.4 Comparison of Economically Stagnant Backtrackers with Other Democratizers by Median Levels of Social Welfare during the 1990s

Indicator	Latin America		Former USSR		Sub-Saharan Africa	
	Econ. Stagnant	Democratizers Overall	Econ. Stagnant	Democratizers Overall	Econ. Stagnant	Democratizers Overall
Infant Mortality (deaths/1000)	34.5	34	17.1	16.9	96	97
DPT Immunization (percent of children < 1 yr of age)	79.5	80	89	92	60	58
Prim. School Enrollment (percent of cohort)	91.2	89	94.1	92.6	50.1	51.1
Malnutrition (percent of children < 5 years of age)	16.5	10.3	4.2	4.2	27.3	25.8

Source: *WDI 2003; Polity.*

region of the three where a statistical difference of note existed in a social-welfare category was Latin America, where childhood malnutrition among the backtrackers in Latin America averaged 16.5 percent versus 10.3 percent for democratizers overall.

We did identify three distinguishing economic features of the recession-related backtrackers in all three regions however: higher inflation, greater constraints on the private sector, and more elevated debt-service levels. Inflation for these backtrackers in the 1990s was roughly double that of the other democratizers in their region (see Table 3.5). In Latin America, this divergence only emerged during the 1990s, reflecting a halving of inflation rates for most democratizers to an average 12.9 percent. By comparison, countries that stumbled on the democratic path maintained average inflation rates of 20 percent.[23]

Peru fits the pattern. Inflation was at the relatively high but stable rate of 87 percent for the 1980–1987 period of democratic governance. Real annual per capita growth was over 2 percent during this time. Inflation then skyrocketed during the next three years, reaching 7,482 percent in 1990. Real per capita incomes declined by one-third from 1988 to 1989 and after a brief recovery in 1990, contracted again in 1991. Alberto Fujimori was elected in 1990. He dissolved Congress and the courts in April 1992 in an auto-golpe, or self-imposed coup d'etat, that was supported by the military.

The divergence in the former Soviet Union is particularly notable. Despite the volatility of prices following the break up of the Soviet Union, the countries with a track record of backtracking in rough economies posted average inflation rates three times as high as other democratizers (79 percent versus 25 percent). Since those who are better off in a society can more easily move resources abroad, the hardships from inflation disproportionately fall on the poor and middle classes. The effect is particularly harsh on those who have built up substantial savings or are on fixed incomes, such as pensioners.

Table 3.5 Comparison of Inflation Levels (as a Percent of GDP) of Democratizers

Region	1980–1989		1990–2001	
	Econ. Stagnant Backtrackers	Democratizers Overall	Econ. Stagnant Backtrackers	Democratizers Overall
Latin America	22.1	24	20.9	12.9
Former USSR	—	—	79.3	24.8
Sub-Saharan Africa	19.7	12.3	17.2	10.0

Source: *WDI 2002; Polity.*

The injurious effects that inflation has on political development are perhaps most memorably illustrated by Germany's experience after World War I. The severe reparations placed on Germany by the victors, the fluid monetary policy pursued by Germany's post-war government to help meet these demands, and the acute shortage of most goods led to a precipitous decline in the value of the German mark. Inflation accelerated after the war —peaking in late 1922 and 1923. The mark declined in value from 8.9 to the dollar in January 1919 to 4.2 trillion to the dollar in November 1923. The wealth of most German households had been nearly completely wiped out. Scenes of ordinary Germans toting wheelbarrows full of marks to the bakery to buy bread are etched into history. The despair and suffering caused by this runaway inflation was, most historians agree, a major influence on Germans' willingness to support radical, autocratic policies in their desire to escape the humiliation of what was perceived as an unfair and exploitative maneuver by the Allies, particularly France, Belgium, and Italy. Hitler won control of the National Socialist German Worker's Party in 1921 and undertook a failed putsch in 1923 before ultimately taking power in 1932.

The second distinguishing feature of countries that tend to slip off the democratic path in economic hard times is the relative weakness of the private sector. This is seen, for example, through proportionately lower levels of private sector access to available credit (see Table 3.6) and a smaller share of capital managed by the private sector in general. This shouldn't be surprising; the private sector's autonomy from political influence reflects a society's commitment to a market economy and its capacity to build viable financial institutions. A society with a robust private sector generally has multiple centers of power, which can then balance arbitrary acts from government officials. Conversely, in societies in which economic opportunity is tied to political relationships, the government has enormous control over the lives and fortunes of virtually every individual in the society. In such an environment, criticizing corrupt practices and engaging in productive entrepreneurship are equally discouraged. In the most acute cases, nearly all economic opportunities are controlled through state-owned or patronage-based enterprises. By contrast, greater private sector autonomy creates a more balanced power structure within a society, spurs more rapid economic growth, creates broader opportunities for economic advancement, and generally expands the number of stakeholders in pluralist governance and therefore contributes to greater democratic resiliency.

Consistent with this reasoning, economically stagnant backtrackers have considerably less autonomous private sectors than other democratizers. In each of the three regions considered during the 1990s, countries that backtracked during economic adversity have levels of private sector access

Table 3.6 Credit to the Private Sector (as Percent of GDP)

Region	1980–1989		1990–2001	
	Econ. Stagnant Backtrackers	Democratizers Overall	Econ. Stagnant Backtrackers	Democratizers Overall
Latin America	21.7	27.9	22.3	28.1
Former USSR	—	—	7.8	8.6
Sub-Saharan Africa	14.8	14.8	9.3	12.0

Source: *WDI 2002*; *Polity*.

to credit that were 20 to 40 percent lower than the median levels of democratizers within their respective regions (see Table 3.6).[24] These differences are robust even when controlling for other factors.

Another issue drawing considerable interest in recent years is the problem of debt burdens for developing countries. The concern is that the debt built up over the years by many developing countries has become so large that debt service dominates discretionary government spending and thus has become a major constraint to economic growth and development. Democratizers whose development is crippled due to debt repayments may be more vulnerable to backsliding. Upon inspection, some differences in debt service burdens between economically-stressed backtrackers and other democratizers do emerge (see Table 3.7). This is most apparent in Latin America and Africa. Debt service burdens were nearly a percentage point of GDP higher in backtrackers in these regions during the 1990s. In Latin America, the difference was 6.6 percent versus 5.9 percent and in Africa 4.4 percent versus 3.6 percent.[25] The divergence in Africa during the 1980s was even more clear-cut.

Although inflation and private-sector autonomy stand out as defining characteristics of economically-challenged backtrackers in all three regions, certain other features distinguish them from the other democratizers within their own regions. In the former Soviet Union, they were much more reliant on fuel exports, which accounted for 40 percent of merchandise they sold abroad in the 1990s, compared with 10 percent for democratizers in the region as a whole. This negative relationship between economic growth and oil exports, coupled with the propensity for oppressive government, otherwise known as "the oil curse," can be seen in other major petroleum producers, including Nigeria, Saudi Arabia, Iraq, Venezuela, and Angola. The easy availability of a natural resource like oil reduces incentives to develop a skilled workforce and an economic infrastructure capable of sustaining national wealth. Simultaneously, the abundance of a commodity that can be easily extracted and sold on the international market at a great profit favors the consolidation of political and

Table 3.7 Comparison of Debt Service (as a Percent of Gross National Income)

	1980–1989		1990–2001	
Region	Econ. Stagnant Backtrackers	Democratizers Overall	Econ. Stagnant Backtrackers	Democratizers Overall
Latin America	7.2	6.9	6.6	5.9
Former USSR	—	—	0.76	1.6
Sub-Saharan Africa	5.5	4.1	4.4	3.6

Source: *WDI , 2002*; *Polity.*

economic power. This works against the expansion of stakeholders in an emerging democracy. The democratic momentum of such a transition, in turn, is more easily reversed in times of economic contraction.

Cereal productivity was another indicator of commitment to democracy in the former Soviet Union. Countries that backtracked in periods of economic stagnation registered average output levels 30 percent lower than other democratizers in the region (or 1,622 kilograms versus 1,855 kilograms per hectare). This is notable because 40 percent of the former Soviet Union's inhabitants live in rural areas, where agriculture is a vital source of income, savings, and investment capital as well as of food. If it does poorly, the population suffers.

In Latin America, too, certain traits set countries that backtrack in the face of economic stagnation apart from those that stayed the democratic course in the 1990s. One of these was higher rates of malnutrition—16.5 percent, comparable to the 1980s, versus 10.3 percent for democratizers as a whole (see Table 3.4). And like higher corruption ratings by indices such as the International Country Risk Guide. Together, these figures indicate relative slippage in standards of living compared to other countries in the region, a slippage that may foster perceptions of exploitation and growing inequality. Such outcomes would understandably contribute to growing frustrations and dashed expectations of the benefits from democratization.

In Africa, the primary factor that separates backtrackers and other democratizers is the size of the fiscal deficit. Countries that retrenched during economic duress averaged deficits of 4.5 percent of their GDP in the 1990s, or 1.5 percentage points higher than democratizers in the region overall.

We can see, then, that policies that provide a foundation for macroeconomic stability are particularly important for reducing the threats to democratization posed by economic contraction. Resilient democratizers have demonstrated a greater ability to temper inflation and build an independent private sector than their more fragile counterparts. They have also generally faced lower debt-servicing burdens. These relative strengths have apparently helped them grow consistently and expand the number of stakeholders in the new system while avoiding the severe political and so-cial strains caused by an economic downturn. They also highlight the value of separating political authority and economic opportunity as an effective means of creating checks and balances in a democratizing society. Openness to the creation of an autonomous private sector requires will-ingness on the part of the political leadership to a certain degree of power sharing. In turn, this creates a channel to funnel entrepreneurial energy that would otherwise be bottled up and expressed through alternative, and potentially more dysfunctional, economic or political mechanisms.

Summary

This chapter has made the case that economic stagnation is a threat to de-mocratization. Over 70 percent of democratic backtrackers experienced economic stagnation in the years preceding their political contraction. Moreover, democratizers with more prolonged recessions had a greater tendency to revert to authoritarianism. Backtracking under economic duress has been primarily concentrated in parts of Latin America, Africa, and the former Soviet Union. Nonetheless, democracy has amazing staying power. In more than 95 percent of the cases of sustained economic con-traction, democratizing states did not backtrack. Furthermore, even for those that eventually did backtrack, 60 percent regained their democratic course after a several-year interval.

Since the frequency of backtracking recedes with the duration of the democratization process, societies that can overcome threats from eco-nomic hard times early in their transition have a much stronger likelihood of sustaining their democratization effort. Although democracies are often born in the economic emergency room, sustained focus on eco-nomic development after a democratic opening helps considerably in maintaining democratic momentum. This provides the space in which these societies can learn the nature of democratic change and adjust their expectations accordingly. As with most political-economy issues, the fac-tors making certain countries more susceptible to backtracking from the democratic path in hard times are not universal. Nonetheless, the key dis-tinguishing characteristics gleaned from this review are macroeconomic in nature—the development of independent financial institutions, control of inflation, and lower debt-service levels. The first fosters the level of cap-ital flowing to the private sector and has the effect of diversifying power within a society. The second, among other effects, vitally protects the pur-chasing power of middle and low-income households that might other-wise strain fledgling democratic institutions. The third greatly increases the flexibility a democratizing government has in addressing social hardships resulting from economic reform as well as enhancing options for building democratic coalitions. Together, these factors create an environment that helps thwart authoritarian ambitions among competing leaders within a democratizing society.

CHAPTER **4**

Democracy and Security

Those who would give up essential liberty to purchase a little temporary safety deserve neither liberty nor safety.

Benjamin Franklin
1775

Since World War II, American foreign policymakers have debated the extent to which the United States should trade off its commitment to democracy abroad for the perceived political stability of dictatorships. In the Cold
War, stability mattered more. But the question can be asked whether the
question was properly framed. In this chapter, we examine some of the
widely held perceptions that underlie the debate, and we attempt to apply
the lessons that can be drawn from American diplomacy in the post-World
War II era to the problems that plague the world today. In the process, we
make two overarching arguments. First, autocracy, poverty, and conflict are
a package deal. The relationship is tangled, but autocracies are more likely
than democracies to generate both poverty and conflict. Poor countries,
meanwhile, are breeding grounds for conflict. The emerging global threat
of militant Islamic terrorism is a new strain of this autocratic pattern.
Global terrorist organizations find havens and most terrorists are bred in
autocracies. Second, U.S. policy decisions to support autocratic governments in the name of stability have, at times, contributed to this vicious circle. The long-term negative effects stemming from these misconceived
alliances are more persistent than is generally recognized and have been especially pronounced in recent decades. This, in part, reflects the changing

nature of the types of autocratic governments the United States has supported. Until we recognize the autocratic dimension of this violent cycle, we will at best be chasing our proverbial national security tail. At worse, we may be greatly increasing the level of risk we face.

The Vicious Cycle of Conflict[1]

War typically knocks off about 2 percent of a nation's annual economic output.[2] Assets and infrastructure are destroyed, capital takes flight, and trade becomes unreliable. Resources are diverted to military spending. Health, education, and agricultural systems are interrupted or dismantled. Populations are displaced. In fact, wars account for virtually all of the 20 million refugees and displaced persons in the world today.

Since the end of the Cold War, nearly all wars have been civil wars. Most have dragged on interminably, lasting seven years or longer in two-thirds of the 54 countries that experienced them in the 1990s.[3] Moreover, once a country has been in a conflict, it has a hard time getting off that track; there is a 40 percent probability that a country will fall back into conflict within a year of ending it. This probability declines only slowly—roughly by a percentage point a year.[4] Furthermore, the devastation is not contained; almost one in three conflicts spills over into neighboring countries.[5] The cascade of wars in the Balkans and West Africa provide vivid examples of this pattern. War in one country also damages the economies of nearby states. Economic contraction, in turn, increases the prospect of war; each percentage point of reduction in growth rates adds a percentage point to the risk of conflict.[6]

Given this chain effect, it is not surprising that the average per capita income of states engaged in war over the past 20 years is substantially lower than the developing country[7] norm—$421 versus $538. Poor countries have a higher propensity to be embroiled in conflict than more prosperous ones. From 1980 to 2002, low-income countries were involved in conflict[8] nearly one year out of five, on average. For countries with per capita incomes in the $2,000 to $4,000 range, the rate dropped to one in eight, and for more wealthy countries, one in 33.

The Democratic Peace

Although the connection between conflict and underdevelopment is obvious, what is less widely recognized is that political regime type is a factor as well. Democratic states rarely, if ever, go to war with one another. This is particularly so since the end of World War II. The concept of a "democratic peace" has enormous implications for the future of humanity. If the global democratization trend expands and is consolidated, then the twenty-first century may become known for its historic decline in politically motivated bloodshed.

Let's look at the recent history on this. At the same time as the number of democracies in the world has been increasing, the number of armed conflicts has been declining. This trend accelerated in the first decade after the end of the cold war. From a peak of 36 countries engaged in war in 1991, this number has declined to just 13 in early 2003 (see Figure 4.1).[9] All but one of these 13 are civil wars. This trend is all the more noteworthy since the number of states in the global system has been increasing.

This scorecard of the past 50 years of conflict reveals another surprising reality. There is a widespread perception that while the cold war was a period of high tension, it was relatively stable. In contrast, the end of the cold war is believed to have unleashed a spate of civil wars as the restraining harness of the superpower rivalry was removed. In fact, the cold war, particularly the 1970s and 1980s, was a time of great turbulence. Although the superpowers did not go to war, there were a mounting number of conflicts (some of which were proxy wars) that were highly destabilizing for the peoples of the affected

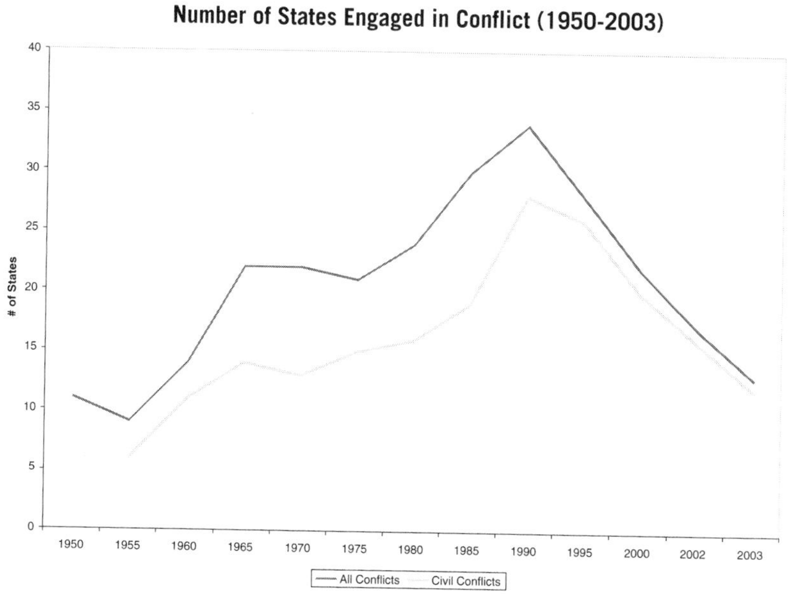

Number of States Engaged in Conflict (1950-2003)

Based on Data from the Center for Systemic Peace (2002); Marshall and Gurr, 2003.

Figure 4.1 The number of states engaged in conflict, including civil conflict, has been declining since the end of the cold war.

regions. It is only with the end of the cold war (and the flows of resources that sustained some of these conflicts) that wars declined sharply.[10] From its peak in 1991, the number of conflicts has decreased by two-thirds.[11]

The democratic peace has traditionally been thought to apply only to relations among democracies. However, there is growing recognition that democracies are also more peaceful overall, even in their relationships with autocracies. That is, democracies are less likely to become engaged in conflict than any other regime type.[12] Taking into consideration the nature of the state that initiates a military confrontation, we see that democracies are typically the instigator less than one time in five. In other words, democracies are more often the victims of aggression than its precipitators. Democracies, however, are victorious in 76 percent of the conflicts in which they become engaged.[13] Meanwhile, authoritarian governments are just as likely to fight one another as they are to fight democracies, making the notion of an "autocratic peace" a contradiction in terms.[14]

Although the concept of a democratic peace was derived from the experience of relations between states, there is also growing evidence that democracies experience fewer civil wars than nondemocracies.[15] The rationale for this is that elected governments are less likely to be challenged as illegitimate than are dictatorships. Facing future elections, they are more likely to respond to the needs of the population and less apt to resort to violence to put down dissent. Some scholars have suggested that democracies' stabilizing effect only sets in once their institutional structures are strong enough to incorporate competing interests politically, provide security against armed factions, and implement a reliable revenue-collection capacity.[16] Using our categorization of regimes, we find that of the 49 low-income countries that faced civil conflicts from 1990 to 2000, only eight were democracies. By contrast, the 25 low-income autocracies were engaged in civil conflict nearly one-fourth of the time.

Democracies' capacity to avoid conflict appears to be particularly important in ethnically diverse societies. Democratic governments generally manage social conflicts by channeling them into conventional politics. When divisive ethnic issues surface in democracies, they usually are expressed in protest rather than rebellion and often culminate in reformist policies.[17] Similarly, whereas ethnic diversity reduces growth by up to three percentage points in dictatorships, it has no adverse effects on economic growth in democracies.[18] Evidently, democracies are better able to incorporate the competing interests of diverse societies than are autocracies. The latter, by relying on a narrow political, economic, and military base of power, tend to direct a disproportionate share of benefits to a single or limited number of ethnic groups. Indeed, this is a central mechanism by which they ensure the loyalty and discipline needed to maintain their hold on power. However, the exclusivity and disenfranchisement of this system stirs resentment and violent opposition.

Democratic government is also a bulwark against state failure—the collapse of a central state's ability to maintain political order outside the capital city.[19] State failure usually results in violent civil conflict and is typified by the experiences of Somalia, Liberia, Sierra Leone, Bosnia, and Afghanistan in the 1990s. A comprehensive analysis of 75 potential predictors of state failure from 1955 to 1996 found that lack of democracy was one of the three most important.[20] (The two others were material well being as measured by infant mortality rates and the level of trade.) In other words, the stronger a country's democratic institutions, the lower the likelihood that it will become a failed state.

Autocracies are also the main culprit in the world's refugee crises. Of the 40 countries that have generated refugees over the past 20 years, 36 were autocracies engaged in conflict.[21] Of the top 10 refugee populations at the end of 2003, all were fleeing conflicts that originated in autocracies (see Table 4.1). Similarly, of the 50 largest instances of annual refugee flows from 1980 to 2003, all originated in autocracies.[22] The most sizable nonautocratic refugee experience was in Sierra Leone in 1999.[23] Yet this event, though it

Table 4.1 Origin of Top 10 Major Refugee Populations in 2003

Country of Origin	Refugee Population	Polity Democracy Score (0–10)	Freedom House Freedom Score (2–14)
Afghanistan	2,500,000	0	4
Sudan	600,000	0	2
Burma	586,000	0	2
D.R. of Congo	440,000	0	4
Liberia	384,000	0	4
Burundi	355,000	1	5
Angola	323,000	1	5
Vietnam	307,000	0	3
Iraq	281,000	0	2
Eritrea	280,000	0	3
Somalia	277,000	0	3

* Establishing a figure for Palestinian refugees is complicated due to the political dimensions of this definition. There are some 3.9 million refugees covered under the United Nations Relief and Works Agency for Palestine Refugees in the Near East (UNRWA). In addition, some 350,000 Palestinians in countries such as Iraq and Libya are monitored by UNHCR.

Source: World Refugee Survey, 2003; Polity Dataset, 2002; Freedom House 2001 to 2003.

generated 487,000 refugees, was only the 88th worst refugee crisis of the past two decades. These figures buttress a key observation made in Chapter 2—humanitarian and economic disasters nearly always take place under autocracies.

The theory that democracy is a force for peace makes sense. Societies built on a respect for human rights and the rule of law have a strong basis for resolving their differences in a nonviolent, legal, and morally defensible manner. And their governments are less likely than dictatorships to seek to dehumanize the leaders of competing democratic states, and more likely to engage in constructive dialogue.[24] These attitudes also appear to apply to those that have not yet achieved democracy but are on the road to it. Public opinion surveys in Eastern Europe and Russia suggest that the more citizens in democratizing states perceive their neighbors as democratizing, the less they expect to fight them.[25]

Democratic leaders and the societies that elected them are also accustomed to balancing multiple and competing interests. Therefore, they accept the inevitability of disagreement and the need for nonviolent compromise. Nondemocratic leaders, in contrast, are more likely to learn their political skills in environments that reward the use of coercion to resolve disputes.[26] Furthermore, by design, democratic executives cannot act unilaterally. They need the support of cabinet ministers and the legislature, and must also take public opinion into consideration—all brakes on their power to instigate war. In the event that two democracies are contemplating a conflict, moderates in each respective society can lobby public opinion to oppose such action.[27] Finally, democracies are risk-averse. Recognizing the high and destabilizing costs of war, their leaders have incentives to pursue moderate policies and avoid conflict when it is possible to do so. If both sides of a disagreement adhere to these norms, then armed conflict can probably be avoided.

Critics of the notion of a democratic peace have focused on the extreme version of the proposition—that democracies *never* go to war with each other[28]—an argument that few proponents actually make. Potential exceptions that these detractors point to include the war between the United States and England in 1812, Spain in the Spanish-American War, Wilhemine Germany in World War I and Finland's siding with the Axis Powers (to fight the Soviets) in World War II.[29] For our purposes, even if these exceptions were conceded by the democratic-peace camp, democracies would still have a substantially lower probability of interstate conflict than other political systems. Using data from 1816 to 1980, two skeptics of the democratic peace argument, Farber and Gowa, note that the probability of democracies fighting one another (0.02 percent) is markedly lower than the rate of war between nondemocracies (0.09 percent).[30] From a policy perspective, it is this lower likelihood rather than absolute guarantees that are most relevant.

Other factors in addition to democracy associated with lower levels of conflict are a country's level of economic interdependence and its participation in international organizations. Each of these components acts independently as a force for peace and mutually reinforces the other two. When a country exhibits all three, its risk of entering into a military conflict declines by more than 70 percent from baseline rates.[31] Economic integration reduces the danger of war because once trade accounts for a significant portion of a country's national income, substantial domestic political interests will lobby for avoiding a course that would be harmful to them. Similarly, the more integrated a state is in the international system, the more it sees common interests with other states in the system. Trade is also considered to be an instrument through which cultural values and norms are exchanged, enhancing cross-national understanding. More generally, it contributes to a greater flow of information between states, enabling their populations to see more clearly what their governments are up to and to analyze their policies and criticize their actions. Participation in international organizations lowers a nation's likelihood of going to war because it gives the government greater access to information about the other members, thereby allaying mistrust and uncertainty, and providing a forum for resolving disputes and the mechanisms for enforcing the rulings on those disputes.[32] Notably, all three of these factors that restrain a nation's penchant for conflict reflect trademark democratic qualities of openness and the rule of law.

A similar pattern is at work in the proliferation of weapons of mass destruction. The lack of openness, independent scrutiny, and adherence to established international regulations in closed political systems allow them greater leeway in pursuing programs to acquire them. The countries that have been the most active proliferators of materials for chemical, biological, and nuclear weapons programs—North Korea, Iran, Pakistan, Belarus, Libya, Syria, and Sudan—are all run by dictators.[33] Russia is also on the list. Although not classified as an autocracy, Russia has a long way to go in establishing democratic institutions that can assure transparency in government behavior and hold government officials accountable for their actions.

It is uncertain how robust the democratic peace will prove to be as we move further into the twenty-first century. The nature of conflict has changed; today, it takes place primarily within, rather than between, countries. Moreover, the large numbers of new, low-income democracies and an increasingly integrated global system have resulted in a world order unlike that of any era of the previous two centuries. Powerful countervailing forces are now at play. For one thing, more democracies today than in the past are poor, a condition that can foster both civil conflict and war with neighboring states. On the other hand, increasing global integration could be expected to mitigate conflict between states (though some would say that the increased contacts are actually a source of greater friction). In any event, we aren't claiming that no two democratic states will *ever* go to war with each other. We are simply describing the remarkable tendency of democracies to avoid armed conflict. As the proportion of the world's population that lives under democratic governments grows, the potential implications for global security are far-reaching.

Democratizing Countries and Conflict

Some concern has been expressed that while democracy is a desirable end, the process of democratization itself is a destabilizing event.[34] By contrast, although they may be repressive, authoritarian governments are considered more stable, particularly among low-income societies. The reasoning is that autocratic leaders' monopoly on coercion within their societies keeps internal challenges to their authority rare. As a country makes the awkward transition from autocracy to more open government, opportunities to challenge the state increase. These can spiral out of control, polarizing ethnic and other group rivalries. Weak politicians may be tempted to fan the flames of ethnic animosity to build a stronger base of support.[35] This would create incentives for belligerent nationalism and exclusionary politics that could increase the likelihood of civil conflict.[36]

Surprisingly, despite the logic of this argument, the rate of conflict in a democratizing society was no higher than the global norm in the 1980-2002 period. Democratizers[37] had a 15 percent likelihood of experiencing conflict in a given year, compared to the 16 percent rate globally. However, these figures do not take into account differences in national income. And as we noted earlier, low-income countries (a group that comprises most contemporary democratizers) are much more likely to become engaged in conflict. A more apt comparison, therefore, is to ask, "Are democratizers more likely to become embroiled in conflict than other low-income countries?" Framing the question in this way finds that democratizers are actually somewhat less likely to face conflict than other countries in their income group. In the 1980–2002 period, democratizers with per capita incomes below $4,000 had an 18 percent probability of conflict in any given year, compared with the 21 percent global norm for this income group. Considering a sample of lower-income countries (that is, below $2,000), the comparable stability of democratizers expands to 17 percent versus 22 percent.

As noted previously, the 1980s were a period of great turbulence. Nonetheless, countries starting down a democratic path during this period of geo-strategic change were no more likely to become engaged in conflict than (the mostly autocratic) low-income states that were not making democratic advances. When we limit our comparison to the period since 1990, the rate of low-income democratizers engaged in conflict declines to 15 percent, whereas the average for the under-$2,000 income category remains above 20 percent. Recalling that the number of conflicts declined rapidly in the post-cold war period, the data here show that the reduced probability of conflict among democratizers was a contributing factor to this trend.

Further perspective on the relationship between democratization and conflict can be gained by examining it by geographic region. In most cases, democratizers had a lower likelihood of conflict than the norm for their regions (see Table 4.2). Only in East Asia in the 1990s were the rates of conflict among democratizers notably greater than the overall levels. And this is largely a factor of the limited level of conflict in the region. There have only been 20 "conflict-years" in the region since 1990. Of these, 12 were in the Philippines (a democratizer), which had been enduring civil conflict since the early 1970s (that is, predating democratization).

Democratizers in Africa and South Asia, meanwhile, have had substantially lower rates of conflict than states in the region overall. This is particularly relevant for Africa (where the rates are 11 percent vs. 19 percent in the 1990s) in that Africa has been plagued by the greatest number of conflicts of any continent since the 1980s.[38] Africa is also home to approximately one-third of the world's democratizers. The fact that autocratic governments are nearly twice as likely as democratizers to experience conflict in Africa bears particular scrutiny by policy makers.

Similarly, democratization is not significantly associated with either the frequency or magnitude[39] of conflict when the variables of income level, trade, infant mortality rates, and level of democracy are included in the analysis. When only the 1990s are considered, the negative relationship between democratization and conflict is increasingly strong and significant. This is consistent with the probability listings in Table 4.2—rates of conflict for democratizers have notably declined in the post-cold war era.

These results support other recent analysis.[40] Russet and Oneal conclude that democratization in no way increases the likelihood or severity of conflict. They find that the wealthier and more democratic a state is, the lower the probability of conflict. In their study, the conflict rate for fully democratic states is 46 percent below the baseline. For fully autocratic states, it is 80 percent above the baseline.[41]

Table 4.2 Conditional Probabilities of Democratization and Conflict*

Region	Probability of Conflict	Probability of Conflict Among Democratizers
For 1980–2002:		
All States	0.21	0.18
Latin America & Caribbean	0.19	0.20
Sub-Saharan Africa	0.18	0.12
Middle East and North Africa	0.22	0.16
South Asia	0.44	0.20
East Asia	0.23	0.25
For 1990–2002:		
All States	0.19	0.15
Latin America & Caribbean	0.15	0.13
Sub-Saharan Africa	0.19	0.11
Middle East and North Africa	0.17	0.17
South Asia	0.47	0.27
East Asia	0.17	0.26
Central Europe	0.07	0.04
Former USSR	0.17	0.16

Conflict data from Center for Systemic Peace; democratization derived from Polity Index.

*For all countries with populations greater than 500,000 and per capita incomes under $4,000.

In summary, conflict among democratizing countries does occur with greater frequency than among democracies. However, compared to other countries of similar income levels, democratizers are no more likely, and are frequently less likely, to experience conflict.[42] We are not suggesting that democratizers are immune from conflict. Rather, while the strife that has bedeviled imperfect democratizing countries like Angola, Croatia, Armenia, Georgia, and Burundi rightfully gives us pause, this must be compared with the even deadlier wars that have engulfed autocratic-led states like Afghanistan, Democratic Republic of Congo, Iraq, Somalia, Eritrea, Myanmar, and Sudan in the same period. And while democratizing countries might be susceptible to violence, they are at least farther along the path to full democracy and thus toward the peace and stability that come with it.[43]

The Linkages Between Autocracy and Non-State Terrorism

Terrorism is a type of conflict that has dominated international attention since the attacks on the World Trade Center and Pentagon on September 11, 2001 as well as the subsequent strikes in Indonesia, Tunisia, Morocco,

Saudi Arabia, Spain, and elsewhere. Yet, given its extraordinary nature, isolated terrorist attacks are not included in the sorts of analysis we have just reviewed. This is so despite the fact that terrorism as a political weapon has existed from the beginning of humankind. Nonetheless, as international terrorist organizations have become more sophisticated and the prospect that they may gain access to modern weapons technology has become more likely, these organizations pose unprecedented potential to cause mass destruction. We are compelled, therefore, to examine the extent to which the systematic links between autocracy, underdevelopment, and conflict apply to this new type of threat.

Much remains unclear about the political, social, and economic factors that contribute to terrorism. That some of the terrorists conducting these attacks apparently come from middle-class backgrounds has led many to conclude that social and economic factors are extraneous to understanding international terrorism. However, this discounts the millions of Arab and Muslim youth who have developed visceral anti-American and anti-Western attitudes over the past two decades—and who represent the pool from which al-Qaeda and other Islamic terrorist organizations draw their recruits. In other words, militant Islamic terrorist organizations were not spawned in a vacuum but rather emerged from an environment in which radicalized views and orientations to targeted violence were actively fomented. As at least 20,000 individuals[44] were trained in al-Qaeda camps during the 1990s, the broader social and political factors potentially underlying the emergence of these organizations bears considerably greater attention.

Indeed, international terrorist organizations are virtually all based in and draw the vast majority of their recruits from autocratic societies. In other words, in addition to exhibiting a higher probability of conflict than democracies and an even higher likelihood of being the aggressor in a conflict, autocracies represent a fertile breeding ground for the most virulent form of contemporary organized violence: transnational terrorism.

Terrorism is perpetuated by states—such as Libya's bombing of Pan Am flight 103 over Lockerbie, Scotland and the Iranian government's alleged involvement in the bombing of the Jewish embassy and cultural center in Buenos Aires—as well as by nonstate players. In the first decade of the twenty-first century, it is the nonstate form that is on the ascent. Therefore, this will be the focus of our analysis.[45] Nonstate terrorists rely on their constituent societies for recruitment and financial support. The felt grievances of these societies form the foundation for this support. As such, there is a strong social, economic, and political dimension to the viability of nonstate terrorists.

The forces that drive terrorist groups vary widely by country and region. In analyzing what makes them tick—what inspires them, what keeps them going—you simply cannot lump together such disparate groups as the Irish Republican Army in Northern Ireland, the Revolutionary Armed Forces of Columbia (FARC), the Basque separatists in Spain, and al-Qaeda. For our purposes, then, we will focus on the most murderous form of terrorism, and the one that poses the biggest threat to world peace: radical Islamic terrorism, and specifically, al-Qaeda and its sister organizations. This is the international terrorist entity with the most established global infrastructure, with cells in 60 countries. Moreover, it has demonstrated a motivation, intent, and capacity to mount repeated attacks against the interests of the United States and the West more generally.

The Political Economy of Terrorist Culture

Terrorism is an act of desperation. Embraced from a position of weakness and perceived helplessness (that is, hopelessness about influencing events by conventional means), its perpetuators undertake violent attacks against civilian populations and symbols of power in the attempt to shock and strike fear in their enemies. In this way, terrorists attempt to gain attention for their cause and exert influence. What is it that leads to such desperation and willingness to turn to violence, the two main attributes of terrorism? Let's look first at the common cultural characteristics of the societies that breed them.

First, they are mired in despair. Individuals and communities in these societies feel powerless to address the problems they face in their daily lives. Their ability to advance their own interests or to influence their governments' behavior ranges from limited to nil. This reflects a society with weak civic associations—the building block for collective action. Such a society may lack the political space, sense of community, or social trust needed for such groups to form. The absence of mechanisms to spur government responsiveness also highlights the lack of a vibrant, independent press. Citizens in cultures that breed terrorists lack outlets through which their grievances can be aired.

To maintain political stability, autocratic governments must typically rely on a high degree of repression. Attempts at citizen participation and self-initiative are beaten down in order to maintain the government's monopoly on control. Trust is fractured by the existence of state security networks that penetrate virtually every institution in society. The likely presence of informants in the most innocuous places squelches open discussion. Neighbor cannot trust neighbor. Professional, social, and economic advancement are dependent on one's loyalty to the political authorities. The disincentives for dissent under such a system are high. Corruption, patronage, and the monopolization of power can thus expand unchecked. Moreover, the dearth of transparency removes a key mechanism for exposing governmental bottlenecks in the allocation of resources to address priority services. Hope for improvement is suffocated. Not coincidentally, the socio-economic conditions of autocratic societies are normally much worse than democratizers or democracies—as shown in Chapter 2. In short, autocratic societies have no shortage of tangible grievances.

The social hardships of nations prone to breed terrorists are compounded by an attitude of relative deprivation.[46] These societies are frequently those that have recently experienced some economic growth, the benefits of which remained limited to a relatively small share of the population or have since contracted. Thus expectations for greater prosperity are generated, though left unrealized for many. This creates frustration, loss of self-respect, and an attitude among the dissatisfied majority that society owes them more than what they are getting. Some scholars have used this observation to explain why those attracted to radical ideologies are often drawn from the lower middle class.[47] These individuals miss out on the limited opportunities for social and economic advancement in these narrowly structured societies, yet have aspirations for a measurable improvement in their status—an ambition beyond that of the truly poor. Lacking outlets to address these grievances or the prospect of systematically changing their rulers, despair is a natural outcome.

Despair on its own, however, does not create a culture of terrorism. Many societies have endured repressive rule without turning to political violence. If terrorism were simply an outgrowth of material deprivation, then sub-Saharan Africa would be the epicenter of terrorist activity. Indeed, despair and helplessness typically lead to inaction and social despondency. These are the attitudes, after all, that allow narrowly supported autocratic rulers to so easily shepherd the cooperation of their populaces. How does such a defeated and inert society spawn terrorism? The answer lies in the fact that despair and frustration are highly combustible elements.[48] When this "kindling" is fused with the match of radicalization, it can be transformed into the fire of anger and violence.

Radicalization occurs through the perpetuation of an ideology that frames a society's grievances as injustice[49] and channels this angst toward a designated group deemed responsible. Intended to rock the status quo, radicalized ideologies are typically initiated from outside the society in which they take root and thereby escape the full force of state repression that would be visited on homegrown agitators. When disseminated through religious networks, a radicalized ideology gains an additional layer of protection.[50] A religious pretext also provides a legitimizing rationale for the use of violence—while moving the righteousness of the ideology's cause beyond reproach. Consistent with its dogmatic nature, radicalization opts for the most extreme of the choices available. All other alternatives are dismissed as insufficient or even treasonous.

The organizational structures that evolve in radicalized movements opposing autocratic governments are themselves typically autocratic.[51] This is the social-political model with which they are most familiar. It is also effective for the simplifying, polarizing strategy they employ.[52] The complex array of social, economic, political, cultural, and institutional factors that contribute to the aggrieved set of affairs are minimized or not acknowledged. However, in cultures of terrorism, where collective mindsets are common, such ideologies, once introduced, spread quickly. The lack of critical debate, again typical of autocratic governance, allows the one-dimensional characterization of a society's problems to proceed unchecked.

The deficiency of critical introspection is also a reflection of underfunded and weak educational systems. Relatively few individuals in these societies have access to schools. For most, the only alternative is the madrassas (Islamic schools). In both cases, though to varying degrees, teaching is done through rote. Students do not gain exposure to critical reasoning, alternative ideologies, or the acquisition of functional skills that would allow them to take on fulfilling jobs in a modern economy.[53]

The weak legitimacy of the autocratic governments in which these radicalized movements emerge compels the authorities to attempt to co-opt rather than confront these challenges. The endorsements of fundamentalist religious leaders are sought, madrassas are left unregulated, and the lines between civil and religious mores are blurred.[54] State media adopt the antiforeigner rhetoric of the radicalizing ideology, which conveniently redirects responsibility for the society's ills away from the government. In some cases, subsidies are provided to leaders of designated religious, educational, or charitable organizations in order to obtain their support and gain leverage over their operations.

One can easily see how the autocracy-poverty-radicalization cycle is perpetuated. The lack of education facilitates uncritical thinking. The absence of a free press or access to alternative viewpoints allows for the widespread acceptance of radical ideologies. The poor caliber of education simultaneously lowers prospects for the high-paying jobs and productivity-enhancing economy that can substantively address the long-standing material deprivation these societies face.

Contemporary Islamic Radicalization

The ideological basis for contemporary Islamic radicalization has its roots in the works of Egyptian philosopher Sayyid Qutb.[55] Qutb was active in articulating his worldview from the 1940s through 1966 when, after more than 10 years in prison, Egyptian President Gamal Abdel Nasser had him executed for his unrepentant radical views. Qutb argued that there is a fundamental discordance between modern life and divinely bestowed human nature.[56] This discordance generated the malaise, skepticism, and immorality that characterize the modern world. Qutb blamed this incongruity on Western civilization's segregation of religion from other spheres of life. Having deviated from a unified spiritual and physical worldview, the West was doomed forever to seek but never to discover harmony, he believed. Qutb further argued that the West's domination of the Arab world in the twentieth century, through colonization and cultural norms, pulled Islam into the same morass. He viewed the secular reformers who emerged in the Muslim world as a Western-inspired threat to Islam's very existence.[57] To reassert Islamic harmony, he argued, Western civilization should be aggressively expelled from the Arab world. Only the "ideological ideal" of Islam could "rescue humanity from . . . the barbarism of technocratic culture."[58] Islam could then be fully reintegrated with other spheres of life. This would lead to a new society based on ancient Koranic principles and the constancy provided by its irrefutable rules for every aspect of life. This "liberating" political system would necessarily be autocratic since there was only one truth, and any attempts to deviate from that path would be symptoms of corrupted Western thought.[59]

Another influential scholar behind the contemporary Islamic radicalization movement is Muhammad Abdel Salam Al-Farag. A member of Islamic Jihad, Farag, also an Egyptian, wrote the manifesto "Al-Faridah Al-Gha'ibah" ("The Neglected Duty") around 1980. In it, he justified violence by calling for jihad against infidels, meaning all those who did not follow a strict interpretation of Islamic law.[60] The first target of jihad should be, he said, the "enemy at home"—infidel leaders who should be uprooted and replaced by those who would institute an Islamic system. Once this was accomplished, the enemy "who is afar" could be combated. Farag dismissed peaceful methods for establishing an Islamic polity. Moreover, deceiving and lying to the enemy was deemed permissible in jihad since it allowed "victory with the fewest losses and by the easiest means possible." Farag was so convinced of the importance of jihad that he proposed that it be added as the sixth pillar of Islam. Farag was executed in 1982 for his role in the assassination of Anwar Sadat, one of the "infidel" leaders against whom he had declared jihad.

The philosophies of these two men contain all the elements for radicalizing a society. They tap into the despair and humiliation felt by many Arabs and they stoke those emotions into anger and hatred toward the West, the supposed source of the dissonance that has infected their societies. They justify violence against perceived enemies of Islam, and glorify those who die in such violence as martyrs.[61] They reject peaceful alternatives as deviations from "the truth." Furthermore, by insulating the belief structure from outside influences, they squelch scrutiny of their ideology and thereby deflect any challenges to its veracity. And they invoke the stagnation of societies that are run by secular Arab nationalists as further proof that the full integration of Islam with all spheres of life is needed.

At the same time as eschewing modernism, radical Islamic ideology has spread on the wave of oil money that started pouring into the Middle East, and particularly into Saudi Arabia, in the 1970s. Religious leaders in Saudi Arabia, closely intertwined with the royal family, took advantage of this windfall to bankroll a global campaign to expand their ultra-conservative interpretation of Islam. An estimated $70 billion has been spent on this campaign since the late 1970s, building and maintaining tens of thousands of Islamic madrassas, mosques, publishing houses, and student associations around the world.[62] Working through the madrassas provides access to not only millions of students, but also a stable organized structure from which to espouse the violent doctrines of the radicalization movement. Although most of these efforts have been aimed at shaping the ideology of the Muslim world, Saudi funds have also been used to build 1,500 mosques, 210 Islamic centers, and dozens of academies and schools in non-Muslim countries since the 1970s. In recent years, particular attention has been given to the newly opened central Asian region. Even in North America, some experts estimate that the Saudis support 80 percent of all Islamic establishments. In a sentence, the Saudis have been the primary financial enablers of extremist Islamist ideology around the world.

Al-Qaeda was established in the 1980s in Afghanistan with help from the head of Saudi Arabian intelligence in order to organize Arab recruitment for the mujaheddin who were then fighting the Soviets.[63] Al-Qaeda and its three principal sister organizations all have their roots in Qutb's and Farag's teachings.[64] In addition to Osama bin Laden's Saudi faction, these include the Egyptian-based Islamic Group and Farag's Islamic Jihad (led by Dr. Ayman al-Zawahiri, later Osama bin Laden's top deputy). The Egyptian groups emerged from an older fundamentalist movement, the Muslim Brotherhood. Qutb was the editor of the Muslim Brotherhood's journal and its principal theoretician.[65] Qutb's brother, Muhammad Qutb, exiled in Saudi Arabia, was one of Osama bin Laden's teachers.

Al-Qaeda thus has deep roots in Saudi Arabia and Egypt.[66] In addition, elements of Pakistani society have provided critical financial and human resources to the efforts of al-Qaeda and the Taliban in Afghanistan. Each of these societies has undergone major radicalizing transformations over the past 30 years. To better understand the political and economic underpinnings of terrorist culture, we will briefly examine the recent development experiences of each of these three societies.

Saudi Arabia

Characterizations of Saudi Arabia frequently conjure up images of vast oil wealth. Indeed, owing to the oil price booms, Saudi Arabia tripled its per capita wealth between 1960 and 1980 from $3,767 to $11,557. However, the Saudi economy has been largely stagnant since. As little productive capacity was built during the oil booms, productivity gains have been insufficient to sustain income growth during the subsequent declines in oil prices. By one estimate, only $800 billion to $1 trillion of the $3 trillion in revenues generated by oil over the past 30 years has been reinvested in Saudi Arabia.[67] The kingdom has simultaneously experienced one of the most rapid rates of population growth in the world during this time period—an average of 4 percent per year,[68] transforming it from a sleepy desert society of 6 million in 1970 to a largely urbanized population of 22 million today. The demographic explosion has caused contractions in per capita GDP in all but five years since the peak in 1980. In 2001, per capita incomes stood at $6,614.[69]

Government expenditures represent 30 percent of GDP—double the level of 1970, reflecting the state's growing control over economic life (and economic opportunity). A considerable percentage of this government spending is for the military, a sector that spins off few economic benefits for the rest of nation. On average, since 1980, the government has devoted 38.5 percent of its budget to the military. Reflecting the decline in per capita incomes and, until recently, the growing threat from Iraq, military spending as a share of total expenditures has increased from 27 percent in 1985 to 43 percent in 1999, compared with the regional median of 23 percent.[70]

Given the government's heavy subsidization of the economy, the shrinkage in per capita wealth has significantly restricted the Saudi government's ability to provide public goods and services. This imbalance has had a negative effect on the welfare of the population, evidenced by key measures of social well being that were already deficient by regional standards. For example, Saudi Arabia's 23 percent adult illiteracy rate is comparable to that of Iran and Syria and substantially higher than that of Lebanon and Jordan, despite the fact that all of these countries have per capita GDP's that are less

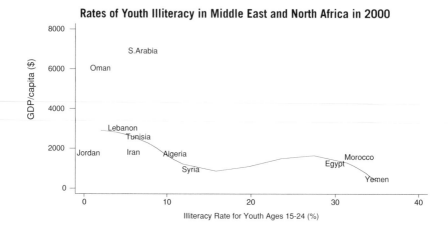

Data from WDI 2002; for countries with per capita income below $8,000. Plot line captures median observations across equivalent literacy segments.

Figure 4.2 Illiteracy rates among youth in Saudi Arabia are comparable to countries in the region with one-fourth the per capita incomes.

than half of that of Saudi Arabia. Illiteracy among Saudis between the ages of 15 and 24 is comparable to countries with per capita incomes one-fourth of that of the oil-rich kingdom (see Figure 4.2). Similarly, the proportion of rural residents in Saudi Arabia who have access to safe drinking water is lower, at 64 percent, than any other Middle Eastern or North African country except Morocco. This places Saudi Arabia on a level comparable to that of Yemen and Syria. In fact, one commentator has described Saudi Arabia as "Yemen with oil."[71]

The period since 1980 has also been marked by rapid urbanization. Rural inhabitants' share of the population fell to 14 percent in 2000 from 30 percent in 1980. Coupled with the declining per capita incomes, this has generated a throng of unemployed youth in Saudi cities. With over half of its population under 16 and a stagnant economy unable to generate enough jobs to support them, socio-economic conditions in Saudi Arabia are expected to worsen. The paradox of growing poverty in a country of such wealth is a formula for despair.[72]

The Saud monarchy has maintained an alliance with the Wahhabi sect of Sunni Islam (founded by Mohammed Abd al-Wahhab) since the late eighteenth century when the al-Saud were rulers of a small emirate. In need of consolidating their political authority, the endorsement of the ultra-orthodox Wahhabis, whose aim is to reinstitute a "pure" version of Islam, provided the regime with the religious credibility to rule. This alliance continues to the present. Even Muslims who do not practice the Wahhabi version of Islam are considered to be heathens and enemies. As part of this partnership, the Wahhabis direct the Ministry of Religion through which they control the messages preached at mosques throughout the country. Moreover, they field religious police to ensure adherence to their strict norms and exert influence on Islamic teaching throughout the Muslim world through their funding of the madrassas. The Wahhabis also appoint judges and supervisors of education. Members of the al-Sheikh family (descendants of al-Wahhab) have been ministers of education for most of the period since 1980.[73] In the mean time, the state-controlled media broadcast anti-Western diatribes as a way of placating the fundamentalists.

Although long linked to the al-Saud clan, the influence of the Wahhabis has grown considerably in recent decades as a result of four turns of events. First, the Israeli victory in the 1967 war left in ruins the ideological foundation of pan-Arab nationalism promoted by Egyptian leader Gamal Abdel Nasser. This created an intellectual vacuum into which religious leaders were able to step. Second, the huge oil revenues during the 1970s gave the Saud monarchy, and by extension the Wahhabis, greater prestige and resources than they had known previously. As millions of Egyptian, Moroccan, Pakistani, and other guest workers poured into Saudi Arabia, they gained exposure to the rigid Wahhabi brand of Islam, which they then took home with them.[74] The Wahhabis, in turn, were exposed to the views of members of the radical Muslim Brotherhood who had been expelled from Egypt in the 1960s. Third, the Iranian revolution and its brandishing of an alternate Shiite model of Islam threatened Saudi Arabia's position as the guardian of true Islam, prompting a sharp increase in Saudi funding for Wahhabi madrassas throughout the Muslim world after 1979. Islamic schools and universities also expanded dramatically within Saudi Arabia. There are now three Islamic universities (out of seven in the country), which account for 20 percent of the Saudi student body. The Imam Mohammed ibn Saud University in Riyadh produced 5,000 graduates in 1980 and 17,000 in 2000, an increase of more than 300 percent. Over the same period, graduates from the main engineering university grew by only 20 percent.[75] Fourth, the Soviet invasion of Afghanistan in 1989 provided a focal point for radical Islam to defend the faith—expanding the number of recruits, funding (including money from the United States), and organizational cohesion for the movement. Both the Wahhabis and the Muslim Brotherhood in Egypt prospered as a result. The ongoing weakness of the al-Saud regime continues to make it dependent on the clerics for credibility with the masses. Although this remains the consensus view, terrorist attacks in Saudi Arabia in late 2003 and 2004, as well as heightened international pressure, may be causing the monarchy to reassess whether its relationship with the Wahhabis is, in fact, posing a threat to its own stability.[76]

Egypt
In contrast to Saudi Arabia, Egypt has experienced rapid and consistent growth over the past several decades. Between 1960 and 2001 its real per capita GDP more than tripled from $360 to $1,230, an average per capita growth rate of 3.1 percent per year. Annual per capita income fell only four times in those four decades.

Despite this extraordinary record, Egypt remains one of the poorest Middle East and North African states, ahead only of Yemen and Syria. It has an infant mortality rate that is double the regional median (68 deaths per 1,000 live births versus 34), higher adult illiteracy (53 percent versus 33 percent), and fewer televisions (107 per 1,000 people versus 158).[77] This abysmal performance holds even after adjusting for income. Take a look at Egypt's position with regard to the percentage of newborns who are underweight, a key measure of both malnutrition and women's access to health care (see Figure 4.3). At 49 percent, the rate in Egypt is three times that of other countries with comparable per capita incomes—Algeria, Iran, Jordan, and Syria. Similar patterns can be seen for other key health and education indicators. This level of social-welfare performance is particularly remarkable in that per capita public expenditures on health and education

Rates of Low Birth Weight in Middle East and North Africa (1999)

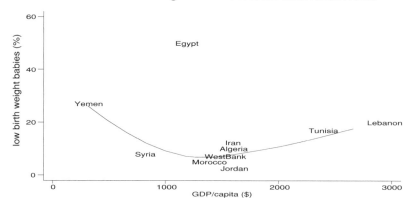

Data from WDI, 2002; for countries with per capita incomes below $3000. Plot line captures median observations across equivalent income segments.

Figure 4.3 Social welfare in Egypt, as measured by the percentage of low-birthweight babies, is far worse than the norm of other Arab countries with comparable income levels.

in Egypt are very comparable to the regional medians. Similarly, Egypt has received official development assistance averaging 5.2 percent of GDP a year since 1980, five times the regional average. Furthermore, many of Egypt's major sources of foreign exchange are controlled by the government—oil, fees from the Suez Canal, tourism, and foreign aid.[78] Therefore, shortage of revenue is not the cause of Egypt's disappointing development performance.

What these statistics reveal is a disconnect between the level of financial resources available and overall social welfare in Egypt relative to other Middle Eastern and North African countries. What might explain this gap? Egypt distinguishes itself on one notable account. It is widely perceived to have higher levels of corruption than other countries in the region. On a scale of 0 to 10 on Transparency International's corruption perceptions index, Egypt has averaged a 3.3 in the late 1990s, with zero the most corrupt and 10 the least corrupt. This compares to the regional median of 4.7. Similarly, according to the International Country Risk Guide's corruption ratings, Egypt has consistently scored a 2 (on a scale of 1 to 6), compared to the regional median of 3. In other words, the pervasiveness of corruption in Egyptian society reflects a lack of accountability that contributes to its underperformance on social indicators. This, in part, explains the appeal of Islamic-inspired organizations that have a reputation for providing services more efficiently than the government.[79]

Meanwhile, opportunities for political expression remain limited in Egypt. It is, in fact, considered a prototype of a semi-authoritarian state: although it has adopted certain trappings of a democratic system, including a parliament and the holding of periodic elections, the ruling party does not allow a genuine contestation for power.[80] Whatever political opening that may have occurred in the early 1990s waned in the latter half of the decade. At the same time, instances of political oppression have increased. Constraints on civil organizations were tightened. Those that demonstrated too much independence from the government were closed or singled out for excessive regulation.[81] The increase in pressure was felt by mainstream democracy advocates. Most prominent among these has been Said Eddin Ibrahim, who has called for greater openness as a means of revitalizing Egyptian culture, modernizing its society and transforming its economy. He has been regularly harassed by the government and was jailed by Egypt's State Security Court in May 2001 on charges of accepting foreign funds without authorization, disseminating false information harmful to Egypt's interest, and embezzlement. The case was dismissed by Egypt's Court of Appeals in March 2003 after extensive international pressure.

Starting as one of the most modern and cosmopolitan nations in the Arab world in the 1950s, Egypt has seen a radical Islamic movement grow steadily over the ensuing decades from the seeds planted by Sayyid Qutb's radical philosophy. Following Nasser's crackdown in the late 1950s, political opposition groups, including the Muslim Brotherhood, were driven underground. Some found refuge in Egypt's many independent mosques that, unregulated by the government, provided fertile ground for the politicization of Islam.[82] With this backdrop, Egypt's signing of the Camp David peace accord with Israel in 1979, under Anwar Sadat, was the spark for the sudden upsurge in violence. Sadat was assassinated in 1981 by Islamic militants. Fundamentalist attitudes were further amplified by the radicalized madrassas, courtesy of funding from the Saudis. This was reinforced by the return of thousands of workers from Saudi Arabia who had been exposed to far more austere versions of Islam than those they had previously known.[83] During the mid 1990s, the militant Islamic groups al-Jihad and al-Jama'a al-Islamiyya led a violent confrontation with the government resulting in the deaths of 1,500 people. Their aim was to devastate the Egyptian economy, weaken the Mubarak government and gain political leverage in the ensuing instability. This killing spree culminated in the slaying of 58 tourists at the Temple of Queen Hatsheput in Luxor in November 1997, an act that shocked the country and the world. The government responded with a ruthless campaign to exterminate these terrorist organizations, and achieved its goal, at least at home, by the late 1990s. However, rather than being stamped out, the Egyptian terrorist movement morphed onto the international scene. Thousands of Egyptians have subsequently trained with al-Qaeda and fought with the Taliban in Afghanistan. Today, a majority of al-Qaeda's members are thought to be Egyptian.[84]

Although terrorism has largely disappeared from Egypt, the radicalized ideology behind it has continued to grow. It now has greater influence in Egyptian society than ever before. And it is not just the poor who are drawn to promises of an Islamic state free of corruption. Although prevented from running for parliament, Islamist candidates routinely dominate elections in professional and trade associations.[85] The trend has alarmed many in the Egyptian middle class. As Muhammad Abu Layla, a scholar of Islamic Studies at Al-Azhar University, laments, "When we have so many problems in Egypt, they just say, 'Islam is the only solution—adopt the values of Islam and your problems will disappear.'"[86]

Pakistan

Although considerably poorer than Egypt, Pakistan shares some of the same development patterns. It has experienced steady economic growth since 1980, nearly doubling its real per capita GDP from $318 to $517 in 2001. It has only experienced two years of economic contraction in that

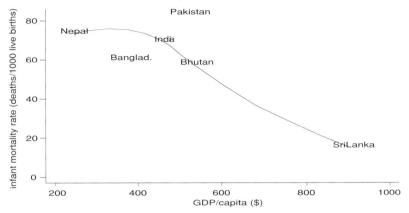

Data from WDI, 2002 for countries with information available. Plot line captures median
observations across equivalent income segments.

Figure 4.4 Pakistan has consistently underperformed on its levels of social welfare compared
to other South Asian countries at similar income levels. Seen here, Pakistan posts noticeably
higher rates of infant mortality.

span. However, when considered in the context of the dynamic South Asia
region, which experienced the fastest per capita growth in the world in the
1990s, Pakistan's achievements appear less impressive. Pakistan has realized
a lower-than-median regional growth rate since 1980, a gap that widened
during the 1990s when Pakistan grew at an average rate of 1.5 percent compared to the regional median of 3.4 percent. Pakistan has also under performed on its social-welfare indicators. Its infant mortality rate of 85 per
1,000 live births, compared with a regional median of 71, was the highest in
all of South Asia in 2000 (see Figure 4.4). Similarly, its adult illiteracy rate
of 65 percent exceeds the South Asian average of 58 percent and is neck and
neck with the rates of much poorer Bangladesh and Nepal. Pakistan has
also distinguished itself for its low level of immunization for infants, at just
39 percent compared with a regional average of 49 percent. Officially,
Pakistani government spending on health and education as a percentage of
GDP has been in line with the regional averages over the past 20 years, so
lack of financial resources is not the sole explanation for the poor socio-
economic performance. Moreover, Pakistan's mediocre social indicators
cannot be attributed to neglect by international donors; on average it received aid amounting to 3.6 percent of GDP a year between 1960 and 2000.

As in Egypt, corruption appears to be a central explanation. Even within
South Asia, which generally ranks at the bottom of corruption measures

compared with other regions, Pakistan fares poorly. According to Transparency International's corruption perception index, Pakistan averaged a 2.25 on a scale of 0 to 10 in the last half of the 1990s, with 0 indicating the worst corruption possible, putting it at the bottom of the heap. Transparency International has consistently ranked Pakistan in the bottom 10 percent of all countries in the world in its annual indices. The International Country Risk Guide ranks Pakistan's corruption 2 on a scale of 0 to 6, with 0 being the most corrupt.

Meanwhile, like Saudi Arabia, Pakistan spends heavily on its military, reserving 27.5 percent of its government budget for the armed forces, more than double India's 13.3 percent. Viewed from another angle, the expenditures account for 6.6 percent of national income, roughly equivalent to that allotted for health and education combined. As with Saudi Arabia, these allocations of resources exert long-term constraints on productive investment.

Unlike Egypt and Saudi Arabia, Pakistan has made repeated attempts to embrace democracy, first during the mid-1960s, then in the mid-1970s, and most recently in the period from 1988 to 1999. In each case, however, the military quashed the process by seizing power, and it remains the single strongest institution in the country. Pakistani governments have also been renowned for the lack of accountability of their local and provincial government officials.[87] Even during its fitful attempts at democratization, these officials were described as managing their municipalities as fiefdoms. Appointed by the central government, they do not face electoral removal. Moreover, weak institutions and the absence of rule of law make them immune from horizontal checks and balances that may be exerted by other government ministries. The control these civil administrators exert over the distribution of land, contracts, and public services makes the local population beholden to them. The patronage and cronyism fostered by the consolidation of political and economic power at the local administrative levels act as a further disincentive to economic investment and productivity.

Pakistan has also experienced an upsurge in anti-Western sentiment during the past 30 years. For most of its early existence after the partition from India in 1947, the country was known for its tolerance. Only in the 10 percent of the Sunni population practicing the Deobandi school of Islam (historically close with Wahhabism) in the far northwest of the country could fundamentalist views be found.[88] The radicalization of Islam, ironically, was begun under secularist Zulkfikar Ali Bhutto (1971 to 1977). Seeking to strengthen national identity in the aftermath of the civil war between East and West Pakistan, Bhutto oversaw the creation of a constitution that made Islam the state religion. A Council of Islamic Ideology was also established to enforce religious orthodoxy. Madrassas were excluded from state regulation. The Islamization of Pakistan was accelerated under General Zia ul-Haq, who led a military takeover from Bhutto in 1977. Zia justified the coup by citing the disorder, inefficiency, and corruption of the elected government—a line used by Pakistani generals before and since. However, Zia went further by embracing radical Islamist ideology to legitimatize his rule. Through the selective use of Islamic punishments, legal strictures, and the imposition of Zakat (an Islamic tax), he was able to weaken civil society and further centralize power.[89] By institutionalizing these changes in the legal system and co-opting clerical groups such as Jama' at-i-Islami, the military was subsequently able to project itself as the guardian of Islamic ideology.[90]

The close relationship between Islamists and the military grew in the aftermath of the Soviet invasion of Afghanistan in 1979. The Afghan mujahedeen were trained and equipped (with American funds and supplies) by the Pakistani army and powerful Inter-Services Intelligence organization. These links continued through Taliban rule of Afghanistan and the establishment of al-Qaeda's base of operations.

The stunning success of the 1979 revolution in Iran, a predominantly Shi'a country, facilitated this radicalization while exacerbating tensions in Pakistan between the minority Shi'a and the dominant Sunnis, who made up 80 percent of the population. In response to the central government's attempt to impose the Zakat tax according to Sunni law, the Shi'a, exerting a new assertiveness engendered by the Iranian revolution, staged a series of religious and political protests demanding that they be allowed to regulate their religious life according to Shi'a traditions.[91] Perceived as an attempt to reshape Islam along Shi'a lines, as part of the broader effort to export the Iranian revolution, the threatened Sunni majority rallied around sectarian Sunni mosques and organizations. The competition between the two religious communities for converts and for the power to define Islam in Pakistan led to the proliferation of madrassas and an increase in sectarian conflict.[92] In the mean time, an estimated 10 million Pakistani workers, or 11 percent of the entire population, left Pakistan in the period from the mid-1970s to the mid-1980s for jobs in the Arab world, primarily Saudi Arabia. When they returned home, many had been exposed to more virulent versions of Islam. Their newfound fervor, plus the increasing urbanization of the country, contributed to the radicalization of Islam in Pakistan.[93]

Zia oversaw the explosive growth of the Islamic educational network. Fairly rare at the time of partition, seminaries have now been established in every region of the country. Dominated by the fundamentalist Deobandis, the seminary curriculum is heavy on Islamic ideology and light on job skills. A third of the schools provide military training.[94] Students often graduate functionally illiterate. Nonetheless, under Zia, seminary graduates were increasingly recruited into government service. As Islamism grew and spread, it began to creep into the government-run secular school system.

The civilian and politically weak governments of Benazir Bhutto and Nawaz Sharif that succeeded Zia's rule made halfhearted attempts to limit the influence of the Islamists, but at the same time curried favor with them to win popular support. Sharif, for example, appointed a prominent Islamist as director general of the Inter Services Intelligence, further entrenching religious ideologues in the military.

The exponential growth of madrassas has contributed to the politicization of Islam in Pakistan. This process was aided by a crackdown by the Zia regime on the media that curtailed debate on the issue and silenced some critics. Once the prominence of the Pakistani clerics was established, they staunchly resisted any official monitoring of the madrassas.[95] But if their exact number isn't known, it is estimated that in 1997, more than 10,000 of them were instructing three million students, largely from poor families, in the strident views of the clerics. In addition, an estimated 10,000 foreign students from neighboring Muslim countries took part in the semi-military training provided by these schools.[96]

The madrassas are exempt from auditing requirements, but their combined spending is estimated at more than $1 billion a year, more than the federal government's budgetary allocations for education and health combined. Three-fourths of this funding is thought to come from abroad— nearly all of it from Saudi Arabia.[97]

Many Pakistani clerics openly expressed their support for the Taliban model of Islam prior to the U.S.-led toppling of the regime in late 2001. Notably, even after the Taliban's fall and the intense international scrutiny this generated, relations between the clerics and the Pakistani state remain as close as ever. General Pervez Musharraf, the latest military leader to seize power in Pakistan, continues to defer to the Islamists while publicly denouncing terrorism. Emblematic of the close relationship between autocracy and radical ideologies, after barring the major established secular political parties[98] from participating in heavily controlled parliamentary elections in 2002, Islamic parties gained 59 out of 342 parliamentary seats, more than at any time in Pakistan's history. They are now a key ally to Musharraf's governing coalition.

A Common Pattern
Though the circumstances varied, the evolution of these three countries into breeding grounds of terrorism displayed three common features—a population mired in poverty and despair, a dictatorial government, and a

radicalization of religion. Since many countries that share the first two attributes do not produce terrorist movements, it would seem that the distinguishing characteristic of countries that do is the third. Saudi Arabia, Egypt, and Pakistan each experienced a dramatic rise in the number of Wahhabi-funded madrassas over the past 30 years, and these infected the minds of millions of students every year with anti-Western attitudes far more virulent than those held by their parents.

This radicalization was not inevitable. To varying degrees, it was facilitated by leaders who exploited religious passion to their benefit, which partly explains why radicalization rarely occurs absent the other two co-factors, autocracy and poverty. The monopolization of political and economic opportunity breeds despair, made all the more acute by the burgeoning youth bulge. Lacking a representative government or a free press, opportunities for channeling this despair toward domestic reforms have been minimal. Instead, drawing on the themes learned in the madrassas, this angst is directed at foreign powers that are perceived to be the source of their misery.

Another distinguishing trait of each of these three countries has been their close alliance with the United States over the years. Egypt and Pakistan have regularly been among the leading recipients of U.S. economic and military assistance. Both have been formally deemed as "major non-NATO allies" by the United States. Although its wealth has made assistance unnecessary, Saudi Arabia has also enjoyed a close military and economic relationship with the United States. From the American perspective, these alliances have all been motivated by genuine economic and security interests that were deemed to outweigh other considerations, such as promoting democracy. These close ties and the perception in the Arab and parts of the Muslim world that the United States is responsible for propping up the repressive and closed political systems in these countries have contributed to anti-American sentiment in the region. In short, the terrorist attacks against the United States in the late 1990s and early twenty-first century reflect the collision of the U.S. short- and long-term interests in dealing with these and other autocratic governments.

With growing global integration, Western economic, cultural, and political influences are increasingly on display in the Arab and Muslim worlds. This is likely to accentuate feelings of relative deprivation in these societies that face ever-growing despair. The West will thus remain a ready target of the anguish and frustration felt by many Arab youths. Left unchecked, the confluence of globalization, authoritarianism, and radical Islamization portend a future of increasing terrorism and instability. This threat is especially serious when one considers that the Saudi-based Wahhabis have sponsored literally tens of thousands of madrassas all over the world at an estimated cost of $70 billion.[99]

Democracy's Dissipating Effect on Terrorism
The flipside of this discussion is that international terrorist networks rarely emerge from democracies. By guaranteeing freedom of expression, the right to political organization, opposition to a party in power, and prospects for political change, democracies provide mechanisms through which dissent can be systematically channeled into recognized public institutions. In this way, terrorist activity—calculated violence aimed at generating a political objective—is discouraged. This system is built on the recognition that in any society there will be varied and competing interests. Rather than repressing all views but those held by the party in power, democracy channels dissent into debate and deliberation. As competing views must ultimately gain the support of a plurality of an electorate to be made policy, there are incentives to appeal to a broader audience by moderating one's position. The process of debate and scrutiny also exposes the risks from pursuing radical policies, positions that can easily flourish in controlled environments. In the process, radical rhetoric falls on deaf ears, rather than mobilizing masses as it does in a repressive state. Militant groups that do emerge in democracies direct their energies inward rather than outward.

Another way of saying this is that force alone will not resolve the threat of global terrorism. Simply killing off terrorist or radical leaders is not enough. That has already been tried—for example, with the executions of Sayyid Qutb and Muhammad Abdel Salam Al-Farag. However, their violent ideologies survived and took on new forms. The crackdown on the Egyptian terrorist organizations served to fill the ranks of global networks like al-Qaeda. Rather, the culture and attitudes that allow these radical ideologies to persist must also be targeted. That, in many ways, is the underlying dimension of this struggle. Defeating these narrowly based and simplifying dogmas is best accomplished in an environment of critical thought and competing views. As democratic institutions are built on norms of openness, they provide systematic mechanisms to temper radical ideologies.[100]

This is not to suggest that democracies are immune from terrorist organizing. Experience has shown that radical Islamic terrorists have taken advantage of the openness and basic protections of democratic societies to move freely across borders, fund raise, and recruit for their operations. Most persuasively, from the terrorists' perspective is that this allows them to prepare and stage their attacks at locations close to their targets. Western Europe, in particular, has had to grapple with the evolving reality that it has gone from being a refuge for Arab radicals, to a staging ground for terrorist attacks elsewhere, to a prize target for Islamic terrorists.[101] Nonetheless, in nearly every case, the individuals and ideologies that drive these terrorist cells originate in countries with autocratic governments and radicalized societies.

Once a terrorist threat has been identified, democracies have a much greater willingness to isolate, target, and remove this threat from within their borders. As discussed in our discussion of terrorist-breeding societies, autocracies are much more apt to tolerate or attempt to co-opt such trends. Sharing values of rule of law and openness, democracies also have greater capacity for cross-national cooperation: one democracy's terrorist is largely seen as another democracy's terrorist.[102] The sharing of information, expertise, details on suspects, and intelligence allows them to track and target transnational terrorist organizations in a more coordinated manner than possible with authoritarian governments. Although terrorist cells may be established in democracies, the havens of choice for transnational terrorist organizations remain authoritarian states.

In short, even as new security threats emerge in the twenty-first century, one thing remains constant: authoritarian governments are at the source.

U.S. Support for Autocratic Regimes

We have argued that promoting democracy is a crucial dimension of international security. Democracies rarely fight each other and they are less likely to instigate conflict. Not coincidentally, most of the world's famines and refugee crises are generated by autocracies. Autocracy, conflict, and poverty are all factors in the growth of militant Islamic terrorism. The repression common to dictatorships creates popular angst that, unable to find constructive outlets, turns into despair. Despair, when radicalized, turns into violence. However, there is another, perhaps more practical, reason to withhold support for autocratic governments: It doesn't work. Historical analysis reveals that this support fails to accomplish the goals trumpeted by those who counsel this course of action—enhanced stability, economic growth, and prospects for the emergence of democracy. As we have seen, all of these underlying assumptions are inaccurate. As discussed in Chapter 2, authoritarian governments have been, by and large, no better than democracies in generating economic growth and have been substantially less capable of fostering social progress. Moreover, middle-income dictatorships have been no more inclined to democratize than low-income ones. Similarly, as we showed in this chapter, autocratic governments have not demonstrated a superior capacity to prevent conflict; on the contrary, they are the third ingredient along with poverty and conflict in the vicious circle that has hamstrung dozens of low-income countries.

U.S. assistance to autocrats has apparently contributed to this ruinous pattern. Autocrats supported by the United States have put on poorer economic performances and shown a greater probability of conflict than other countries receiving U.S. assistance. The same pattern applies when comparing U.S.-supported autocrats to countries in similar income categories that did not receive U.S. aid.

Over the years, the United States has allied itself with numerous autocratic governments, notably in its struggle with the Soviet Union. Responding to a threat to its very survival, the United States made stemming the advance of communism its foreign policy priority. Providing political, military, economic, and covert support to governments that disavowed communism was a key part of that policy. Long-term assistance for autocracies such as Marcos's Philippines, Pinochet's Chile, the Shah in Iran, and Mobutu in Zaire, among many others, was provided on this basis.

A review of the published record shows that the United States gave preference[103] to 104 autocratic countries with military or economic assistance at some point from 1950 to 2000 (see Appendix D). The median level of annual military aid[104] received over this period was $600,000.[105] However, allocations of military assistance have been highly skewed to the top recipients. The average annual allocation for the top fourth of recipients was $8.2 million, and to autocrats in that group, $37 million. A similar pattern applies to economic assistance.[106] The median recipient of U.S. economic assistance in the 1990s received an annual allocation of approximately $17 million. The top fourth of recipients received an average $47 million. For the autocrats among them it was $54 million. In summary, U.S. support to autocratic governments since 1950 has been substantial and sustained.

Let's examine this history in more detail by assessing the performance of U.S.-supported autocrats in each of the three spheres frequently invoked to justify this support: economic development, political stability, and advancing democracy.

Economic Impacts

Three key economic observations emerge from a review of U.S. assistance from 1960 to 2000.[107] First, economic assistance has had a marginal effect on economic growth. That is, controlling for income level across multiple decades, U.S. economic assistance has not been statistically linked to rates of more rapid economic advancement. Though this relationship is consistently positive—countries receiving more aid generally grew more rapidly—it simply is not strong enough to demonstrate a statistically reliable effect. Given the fact that U.S. economic assistance was often primarily used to reward friendly governments rather than advance development, this finding is not terribly surprising.

There was one exception, however, leading us to the second observation. The positive pattern between economic assistance and growth strengthened in the 1980s and 1990s. And when the 1990s are considered in isolation, a significant positive relationship does emerge. Interestingly, it parallels a strengthening pattern between democratic recipients of assistance and growth during this time period. In other words, economic assistance was associated with economic development only when the relationship between democratic recipients and economic performance was also quite strong. In the 1960s and 1970s, little distinction in growth levels among economic recipients is detected based on level of democracy. However, this changed in the 1980s and 1990s when the number of low-income democracies was increasing. (Democratic recipients of economic assistance still only accounted for less than a third of the total recipients in the 1990s, however).

In contrast, autocratic recipients of U.S. assistance[108] performed much more poorly during those latter decades, averaging less than half of the growth rates of democracies (see Figure 4.5). Notably, this difference is not explained by conflict. That is, even when controlling for conflict, growth rates of autocratic recipients of economic assistance in recent decades have still been markedly slower than those of democracies. Moreover, when the performance of autocratic recipients in the top fourth of allocations is considered, the results are even more striking. During the 1990s, the median level of per capita growth for this group was 0.03 percent, or effectively flat. Therefore, to the extent that the United States can point to a positive

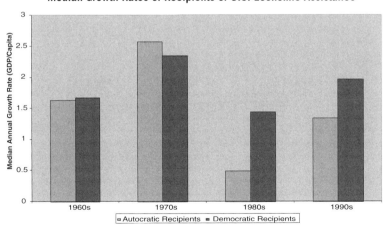

Data from *USAID, 2002; Polity.*

Figure 4.5 Autocratic recipients of U.S. economic assistance have realized economic growth rates half that of democratic recipients during the 1980s and 1990s.

impact on economic development from its economic assistance in recent decades, this is associated with the relatively stronger performance of its democratic recipients.

This brings us to the third key observation regarding the relationship between U.S. economic assistance and economic performance. The weak relationship between assistance to autocratic governments and growth that emerges in recent decades appears to be persistent. Not only did autocratic recipients of U.S. assistance fare worse at the time, these countries tended to grow more slowly than other recipients five and 10 years later (see Figure 4.6 and Figure 4.7). Stated differently, autocratic recipients of U.S. economic assistance in the 1980s such as Cameroon, Haiti, Morocco, Togo, and Zaire (now Democratic Republic of the Congo) performed markedly worse than the norm in the 1990s. Those autocratic recipients that were in the top 1/4 of beneficiaries during the previous five-year and 10-year periods realized particularly weak subsequent growth. Most notably, the top autocratic recipients from the late 1970s and 1980s experienced average annual per capita economic contractions of 0.57 percent of GDP five years later (Figure 4.6). Honduras, Liberia, Mauritania, Panama, Syria, and Tunisia were among the countries that fit that pattern. Likewise, top

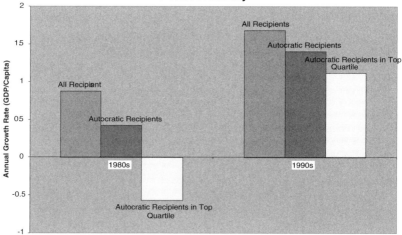

Data from *USAID, 2002; Polity.*

Figure 4.6 Autocratic recipients of U.S. economic assistance had slower growth rates five years later than other aid recipients. Among autocratic recipients, those in the top quartile of per capita funding subsequently posted the slowest growth rates.

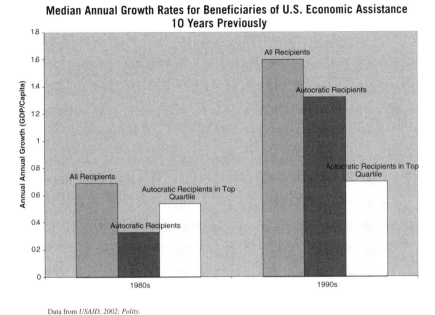

Data from *USAID, 2002; Polity.*

Figure 4.7 The persistent economic malaise seen in autocratic recipients of a U.S. economic assistance is apparent even 10 years after the funding was allocated.

autocratic recipients from 10 years previously still had growth rates that were only half that of other recipients in the 1990s (Figure 4.7). Pouring more economic assistance into autocratic governments did not help; they performed even worse.

In short, since the 1980s, economic assistance to autocratic governments has coincided with lower levels of growth relative to other beneficiaries (and the global median for lower-middle income countries). The largest autocratic recipients demonstrated the most disappointing outcomes. Moreover, economic assistance to autocratic governments appears to contribute to a prolonged economic malaise in these countries; they grow more slowly for some years to come. This implies that autocratic beneficiaries of U.S. assistance were less able to convert these resources into long-term productive advantages for their economies than other recipients.

Propensity for Conflict

Let us now consider how U.S. economic and military support over the years has affected the stability of those countries. We will do so through the prism of warfare in the years 1946 to 2002, looking both at the frequency of engagement in conflicts and the magnitude of those conflicts.[109] Considering magnitude of conflict allows us to factor in a country's size, population, and economy to gain a clear picture of a conflict's impact. An armed confrontation in some remote district of China, after all, would have fewer repercussions on the society at large than one of the same scale in Sierra Leone. Our review of American assistance also takes into account the recipients' wealth and trade activity, as research has shown a strong linkage between those two factors and a nation's diminished likelihood of becoming embroiled in conflict.[110]

The single best predictor of conflict is recent history of conflict. Forty-eight percent of countries that were engaged in conflict in the 1990s had been at war 10 years earlier, and 43 percent 15 years earlier. In short, fighting is easier to start than end. The duration of civil conflicts appears to have been growing in recent decades and today averages seven years. Moreover, countries that have recently concluded conflicts are highly vulnerable to falling back into them. A country that is just emerging from war may have up to 10 times the risk of sliding back into it than it had in the first place.[111]

Beyond its persistence, there is also a strong link between the level of U.S. assistance to a country and its propensity for armed conflict. Controlling for income and trade levels, we have found that throughout the 1960–2002 period, countries receiving greater levels of economic and military assistance from the United States had a higher proclivity for frequent and devastating conflict than those receiving lower levels of aid. On the surface, this is not surprising as this may simply reflect U.S. aid flows tracking countries in conflict. However, this effect was long lasting.[112] Even when taking into consideration a country's previous history of conflict, countries receiving greater levels of U.S. assistance in 1980 were more likely to be engaged in an intense conflict in 1985, in 1990, and even in 1995, than those that did not. The relationship was particularly strong between level of military assistance and subsequent magnitude of conflict.

We find that countries receiving U.S. economic assistance typically had a 20 percent to 40 percent higher probability of conflict in subsequent years than the norm.[113] This finding is somewhat counterintuitive, suggesting that economic assistance is not an unmitigated good. But it shows that, when interjected into unstable situations and into the wrong hands, aid can actually foster violence rather than work for the good of society. (Recall that some 70 percent to 80 percent of recipients of U.S. assistance have historically been autocracies.) Thus, these resources may serve to entrench a repressive leadership, pushing political opponents to resort to armed conflict to overthrow them. A list of some of the autocratic recipients of U.S. economic assistance in the 1980s illuminates our point: Angola, Afghanistan, Burundi, Chad, Congo, Ethiopia, Guatemala, Indonesia, Liberia,

Myanmar, Philippines, Rwanda, Sierra Leone, Somalia, Sudan, and Zaire. These countries were engaged in some of the most wrenching conflicts of the 1990s.

Reviewing the case of Liberia may give a better sense of the dynamics of this phenomenon. The United States had long been a close ally of this West African state founded by freed American slaves. Its support not only continued uninterrupted after Samuel Doe seized power in a military coup in 1980, it grew rapidly over the next few years, averaging $75 million and reaching one of the highest per capita levels in the world. In return, Liberia provided the United States landing rights for its military aircraft as well a base for the CIA's regional communications network. When Doe claimed victory in the 1985 presidential elections that he was widely thought to have lost badly, the United States issued only a mild rebuke. Economic assistance continued unabated (though military assistance did subsequently slow). Economic conditions declined rapidly over the next several years, due in large part to widespread public corruption. Doe put down a coup attempt after the stolen elections, but a civil war broke out in late 1989 and continued largely uninterrupted through 2003, though Doe himself was killed in 1990. Over the course of the next decade, all of Liberia's neighbors—Sierra Leone, Cote d'Ivoire, and to some extent Guinea—were pulled into the cesspool of instability that originated in Liberia.

The relationship between autocratic governance and conflict, adjusted for trade and income levels, is particularly strong in the post-cold war period. In other words, while autocracies were always more likely to be involved in conflict, starting in 1987 this difference became more pronounced statistically.[114] Recall that almost all conflicts since then have been civil wars. Similarly, among countries receiving U.S. military and economic assistance during this period, autocracies were significantly more likely to be engaged in more frequent and damaging conflicts.

The relationship between American military assistance and the recipient's future likelihood of going to war has also been very strong over the years.[115] This peaked in the 1980s, when one in three nations that had received such aid 10 to 15 years earlier was still engaged in conflict. In other words, military assistance allocated in the late 1960's and in the 1970s was closely tied to the frequency and ferocity of conflicts in the 1980s.[116] However, the association between American military assistance and the frequency (though not the magnitude) of future conflict weakened in the 1990s. A likely explanation for this is that conflicts in this decade were primarily civil wars largely fueled by internal factors such as an escalation of long-standing disputes, attempts by distinct ethnic groups to gain separation from a central authority, competition over black-market commodities like diamonds and drugs, illicit trade, and the spread of regional instability.[117]

In summary, the track record of the relationship between U.S. economic and military assistance to developing countries and their tendency to go to war five, 10 or 15 years down the road is sobering. To be sure, a variety of factors contributed to this linkage. U.S. funding was heavily oriented toward assisting countries in conflict, as well as toward cementing cold war alliances and providing humanitarian assistance to war-torn regions. However, the stubborn persistence of the relationship cannot be easily dismissed. Recipients of U.S. assistance from 15 years ago are still more likely to be engaged in more serious conflicts today than are nonrecipients. And this is especially true of autocratic recipients of such aid. Although the number of conflicts in the world is declining, the probability of conflict in autocracies, including autocratic recipients of U.S. assistance, is increasing. This raises questions about the implications of this assistance and to what extent the United States may be playing an enabling role to these autocracies, leading to greater levels of subsequent conflict.

Impact on the Emergence of Democracy
Another important dimension of U.S. military and economic assistance is the consideration of what, if any, long-term impact it has on the emergence of democracy. After all, all sides of the national security debate agree that stable democratic societies are least likely to pose a threat to the United States. Disagreements have revolved around how to best foster such outcomes. Alas, our review finds that U.S. aid to autocracies significantly slows a country's evolution toward democracy.[118]

Consider economic assistance. Controlling for income, it appears to be an important contributing factor to higher levels of democracy five to 10 years into the future.[119] That is, over all, countries that received greater levels of economic assistance were likely to be more democratic in the future than other countries.[120] That tendency, however, does not hold for autocratic governments—they are significantly less likely to be democratic, even 15 years into the future. The negative relationship is even sharper for those autocracies that were among the top quartile of recipients of U.S. economic assistance. In other words, the top autocratic recipients of U.S. economic assistance were even less likely to be democratic up to 15 years later than other countries at similar income levels—including other economic aid recipients.

The consistency of this dichotomous pattern is portrayed in Figure 4.8. This summarizes the results from six different groupings of aid recipients and their subsequent level of democracy, controlling for income and other factors. The three on the left include samples of all economic recipients from five, 10 and 15 years previously throughout the 1960 to 2000 period.

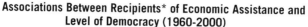

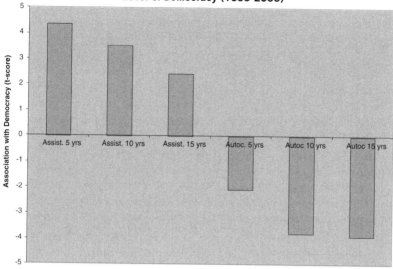

*Assist-5, 10, 15 refers to all recipients of economic assistance five, ten, and fifteen years previously, respectively. Autoc 5, 10, 15 reflects the experience of autocratic recipients of economic assistance during those same time intervals. Data from *USAID, 2002; Polity.*

Figure 4.8 Recipients of U.S. economic assistance were subsequently likely to become more democratic. However, autocratic recipients of U.S. economic assistance were still more likely to be autocratic than other recipients up to 15 years later.

Meanwhile, the three columns on the right represent autocratic recipients of economic assistance for those same three time intervals.[121] What we see in the three columns on the left is that the typical recipient of economic assistance was likely to be more democratic in subsequent years. This relationship is strong and consistent. Countries receiving economic assistance 15 years previously were somewhat less strongly associated with advanced democracy scores than those receiving assistance more recently. Nonetheless, the relationship is still significant.

When economic assistance to autocratic recipients is considered (that is, the three right columns), we find it is strongly negatively related to the subsequent level of democracy. This relationship shows up 15 years into the future. For example, Egypt, Liberia, Oman, Haiti, Mauritania, Somalia, Sudan, Swaziland, Burkina Faso, Togo, and Tunisia were autocratic countries that received significant levels of U.S. economic assistance on a per capita basis in the 1970s and 1980s, yet had below-average democracy scores in the 1990s.

A notable observation of the autocratic-recipient columns is the relative weakness of the five-year time lag. We would expect this to show up most negatively given the relatively short time period it allows for a democratic transition. That the five-year time lag is relatively weaker reflects a considerable level of fluctuation among autocratic recipients on a short-term basis. In fact, reflecting the major transitions of the 1990s, when that decade is considered on its own the five-year autocratic recipient category is neutrally associated with democracy (not shown). Therefore, autocratic recipients need not always remain autocratic. Near-term changes are possible.

Another way of looking at this relationship is to compare the progress toward democracy of the autocratic recipients of U.S. assistance relative to the norm. In this case we will focus on the 1990s, the period of most rapid democratization for many low-income countries. In fact, during that decade, the average low-income country realized an increase in its Polity democracy score from 0 to 3 on the eleven-point index. This generated decade averages for countries with per capita incomes below $2,000 and $4,000 of two and three, respectively. Most recipients of U.S. economic and military assistance subsequently met the global median levels of democracy for their income group.

When we consider the autocratic recipients of U.S. assistance, we find that their democracy scores consistently fell below these median levels—including up to 15 years after the assistance was provided. This trend is most pronounced among the autocratic recipients of economic assistance. With scores of 0 and 1, these countries were consistently one to two points below the global democracy norms for their income groups. This is not necessarily surprising for countries that had received aid just five years earlier, a relatively short interval for making the transition from dictatorship to democracy. However, the fact that it holds true for countries 15 years after the aid was received is striking. Their sluggish progress toward democracy as others in their income group were moving at two to three times their pace is depicted graphically in Figure 4.9. Autocratic recipients of economic assistance in the late 1970s and 1980s had a median democracy score of 1 during the 1990s, in both income categories considered.[122] This was below the global medians of 2 to 3 for low income countries and for aid recipients overall.

The key theme that emerges from this review of U.S. economic and military assistance is that support to autocratic countries has persistent long-term negative consequences.[123] Democratization is delayed and these countries are substantially more prone to conflict. In the late 1980s and 1990s, noticeable divergences in rates of growth also emerged. Bluntly put, where the United States has generously aided autocratic governments, the citizens of these countries and their neighbors have had to endure the con-

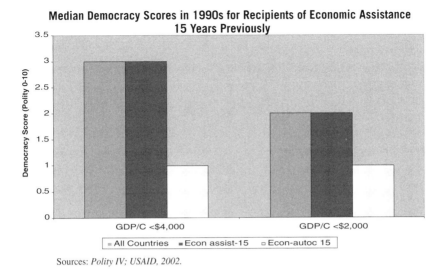

Median Democracy Scores in 1990s for Recipients of Economic Assistance 15 Years Previously

Sources: *Polity IV; USAID, 2002.*

Figure 4.9 Autocratic recipients of U.S. economic assistance 15 years previously had democracy scores two to three times lower in the 1990s than other low-income recipients.

sequences of misgovernment for a longer period of time. Recognition of this pattern should prompt U.S. policymakers to consider a longer time horizon when making decisions about which governments it will support. Although such alliances may produce short-term tactical gains for the United States, they can also be disastrous over the long term for the developing countries in question, pushing them into a vicious circle of autocracy, underdevelopment, and conflict. And as experience has shown, the effects from this cycle do not remain isolated.

In other words, while there has been an active and ongoing debate over whether the United States and the West should promote democracy in the developing world on security and economic grounds, a primary lesson to be drawn from the historical record takes us in the opposite direction. U.S. foreign assistance to autocracies has contributed to undercutting economic development, stability, and democracy in these countries.

Our review of the social, economic, and military consequences of U.S. assistance also reveals a chronological divide: those autocratic recipients of aid in the 1950s and 1960s, notably Taiwan, South Korea, Turkey, Greece, Spain, Yugoslavia, Portugal, and Singapore, fared much better those that received aid in subsequent decades. These European and East Asian countries exhibited stronger governance institutions than has been typical of dictatorships overall. Moreover, poor though they were, these earlier autocratic recipients generally enjoyed socio-political conditions conducive to growth, like a clear national identity and geographic location in an economically dynamic region.

In contrast, the leading autocratic recipients of U.S. military and economic assistance in the 1970s, 1980s, and 1990s were countries such as Egypt, Ecuador, Panama, Liberia, Honduras, Zaire (Democratic Republic of Congo), Oman, Djibouti, Chad, Sudan, Gabon, Equatorial Guinea, Eritrea, Bahrain, Guinea-Bissau, and Haiti, whose governments tended to be more narrowly based and corrupt. They also reflect a shift in geographic focus to Africa, Latin America, and the Middle East—regions that had just thrown off the shackles of colonialism and were grappling with the challenges of establishing a national identity. In general, they were plagued by sharper class differences than the earlier group. Because of that, political and economic power was concentrated in fewer hands. That meant that the rulers were more likely to manage national resources in a way that reinforced their hold on power, rather than alleviating the conditions of the masses.

This analysis does not attempt to weigh the strategic value of U.S. support to these autocratic governments. However, our observations suggest that a policy of support to autocracies established during the early stages of the cold war was later applied to a much broader collection of autocratic states. Specifically, if the assumption that autocracies were better guarantors of stability and growth was ever valid, it was valid only for the earlier group. Yet scholars and foreign policy analysts have persisted in applying it to subsequent generations of dictatorships, failing to account sufficiently for their vastly different circumstances. Thus American aid was poured into countries that lacked the institutional and political advantages to utilize it for economic development. Instead, it had the contrary effect of perpetuating economic malaise, conflict and repression.

The fact that divergences between autocratic countries and other recipients of U.S. aid appear to be widening in the aftermath of the cold war with regard to their progress toward democracy, economic development, and peace is further impetus for U.S. policymakers to rethink how they allocate that assistance. Whereas support to one genre of autocratic governments in the 1950s, 1960s and 1970s may have had a persuasive national security rationale, the disadvantages of providing even economic help to autocratic governments in the post-cold war period are multiplying.

Summary

Autocratic governments are a threat to international security. Over the last 40 years, these governments have been more likely to instigate war with other countries, become embroiled in civil conflict, precipitate refugee crises, and trade in illicit goods. In short, autocratic governance is a key feature in the nexus between poverty and conflict. This is so even in comparison to countries undergoing democratic transitions, which while they may face ethnic or separatists challenges, are no more likely to face armed conflict than are autocracies. In fact, the autocracy–conflict linkage has become more pronounced in the 1980s and 1990s with the end of the cold war.

Over the past 50 years, the United States has supported numerous autocratic governments—mainly to combat communism. Unfortunately, as the communist threat has faded, the instinct to ally with autocratic governments in pursuit of an immediate economic or security interest has not. We recognize that, at times, there are certain short-term merits in this approach. However, experience shows that there are also immense long-term costs. On average, autocratic beneficiaries of U.S. assistance have subsequently endured slower rates of economic growth, a higher probability of conflict, and a greater resistance to democratization. Indeed, the dominance of autocratic recipients in the U.S. foreign assistance portfolio over the years is a key reason for the Unites States' poor track record in promoting development.

In an increasingly globalized world, the instability engendered by these autocratic states will not be confined to national boundaries. With the prospect of transnational terrorist organizations gaining access to weapons of mass destruction, the costs of alliances with autocratic regimes are escalating. At the same time, distinctions between short- and long-term costs are blurring. Yet these costs are insufficiently weighed when policy decisions to enter these partnerships are made. A new policy equation is needed in relation to autocracies with which the United States may share certain aims. Whereas in the past cooperating with them was rationalized on the grounds of national security, that argument can no longer be convincingly made. Quite the opposite: U.S. security is closely aligned with the promotion of democracy.

This is particularly true for the principal terrorist-breeding countries—all of them long-time beneficiaries of U.S. support. They are clear examples of how autocratic governments do not produce true economic development even when they realize economic growth. Lacking incentives to respond to a broader range of their citizenry, these countries are susceptible to becoming trapped in the downward spiral of autocracy, relative deprivation, and the allure of radicalized ideologies.

In other words, enhancing global security is tied to promoting democracy. Creating transparency in the use of public resources, reducing corruption, professionalizing the civil service, and enhancing adherence to the rule of law will augment the delivery of public services and increase government credibility. Moreover, promoting a free press, legalizing independent associations, and respecting basic human rights will strengthen civil society and provide the basis for the separation of private and public spheres and for protections against government abuse.

The record of democracies as a force for peace offers a vision for a more stable future. The movement of so many low-income countries toward democracy since the 1980s is an encouraging step toward the realization of this vision. However, a third of the states in the global system remain autocratic. Given the overlap of autocracy, poverty, and conflict (including terrorism), these states will continue to absorb a disproportionate share of international attention in the coming decades. As the United States contemplates its relations with these states, it will need to take a hard look at whether its actions are fostering the creation of a global network of stable democratic states or if, instead, they are perpetuating autocratic governance, with all the risks to international security that this entails.

CHAPTER 5

Making Development Safe for Democracy

Expansion of freedom is viewed both as the primary end and the principle means of development. Development consists of the removal of
various types of unfreedoms that leave people with little choice and
little opportunity for exercising their reasoned legacy.

Amartya Sen
Nobel laureate economist

Economic stagnation, Chapter 3 showed, stymies democratization in poor
countries. But so does the wrong type of economic reforms—those that pay
insufficient heed to political, social, and institutional considerations.
Indeed economic reforms, when poorly conceived, can undermine the very
economic growth they are supposed to achieve. This chapter documents
such outcomes through a series of case studies. A recurrent theme is that
timing and sensitivity to the political realities facing reformers is vital.
Reforms must be customized to the specific needs of individual countries
and sequenced carefully. Meanwhile, unconditionally granting aid to countries with a history of unaccountable governance creates disincentives to
both economic and political progress.

The Case of Russia

Emerging from the collapse of the Soviet Union after seven decades
of communism, Russians looked expectantly to the 1990s. Multiparty

elections in June 1991 gave Boris Yeltsin 57 percent of the vote, making him the country's first freely chosen leader. He was joined by a team of young reformers intent on opening the political system and transforming Russia's centrally controlled economy into a free market system. Visions of greater freedom and prosperity filled the imaginations of many ordinary Russian citizens.

The new Russian policymakers were aided by highly touted western economic advisers, largely from the United States and the International Monetary Fund (IMF). They advocated a series of rapid, fundamental reforms to dismantle the communist economic structures. This "shock therapy" was justified on the grounds that only a complete break with the past could prevent a resurgence of the old regime. Moreover, it was argued that such a policy would shorten the painful transition to a market economy and thus hasten the onset of a long-term upturn in economic growth.

Whether Russia pursued shock therapy as intended by its advocates is a matter for academic debate. But whatever the answer, Russia embarked in 1992 on a strategy of rapid economic liberalization, stabilization, and privatization.[1] Liberalization involved freeing prices from the levels fixed by central planners—the first step in creating incentives for private suppliers. However, without a history of entrepreneurship, a legal code geared to a capitalist economy, a sophisticated banking system, or the delivery and marketing resources required to match supply and demand, few firms were in a position to respond. Consequently, the sudden lifting of price controls on virtually all goods and services resulted in a sharp and prolonged spike in consumer prices. The situation was exacerbated by mismanagement at the Russian Central Bank, which, led by former Soviet bureaucrats, showered state banks with cheap credit, weakening the ruble. The result was hyperinflation of more than 2,318 percent in 1992. This eviscerated the savings of millions of Russian households, shifting fully one-third of the largely middle-class society into poverty. This loss of savings simultaneously eliminated the capital base upon which small businesses could be expected to rely. Once the Central Bank tightened monetary policy, it did so dramatically. The resulting 100 percent interest rates[2] severely limited access to capital, further constraining the economic growth needed to stimulate the supply of goods and creation of jobs.

Despite these obstacles, those implementing the shock therapy strategy pushed ahead with the privatization element of the program, encouraged by the U.S. Department of Treasury, the IMF, and the World Bank. As a result, government-owned enterprises and natural resource concessions were sold off without competitive bidding or the legal and regulatory oversight of the sort found in the United States and western Europe. This enabled a small number of well connected people with access to capital—most of them friends and allies of government officials—to grab these national assets cheaply.[3] Moreover, because the nation rushed into privatization before the Russian tax code was overhauled and tailored to the needs of a market economy, many of these freshly minted oligarchs paid no taxes, creating a fiscal crisis for the government. Consequently, the government did not have the revenues to provide essential services in schooling and health care. Pensions for the elderly and social programs for the poor went unfunded. Military programs were terminated and salaries cut. The government was forced to borrow billions from the IMF.

Recognizing the fragility of the economic environment, the new owners had stronger incentives to engage in asset stripping than increasing their firms' productive capacities. The dismemberment and sale of these assets earned the new entrepreneurs far more than they had paid for the firms, whose bankruptcy threw millions out of work. Those owners who acquired monopolies they saw as viable would oftentimes use their disproportionate influence with government officials to alter governmental tax, regulatory, and antitrust policies to lock in their advantageous position, a process known as "state capture." The oligarchs strengthened their capacity to enforce these regulations by creating their own private armies among the thousands of discharged military personnel. Taking advantage of liberalized capital regulations intended to promote investment, Russians who were better-off transferred their assets out of the country where they could be protected from hyperinflation and the insecurity of domestic financial institutions. The result was capital flight of an estimated $40 billion in 1992[4] and an average of $20 billion to $25 billion per year for the decade.[5]

Russia's economy experienced a near uninterrupted tailspin in the five years following the initiation of the reforms. From 1992 to 1994 alone, per capita GDP contracted by 34 percent. By 1997 the situation appeared to be stabilizing, with Russia's per capita output growing by 1.2 percent. Nevertheless, weak institutions, unstable macroeconomic fundamentals, widespread corruption, an overvalued currency, and a decline in oil prices—the source of much of the government's revenue—exposed the economy's ongoing vulnerability. The East Asian financial crisis in 1998 pushed it over the edge. Jittery investors fled, and the outflow of capital and accompanying speculation against the ruble triggered another spike in Russian interest rates, to 50 percent, a risk premium of 45 percentage points over U.S. Treasury bills. Despite a rescue package of $22.6 billion organized by the IMF and World Bank, Russia defaulted on its debt repayments in August. Per capita GDP slipped another 4.6 percent.

Although painful, the devaluation of the ruble in 1998 did serve to make Russian exports more competitive. Combined with a steady rise in oil prices, Russia has enjoyed annual growth in GDP of 6 percent since then.

Official unemployment has declined from 13 percent in 1999 to 7 percent in 2002. Nonetheless, the transition has left Russia dominated by oligarchs whose unchecked control over the economy creates structural inefficiencies. From 1989 to 1998, per capita incomes had been cut almost in half—from $3,800 to $2,130.[6] In the process, the level of inequality effectively doubled.[7] Life expectancy for Russian men declined from 64 to 59 years.[8] Workers' salaries often arrived months late.

Compounding this economic debacle, Russia's political evolution has been problematic. U.S. officials involved in the transition, drawing directly from Lipset, firmly believed that economic reform would facilitate the emergence of democracy in Russia.[9] Moreover, fearing the challenges of simultaneous economic and political transitions, efforts to instill democratic institutions were put on the back burner. This tentativeness was augmented by the absence of a clear model for political reform as a counterweight to the liberalization, stabilization, and privatization tenets of the economic reform strategy.[10]

Popular support for reforms quickly fragmented as economic disparities, "theft" of public enterprises and widespread corruption became apparent. In the fall of 1993, as a result of a power struggle between the Parliament and President Yeltsin, communist and nationalist hardliners led by Vice President Alexander Rutskoi seized the Parliament building and declared themselves in charge. This precipitated a constitutional crisis that was resolved only when Yeltsin ordered Russian army tanks to fire on the parliamentary building. An estimated 193 people were killed and 1,338 arrested.[11] Although the crisis was settled, popular disillusionment continued. In December 1995, the Communist Party won a plurality in parliament and seemed poised to win the presidency. However, after starting the year trailing badly in the polls, Yeltsin narrowly came out on top in the first round of the 1996 presidential elections. He then won the runoff in July against Communist Party candidate Gennady Zyuganov with 54 percent of the vote. To secure popular support, however, Yeltsin suspended many of his free market reforms. The ongoing fractionalization of Russian politics and Yeltsin's deteriorating health contributed to an extended period of fecklessness in economic policymaking that culminated in the 1998 default.

Following Yeltsin's abrupt resignation on New Year's Eve 1999, Vladimir Putin ascended to the presidency. Using the Kremlin as a platform to pressure regional governors and the media, Putin won the March 2000 elections with 53 percent of the vote. His Unity Party, formed only six months previously and propelled by widespread popular support for military operations in Chechnya following apartment bombings in Moscow, provided Putin a base from which to consolidate power in the executive branch. He has steadily imposed ever more substantial restrictions on the media and has shown intolerance toward criticism. All national television outlets are now state-owned. Putin allies from his days at the KGB have been appointed to key ministerial and public enterprise posts, allowing him to extend executive control. Laws are seemingly enforced arbitrarily and the government at times seizes private sector assets. In short, the checks and balances that typify an accountable, democratic system, never fully established in Russia, have been appreciably eroded. This was vividly displayed in the March 2004 presidential elections in which intimidation of opposition candidates and fawning press coverage of Putin made the result a foregone conclusion. Putin "won" with 71 percent of the vote in a process that was deemed by international observers to have fallen considerably below "free and fair" standards.

The Russian experience is a classic case of how disregard for the institutional base upon which a market economy relies—particularly one created from scratch—can lead to disaster. Property rights, the capacity to enforce contracts, regulation of financial institutions, rules for the creation of corporate entities, standards of corporate governance, and norms for financial disclosure are just a few of the institutional conditions that must be created for capitalism to flourish. These rights and regulations are interconnected, and may need to be introduced gradually. Gradualism enables individuals, corporations, government bodies, and other organizations to adjust to change. It also cultivates three ingredients for a successful transition to a market economy: economic competition, full employment, and social stability.

Russia illustrates the risks of hasty policymaking. Poorly designed, poorly timed, and poorly implemented reforms not only can damage the economy, they also can have an undesirable impact on the political landscape, for example, by breathing new life into discredited antidemocratic forces. Fifteen years after it began its transition, Russia has reemerged as a semi-authoritarian state. Economic growth remains heavily tied to surging global oil prices and is independent of the rule of law. State corruption is on the rise. The vision of a more prosperous and democratic Russia that many Russians had hoped for would arguably be closer to reality today if Russia had pursued a more balanced development strategy, one that gave relatively greater attention to the tasks of building stable, democratic political institutions.

Development Reforms Can Undercut Reformers

Machiavelli once observed that there is nothing more difficult to carry out, more doubtful of success, nor more dangerous to handle than reform.[12] Reforms change the rules of the game. Development reforms are about increasing transparency, fairness, and accountability in the use of public resources. They are intended to improve the responsiveness of public officials to citizens' concerns and improve the efficiency of markets. Reforms typically take the form of increasing competition (for example, increasing access to the market, reducing special-interest privileges, and granting contracts and positions on the basis of merit), which in turn enhances incentives for superior performance. The resulting improvement in efficiency increases the accessibility of goods and services and improves social well being. Opponents of reform are usually those who have prospered under the old, undemocratic rules. Since these special interests are, by definition, a small group relative to the rest of the society, they readily recognize they have much to lose with a change in rules. Their small size means they can be easily organized. In contrast, since the benefits to society from reforms are likely to be diffuse and the beneficiaries difficult to organize, the ability to mobilize and maintain support for change is considerably more difficult.

Yet economic and political reform requires building and maintaining just such broad social coalitions. Consider initiatives that promote small- and medium-sized enterprises. These businesses are major drivers of new employment, increased economic output, greater competition, and lower prices for consumers. Nonetheless, even though the net benefit for society is positive, certain firms, particularly those enjoying regulatory protection, will be threatened. Garnering public support for such reforms requires raising public awareness of the benefits of the change, mobilizing key constituencies around the issue, drafting legislation, and seeing these changes put into practice. Opponents of reform will attempt to derail the process each step of the way. The struggle for reform, therefore, could be characterized as a battle between competing coalitions—those that aim to broaden economic participation versus those who strive to maintain privileged control.

Bulgaria

Bulgaria realized its democratic opening in 1989. Taking advantage of the end of the Cold War, reformers were able to force the resignation of the dictator, Todor Zhivkov, and compel the ruling communists to begin separating the responsibilities of the party from those of the state. The communists managed to retain enough institutional and financial clout to win a disputed election in June 1990. However, by failing to adjust to the rapidly changing external economic environment (80 percent of Bulgaria's trade was with the USSR), the communist government defaulted on its $11 billion debt (much of which was amassed in the latter half of the 1980s).[13] Popular protests and strikes led to the election of the opposition Union of

Democratic Forces, or UDF, under the leadership of Filip Dimitrov, in October 1991. Formed less than two years previously, the UDF represented a coalition of 19 democratic parties whose main unifying theme was their opposition to communism.

The UDF was zealous about economic reform, in large part motivated by a desire to destroy the communists' long stranglehold on the economic levers of control that provided disproportionate benefits to party members. The strategy was to decentralize and de-monopolize as quickly as possible.[14] In practice, because of the Bulgarians' lack of proficiency in these matters, the initial reform package was almost entirely designed by the IMF.[15] As such, the program closely followed the orthodoxy of the time: rapid liberalization, macroeconomic stabilization by pursuing monetary, and fiscal austerity and privatization. The UDF simultaneously lifted price controls, cut farm subsidies, curtailed soft loans to state-owned enterprises (that comprised 95 percent of Bulgaria's firms), and initiated the privatization of state-owned industry.[16] The process of land reform—reconstituting state-run farms to their pre-communist owners—was also begun. The austerity measures aimed at the agricultural sector were particularly sensitive given that 35 percent of the Bulgarian population was rural-based. In April 1992, a standby $212 million agreement with the IMF was negotiated.[17]

In response to the liberalization, Bulgaria's annual inflation rate shot up to 450 percent. The consequent tightening of monetary policy led to interest rates of 50 percent, severely limiting access to capital. Per capita GDP contracted by 7 percent in 1992, following a 6 percent decline in 1991. Nonetheless, reflecting popular support for change, these hardships did not generate civil unrest, seemingly affirming the observations of some western diplomats that the Bulgarian population was as prepared for the difficulties of transition as any in central Europe.[18]

The reconstituted communists, the Bulgarian Socialist Party, or BSP, however, did not simply shrivel. They had profited handsomely under the state-dominated economic system and, as such, had the means, motivation, and acumen to fight back. They held the second largest number of seats in parliament and challenged the reformers whenever possible. The BSP played on the population's xenophobia and fears of exploitation by asserting that land reform would result in displacement of Bulgarians by wealthy outsiders.[19] It denounced privatization as a giveaway of national wealth to foreign interests. And it described the UDF efforts to restore land to its pre-communist owners as evidence that it cared mostly for the rich.[20]

Responding to the divisive tactics of the BSP and the strained economic environment, a small party representing Bulgaria's Turkish minority switched its allegiances from the UDF to the BSP in October 1992. After only 11 months in power, the Dimitrov government was forced to resign after losing a no-confidence vote. A pro-BSP coalition subsequently came to power and the reform process was stalled. Due to worsening factionalism within the UDF, the BSP won the 1994 parliamentary elections. It went on to reverse some market reforms, to pour millions of dollars into the faltering state-owned enterprises, and to favor farming cooperatives over private farming. Local BSP strongmen used coercive tactics against "peasant capitalists," and price controls were reinstituted on over one-half of all consumer products.[21]

These BSP policies led to disastrous economic consequences. Per capita income contracted by 16 percent in the years 1996 and 1997. Fiscal deficits averaged 9.3 percent of GDP from 1993 to 1996. Hyperinflation returned with a vengeance, reaching 1,058 percent in 1997 and hammering the Bulgarian currency. Nationwide strikes forced a new round of elections, which saw the reshaped UDF returned to power in 1997. After a five-year retrenchment, Bulgaria was back on the path of reform. In the interim, however, per capita income had shrunk from $1,487 to $1,349. The inability to maintain a reform coalition in 1992 had been costly.[22]

Bulgaria's experience is similar to that of other countries making the transition to democracy and illustrates the need for balance in carrying out reforms. Although all politicians prefer to advertise a policy's immediate benefits and push off its costs into the future, economic reform forces them to do the opposite. They must spell out the economic pain to come and wait for the benefits to accrue. Reformist politicians must therefore calculate the trade-offs, seek compromises, and provide sufficient assurances to an anxious public undergoing a dramatic change in circumstances in order to maintain a wide enough base of support for reform. This is particularly the case in parliamentary systems, where small shifts in coalitions can easily result in policy reversals. As the reform process moves forward, the social equilibrium must be recalibrated. If the benefits of reform are readily discernible, then the process can be accelerated. If, on the other hand, the initial costs are acute due to actual hardships or apprehensions stoked by misinformation, then greater attention to coalition maintenance will be required. In short, reform movements in democracies must be constantly cognizant of how the proposed reforms will affect the average voter.

Adding another layer of complexity to the dynamics of reform is that the opposing sides are often sharply divided along class, ethnic, or religious lines. For example, in Kenya, President Daniel arap Moi's minority Kalenjin tribe heavily dominated the long-ruling Kenyan African National Union (KANU) party. KANU's control of government ministries provided ample opportunities to hire patrons and award public contracts. This maintained a strong financial base of support for KANU, despite the deleterious effects on the country's economy. Electoral regulations allowed Moi to handpick members of the electoral commission and draw up constitutional districts to maximize KANU representation.[23] Moreover, prohibitions against coalition governments and cabinet appointments from outside a president's party undermined the opposition efforts. The state-controlled media's favorable coverage of the government further complicated opposition parties' efforts to challenge KANU. Exploiting its disarray, Moi was able to engineer electoral victories in 1992 and 1997 with only 35 percent of the popular vote.[24]

Given the difficulty of building political coalitions to pursue reform by democratic means, some people ask whether a benign dictator might move the process along more efficiently. That is a bit like putting the fox in charge of the henhouse. The presumably well-intentioned autocrat has usually created the very political and economic monopolies that the reforms are meant to break up. And he continues to be beholden to the narrow constituencies that those monopolies benefit. The "economics of autocracy" works well for the ruling elite, but is inefficient for the society as a whole.[25] As there are no institutional incentives short of political instability to widen this base, any reforms undertaken by a benign dictator are indeed reliant on his or her good will.

Although time-consuming and energy-intensive, the democratic process of reform does create ongoing incentives for improvement that are independent of a single individual. Furthermore, this process has the advantage of educating and building deeper public support for change. Once adopted, this facilitates social acceptance and adherence to a reform, reducing the costs for enforcing compliance—a facet to which governments ruling by fiat must commit considerable coercive energy.

The political and social dimensions of maintaining reform coalitions in democracies have direct implications for international development assistance organizations. In particular, they call for flexibility. The types and timing of reforms that can be most successfully pursued are going to vary depending on the makeup of a developing society, the level of political support for its leaders, the coherence of opposition, and its political and economic history. Nuance and flexibility, not some boilerplate formula, are required for the success of a development-reform strategy.

Ecuador
Although Ecuador has been considered a democracy since 1978, its democratic institutions are still weak. There are ill-defined divisions between the legislative and executive branches, which combined with the highly

inequitable nature of Ecuadorian society[26] exacerbate the unavoidable power struggles between these two bodies. For example, until 1998 Congress had the authority to fire cabinet ministers. Moreover, it is the legislature that appoints members of the Supreme Court. In 1997, Congress deposed the president, Abdala "El Loco" Bucaram, winner of the 1996 elections, on charges of "mental incapacity."[27]

Into this context, Jamil Mahuad, representing the center-right Popular Democracy-Christian Democratic Union party, or DP-CDU (using its Spanish acronym), took office in August 1998. Elected as a pro-business candidate, the successful two-term mayor of Quito and holder of a master's degree in public administration from Harvard had promising reformist credentials. Reflecting the fragmentation of Ecuadorian politics, however, Mahuad's DP-CDU controlled only 33 of the 121 congressional seats. It therefore relied on the support of the market-oriented Social Christian party, or PSC, to pursue its agenda.

Inheriting a stagnant economy (growth had been flat over the five previous years), a fiscal deficit of 7 percent of GDP and annual inflation of 40 percent, Mahuad was anxious to launch a recovery program. However, debt service payments consuming 40 percent of the federal budget[28]—or twice the amount spent on social programs[29]—limited his options. Recognizing he needed the support of both his business constituency and the mostly poor indigenous Amerindians who made up more than three-fourths of the population to successfully pursue reforms, Mahuad advocated a course of fiscal discipline while expanding emphasis on education, health, and employment programs to combat poverty.[30] This included a 'solidarity voucher' that provided $15 per month to mothers of poor children.[31] However, Mahuad's attempts to secure $530 million in multilateral loans were rebuffed by the IMF, which insisted on a more rigorous program. IMF Managing Director Michael Camdessus remarked in November 1998, "We agree with the medium-term objectives such as reducing the fiscal deficit, single-digit inflation, and growth to satisfy social objectives, but the problem is defining precisely how to get there."[32]

Mahuad proceeded with a series of fiscal austerity policies anyway, despite a weak economy hurt by low oil prices (the country's main export earner) and $2.6 billion[33] in El Nino-generated flood damages that devastated coffee and banana exports. With the aim of increasing the export competitiveness of the economy, Mahuad let the overvalued national currency, the sucre, float freely, causing a 36 percent drop in its value.[34] Additional austerity policies included ending fuel subsidies (that precipitated price hikes of 400 percent, particularly affecting the poor through higher prices for food and public transportation), freezing wages for public employees, accelerating the privatization of state-owned energy and telecommunications assets, overhauling trade tariffs, imposing a new car tax, stepping up efforts to jail tax evaders, and seeking to eliminate sales tax exemptions on all products except food and medicine.[35] In the attempt to rein in inflation, the newly independent central bank pursued a stringent monetary policy, holding interest rates at 100 percent.[36] Mahuad's austerity actions were met with national strikes led by Ecuador's powerful leftist unions, students, and Amerindian groups. Several people were killed in the protests.

A rash of bank failures made the crisis worse. Within three months of Mahuad taking office, four major banks, including the nation's largest, had failed. Mahuad ordered an emergency bank holiday to prevent mass withdrawals amid fears the financial system was nearing collapse. Eventually, the government would bail out 18 financial institutions. This amounted to a transfer of $6 billion, or 23 percent of GNP, from the government to the banking sector during Mahuad's first 16 months in office. This transfer of resources, popularly seen as another instance of the poor propping up the rich, did much to erode popular support for him.[37] His reputation as an honest technocrat was further damaged when in late 1999 he was accused by a major campaign contributor, a former bank president jailed for his role in the bank failures, of misusing $1 million in campaign funds. Mahuad's party denied the charges. But his approval ratings, which had climbed as high as 60 percent, declined to single digits.[38] More ominously, according to a 1999 poll, only 6 percent of the population had confidence in political parties and only 11 percent trusted Congress.[39]

Mahuad badly needed an agreement with the IMF. By mid-1999, he was seeking a $250 million standby loan.[40] This would allow him to renegotiate Ecuador's debt arrears with the Paris Club of bilateral creditors and open the door to new lending from other multilaterals to revive the banking sector. Nevertheless, despite the draconian measures adopted by Mahuad, the IMF remained coy, indicating willingness to support an agreement with Ecuador "once agreed policy measures have been implemented and provided Ecuador is making good faith efforts to reach a collaborative agreement with its creditors."[41]

In the absence of an agreement with the IMF, in October 1999 Ecuador defaulted on its Brady Bonds payments on rescheduled public debt of $5.9 billion, which accounted for nearly half the country's $13 billion foreign debt.[42] Nonetheless, the IMF refrained from stepping in to help the government resolve the crisis. The Fund was taking a hard line with Ecuador as a way to show, through a small country that would not destabilize world financial markets, that it could get tough on creditors. By holding back on bailouts for private creditors who made risky investments, it hoped to compel a restructuring deal between Ecuador and its bondholders.[43]

Facing an increasingly destabilized economy and escalating political unrest, Mahuad took the extraordinary step on January 9, 2000, of adopting the dollar as Ecuador's currency to staunch capital flight, which was estimated at $2 billion[44] since the crisis began—from a country with a GDP of under $18 billion. The announcement boosted Mahuad's approval ratings to 26 percent from less than 10 percent.[45] Nonetheless, within two weeks of the switch, with protests by students, unions, indigenous groups, leftist parties, and low-level military forces spreading throughout Ecuador, Mahuad was deposed in a coup by a three-man military-civilian junta. After intense international pressure, the junta agreed to relinquish power within 24 hours to Mahuad's vice president, Gustavo Noboa Bejarano. A business magnate described as the richest man in Ecuador, Bejarano, by virtue of having lost the runoff election to Mahuad in 1998, was now president.

Six weeks after the coup, the IMF, the World Bank, the Inter-American Bank, and the Corporación Andina de Fomento, a multilateral public-private development bank, announced a $2 billion relief package "to support the Government of Ecuador's ambitious program of economic and structural reform."[46] The chief goals were to smooth the way to adopting the dollar, to resolve the nation's banking crisis, to strengthen public finances, and to mitigate the effects of these policies on the poor.

In November 2002, Lucio Gutierrez, a member of the coup junta, was elected president, taking office in January 2003. A populist candidate, Gutierrez had railed against the constraints set by previous agreements with the international financial institutions (IFIs) like the World Bank and International Monetary Fund and had pledged not to undertake policies that would harm ordinary Ecuadorians. This pledge would prove difficult to fulfill, given that Gutierrez's party controlled only 17 of the 100 seats in Congress and he had to contend with the class tensions that have long beleaguered Ecuador.

Ecuador's experience of the late 1990s demonstrates the perils for the United States and the international organizations it supports in carrying out development assistance in poor countries. By sticking to a dogmatic course, the IMF had unwittingly contributed to the unconstitutional removal from office of a genuine pro-business democratic reformer and to his replacement by a populist military officer with antidemocratic leanings and an ambiguous position on economic reform. The parallel irony of its strategy was that it ended up having to provide a much larger bailout package than was ever on the table during discussions with the Mahuad government. In the end, Ecuador's people, its government, its international lenders, and the IMF all came out worse off than they would have if a deal had been struck in 1999.

Civil Society

Development policies that seek the laudable goal of economic reform in poor countries but fail to take account of their impact on civil society hold the potential of undermining democratization. Civil society—neighborhood associations, social service organizations, civic groups, and independent media—is the lifeblood of a dynamic democracy. As a country makes the transition to democracy, these groups multiply and flourish, and any policy aimed at improving the economy should nurture them. They are the vehicles through which ordinary people can participate in public life and take action on issues of greatest concern to them. As such, they grease the wheels of democracy by stimulating independent thought, tolerating and even encouraging minority viewpoints, and acting as an indirect check on government power by forcing public officials to be more responsive to the needs of their constituents and more open about their decision-making. Development policies that weaken civil society, then, undercut a potentially moderating influence on policymakers and a key force in economic reform.

One example of how this can happen was a campaign in the 1990s by the IFIs, in concert with the U.S. Treasury, to get developing countries to improve tax collection as a way of easing their chronic budget deficits and providing a more stable revenue stream for their public expenditures. A laudable goal, to be sure, but the way some governments carried out the reform was counterproductive. Lacking strict guidelines from the IFIs, these governments began taxing nonprofit organizations for the supplies, property, and staff they needed for their development projects.[47] In some cases, these taxes amounted to 40 percent of income and 100 percent of imported goods.

The predictable consequence was that resources intended to be used for social services were redirected toward governments' general budgets. Fewer services were provided to communities. Although civic groups have varying degrees of capacity and scale, it is widely acknowledged that their efforts direct a greater share of resources at the grassroots level than official development agencies.[48] Consequently, the tax policy had the perverse consequence of reducing the effectiveness of those organizations most directly targeting poverty. (Notably, those development entities representing states —the IFIs, bilateral donors, and UN agencies—are tax exempt, even though they represent 93 percent of official development assistance.)

From the civic groups' perspective, such levies have compounding complications. Given that most nonprofit organizations are evaluated by the percentage of their resources devoted to overhead, the requirement to pay more in taxes places them at a distinct disadvantage. More broadly, the push to tax civic groups, often called "nongovernment organizations" or

NGOs, reverses a long-established norm of according nonprofit development agencies tax-free status. This norm evolved as a way to create an enabling environment for NGOs in the recognition that the development activities they undertake are for the public benefit and taxing them would be counterproductive.[49]

From a democratization perspective, the reduction in the number of NGOs and the activities they are able to undertake is a blow to civil society. It lowers the number and quality of independent players, reduces empowerment opportunities, and limits sources of information in a society. Donor-driven tax initiatives that fail to explicitly exempt them give governments with little enthusiasm for democratization the excuse they need to stifle what are often some of the only independent voices in society. Even when intended to apply only to for-profit firms, such measures provide a readymade lever by which these governments can clamp down on non-profit organizations. Taxes can be applied selectively to scrutinize and penalize those groups a government feels are too independent.[50] Those that protest can be closed for violating the law. In turn, as James Scott has observed, " . . . an incapacitated civil society provides the level social terrain on which (authoritarian states) can build."[51] In short, even a seemingly uncontroversial economic reform can have unintended negative repercussions on civil society. This, in turn, washes away some of the fertile topsoil in which a stable, accountable democracy can take root.

Development Policies Can Diminish Democratic Representation

Differences over competing development priorities are a common source of tension between donors and developing countries. Since the mid-1980s, major donors have emphasized the preeminence of macroeconomic fundamentals. Coined the "Washington Consensus," this strategy aims to promote fiscal responsibility by managing deficits, limiting inflation through strict monetary policy, and maintaining exchange-rate stability. The desirability of macroeconomic stability is widely accepted. However, the means and timing for achieving it are hotly disputed. Donors can legitimately preach the benefits of cutting public-sector expenses and employment, selling state-owned enterprises, removing price subsidies, and maintaining high interest rates; all of these measures unquestionably increase economic efficiency even while creating short-term economic pain. But that prescription puts leaders of democratic societies in a spot. They know the measures are necessary for the good of the nation, but they also know they can be political suicide if pushed on a reluctant public. They also understand the value of pursuing other worthy economic goals like maximizing job creation, fostering the geographic distribution of development, and ensuring the fair distribution of the costs and benefits of reform. Having been elected to represent their compatriots' interests, it is the responsibility of democratic leaders to strike the balance required to maintain support for reforms. Reflecting on these tensions, Joseph Stiglitz has argued that pursuing the IMF's priorities to the exclusion of those of a democratic leadership compromises a country's sovereignty.[52]

As we saw earlier, economic policymaking has important social and political components. Pursuing austerity measures without taking these into consideration can diminish or destroy the public's backing for reform. Although Bulgaria's Dimitrov and Ecuador's Mahuad were popular with western governments, they lost the support of their key constituencies. The implication for the post-Washington consensus era is that donors should work more collaboratively with democratic governments to identify the best combination of initiatives to spur macroeconomic stability in their societies without alienating the general population on whose sustained support these reforms depend.

Timing presents other difficulties. There may be instances, some economists argue, in which shock therapy is necessary—for which gradual reform would almost certainly lead to no reform. But shock therapy as a strategy requires the quick introduction of many reforms, making execution difficult and the human strain of adjustment more acute. Moreover, societies require at least a modicum of functional laws and institutions on which reforms can be anchored. When reforms can be introduced in sequence, people and institutions can adjust. The ensuing progress builds confidence and momentum.

Sequencing does not imply inertia. Former Polish Finance Minister Leszek Balcerowicz labeled the initial stage of transition "a period of extraordinary politics" where entrenched interests can be dislodged, popular support for change won, and a high degree of legitimacy in the new political leadership established.[53] The early stages of democratization frequently represent windows in which substantive changes are possible. International development actors need to be sensitive to this finite period. However, rather than using this window of maximum enthusiasm only to induce the most painful aspects of transition, development agencies can play a critical role by providing timely and balanced assistance. Done in a way that generates some tangible benefits (that is, a "democracy dividend") to what are frequently long-suffering populations, gains made during this early period can build momentum for further political and economic reforms. Conversely, failure to advance popular interests at an early stage of the democratization process blurs differences with the previous, undemocratic governance structure and can contribute toward "democratic disillusionment," opening the door to a return of authoritarianism.[54]

Another common timing-related oversight made by donor nations is to scale back development assistance to democratizing countries once they have conducted their first multiparty elections. Minxin Pei and Merritt Lyon of the Carnegie Endowment for International Peace find that the level of official development assistance made available to countries in the three years after they have made a democratic transition is less than that provided in the years preceding it.[55] Phasing out development assistance following the first election overlooks the substantial level of institutional reform that is required in order to consolidate a democratic political structure. The government faces the daunting tasks of making revisions to the constitution, breaking up patronage networks in the civil service, reducing political influences in the judicial system, instituting a productivity-enhancing regulatory environment and creating a system for orderly political succession. It needs all the international support it can get in carrying out these political reforms, almost always in the face of strident opposition from the forces of the old dictatorial order. Our review of the rate of democratic backtracking in Chapter 3 underscores the difficulties democratizing countries face in consolidating their gains. Not until a democracy achieves a per capita income of about $4,000 does it appear to cross the consolidation threshold. This reality compels donors to remain engaged in democratizing countries as they mature. The cost of failing to pursue a sufficiently extended phaseout strategy is the substantially greater assistance that will be required to resuscitate a country once it has contracted economically or politically.

The point we are making is that the opportunity to build democratic momentum is often missed. Policymakers from donor countries frequently fail to reset the parameters of their relationships with a developing country when a democratic breakthrough occurs. Instead, the same policies, procedures, obligations, and timetables are applied to the democratic government as those that were negotiated with the previous, discredited authoritarian leadership. Take, for example, debt. New democracies typically inherit debt levels amounting to 59 percent of GDP, ten percentage points more than the developing country norm.[56] The debt, incurred by an unaccountable leadership, (at times to the IFIs), typically has been squandered without advancing development. Yet, its servicing substantially limits the flexibility and reduces the potential for rapid developmental gains and reforms among new democracies.

Nigeria

Consider Nigeria's democratization effort in the late 1990s. After a 15-year string of military governments Nigeria returned to democratic rule in May 1999. Having won the February elections, Olusegun Obasanjo, a prisoner under General Sani Abacha's autocratic reign, took office with the long-unrealized aspirations of a nation on his shoulders. A former general, Obasanjo came to the presidency with strong democratic credentials. After acceding to the presidency in 1976 following the assassination of General Murtala Mohamed, he gave up power to an elected government in 1979—the only Nigerian ruler ever to have done so.

In his first two months in office, Obasanjo retired 200 top military officers, fired the heads of two key state companies, and established panels to look into past corruption and human rights abuses.[57] He unveiled an economic stimulus plan aimed at providing a "democracy dividend" to the long-suffering nation,[58] Africa's most populous with 130 million citizens, most of them living on $1 a day.[59] The dividend was conceived as a combination of more jobs, improved access to social services, and increased monetary discipline. Obasanjo also sought to reduce corruption, pump money into the rural areas where most Nigerians lived, and sell off unproductive state-run firms.

Central to accomplishing these aims was renegotiating $30 billion in debt inherited from the previous military governments. Two-thirds of this debt was owed to official lenders, requiring $3 billion a year to service—or half of Nigeria's annual income.[60] Obasanjo reflected on the paradox, "[High expectations] can only be sustained if Nigerians have a democracy dividend in terms of an improvement in the quality of their lives. That will not happen if we have to service debt [at current levels]. We need to show Nigerians that democracy not only has intrinsic value but value in the real sense of the word . . . We are not only talking about the morality of the re-payment of debt, some of which has a sordid genesis. We are saying that it [debt relief] is not only in our own interests. It's in the interests of Africa and of the world that democracy should be sustained in Nigeria."[61]

In addition to calling for donor forgiveness of Nigeria's debt burden, Obasanjo set out to negotiate a $1 billion standby agreement with the IMF by the end of 1999 in order to pursue his stimulus plan. Despite public pro-nouncements of support for Nigeria's democratic transition, the IMF's Michel Camdessus insisted Nigeria rigorously stand by its agreements with creditors.[62] Furthermore, negotiating an economic reform program with the IMF, generally a prerequisite for any debt rescheduling, was slow in coming. The IMF wanted the new government to first demonstrate its ca-pacity to pursue macroeconomic stability lest it draw down on its reserves, fuel inflation, and put increased pressure on the naira. In fact, according to the IMF's own assessment, the government did take decisive action to re-store macroeconomic stability and tackle corruption.[63] The new leaders balanced the federal budget in 1999 after inheriting a projected 8 percent of GDP deficit in May. With the benefit of higher oil prices, a 13 percent sur-plus was achieved in 2000.[64] The annual inflation rate declined to 7 percent from the 12 percent clip inherited when Obasanjo took over. Nonetheless, it took until August 2000 before the IMF would approve the standby loan. As of mid-2004, Nigeria had yet to qualify for the World Bank's Heavily Indebted Poor Countries program for negotiating debt forgiveness.

Subsequent negotiations with the IMF on a medium-term agreement continued throughout Obasanjo's first term without a breakthrough. The IMF wanted the new government to take further action on structural re-forms, specifically the privatization of Nigeria's power and petroleum sectors. Although the government had taken steps to liberalize the telecommunications sector, it preferred to pursue privatization more slowly given the unemployment and disruptive economic impacts these actions would have on the economy. This included plans for the petroleum sector, which had been a centerpiece of the Obasanjo strategy to attract capital and expertise into the refineries.[65] There were also concerns that rushing the process would simply result in transforming state monopolies into private monopolies.[66] Although external economists emphasized the need for radical economic reform, the Nigerian government reasoned that the social tensions inherited from the military authorities merited a more cautious approach.[67]

Without IMF backing, the government proceeded with a scaled-down antipoverty campaign that disappointed many Nigerians and cost Obasanjo some support among labor unions and civic organizations and triggered several large strikes. According to labor leaders, the austerity measures resulted in "mass unemployment, reduced government expenditure, collapse of the middle class, and worsening poverty."[68] Disenchantment was particularly deep among the poor, who tended to blame the government for their woes without giving much reflection to all the historical and political factors involved in its decision-making.[69] Some analysts have attributed the increase in the ethnic and religious clashes Nigeria experienced under Obasanjo to the mounting economic stresses.[70] The Nigerian government subsequently slowed the pace of privatization.[71] "The president has had to ask himself each time: 'If I do things the way I should, will I carry the country with me?'" said Magnus Kpakol, economic adviser to President Obasanjo.[72] Social unrest also increased pressures to boost public spending and with it, the risks of setting off inflation.

In February 2002, Nigeria suspended further negotiations with the IMF. Asked whether Nigeria was better off without an agreement, Obasanjo replied, "It is not a question of better off. For three years, I can't really say we have got much out of the IMF. But I won't say because of that I don't want the IMF. One thing I enjoy is that they give an opinion that is reasonably uninvolved. But you know one of the problems we always have with the IMF is that the IMF wants 10 out of 10 . . . Nine and a half is not good enough for the IMF. They want targets. They wanted me to say 'This will be the level of expenditure in 2002. This will be the level of inflation. This will be the exchange rate.' I couldn't do that so I thought it's better—and we agreed to this —that once the budget's approved (by the National Assembly) we will call them back."[73] In December 2002, following congressional approval of the new economic plan, talks with the IMF were resumed.

As cynicism grew among Nigerians, perilous alternatives became more attractive.[74] President Obasanjo appeared as wary as anyone about the future. "Because the weaknesses of our political structures pervade the entire social system, violence, not just in the electoral process, but also in virtually all spheres of life, is threatening to assume an endemic presence," he said. "We have very little time to sort out many pending problems and disputes that will determine the survival of democracy or even the security and survival of the nation."[75]

Nigeria is a case study of the challenges that leaders of fledgling democracies and the international community face in plotting an economic development strategy that will start the country on the road to economic reform without alienating the population. Too often, the sound macroeconomic prescriptions of the IMF and the major industrialized countries that finance it clash with the government's need to win over a distrustful electorate already boiling with anger at years of dictatorial misrule. This is a dilemma even when the economy is growing; indeed, in Nigeria, real GDP growth averaged 3.7 percent per year from 2000 to 2003, better than at any time during the previous decade. By failing to shift its policy to take account for the dramatic turn of political events in that country, the IMF missed a golden opportunity to build on the period of "extraordinary politics" that is typical of democratic transitions. Had it paid closer attention to the political and economic implications of its policy formula, it might have adjusted it in ways that spur long-term reforms while simultaneously fostering short-term economic growth. Although not without its shortcomings, the new democratic government was clearly more reform-minded and willing to cooperate with the international financial community than the military governments preceding it. However, by treating both regimes similarly, the IMF may have actually slowed the pace of reform. Obasanjo won reelection in April 2003 with 62 percent of the vote, the first successive civilian administration in Nigeria's history. Even so, democratic institutions remain weak. By forcing the Nigerian government to go its own way, the IMF's inflexibility increases the risk that a fragile democratic experiment will fizzle, dimming the prospects of economic reform.

Development Policies Do Not Provide Incentives for Democracies

Since the 1990s, many donor nations have increasingly funded initiatives to promote democracy as well as development in low-income countries. Even the multilateral development agencies have expanded funding for "good governance" initiatives. Nevertheless, a review of official development assistance disbursements reveals that donors do not pursue the twin goals of democracy and development in a complementary manner. Despite the higher profile given to political governance, development policymaking does not create incentives for reform.

Over the past 40 years, autocracies have been as likely as democracies to receive economic development aid (see Table 5.1).[76] Among countries with per capita incomes under $1,000, both autocracies and democracies have typically received official development assistance around 6.5 percent of GDP. Donors are supporting autocracies such as Syria, Guinea, Cameroon, and Egypt to the same extent they do democracies in Bolivia, Senegal, and Papua New Guinea. This neutral relationship holds under more rigorous analysis.[77]

If we consider developing countries that are relatively better off, autocracies have realized a perceptible advantage in the official development assistance (ODA) levels received. Those with per capita incomes of $1,000 to $2,000 received an average of 1.8 percent of GDP in the years 1960 to 2001, compared with 1.3 percent for democracies. This means countries with authoritarian governments like Morocco, Tunisia, Fujimori's Peru, Swaziland, and Equatorial Guinea have been favored for development investment by donors over democracies such as Jamaica, Latvia, Lithuania, Dominican Republic, and the Philippines.

Although the funding advantage to lower-middle income autocracies is slight, it has disturbing implications. Aid for low-income autocracies can be justified on the humanitarian grounds of alleviating poverty, wherever it may be. However, robust levels of assistance for higher-income autocracies suggests other motivations are at play. Since the figures we are using are median levels, they reflect a broader pattern of support than can be ex-

Table 5.1 Levels of ODA (Percent of GDP) for Democracies and Autocracies 1960 to 2001

GDP/Per Median Capita	Democracies	Autocracies
$2,000–$4,000	0.85%	0.65%
$1,000–$2,000	1.3%	1.8%
$500–$1,000	6.7%	6.6%
$0–$500	8.1%	8.0%

Based on *WDI 2003* and *Polity* data.

plained by strategic assistance to a single country or group of countries such as the U.S.'s annual aid package to Egypt.

The overly generous pattern of aid to autocracies across time goes beyond Cold War considerations. Similar, and in some ways even more distinctive, patterns are seen for the post-Cold War period of the 1990s (see Table 5.2). Aid levels to autocracies exceeded that to democracies at every income level considered. This is particularly evident in the middle income ($2,000 to $4,000) and below $1,000 per capita GDP categories, in which autocracies received assistance amounting to a percentage point of GDP more than democracies (10.8 percent versus 9.9 percent). The consistency with which aid has been dispensed to autocracies demonstrates that the pattern cannot be simply explained as an aberration. Nor is it the result of a shortage of low-income democracies. The emergence of numerous developing country democracies in the 1980s and 1990s did not result in a significant tilting of assistance toward democracies. Ironically, this stands in stark contrast to the trends in foreign direct investment (FDI) discussed in Chapter 2. Since the mid-1980s, median levels of FDI, as a share of GDP, has swung sharply toward democracies in the developing world.

The record of undifferentiated development assistance holds for Africa, Latin America, central Europe, the former Soviet Union, and South Asia. Democracies in these regions have not received perceptibly greater levels of development assistance than have neighboring autocracies. For example, sub-Saharan Africa is arguably the world's poorest region and of the least strategic importance. Yet, from 1960 to 2001, among countries in this region with per capita GDP below $2,000, autocracies typically exceeded democracies in aid levels allocated (8.2 percent versus 6.5 percent).[78] The levels are comparable (12.1 vs. 11.8 percent) when only the 1990s are considered. Only East Asia fails to fit into this pattern. Among countries with per capita incomes below $4,000, democracies (Fiji, Papua New Guinea, the Philippines), on average, received more official development assistance than autocracies (3.1 percent versus 1.3 percent of GDP). Notably, however, this disparity diminishes in the 1990s. In the 1990s, the autocracies of Vietnam, Laos, and

Table 5.2 Levels of ODA (Percent of GDP) for Democracies and Autocracies 1990 to 2001

GDP/Per Median Capita	Democracies	Autocracies
$2,000–$4,000	0.6%	1.1%
$1,000–$2,000	1.3%	1.5%
$500–$1,000	9.9%	10.8%
$0–$500	12.2%	13.0%

Based on *WDI 2003* and *Polity* data.

Cambodia benefited from donor assistance at levels equivalent to democracies such as Mongolia, the Philippines, and Thailand—roughly 3 percent.

Despite the increased attention given to the importance of good governance to development and the recent global democratization trend, development assistance continues to flow unimpeded to autocracies. Although donors may state a preference for democracy in their development strategies, this has not been translated into their resource allocations.

Systemic Disincentives

The absence of any development funding advantage for low-income democracies can be attributed to both systematic and administrative disincentives in donor countries to weighing democratic criteria in the allocation of assistance. This reflects the multiple and at times competing priorities in their relations toward the developing world. The end result is an international assistance system that sends mixed signals regarding support for democratization.

Strategic Considerations As discussed in Chapter 4, strategic considerations have often been at the forefront of development decision-making. Foreign assistance has typically been seen and used as an extension of a donor nation's foreign policy. The United States, as a superpower and a major donor, has been in the lead in supporting developing countries on a strategic basis (that is, to gain increased influence or reward global partners).

A review of other major donors and the countries they support suggests that the United States is not alone in emphasizing the strategic dimension of development funding. Eight of the top 10 recipients of French assistance are former French colonies—and a constant of France's foreign policy has been to maintain French influence, language, and culture on the global stage. Sixty-five percent of official French development assistance is directed to Africa.[79] Of those African countries on France's list of top 10 recipients, the median income level is 35 percent higher than the regional norm. Similarly, the Department for International Development, the United Kingdom's development agency, focuses its funding on Commonwealth countries (that is, those with colonial or other historical ties to the UK). All of the top 10 of the agency's program recipients (excluding humanitarian assistance) in 2001-2002 were Commonwealth members.[80] (Notably, these 10 generally had lower per capita incomes than the norm for their regions and higher democracy scores). A similar pattern applies to Japanese assistance. Eight of the top 10 recipients of official Japanese aid in 2000 were in Asia.[81] One non-Asian country that made the top 10 list in the 1990s was Peru—whose president at the time, Alberto Fujimori, was born to Japanese parents. Perhaps unsurprisingly, Japanese aid to Peru continued at the same level even as Fujimori transformed the country from a recognized democracy to a dictatorial system. Japanese aid has also long been used strategically to support Japanese exporters by such means as tying it to purchases of Japanese goods or to the elimination of trade barriers that block access to Japanese exports.[82] Even with the end of the Cold War, donors are inclined to support those countries with which they share common political or cultural interests, whether or not they have made the transition to democracy.

Failure to Make a Democratic Distinction   Aside from the strategic influences, possibly the most direct explanation for the lack of democratic differentiation in development funding is the fact that donors simply do not categorize recipients by their democratic credentials. They divide countries by region, income level, colonial history, or language. But they often ignore democratic posture. Therefore, while most of the major bilateral donors cite the desirability of democracy in their development strategies and fund democracy promotion activities, none has made democracy an explicit criterion in the allocation of development assistance.[83]

Why is this? It would seem that donors fail to grasp and value the link between democratic governance and sustained, broad-based development. By not demonstrating preference to democratic governments, in turn, their policies have the effect of dampening incentives for political reform. Developing country leaders who are accustomed to interpreting donors' priorities based on their actions rather than on their rhetoric, logically infer that donors are indifferent about democratization.

Multilateral financial institutions are also major forces in establishing official development assistance norms. In terms of dollar volume they provide one-third of all such aid. Moreover, because IMF agreements are typically required before donor countries commit funding, the allocation of development aid is significantly influenced by the policies and funding decisions of the IFIs. Contrary to most bilateral donors, the IFIs do have an explicit policy regarding democracy—they are prohibited from considering it! This regulation was instituted to emphasize technical factors in financing decisions. However, it has resulted in the systematic exclusion of political governance considerations from decision-making, despite the growing recognition of its centrality to effective development.

Stipulation That Ifis Resources Pass Through Central Governments The manner in which the World Bank and other international aid organizations allocate their development assistance can also retard democracy. Specifically, their bylaws stipulate that their financing must be go directly to the recipient nations' central governments and not to other organizations that fight poverty. This requirement reflects the reality that the IFIs are comprised by states as well as their original macroeconomic stability rationale. It is also based on the premise that aid provided to national governments strengthens their capacity to provide public services. A large share of bilateral funding also goes directly to national governments (a convenient way to solidify bilateral relationships). Perhaps it is unsurprising, therefore, that only 3 percent of total bilateral assistance in 2000 was provided to nongovernment organizations.[84]

One can easily see how a vicious circle develops under this arrangement. Donors intent on reducing poverty provide resources to countries facing deprivation. Because of the institutional strictures, these resources flow almost exclusively into the coffers of the central government. Yet if these countries are poor *because* their governments misuse resources, then development assistance will do little good. Rather, the greater likelihood is that these resources will contribute to reinforcing the dysfunctional, predatory, or autocratic tendencies of these governments. In the end, the country remains poor while the donors' compulsion to provide assistance is perpetuated.

Such a cycle is fueled by the false premise that development assistance, even if poorly managed, will actually do what it is supposed to do. The attitude of the donors seems to be that by providing more aid, there is a better chance that at least some will reach the poor. In fact, the manner in which it is administered may have more impact on poverty than the actual dollars committed. Well-designed programs ensure broader participation and strengthen incentives for improvements, which in turn lay the groundwork for future advances. Conversely, increasing or continuing development assistance to a dictatorial government while turning a blind eye to its rampant cronyism and inefficiencies can only prolong these dysfunctions. The rigid institutional requirement to provide virtually all development assistance through central governments gives unresponsive national authorities very little reason to change. For autocracies, such an arrangement serves their aims (to strengthen their hold on power) quite nicely. Aid resources allow them to feed their patronage networks, perpetuating the economics of autocracy.

Aid effectiveness could be enhanced if the professionals in donor countries and international development agencies had the flexibility to funnel the aid wherever it could do the most good, whether the recipients were civic organizations, state or local governments, or even private companies. Not only might those entities do a better job of advancing development efforts but the central government, facing the sudden prospect of losing access to these resources, might also become more responsive to their populations.

Floods, famines, and other humanitarian disasters are events in which the weaknesses of dictatorships are sharply exposed. In a classic review of the economic and political dimensions of such catastrophes, Fred Cuny noted that historically these crises were occasions for societies to rid themselves of poor leaders. Cuny reasoned that such national disasters expose the emptiness of an autocrat's claim to authority while simultaneously crystallizing a society's recognition that major changes are required to deal with the catastrophic circumstances. Whatever nominal support an autocrat might have had quickly erodes. He cites as an example the 1974–1975 famine in the Sahel region of Africa and the inadequate responses of national governments to it. Every government affected by the famine subsequently fell.[85] Today, the donor community's desire to prevent humanitarian catastrophe may (without reducing a population's privations) unintentionally prop up illegitimate governments that would otherwise have been swept away.

When autocratic governments oversee catastrophe, it is plain to see. However, when development assistance helps bolsters a dictatorship in good economic times, the damage it is doing to the nation may not be readily apparent to the outside world. But when the economy inevitably crashes, it is apt to do so spectacularly, with devastating results for both the population at large as well as for investors.

Indonesia

Indonesia's experience under Soeharto illustrates the phenomenon. On May 21, 1998, after six months of street protests and economic turmoil, President Soeharto resigned. The economy was in free fall, with per capita output in 1998 slumping by 14 percent; the rupiah sliding by 80 percent against the dollar, one of the worst currency depreciations since World War II; capital flight accelerating to somewhere between $30 billion and $50 billion, a vastly greater sum than total net private capital inflows of $12 billion for the entire decade of 1985 to 1995; and national debt surging to 72 percent of GDP, creating an onerous burden on Indonesians that will last for years.[86] The human costs of the collapse are even more sobering, though difficult to quantify. Between 15 million and 25 million Indonesians were thrust into poverty.[87] Runaway inflation of 58 percent was eroding their purchasing power and wiping out their savings. Soeharto himself, although leaving office in disgrace, was in somewhat better economic shape: in 35 years of rule, he and his family are believed to have amassed a personal fortune of up to $40 billion, much of it stored safely abroad.[88]

The underlying causes of Indonesia's financial implosion are generally accepted. Cronyism drove the bidding process for government contracts, access to capital, and the ability to establish new businesses. The lack of autonomous regulatory institutions with real teeth enabled firms to grossly misreport their financial status and banks to extend untenable loans. Accounting standards were highly discretionary and audits largely perfunctory. Corporate boards were frequently ceremonial positions used to reward friends and loyalists.

The virtual absence of accountability structures in Indonesia is typical of autocratic regimes. There were few checks on the executive branch and incentives were oriented to promote conformity with its interests. What is more noteworthy is the two-fisted endorsement of the Soeharto government given by the IFIs. Indonesia was one of their stars and the beneficiary of sizeable, long-term assistance. The World Bank averaged $1.1 billion in annual disbursements to Indonesia from 1989 to 1998. From 1969 to 1998, the World Bank disbursed $25 billion in grants and loans to Indonesia for 278 projects.[89] Indonesia was typically within the top four recipients of World Bank assistance during the 1980s and 1990s. The Asian Development Bank was the second leading donor to Indonesia, providing approximately $1 billion a year in loans in the years preceding the crisis and $17.9 billion since 1969.[90] By the nature of their long-term relationship with the Soeharto government, the IFIs abetted the autocrat's construction of the fragile, cronyistic structures that would lead to the economy's collapse.

The first World Bank project with the Soeharto government was in 1969. This coincided with the onset of Indonesia's period of rapid growth, which was to average 5.4 percent per year per capita for the next 30 years. However, charges of high-level corruption were leveled at the Soeharto government from almost its first day in office. A blue-ribbon "Commission of Four" that was established in response to these criticisms reported in 1970, "corruption was so rampant that people no longer knew what was corrupt and what was not."[91] Despite the commission's findings, none of the recommendations identified as needing "urgent action" were pursued by the government.[92] Similarly, in 1971 Hugeng Santoso, the reform-minded police chief, uncovered a car-smuggling racket in Jakarta, in which it appeared Soeharto's wife was involved. Hugeng was fired and the investigation dropped.[93]

Having taken power in a military coup, Soeharto brought his close ties with the military into the economic sphere. Military-owned companies and joint ventures between the military and private capital expanded rapidly in the 1970s.[94] These were closely aligned with the dominant ethnic Chinese business sector and with foreign firms. The nation's business interests gave the military access to capital and the military gave investors political protection. Military officers in strategic positions were able to funnel export credits and state contracts to their allies. Although justified as a means of raising revenue for the underfunded military, the military companies were mechanisms through which individual officers could increase their own political and economic power.[95] This, in turn, strengthened Soeharto's tightly controlled patronage network.

In the 1980s, Soeharto established a committee known as "Team Ten" to oversee government purchases of goods and services worth more than $800,000 (later reduced to $300,000).[96] This enabled him to centralize and expand the patronage network. Members of Team Ten and its beneficiaries were selected for their political and social connections as well as their geographical roots to shore up support for Soeharto where it was weak.[97]

As is common in bubble economies, the euphoria that results from rapid growth and easy profits drives out cold-eyed analysis and the will to create the regulatory safeguards that can increase transparency and help filter out illegitimate transactions. In dictatorships, however, the government plays a central role in the process. For example, while the deregulation and economic reform campaign undertaken in Indonesia in the late 1980s was touted as a means to maintain rapid growth and curb corruption, in reality it provided additional leeway for Soeharto to expand the business empires controlled by his children. It is estimated that by the mid-1990s, virtually every major infrastructure contract in Indonesia was awarded to a firm with ties to at least one Soeharto relative.[98] Many of the schemes were aimed at increasing access to capital, particularly the vast deposits collected by Indonesia's state-owned banks. Soeharto's cronies relied heavily on these funds to pay for their projects. In the 1990s, they also turned increasingly to a consortium of foreign and Indonesian state banks for financing. The foreign banks were prepared to overlook the questionable prospects of repayment as long as a state bank was also a lender to the project, thereby giving the project a de facto government guarantee.[99] Any financial regulator who attempted to apply prudential rules to connected institutions or transactions was removed.[100] Such lending practices were a major factor in the escalation of Indonesia's debt from 31 percent of GDP in 1985 to 72 percent in 1998.[101]

The IFIs played directly into these unaccountable structures. Over the years the World Bank devoted 35 percent of its lending in Indonesia to the electric power and transport sectors.[102] However, the state enterprises and regulatory agencies in these sectors were major sources of patronage funds. The power plants the state electricity board built and operated through the mid-1990s incurred roughly double the costs of comparable projects, an extra expense of between $600 million and $1 billion per plant.[103] In 1993, top government officials imposed an irregular tariff on every kilowatt of energy generated. Nengah Sudja, a former head of research for the state energy utility, explained, "Everybody knew it was nepotism, but we couldn't do anything about it."[104]

Despite these recognizable warning signs, the IFIs continued to be bullish on Indonesia. They were no doubt enthralled by its blazing economic performance and blinded by the "halo effect" of other states in the dynamic East Asian region. Believing Indonesia could do no wrong, they gave rave reviews of its economy and plowed considerable amounts of their own money into it. Investors' subsequent failure to take notice of Indonesia's weak financial institutions is, therefore, partially comprehensible. They were swept up in the feeding frenzy of seemingly assured profits promised by Indonesia's skyrocketing economy. As capital controls were relaxed, a policy urged by the IFIs as a way of increasing foreign competition and embraced by the government as a means of increasing access to capital, investors leaped in.

The glowing endorsement of Indonesia reflected a broader perspective of the IFIs management during this era, as captured in the World Bank's 1993 report, *The East Asian Miracle*. The well received, though later highly criticized, report praised the economic governance structures of the East Asian miracle economies, going so far as to suggest that the authoritarian nature of governments in this region gave them an advantage in pursuing efficient economic policymaking. The World Bank's confidence in Indonesia was exemplified by its lending strategy in the late 1980s and early 1990s. Uncharacteristically for that time, it attached no "policy conditionality" to the loans because "there was an understanding that the Indonesian government's prior actions were part of a medium-term program that would be implemented."[105]

Rather than reforming the patterns of corruption created by the Soeharto machine, the IFIs were swept up by them. Consider the World Bank's $307 million Financial Sector Development Project initiated in 1993. The Bank's largest undertaking in Indonesia up to that point, it was intended "to support recapitalization and improvements in the operations of the State Commercial Banks (about roughly half of the banking sector), as well as technical assistance to the Central Bank."[106] Ironically, in the previous year, a World Bank report had warned "that deregulation in the financial sector had moved faster than the development of the legal and accounting structures and the capacity to supervise."[107] Nonetheless, the Bank pushed forward. The project was later found by a World Bank evaluation in 1996 to be "unsatisfactory on all counts;" the report also noted that

"Indonesia's State Banking Sector was in disarray, riddled with insolvency."[108] However, the World Bank "downplayed the evidence presented in the 1996 supervision report and rejected the proposed cancellation of the remainder of the loan for several months (until a new Banking Reform Assistance project was approved in November 1997), arguing that such action would do serious damage to the World Bank–Government relationship. This process also triggered perceptions of unjustified penalties to the career prospects of some Bank staff who had brought these issues to light."[109] All told, leaked estimates from World Bank staff suggest that up to one-third of all Bank funding in Indonesia was misused. In other words, of the roughly $30 billion the World Bank provided to the Soeharto government, some $10 billion was diverted by corrupt officials.[110]

As international public institutions, the IFIs have a responsibility to generate global public goods. One of these goods is to provide an objective assessment of the state of an emerging market's financial infrastructure. This requires reporting on the extensiveness of accountability institutions that increase the quality of information available to financial decision-makers while mitigating financial disasters. It was here that the IFIs failed miserably in Indonesia. They were publicly promoting Indonesia right up to the point that the economy went over the cliff.

The IFIs have acknowledged their negligence in failing to confront the Soeharto regime about its corruption. An internal World Bank report released in February 1999 states, "The Bank knew of many problems but did not want to offend Soeharto's government or threaten the image the World Bank had promoted of Indonesia as one of its great success stories." The report concludes that "Indonesia's rapid growth created a 'halo effect' in its relations with Soeharto that made the World Bank's top managers unwilling to deliver tough messages to the aging leader."[111] Some of the tough messages that should have been delivered would have focused on "important structural problems—a weak financial sector, a fragile social situation, major issues of governance, and corruption—(that) persisted." Yet the World Bank still chose not to respond.[112] It was not until 1997 that "corruption entered the Bank's explicit public vocabulary" in relation to Indonesia.[113] When the financial crisis finally hit in December 1997, the World Bank, like many others, was taken by surprise. It might have been better prepared, it said, "had past successes not bred overconfidence."[114]

As the crisis unfolded, the IMF and World Bank shifted their best staff to deal with it, and quickly concluded that it was "not merely economic but also political."[115] What was needed was the recovery of confidence in the political system. Even then, though, the IFIs had not yet fully grasped the core of the problem and their role in perpetuating it. In an effort to stem capital flight during the early stages of the crisis, the IMF decided on a blanket guarantee scheme for Indonesia's banks. The initiative was administered by the state-run Indonesian Bank Restructuring Agency, which would also decide which banks to close. Over the first three months of 1998, an infusion of $16.6 billion was pumped into the 14 most troubled banks. Much of this money went straight from the Bank of Indonesia into bank accounts and out again—into the bank owners' offshore accounts or into their businesses.[116] Thus, at the height of a financial crisis that had its roots in corruption and cronyism, some of the IMF's best minds tried a cure that ended up being a new way of transferring money straight from Indonesian taxpayers to Soeharto cronies! Rather than calm the markets, this brainstorm only resulted in increased pressure on the rupiah.[117]

It was also during these early months of 1998, after negotiating three separate agreements with the IMF amounting to a $46 billion bailout package, that Soeharto reinstated 15 big-ticket projects that had been forced to close—all of which were controlled by his children.[118] Similarly, two banks owned by Soeharto relatives refused the Bank of Indonesia's order to close. One, owned by Soeharto's half brother, filed suit against the Central Bank governor and demanded the finance minister's removal. Instead of punishing his relatives, Soeharto fired four senior Bank of Indonesia directors.[119] The IMF made no public protest.

The relationship between international donors and the Soeharto regime in Indonesia is an instructive case of how development resources channeled through an autocratic government—even one that is apparently overseeing dynamic economic growth—contributes to the construction of dysfunctional political and economic structures. Developmental strategies compelled to direct their funding to central governments can only be effective if that government is committed to alleviating poverty and enhancing development. If instead, the government *is* the problem, then increasing the level of resources going to it will only reinforce the dysfunctionality. Since many donor agencies have yet to align themselves to this reality, much development assistance continues to be ineffective.

Administrative Disincentives
In addition to the institutional disincentives, there are factors internal to the administrative processes of international development agencies that work against considering the democratic legitimacy of potential recipient governments.

Lack of Donor Discipline The inability of donors to pull out of an unproductive relationship with recipient governments when and if they recognize corruption fuels the vicious circle of government unaccountability, poverty, and the requirement for more aid. The truth is, overall, official development assistance has had little impact on economic growth. This does not mean, as some are quick to assert, that such aid is useless. On the contrary, it highlights the ineffectiveness of imparting aid without tying it to development advances.

From 1970 to 1995, Zambia received consistently and ever larger allocations of outside aid, yet it experienced negative growth in three years out of four, resulting in a contraction of per capita incomes from $700 to $390.[120] This economic performance was clearly the result of macroeconomic mismanagement by the Zambian authorities. However, donors also bear a share of the responsibility, for it is they who continued to increase resource commitments year after year.

The black market exchange rate premium, the difference between the black market exchange rate and the official one, is frequently used as a measure of the level of distortion in a country's financial markets. Countries with overvalued exchange rates commonly have thriving black markets as individuals with hard currency attempt to maximize the value of their assets. Governments frequently profit from exchange rate differentials since they will purchase hard currency at the overvalued rate, then use this for external payments. Unsurprisingly, the correlation between countries with high black market premiums and corruption is quite high. Nonetheless, as William Easterly has observed, the existence of black markets has little effect on donor funding. He notes that Bangladesh, Ethiopia, Guyana, Mauritania, Nicaragua, Sierra Leone, Sudan, Syria, Uganda, and Zambia have all had black market premiums of more than 150 percent during the 1980s and 1990s, yet still received development financing averaging 12.2 percent of GDP.[121]

Certain countries seem to benefit from a seemingly inexhaustible supply of donor patience. Albania, Armenia, Bangladesh, Bolivia, Burkina Faso, Egypt, Ethiopia, Guinea Bissau, Guyana, Haiti, Honduras, Indonesia, Lebanon, Moldova, Niger, Pakistan, Togo, Uganda, Vietnam, and Zambia have consistently gotten substandard corruption ratings,[122] yet received more aid than the median for their regions. This tendency continued through the 1990s, even though this was the period in which the emphasis on good governance came into vogue.

Restricting access to development resources may prod autocratic governments to be more responsive to the population's needs and will at the very least deprive them of money they could use to artificially prop themselves up. Inversely, to the extent that developing country governments view donor support as something that is earned, it creates a healthy competition to demonstrate the effective use of development resources.

Consequently, donor discipline in aligning development assistance to those countries with better track records will have positive institutional effects beyond the monetary value of the funding itself.

Structuring development assistance so that it creates incentives for reform, however, requires a certain degree of donor coordination. To make their priorities clear, they should ensure their actions match their words. And one of these priorities should be to disqualify governments responsible for policies antithetical to development, such as widespread state corruption, the absence of the rule of law, and the lack of accountable leadership. This, of course, requires a working consensus among key donors on what behavior to reward and common measures for judging whether those standards have been met. The failure to act with some degree of harmony risks sending mixed signals and thus erodes the perceived seriousness of donors' commitment to the identified behaviors.

A case in point applies to actions taken by the international community toward Robert Mugabe of Zimbabwe. In 2002 the European Union, the United States, the Commonwealth, and other donors sanctioned Mugabe for stealing national elections and gross violations of human rights. To isolate and delegitimize his claims on power, he and his top aides were barred from traveling to any European or North American country. This policy was designed to register the loss of credibility that results from such a usurpation of power. The signal was diluted, however, when in February 2003, France invited Mugabe to Paris as part of its "Franco-African Summit"—a biannual event aimed at enhancing France's standing and influence among African countries. France had decided that its strategic gains in inviting Mugabe outweighed the potential benefits to the world of isolating an autocratic leader.

In the private sector, investment-friendly environments are rewarded with higher inflows of capital. So too should the aim of development assistance be to reward countries that have created contexts that are best able to use development assistance effectively. Simply put, development funding should be treated as an investment. In this vein and recognizing that in most cases domestic financial, physical, and human resource commitments far exceed the development funding provided by the international community, to the extent that transparent, accountable, and rule of law based institutions can be strengthened through development assistance, the multiplier effects can be great. Stimulating this virtuous circle, however, will only occur if donors act sufficiently in concert that countries employing these institutions are clearly rewarded.

Donor Emphasis on Volume   A partial explanation for the lack of differentiation in the allocation of official development aid between democracies and countries with perpetually poor track records has to do with the incentives within development agencies themselves. Donors have regularly emphasized volume of funding as a concrete, objective criterion to measure staff effectiveness. Dividing the size of the funding portfolios by the number of staff members represents a seemingly clean measure of performance efficiency (never mind complicating variables of population size, poverty levels, or development histories of the respective countries). The staff is thereby rewarded for making frequent and large-scale loans. Moreover, as with many bureaucracies, budgets for individual offices within donor development agencies are based upon the level of spending incurred the previous year. Bureaus that handle a larger volume of funding are considered more prestigious and have leverage in hiring the best staff.

Development, however, is rarely so easily quantified. In addition to improving certain basic indicators of well being, development is a process of building capacity in a society so that it can identify and address its own problems over time. As such, sometimes the most effective development intervention involves providing relatively low-cost technical assistance rather than large-scale infrastructure projects. This reality is not captured in performance measures based on volume. Few indicators of project effectiveness, social welfare impact, corruption, or level of community participation are included in these staff assessments. Consequently, donor officials have few incentives to consider factors, such as whether a potential recipient is a democracy, that may constrain their lending opportunities.

This short-sightedness reflects the fact that multilateral development banks are set up to function much like commercial banks. A private bank earns its profits by making loans against which interest can be accrued. Larger loans are potentially more lucrative. Perhaps it is unsurprising, therefore, that in recent years roughly 40 percent of new development commitments from the World Bank were large, nonproject, quick-disbursing loans and credits.[123] However, this emphasis does not take into consideration the multilateral banks' goal of reducing poverty. The existing incentive structure works against maximizing the effectiveness of development resources by targeting them for each unique context. The process is all the more difficult in that in many cases the benefits from most grants and loans are not observable until several years after the funding has been provided. By this time, the responsible donor officials will have already been promoted—and face little accountability for the lending choices made while in their previous roles.

Another variant of this pressure for volume plays out in terms of staff shortages. The decline in aid agencies' budgets since the end of the Cold War has resulted in substantial staff reductions. The United States Agency for International Development, for example, saw a 35 percent decline in its professional staff from 1992 to 2000.[124] A logical adjustment to such circumstances is to increase the relative size of each respective loan or grant. It doesn't require that much extra effort to make a large loan than a small one. Thus, a busy staff has incentives to make fewer, though larger loans. This administrative constraint reduces the flexibility of targeting smaller loans to meet specific sectoral or provincial-level needs in a developing country. Given the small size of many developing country economies, larger loans also pose greater risks of distorting markets. Finally, larger loans and larger loan-to-oversight ratios create greater opportunities for misuse and corruption. Staff reductions resulting in a leaner aid program do not necessarily make it more cost effective.

In summary, a significant factor in donors' effectiveness is the internal incentive structures by which they operate. In certain cases, current administrative incentives are such that there are few reasons for staff of donor agencies to complicate their jobs by giving preference to governments with strong democratic credentials or, conversely, questioning the validity of maintaining a high volume of assistance to autocratic recipients.

Development Can Complement Democracy

We have described several ways in which democratic processes can be inadvertently undermined by narrowly designed or poorly sequenced development assistance. The list is clearly not exhaustive. Neither is it necessarily representative. We have highlighted these problem areas to illustrate how the international system for providing development assistance must evolve in order to reinforce the positive development effects resulting from good political governance. As we showed in Chapter 2, developing country democracies realize consistently superior development performance compared to dictatorships. The enhanced institutional checks and balances typically created under democracies foster developmental progress. The diffusion of power fosters moderation and flexibility in policymaking, creates incentives for politicians to be more responsive to the public's needs, enables more entrepreneurs to pursue economic opportunity regardless of their political allegiance, permits greater scrutiny of government action, and lays the groundwork for an orderly transfer of power. By taking these factors into account, aid donors can make properly targeted and timed development assistance a positive influence in both enhancing development and strengthening the democratization process.

Mali

Mali's experience during the 1990s is one illustration of the potential synergistic benefits of targeting development assistance to a country making democratic advances. Under Moussa Traore's one-party military rule, Mali exhibited characteristics typical of many authoritarian governments. From 1980 to 1990, it experienced negative growth in eight years out of 10, underwent a 20 percent decline in per capita income to $250 and recorded unending fiscal deficits that doubled the national debt to 98 percent of GDP. These deficits were in part driven by the Traore government's need to maintain a bloated patronage-based workforce from whom it derived its support. The generous benefits package these government employees received —free health care and education plus early retirement[125]—made this a very loyal and vocal constituency. Their cooperation was further solidified by government subsidies for food, fuel, and electricity in urban areas.[126] Unsurprisingly, corruption and tax evasion were widespread, discouraging investment and economic activity. An overvalued currency made goods cheaper for urbanites even as it inhibited exports. Despite the fact that aid averaged over 20 percent of GDP for this decade, donor adjustment programs were ineffective in initiating reforms.

As the winds of change spreading from the fall of the Berlin Wall swept over West Africa, Traore's military government was forced to tolerate some independent press and political associations in 1990, after 23 years in power. While making these concessions, Traore insisted that Mali was not ready for democracy.[127] Widespread public dissatisfaction led to antigovernment protests supported by students, labor unions, civic organizations, and the media. On March 26, 1991, four days after hundreds of protesters were killed by military forces, a group of 17 reform-minded military officers arrested Traore. Within days, the officers joined with the Coordinating Committee of Democratic Associations to form a predominately civilian 25-member ruling body, which in turn appointed a civilian government. A national conference held in August 1991 produced a draft constitution (approved in a referendum on January 12, 1992) laying the framework for a democratic government. Between January and April 1992, a president, National Assembly, and municipal councils were elected. On June 8, 1992, Alpha Oumar Konare, a former archeology professor, was inaugurated as the president of Mali. He had won 70 percent of the presidential vote in a runoff election, while his Association for Democracy in Mali gained 76 out of 116 seats in the National Assembly over dozens of new political parties. Konare then included several opposition party leaders in his cabinet based on his "deepest conviction that democracy does not work without an opposition."[128]

Konare set out an active reform agenda that involved rooting out corruption, ending entrenched patronage, increasing taxes, scaling back public expenditures, trimming "ghost" workers from the payroll, decentralizing government decision-making, promoting small industries, and privatizing a number of public enterprises.[129] The government expressly pursued these measures to rectify the unjust gains of those who benefited under single-party rule. Privatization was undertaken selectively to mitigate the impact on the economy, for example by allowing entrepreneurs untainted by corruption to take over inefficient state-run firms rather than just let them go under.[130]

Donors responded decisively during this critical early period of the transition.[131] From 1992 to 1994, official development assistance as a share of GDP increased from 15 percent to 25 percent. This financial bonanza enabled the Mali government to launch a drive to raise the standard of living, reduce poverty, and improve the country's natural-resource management, even in the midst of its economic restructuring program.[132] As part of this program, it sought to increase primary school enrollments, improve the public healthcare system, and ensure the availability of essential drugs. Acting quickly, the IMF signed a three-year enhanced structural-adjustment loan with Mali in September 1993, which preceded a 50 percent devaluation of the West African regional currency in January 1994[133] and thus softened the blow of the monetary realignment on the nation's economy.

Nevertheless, the drop in purchasing power created by the devaluation generated strikes by teachers, labor unions, and students. Several government supporters' houses were burned.[134] Escalating Konare's woes, six deputies from the left wing of his party abandoned it for supposedly not moving quickly enough to stem corruption. Speculation was rife of an impending military coup. Some longed for the firmer hand of a military government.[135] Even Konare acknowledged "a big risk of a social explosion," stressing the importance of foreign aid to help Mali's democracy. "In a new democracy, the road is never a royal one," adding that "democracy is a process" that must be allowed to be "self-correcting."[136]

The economy responded to the policy shifts, achieving real growth in 1994 of 2.5 percent. The 23 percent inflation rate was more moderate than the 40 percent expected.[137] By 1995, inflation had dropped to 13 percent, halving again the following year.[138] From 1992 to 1996, cereal yields expanded by more than 40 percent, raising living standards for the three-fourths of the population involved in farming. Infant mortality rates declined from 150 to 118 deaths per 1,000 live births. Meanwhile, primary school enrollment rates increased by nearly half over the four-year period, to 35 percent of the school age population. Per capita economic growth has averaged more than 2 percent per year since Mali began its democratic experiment.

In 1996, Konare negotiated an end to a low-intensity civil conflict with rebels from the minority Tuareg ethnic group who had been resisting central authority since 1990. This was accomplished through a comprehensive decentralization effort coupled with administrative reforms.[139]

Konare was reelected with a commanding majority in 1997 against a collection of opposition parties coalescing around the former single-party government. The voting process was not without its flaws. Government officials and the Malian Supreme Court acknowledged that the first round of legislative elections were poorly organized.[140] There was widespread confusion at polling places regarding who was eligible to vote. Many of the polls opened late. Others never received all of their voting materials.[141] With the results showing an overwhelming victory for Konare's party, the opposition claimed fraud. Eager to maintain international credibility, Konare agreed to reschedule the elections. Radical elements of the opposition, threatening violence, called for the release of militants, a suspension of the electoral process, and for the government to resign.[142] On the eve of the subsequent presidential election, with opinion polls showing an overwhelming Konare lead, the opposition called for a boycott and carried out a series of attacks on the offices of the governing party, leaving at least one person dead. Nonetheless, Konare won with 84 percent of the vote.

The IMF extended three additional loans to Mali from 1996 to 1999 totaling $110 million to combat corruption, improve the efficiency of the state bureaucracy, ensure tax compliance, and strengthen judicial institutions. In 1997, an effort was made to strengthen and privatize Mali's banks and encourage the development of microfinance and private guarantee funds. Demonstrating his intolerance for corruption within the government, Konare fired his long-time appointed prime minister, Ibrahim Keita, after he was implicated in a corruption scandal in 2000.[143] Mali became eligible for debt relief under the World Bank's Heavily Indebted Poor Countries program in 1998, qualifying for $870 million in debt forgiveness in 2000[144] out of a total debt burden of $2.9 billion.

In 2001, a series of economic jolts, including a severe drought, rising oil prices, and higher transport costs caused economic growth to stall. Nonetheless, in a survey that year, more than 70 percent of Malians rejected the notion of a return to one-party rule—the same percentage of respondents who in 1996 opposed a return to military rule even "if the democratic institutions ceased to function."[145]

With Konare's two-term limit ending, Amadou Toumani Toure won a runoff election with 64 percent of the vote in May 2002. He defeated the governing-party candidate, leading to a successful transfer of power between parties. The Association for Democracy in Mali, however, did retain a majority of seats in the legislature. Toure is widely respected by most Malians, being one of the generals who ousted the autocrat, Traore, in 1992, then turning power over to a civilian government. He has publicly committed himself to continuing the reforms put forward by Konare.

Mali represents a case where targeted and timely development assistance provided to a new democracy can have positive effects on economic fundamentals, poverty alleviation, and the strengthening of democratic institutions. As one of the poorest countries in the world, it shows how promoting development can go hand in hand with promoting democracy, no matter what the income level. Mali benefited from a broad-based social commitment to political transformation, a noncorrupt leader committed to the principles of democracy, and a discredited former governing system. However, these factors alone did not guarantee a successful outcome. Donors exhibited sufficient flexibility and timeliness in their support for Mali to enable a sequential targeting of required reforms. This allowed time for reforms to take effect and the population to adjust. Consequently, the credibility of the reform process and the requisite social commitment to it were maintained.

Summary

Political governance matters to development. After all, at its essence, government is the manner in which a society organizes itself to pursue its priorities. Since development assistance involves an allocation of resources to pursue these priorities, clearly the system of governance in place is central to the development outcomes to be realized. Governments that have incentives to respond to the well being of their populations stand to use development assistance more effectively. Indeed, this is consistent with our findings from Chapter 2—democracies score consistently better on a range of development indicators.

Despite the increased recognition of the importance of governance to development, the current allocations of development assistance do not reward developing country democracies. Evidently this reflects both a lack of recognition of the strong positive linkage between democratic governance and development as well as bureaucratic disincentives that prevent donor agencies from reconciling their stated preference for democracy with their resource allocations.

At times, donors' development policies have had negative consequences on democratization. There are multiple internal and external causes for this. The most elementary is their failure to distinguish between democracies and dictatorships in a clear and consistent way. Should they do so, they could differentiate their development strategies, allowing leaders who are accountable to their populations a greater say in how the money is spent —and preventing leaders who are not from squandering the aid to reinforce their narrow, patronage-based rule. Donors would also be able to adjust their funding practices to meet the time-sensitive and customized needs of new democracies including alleviating the massive debt burdens they have inherited.

More broadly, donors need to recognize that economic reforms can't be pursued in a vacuum but must be implemented in a measured way, taking into account the social and political circumstances of the country, in order to minimize disruptions to people's lives and thus to maintain their support. Otherwise, a popular backlash against the reforms could develop, retarding or even blocking them and possibly paralyzing the new democratic government that had been championing these changes. Here, too, donors must exhibit flexibility, notably by showing a willingness to relax their timetables for change. A "gradualist" approach, allowing time for institutions and attitudes to adjust to changing incentives, would appear to be particularly appropriate for economic reform strategies in democratizing countries.

The contemporary era of democratization brightens future prospects for more consistent and broad-based development. However, this process must be encouraged by ensuring that the incentive structures reinforced by international donors are institutionalizing patterns of accountability and responsiveness to the public.

CHAPTER 6

Democracy as the Default Option

Democracy is not based on governments. There are many governments in this world today that pretend that they are democracies or that they're working on democratic values but in fact they are not. Unless the people are allowed to be heard, unless the people are allowed not just freedom of speech and freedom of association, but . . . freedom after speech and freedom after association, we shall not be able to build up our democratic institutions.

Aung San Suu Kyi
democratically elected leader of Burma (Myanmar),
held under house arrest by Burma's military junta

Development assistance spending by the United States and other major donors has been on a downward path since the 1960s. In proportionate terms, the United States provides less development assistance than any other industrialized country—$29 per person, compared with a median of $70.[1] This amounts to 0.12 percent of GDP. Nonetheless, with annual outlays of roughly $13 billion,[2] it is the biggest bilateral donor. Moreover, to a greater extent than other donors, U.S. foreign assistance encompasses all developing regions—Latin America, Africa, the Middle East, South Asia, and East Asia. The United States also remains by far the single largest shareholder in both the World Bank and the IMF, at roughly 17 percent. Given the level of its assistance and its position on the world stage, the United States carries substantial influence in setting the direction and priorities in global efforts to promote development and democracy. We therefore focus our bilateral policy recommendations on actions that can be taken by the United States. However, we believe they are also broadly applicable to other bilateral donors.

We have argued throughout this book that democracy and development are compatible and mutually reinforcing processes, even among low-income countries. As described in Chapter 2, democracies, by and large, demonstrate superior developmental performance. This is due, at least in part, to their more robust institutions of accountability that foster greater responsiveness to the priorities of the general population, more informed and extensive policy dialogue, moderating influences on the chief executive, and a fairer dispersion of opportunities generating greater economic efficiency. For those countries with political structures that are antithetical to accountability, be they personalistic, totalitarian, or monarchial regimes, at least some democratic opening is a prerequisite to development.

Taking and sustaining the difficult steps of democratization are ultimately up to the citizens of a given country. Genuine reform requires a commitment by all major elements of a society to the principles of shared power, freedom of expression and association, and tolerance for opposing points of view. Consequently, no type or level of external development assistance, regardless of how robust or well conceived, will be effective in stimulating development progress on its own. Recognizing this, we propose that U.S. development assistance[3] be targeted so as to *generate stronger incentives for internal political and economic reform*. In this way, it can be leveraged toward the vastly more substantial levels of private investment, entrepreneurial energy, and the competition of ideas that are unleashed by more representative, transparent, and meritocratic governing institutions. Lacking such institutional checks and balances, development assistance will likely not only be ineffective but by reinforcing skewed distributions of power, could very well be deleterious. Furthermore, the internal self-correcting mechanisms that are built into democracies and which could reverse this pattern do not exist in autocratic governments. Therefore, development assistance should primarily be provided only to those countries where the seeds of reform have begun to germinate.

Some may argue that development assistance in the age of global capital flows is irrelevant. Total annual official development assistance of roughly $55 billion compares to an estimated $151 billion of net private direct investment that flowed into emerging markets in 2002[4]—even after the exodus of capital from emerging markets following the East Asian financial crisis of the late 1990s. Nonetheless, development assistance remains an important resource for poverty alleviation and economic growth in many developing countries. Most private capital flowing to emerging markets is concentrated in a handful of countries. Some 80 to 90 low- and lower-middle-income countries do not have access to international private capital.[5] Furthermore, capital flows are notoriously volatile. Excluding direct investment, private capital flows have been negative for emerging markets in recent years.[6] Even for those countries that do have access to international private capital, this may not be available for the sectors and locations that are most strategic for broad-based growth or addressing poverty. Moreover, as in the industrialized world, markets rarely form around the provision of public goods such as the establishment of rule of law and investments in education, health services, and public infrastructure—the existence of which much development depends. For these reasons, improving the effectiveness of development assistance remains vital to the prosperity-enhancing prospects for most countries in the world.

Democratic Selectivity

The first priority for a U.S. bilateral assistance strategy aiming to enhance developing countries' incentives to reform is to reverse the current antidemocratic bias in foreign assistance. As discussed in Chapter 5, low- and middle-income autocracies have historically received levels of official development assistance as a percentage of GDP equal to that of democracies. Given that virtually all development assistance comes from established democracies, the current arrangement sends the unfortunate message that the industrialized democracies are just as happy funding autocracies as they are democracies.

Similarly, if we consider development allocations as a type of investment aimed at generating long-term returns (which they are), then the failure to distinguish between these two widely divergent types of regime is hard to justify. As we saw in Chapter 2, economic volatility in low-income autocracies is twice that of democracies. It is as though an investor faces the choice of putting money into a fund that generates a modest though generally consistent 8 percent to 10 percent annual rate of return versus an option that has a 5 percent probability of yielding 15 percent to 20 percent, and a much greater chance of costing him his shirt. Donor governments have been willing to roll the dice on the high-risk option just as often as not. Foreign aid's weak track record, therefore, should come as no surprise. Taken in aggregate, the current system provides no overt incentive to developing countries to democratize.

To correct this bias, the U.S. government and other bilateral donors should give preference to democracies when providing development funding. That is democracies—delineated by the high bar we have been using throughout this book—should qualify for more types of funding support and should receive a larger proportionate share of resources targeted to developing countries. This should apply not only to USAID funds commonly associated with development, but also with other agencies regularly engaged with low-income countries. For example, the Overseas Private Investment Corporation (OPIC), which helps mobilize U.S. private capital in developing and transitioning countries, as well as the Trade Development Authority, which aims to expand the capacity of emerging markets to engage in trade with the United States, have considerable impact on the prospects for development in the countries in which they are working. Reconciling the preference for democracies among all of these agencies will not only augment their overall effectiveness but will send a stronger signal of the advantages from genuine political reform. Any funding for autocracies should be contingent on the explicit approval of the respective executive officer in these agencies, endorsed by the interagency development policy coordination panel (to be discussed shortly). By giving preference to democracies, U.S. taxpayers will have greater assurances that they'll get the biggest bang for their foreign assistance buck—while simultaneously strengthening incentives for democratization around the world.

Although preferences should be given to democracies for development initiatives that involve actual financial transfers and technical expertise, we resist calling for special advantages for democracies on the international trade front. Autocratic governments willing to open themselves to international standards of rule of law, transparency, and exchange is a positive development. This is consistent with the aims of building institutions of accountability and democratization that we have emphasized throughout this book and should be encouraged.

Giving democracies preference in development funding would also minimize instances where sound development initiatives by democracies go unfunded. Indeed, channeling resources to developing countries with accountable governments in an effort to eradicate abject deprivation should be the aim of development assistance. That these efforts are limited due to resources that are squandered in low-accountability countries is the real tragedy of the current arrangement. The unfortunate flipside of this reality is that much global poverty cannot be currently remedied by additional funding. Thomas Freidman has described this phenomenon well using the metaphor of a light socket for development. If you have a damaged socket (that is, dysfunctional governance institutions), then increasing the electrical charge (or development resources) will have no effect. However, democracies represent institutional environments where the electric socket is in working order—and it is through these countries that we should be scaling up our support.

A target for U.S. development policy therefore would be to allocate sufficient levels of development assistance, commensurate with its share of global GDP, to substantively support all viable poverty-alleviation initiatives in low-income democracies. The following qualifications would apply to democracies considered: the macropolicy environment should be stable and the initiative well conceived; sound development practices such as enhancing community participation, investment in human capacity, creation of public goods, and strengthening accountability institutions must be employed; and countries tainted by widespread corruption should be disqualified. (Recalling our discussion in Chapter 3, corruption trumps democracy's developmental advantage. Although democracies generally have a better track record when it comes to control of corruption, they are not immune.) Where low-income democracies have met the necessary prerequisite conditions, the United States and other donors should pull out the stops to ensure sufficient funding is available to undertake these high-potential development initiatives. It is a good investment. It promotes both development and democracy. And it gives incentives to reform—both for democracies and those countries not yet on a democratic path.

Millennium Challenge Account
Some readers will no doubt be remarking at this point, "This sounds an awfully lot like the Millennium Challenge Account (MCA)." Indeed, we are strong supporters of the initiative, proposed by President George W. Bush in March 2002 in advance of the International Conference on Financing for Development in Monterrey, Mexico. As proposed, the initiative would represent a 50 percent increase in U.S. development funding and would be targeted to countries with per capita GDP's below $1,465 deemed (1) to be ruled justly, (2) to respect basic economic rights, notably property rights and the rule of law, and (3) to be making sufficient investments in public health and education. Multiple criteria for each of these three categories—16 in all—have been identified to assess a country's relative level of attainment. In order to qualify for assistance from the Millennium Challenge Corporation, the entity established to manage the initiative, a country must be (a) in the top half of all potentially eligible recipients on the corruption-control indicator and (b) above the median among all potentially eligible countries in at least one-third of the criteria for each of the three categories. The first condition would lessen the likelihood that account funds are misused; the latter ensures that countries are progressing on multiple fronts.

Although the structure and management for the account is still emerging, the innovative program could represent an additional $5 billion a year in development funding.[7] What is clear is that this initiative is intended to take a new approach to development and represents a significant step toward structuring development assistance so that it gives developing countries incentives for reform. The "ruling justly" criterion, partially based on Freedom House's index on political rights and civil liberties, means that the MCA is systematically including democracy criteria in its development decision-making as we have recommended (though we would prefer if this category were explicitly labeled "ruling democratically"). This is an important conceptual step forward.

Our main criticism of the MCA is that it equivocates on the importance of democratic governance. Just as the initiative sets a precondition that all recipient countries must rate in the top half on the "control of corruption" measure, we feel a similar litmus test should be made for democratic governance. Lacking this, the initiative leaves open the possibility that certain autocratic governments could be rewarded with development assistance. Encouragingly, the first contingent of eligible countries Armenia, Benin, Bolivia, Cape Verde, Georgia, Ghana, Honduras, Lesotho, Madagascar, Mali, Mongolia, Mozambique, Nicaragua, Senegal, Sri Lanka, and Vanuatu suggests that the "ruling justly" criterion was given serious consideration, even if questions can be raised over the selection of particular countries. Still, under the current arrangement, several candidate countries, including Bhutan, Burkina Faso, Cambodia, China, Guinea, Rwanda, and Vietnam, could technically qualify despite having highly repressive governments.[8] They score well enough on the "investment in people" and "economic rights" factors to qualify in those categories. They slip through in the "ruling justly" category because of the odd manner in which the criteria for this measure are defined. Two economic rights-oriented factors, rule of law and governmental effectiveness,[9] plus corruption control account for three of the six factors for this category. By meeting the median for these three factors—all meritorious but not measures of democratic government—they qualify as countries that are ruling justly. This despite the fact that they are far below the median on the Freedom House measures of political rights and civil liberties, as well as the World Bank's voice and accountability index—the other three criteria in the ruling-justly category. Thus, the actual implementation of the initiative is vulnerable to falling far short of the democratic themes used in describing it.

A rationale made by some for supporting certain autocracies through the MCA is that these countries may be growing and "in the interest of development" allocating MCA monies to them will enhance economic development and facilitate their eventual democratic transition. However, as we have seen in previous chapters, both of these assumptions are dubious. Autocratic governments are renowned for orchestrating exceptional growth spurts followed by economic collapse. In the meantime, the funding that goes to autocratic governments tends to perpetuate their hold on power rather than hasten a democratic transition. Similarly, there will be strong pressures to expand the number of countries that qualify under the initiative so that this potentially sizable new source of development assistance can benefit more countries. Yet, this impulse should be resisted. Unless the governance criteria are applied scrupulously, the key innovation of this development initiative as well as the incentive impetus it provides to nonqualifying countries would be eliminated. The upshot would be that the democracy objective would be sidelined and a relatively larger share of the account's funds would stand to go for naught. Rather than diluting the aim of the MCA due to the scarcity of general development assistance funds, this problem should be addressed head-on—by increasing the development account of USAID.

Although certain autocratic countries may qualify for the MCA under the current arrangement, several low-income democracies that appear to pass the corruption test, including India and the Philippines, are deemed ineligible since they fall short on measures like educational attainment and healthcare spending—even though their low scores in those areas are arguably more a reflection of their poverty than of their insufficient commitment to investing in their people. In short, the MCA could be strengthened by making democracy more central. A greater share of development resources would then be targeted to countries with pluralistic political institutions—improving the effective use of these funds and strengthening countries on the path to reform.

Nonetheless, the initiative is valuable in that it provides developing countries an incentive to strengthen their institutional capacities in the areas of economic rights, public welfare, and improved governance. More generally, it is a welcome source of new financing in a parched development landscape.

Although the birth of the MCA is a hopeful step, it would still not erase the mixed signals that *existing* development-funding programs send about the importance of democracy. After all, the conventional aid program would continue to represent the largest pot of U.S. government development resources. Consistent with our democratic selectivity framework, therefore, it is our view that *all* U.S. bilateral development funding should give preferential treatment to democracies.

Democratizers and the Community of Democracies

Thus far, we have focused our discussion on democracies. And, indeed, this is where we feel the priority should be given. Developing countries that are democratic and excluded from the MCA for reasons other than corruption ought to be given preferential treatment in the regular bilateral assistance program. However, there are many other countries on the path to democracy that merit additional attention. These "democratizers" may not yet have the full mix of institutions that qualify them as democracies, but they are making fundamental reforms nonetheless. Practically speaking, there are roughly 45 low-income countries that have made some progress in strengthening their democratic institutions since 1990 but that do not yet meet the standard of an established democracy.

We recommend that once the United States has targeted meritorious democracies, it make as its next priority doing the same for democratizers. By singling them out and giving them preference over countries that are making no serious effort at reform, Washington would be creating incentives for countries inching their way to democracy to continue on the journey and even speed up the pace. This would further knit together the respective roles of USAID and the new MCC.

As with the MCA, independent measures of democratic progress could determine which countries qualify as democratizers.[10] Such a method would leave little room for dictatorships to complain they were left out because of the subjective judgments of this or that donor, and would keep the pressure on aid recipients to continue in their reforms. It would also constrain donors from doling out development aid to dictatorships for strategic purposes.

An alternate mechanism for identifying democratizers would be to work off the roster of the Community of Democracies, an organization established in 2000 of countries that have committed themselves to the democratic principles of the separation of powers, freedom of expression and association, and respect for human rights.[11] By 2002, membership had grown to 118 states of all income levels and in every region of the world. The community's vision is to build on their shared principles to protect the integrity of democratic processes in societies that have chosen them and to coordinate their policies to enhance the effectiveness of democratic governance. Because participation in the community is based on a set of principles and not on regional, economic, or strategic considerations, it has the potential to serve as a platform to generate collaborative solutions to common problems facing rich and poor countries.

Although 27 members of the Community of Democracies fail to qualify as full-fledged democracies using the Polity or Freedom House indices described in Chapter 2, all but five of this group are considered democratizers by those same standards.[12] Given this proclivity for democracy, we believe membership in the Community of Democracies merits preferential treatment by the United States and other donors.[13] Such a policy would have the double advantage of motivating countries that are not yet members of the community to make reforms that would qualify them to join and providing incentives to those that are members to deepen their commitment to democracy. For donor countries, using the Community of Democracies as a proxy measure for democratizers would be practical, meaningful, and administratively efficient. It would provide aid to countries on the path to democracy, reinforce incentives for them to pursue further democratic reform, and strengthen the cohesion of this potentially influential new international body. Since the selection of new members (and the expulsion of existing ones) is made by a consensus of the 10 convening group countries,[14] the process has protections against excessive politicization. In other words, a consultative peer review process exists that moderates against the excessive influence of a single state. Nor are the selection decisions made casually. Twelve countries welcomed aboard in 2000 were relegated to observer status in 2002.[15]

What to Do About Autocracies and Failed States?
Autocratic governments—those that demonstrate no real power sharing, political competition, or popular participation—would not qualify for any bilateral assistance. Development funding to these countries would be channeled through private development agencies, to the extent these exist. In the event of a humanitarian emergency or global threat like the AIDS pandemic, assistance to autocrats could proceed provided that sufficient transparency measures were in place to ensure it is used for the designated purposes. If such measures were not adopted, then autocratic governments would be excluded from development allocations altogether. Although some may view this as overly harsh, we contend that since these funds are drawn from a finite pot of resources, there are inevitably trade-offs. Monies sent to an autocratic government without minimal transparency requirements are resources that are taken away from poverty alleviation efforts in another country with greater levels of accountability. Furthermore, resources provided to an autocratic government lacking adequate oversight are hardly guaranteed to ameliorate humanitarian concerns, even if there is a crisis. Rather, the money is more likely to be diverted to the ruling party's coffers and used to beef up its security network, buy off political allies, and otherwise tighten the autocratic regime's hold on power. Given the high risk of such misappropriation of funds, cutting them off instead seems to be a justifiable, if difficult, choice.[16] This approach recognizes that most humanitarian crises have entirely political origins and redressing the human suffering requires dealing with the political context precipitating it.

A case in point is Zimbabwe, which has been ruled by Robert Mugabe and his ZANU-PF party since independence in 1980 and is widely viewed as having grown increasingly autocratic in his years of power. The opposition candidate, considered by most observers to have won the 2002 presidential election, is facing treason charges and his supporters regularly face physical intimidation and imprisonment. Economically, Zimbabwe seems on the brink of implosion. In 2004, inflation is at 450 percent, official corruption is rapacious, and food production in this once maize-exporting country has plummeted, leaving some 60 percent of the population dependent on food assistance. International efforts to provide food aid, however, have been blatantly directed to ZANU-PF supporters. Similarly, a land distribution initiative implemented by Mugabe to mobilize popular support has widely been seen as a land grab by top party officials. Efforts by international agencies to monitor the assistance are heavily restricted. The press has been smothered and international journalists covering stories in the country must do so clandestinely. Simply put, contributing more international assistance in Zimbabwe is unlikely to benefit the people who need it most. It would, however, boost members of Mugabe's party—and augment their hold on power. International efforts to assist ordinary Zimbabweans should focus on supporting private humanitarian assistance agencies and on ensuring reliable monitoring mechanisms are established, ideally including the unrestricted reporting by independent media. Until such measures are in place, additional assistance to the government should not be forthcoming.

Similar principles apply to failed states—nations that are so weak that the government's authority and ability to provide security does not extend beyond the capital. In some instances, no government at all can be said to exist—at various times the reality in Somalia, Liberia, and Sierra Leone in the late 1990s and early years of the twenty-first century. These are crises that merit an international response provided that there are minimal assurances that these resources can benefit those who need it most. Rather than dealing with a corrupt and oppressive government, however, these judgments must be made in relation to local warlords. Establishing a context in which international assistance can benefit those in need and not in the process become a magnet for competing armed factions may require a military component to the intervention.

Some may wonder whether withholding assistance to autocrats may precipitate a country becoming a failed state. In fact, the dysfunctionality created by governance systems that both lack legitimacy and the competency to provide any public goods and services are far more influential factors leading to this outcome. However, holding out the prospect for emergency assistance to failing states that do agree to minimum standards of transparency and oversight does represent a tangible lifeline to those states that are sinking.

Debt Relief

A country's commitment to democracy should also be a factor in whether it is granted debt relief. Debt relief has been on the international development agenda for more than 20 years[17] but became a hot issue at the turn of the millennium as public figures ranging from Bono, of the rock group U2, to the Pope joined a movement advocating it. Their argument was, and is, that it is the only hope for some developing countries to escape poverty, especially those whose debt payments are growing faster than government revenues or export income. As a result of such pressure, the World Bank has accelerated its Highly Indebted Poor Countries (HIPC) debt-relief process and has so far slated 42 countries for debt reduction once they pass through several qualifying stages to demonstrate their commitment to fiscal discipline and human-capital development.

Although such help sounds like the right thing to do, policymakers have to be careful about whom to reprieve and by how much. In his book, *The Elusive Quest for Growth*, William Easterly has described how debt-relief efforts thus far have not led to subsequent improvements in economic performance.[18] In fact, debt forgiveness has led certain countries to incur even larger debts. He notes that under the current arrangement, a commitment to repaying debt is unrelated to a country's future likelihood of receiving loans. In other words, incentives for fiscal discipline are not built into the debt-relief package. Nonetheless, international public pressure to relieve debt has led a further relaxing of the criteria needed to qualify for the HIPC program. Even countries that have failed to meet the debt-relief targets are kept on track for debt amnesty.

We concur with Easterly that debt relief should only be made available to those countries that have reduced their profligate spending both before and after their debts are forgiven. After all, the goal of debt relief should be economic growth. But we would also make the recipient nation's political orientation an important factor in deciding its eligibility for relief, for reasons of both fairness and practicality. Many new democracies start with a mountain of debt incurred by their autocratic predecessors (Nigeria, Indonesia, and Yugoslavia being prominent examples). In fact, countries starting down a democratic path since 1980 have, on average, inherited debt-service payments equivalent to 17.5 percent of exports—one-fifth more than the norm for low-income countries.[19] We submit that democratizing countries that have assumed crushing debt from a previous autocratic government deserve to be leading candidates for rapid and comprehensive debt relief.[20]

That's the fairness part. The practical side of the argument is that debt relief will help a democratizing country stay on the path of reform by removing a major drag on its economy and thus, as we saw in Chapter 3, a major impetus for it to backtrack. Consider the choice of newly elected leaders in a nation saddled by debt: either pursue an austerity package that will spark public disenchantment or continue deficit spending to the detriment of economic stability and long-term economic recovery. Failing to consider changes in regime type risks penalizing new democracies for the sins of their autocratic predecessors. The paradoxical result may be fewer successful democratizers with a genuine commitment to economic reform.

Although democracies are frequently born in the economic emergency room, donor countries that are interested in the development-enhancing benefits of debt relief or in spurring development to advance democracy, have a strong rationale for forgiving debts of new democracies. Reforming countries would have an opportunity for a new start. As icing on the cake, a clear message would go out to the world that democracy pays—and dictatorship doesn't.

Timeliness and Flexibility

As we pointed out in Chapter 5, timeliness is crucial in supporting democratizing societies, which, if they backtrack, tend to do so in the first three years of their effort to shed their old authoritarian ways. So getting development assistance to them early, when the costs of making the transition are highest, is important. Given their relatively smaller size and greater political sensitivity, bilateral donors may have a particular advantage in undertaking timely initiatives that generate quick-hitting impacts. The World Bank, in contrast, is notoriously slow and bureaucratic in its funding of development initiatives. It typically takes one to two years *after* a project has been approved (a laborious process in itself) for Bank funds to arrive in a country— though the Bank has demonstrated a greater capacity for responsiveness in certain post-conflict settings. Timely, targeted assistance has a good chance of increasing the stability of a new democratic government, adding credibility to reformist politicians in the eyes of the population and giving a focus, means, and momentum for further change. It is much more likely to produce a "democracy dividend" than aid that dribbles in years later.

The issue of timing also raises questions about how long new democracies should be supported. There has been a tendency for international donors to support democratizing countries up through their first democratically held election. Assistance frequently drops off after this "success" threshold has been reached.[21] Meanwhile, democracy promoters talk of two successful leadership transitions as being the benchmark of democratic consolidation. Recall from Chapter 3, however, that the path to democracy is frequently more ambiguous. Early progress is not a guarantee of democratic consolidation. Income level does represent something of a threshold indicator precluding democratic backtracking. With the exception of Argentina in 1976, no democracy that has attained a per capita GDP of $4,200 has ever slid back.

Based on this experience, we recommend that democracies should continue to be accorded preferential treatment in the provision of development assistance until they have reached this mid-income level. As funding for the MCA increases, we support the proposed expansion of the per capita income constraints to the $2,975 level.[22] Although there are valid concerns that this approach would short-change poorer countries, and establishing minimum benchmarks of MCA resources to be allocated to lower-income countries is justified, we hold the view that so long as the development funding is generating positive outcomes, then it is an investment well spent—especially if it contributes toward more democratic successes. Moreover, the benefits are not isolated. All countries in question are in developing regions. The economic growth of a mid-income democracy stands to create trade, investment, and labor opportunities for its poorer neighbors. These mid-income countries, therefore, have the potential to be engines of development in their respective regions. As thriving democracies, they would also be setting an example that their neighbors might find contagious.[23]

If getting aid to democratizing countries early in the game is important, so is deciding for what projects it will be used. Our recommendation is to leave that to the democratic leaders, with the obvious requirement that they stick to sound development policies—such as managing inflation, avoiding major deficit spending, investing in citizens and infrastructure, strengthening an economy's financial structures, and so forth. It sounds straightforward, but this approach would demand greater flexibility than donors have historically shown. Rather than relying on a standard set of prescriptions or undertaking prolonged preliminary analysis, they would have to let the recipient country's democratic leaders set the course. After a designated period of, say, three years, donors could then evaluate the effectiveness of their assistance and target their future support accordingly. A variation of this approach would be for donors to agree to support multiyear development strategies devised by democratically governed developing countries. Loans would be incrementally converted into grants pending each year's successful progress against the mutually agreed-upon benchmarks.[24]

Letting democratic leaders call the shots would be a public recognition of their right to represent the interests of their citizenry and, by implication, a repudiation of the right of dictators to do so. This would send exactly the right signal to these populations—that democracy works and that working through the system gets results. They after all chose their leaders and expect them to act on the nation's behalf. It would also give the newly elected leaders a chance to practice the art of democracy—instituting reforms at the right pace and in the right sequence to build momentum for reforms while building the political coalitions needed to sustain them. Countries that are democratizing but have still not crossed the democratic threshold would not be accorded the same degree of flexibility and would be legitimately subject to varying degrees of conditionality in the provision of development assistance.

If willingness by donors to cede or share decision-making with elected leaders about the use of financial aid promotes democracy, a rigid adherence to the old way of doing things can backfire. Joseph Stiglitz, a Nobel laureate and former chief economist of the World Bank, has argued that international development agencies that contravene the priorities of a democratic government are, to some extent, undercutting the quality of democracy in that country.[25] We would go even further and assert that donors who stick stubbornly to their notions of what is best for the country risk subverting the will of the general population. That is not to say bilateral funding agencies should sponsor initiatives they don't consider to be viable. It is to say, however, that within the realm of sound economic principles, given the myriad needs facing most developing countries, there is plenty of room for flexibility about the exact actions to take. If the initiatives that are funded are sought by the democratic leadership (and are perceived as such), the potential benefits for building societal commitment to continued reforms, international cooperation, and democracy in general will be enhanced.

Building on a Precedent: Support for East European Democracy (SEED)
Making democracy a systematic consideration in development funding is not a Herculean stretch for the U.S. government. The 1989 congressional legislation (H.R. 3402) creating the Support for East European Democracy —or SEED—program[26] cited promoting democracy as the first of its three core objectives.[27] It was quite precise about this, saying that its aim was to

1. contribute to the development of democratic institutions and political pluralism characterized by:
   a. the establishment of fully democratic and representative political systems based on free and fair elections
   b. the effective recognition of fundamental liberties and individual freedoms, including freedom of speech, religion, and association

c. the termination of all laws and regulations that impede the operation of a free press and the formation of political parties
d. the creation of an independent judiciary
e. the establishment of nonpartisan military, security, and police forces

The authors of the measure were likewise explicit in laying out the conditions under which assistance would be suspended, namely if:

1. the president or any other government official of that country initiates martial law or a state of emergency for reasons other than to respond to a natural disaster or a foreign invasion; or
2. any member elected to that country's parliament has been removed from that office or arrested through extra-constitutional processes.

Furthermore, recognizing the advantage of pursuing these efforts in concert with the multilateral institutions, the SEED Act called on the executive branch to mobilize the World Bank and the IMF to provide timely and appropriate resources as well as debt relief, "*to the extent that Poland and Hungary [and subsequently other former Eastern Bloc countries] continue to evolve toward pluralism and democracy* and to develop and implement comprehensive economic reform programs" (italics added).

One of the more successful facets of the SEED Act has been the establishment of ten "Enterprise Funds" in Eastern Europe and the former Soviet Union as a means of spurring investment and momentum for a market economy. The Funds are operated independently and much like a venture capital firm, albeit in a high-risk environment. USAID and the State Department have oversight responsibility. The funds have concentrated their attention on small and medium-sized businesses as a means of building a middle class. Thus far, they have injected capital into small businesses that together have hired a total of 150,000 people, created or financed 24 freestanding financial institutions with more than 100 branches, and made more than 50,000 small business loans with a default rate averaging less than 4 percent. The funds have also been matched—sometimes more than matched—by grants made by the partner national governments.[28] Although there have been disappointments, the 10 funds had a capital base of $1.3 billion a decade after the SEED Act was established.[29]

The logic of including democratic criteria as a means of enhancing the effectiveness of U.S. development assistance (and facilitating the transition to a market economy) for the newly democratic nations of eastern Europe was apparent to U.S. lawmakers at the end of the Cold War. Rather than undermining development efforts, the democratic emphasis has arguably contributed to what have widely been regarded as successful initiatives. Our recommendations are extending the same logic to other types of U.S. bilateral assistance.

Structural Changes in U.S. Bilateral Development Assistance

To create a more coherent U.S. development strategy, including the systematic consideration of democratic governance in the allocation of foreign assistance, will require fundamental changes in the manner in which the various U.S. government agencies with interests in the developing world undertake their missions—the cross-purposes of which are predictably self-defeating.

Establishing a Development Policy Coordination Panel

The Treasury Department represents U.S. interests at the World Bank and the IMF in accordance with those bodies' charters, which stipulate that their official link to member governments must be through their finance ministries or central banks. Unfortunately, this requirement limits American development effectiveness. Treasury officials do not see their mandate in relation to the IFIs as promoting development, let alone democracy. Rather, their efforts are directed at promoting macroeconomic stability—establishing sound fiscal, monetary, and exchange rate policies in developing countries, thereby creating an attractive economic environment for investors. They assume social conditions will improve as the economy grows, but take no direct action to make that happen.

Although we have no quarrel with the Treasury Department's objectives, we also believe that they alone are insufficient to advance a country's economic development. Yes, getting the macroeconomic fundamentals right is crucial, but so is cultivating all the other components of a healthy society, like accountable political institutions, local community participation, generating public goods and services, a skilled and healthy labor force, bureaucratic efficiency and responsiveness, and access to information. To pursue a truly effective development agenda, therefore, requires the engagement of policymakers with the awareness, skill, and political will to focus on these issues. In the U.S. government, most such experts inhabit the halls of the State Department and USAID. And there's the rub: The founding protocols of the World Bank and IMF make them unwelcome there.

That is all the more ironic given that the World Bank switched its focus from post-war rehabilitation to poverty alleviation in the late 1960s under the leadership of Robert McNamara, explicitly recognizing that sound macroeconomic policy alone is inadequate to the task of economic development. But while the aims of the World Bank shifted, their institutional underpinnings did not. Furthermore, since in practical terms the World Bank does not make loans to countries that are not certified by the IMF, macroeconomic fundamentalism continues to pervade decision-making at international lending organizations.

Another shortcoming of the current arrangement is evident in the political realm. As we have described previously, a country's political institutions are a critical factor influencing the effectiveness of development resources. More representative and accountable political institutions are linked with more rapid and steady development progress. Within the U.S. government, it is the State Department that has the expertise for assessing the integrity of a country's political institutions. Indeed, U.S. foreign assistance and economic policy is a central element of U.S. relations with most nations in the world (two-thirds of which are developing countries). Yet the State Department does not have a formal relationship with the international lending institutions to discuss U.S. development strategy.

An illustration of how the competing visions of the Treasury Department and State Department have affected the conduct of U.S. policy can be seen in relations toward Nigeria, Indonesia, Ukraine, and Colombia. In the late 1990s, these four countries were identified by the State Department as being strategic priorities for U.S. foreign policy. All were new or struggling democracies, with large populations and economies that were highly important to their regions. Several had sizeable large Muslim populations or faced internal tensions that could have thrown them into conflict if not managed with care. In an effort to devise comprehensive strategies for assisting these target countries, the State Department attempted to initiate a dialogue with the World Bank. However, before a scheduled breakfast meeting between the secretary of state and the World Bank president could take place, the Treasury Department secretary intervened in an attempt to scuttle the meeting. In the end, the breakfast was held—though with a Treasury Department representative present—changing the breadth and tenor of the dialogue.

The Treasury Department's influence over development policy extends beyond direct meetings with World Bank officials. Economists within other U.S. government departments engaged with developing countries have reportedly dropped certain development initiatives pursued by their own agencies out of fear of being excluded from subsequent Treasury Department-led interagency meetings.

To address these shortcomings in the U.S. government's approach to development policy, we recommend the creation of a formal development policy coordination panel composed of the Secretaries of Treasury and State as well as the administrator of USAID, and the head of the MCC. Each of the four individuals would represent a unique and vital perspective to

development policy globally and toward individual countries. Consequently, each would have an equal voice on the development policycoordi-
nation panel.[30] As the primary agency responsible for coordinating U.S.
foreign policy, the secretary of state would chair. Policy coordination with
the international financial institutions would be undertaken with the development policy panel rather than solely with the Treasury Department,
as has been the case historically. Similarly, nominations and authority for
the positions of U.S. executive director to the respective IFIs—the
American official who sits on these institutions' boards—would come from
the panel. The aim of this arrangement would be to incorporate a broader
range of considerations, including development and democracy objectives,
into a framework of sound macroeconomic policy support. Although some
would argue that this would be an unwieldy arrangement, the U.S. government's designation of the secretary of state to chair the board of the newly
established Millennium Challenge Corporation is a tacit recognition not
only of the complementarities but the centrality of political considerations
to the effectiveness of development policy. In addition, with the international lending organizations increasingly being asked to pursue objectives
beyond the purely economic, it just makes sense for Washington to expand
the basis of its dealings with them.

The development policy coordination panel would also be a point of
high-level intersection with other U.S. government agencies having dealings in the developing world. The creation of such a forum would provide
an opportunity to fashion a coherent U.S. government strategy on development issues, and toward the developing world in general—something
that has not existed since the 1960s. Currently, much policy affecting developing countries occurs on an ad hoc basis. What coordination does
occur is largely informal. The departments of Commerce, Agriculture,
Labor, and Defense, as well as the Overseas Private Investment
Corporation, the Trade Development Authority, the Office of the U.S.
Trade Representative, and Environmental Protection Agency, would be logical interlocutors with the development coordination panel. Their participation would ensure that a broad array of issues beyond just financial
assistance would be considered in forging development policy. The
Commerce Department's engagement with the panel, for example, would
forge a stronger relationship between development policymakers and international investors. Currently investors face a major informational challenge in delineating stellar reformers. All countries in certain regions are at
times lumped together—and are thereby unjustly downgraded by reports
of political instability or malfeasance by one of their neighbors.[31]
Commerce's interaction with the development panel would facilitate
clearer "signaling" to private investors as to which developing countries

were felt to be making genuine progress toward a reliable system of rule of law, transparency, and political accountability—and thus to lower-risk status. The investment subsequently directed to these countries would further reinforce the advantages of reform.

Similarly, the development policy panel would be a mechanism to coordinate the United States' sometimes clashing domestic and international agendas toward the developing world. The United States' proselytization of the merits of free trade to the largely rural-based economies of the developing world while simultaneously deepening subsidies to its corporate agri-businesses and textile sectors is a case in point. Domestic political pressures undercut logical avenues for development for many poor countries, and global commitment for a liberalized free market economic structure suffers as a result. The policy coordination panel might not be able to fix this contradiction, but at least it would provide an executive-level forum for addressing it.

The overhaul we are proposing would mirror to some extent the European Bank for Reconstruction and Development's model of forging ties with the foreign ministries as well as the finance ministries of member states. The explicit recognition of the broader considerations involved in development policy would be an important step forward. Moreover, a systematized interagency policy structure would allow for greater sensitivity to the democratic consequences of economic stagnation or lethargic development assistance. In the process, the door to a more innovative foreign policy in relation to the developing world could be opened.

Security Waiver

National security concerns have been a major impediment to democratization and development progress over the past half-century. The threat of communism and the desire to maintain military access to geographically strategic areas around the world have compelled the United States to support numerous autocrats in the interests of national security. As we argued in Chapter 4, the subsequent setbacks to democratization and economic development were frequently deep and long lasting. The fallout from this continues to be felt, not least in the widely held perception that development assistance is a waste of time and money. The persistence of conflict among U.S.-supported autocrats has posed further serious obstacles to development and democracy in these countries.

Given the longstanding deleterious consequences stemming from U.S.-supported autocracies over the past 50 years, the United States should henceforth refrain from providing development assistance and other budgetary support to autocratic governments. The obvious short-term benefits of such relationships often obscure the much more unpredictable, multifaceted and intractable long-term costs. We don't wish to be dogmatic about this; we realize that in some instances the United States might have to collaborate with an autocratic leadership for reasons of national security. Should this determination be made, however, we recommend the following guidelines be adopted to mitigate the potential long-term costs:

1. Require a Security Waiver. Assistance to an autocratic government should be identified for what it is—a security relationship. A "security waiver" acknowledging a deviation from the established policy of supporting democratization should thereby be invoked by the president. To limit the damage to America's reputation as a champion of democracy, any financial or material support subsequently provided to this new ally should not be drawn from existing development, humanitarian-assistance, or economic-support funds, but should come entirely from national security accounts. This requirement would not only preserve development money for its intended recipients but would also give consistency to America's strategic objective of promoting democracy around the world.

2. Set a Time Limit. Aid to a dictatorship should end as soon as the security concern has been addressed. Naturally, this is easier said than done. Relationships between states, once initiated, often build a momentum of their own, and further justifications emerge for maintaining them. To assure a meaningful continuation of a security waiver, it should be recertified annually by the president. Resistance to reverting to the default pro-democracy policy can be expected. The "constructive engagement"[32] argument is surely to be invoked. However, if U.S. foreign policy leaders recognize the short- and long-term security and development rationale behind a democratic policy orientation and are committed to its implementation, then these arguments must be overruled. Sticking to a policy that favors democracies will not only advance U.S. national interests more efficiently than open-ended exceptions, but it will also send a message to developing countries that Washington is genuine about its commitment to democracy. This will, in turn, uphold democracy as the requisite credential meriting international legitimacy and financial support.

3. Limit the Scope. The United States should make it clear from the start that any support for an autocratic regime will be strictly limited and should not be construed as an endorsement of the regime or its policies. The United States might also spell out reforms that the ally-of-convenience could take that would lead to a long-term improvement in relations—a long shot, to be sure, but worth trying. Such a

stance would put the government on notice that the United States is keeping it at arm's length and in no way giving the green light for extra-constitutional or repressive actions.

4. Set a Clear Exit Strategy. In supporting an autocratic government, the United States should follow the military rule of thumb of establishing not only its objectives before launching an engagement, but also an exit strategy. After all, however temporary, helping out a dictatorship is a Faustian bargain with a partner that is inherently unstable and holds the potential for turning into a security threat. The United States should therefore approach it with the same cautious attitude it would an armed conflict—something to be avoided if possible and to be pursued efficiently if undertaken. The very process of devising an explicit exit strategy will drive home the point to policy makers that this is a limited operation. It will also compel them to establish a clear rationale for entering into such relationships, define the goals of those relationships, and set down the circumstances for ending them. Although events will unfold in a fluid and unpredictable manner, just as they do in combat, better defining the endpoint during the planning process will give United States policymakers clearer guidelines for subsequent courses of action.

Improving the Process of Bilateral Development Assistance

As necessary as a fundamental reorientation of U.S. agencies dealing with the developing world is, this is insufficient to improve the effectiveness of development assistance efforts. Certain less formal but important procedural changes and reweighting of priorities are also needed.

Support Institutions Not Individuals

As we have said before, donors who are intent on supporting democracy and development should focus their attention on institutions, not individuals. Politicians might have charisma and enjoy great popularity, both among their own people and within the donor community, but they won't be around forever. Robust institutions are much more durable. And placing too much faith—and money and political capital—in individuals might give even the most democratic among them an unhealthy taste for unchecked power and tempt them into despotic ways. Donors need to focus on institutional reform, through which the prospects for sustained development and successful democratization are systematically strengthened for both the short- and long-term. In other words, donors should be less focused on the identity of a particular leader or even the policies he or she may pursue. Rather, their attention should be on the processes by which that leader came to power. To the extent that these are democratic—participatory, representative, and transparent—the greater the likelihood that democracy's moderating and self-correcting forces will be activated. Not only will more effective development policies result but the burden for correcting poorly designed schemes will shift to the domestic political institutions from international development agencies.

We acknowledge that separating personal ambitions from institutional development may at times be difficult. However, it is important for the United States to make the distinction and to advance the latter rather than the former. If a leader is democratically selected, there is a greater likelihood than if he were not that the development initiatives he or she pursues will address the needs of the population. That he or she benefits under these circumstances is simply part of the incentive structure that makes democratic government work. In this process, donors should aim to strengthen what we call "accountability institutions." By that, we mean institutions such as a free press, an independent judiciary, a meritocratic civil service, an independent private sector, market-based financial and capital institutions, standardized accounting and audit norms, opposition political parties, an empowered legislature, a vibrant civil society, an anticorruption office, and an independent central bank. These institutions will enhance political competition—thereby fostering a competition of ideas, increased transparency, and improved responsiveness on the part of the government. They will also contribute to increased economic efficiency by rewarding innovation, facilitating the equitable access of credit and business opportunities to entrepreneurs, and increasing openness to new technologies.

U.S. development assistance should aim to ensure their resources are facilitating the creation of these accountability institutions. Some may argue that such a focus is too long-term in nature to be of relevance for policy guidance. To this we point out that institutions evolve. In the process, incremental development benefits are realized. As important from a development policy perspective, therefore, is the direction in which these institutions are changing rather than their current level of robustness. The key question is, are these institutions growing more accountable, more transparent, and more representative?

Support Civil Society

Of particular importance to a democracy-oriented development strategy is the strengthening of civil society. This is the network of nonprofit public service organizations such as neighborhood associations, civic groups, social welfare organizations, think tanks, human and labor rights groups, and advocacy organizations that are independent of the government. In addition to the direct benefit these organizations provide, they are incubators of independent thinking and instruments for exposing the influence of special interests and keeping public officials honest and responsive to the citizens.

Active support for civil society is a central part of an effective development strategy. The more the community becomes involved in development activities, the more it will support and sustain them. This hands-on participation also generates experience in the exercise of democratic processes. In societies stultified by long periods of dictatorial rule, of course, civil society may be nearly nonexistent and building it up from scratch will require funding, education, and technical support. In others, less effort will be needed. Regardless, donors must approach this process judiciously. Semi-authoritarian[33] governments are becoming more sophisticated at co-opting civil society in the post-Cold War era by allowing the appearance of a robust civic life to flourish while withholding registrations, directing funding to favored agencies, discrediting the integrity and effectiveness of civic organizations they don't like, and creating pro-government front organizations.[34] Using these techniques, they are able to give the impression of creating a more open society while stymieing truly independent action.

The evolving strategies to mask authoritarian control of civil society demand commensurately greater perceptivity and sophistication on the part of bilateral donors. Vitality of civil society is a tangible measure of openness and a critical element in the categorization of governments as democratic, democratizing, or autocratic. Governments that have attempted to co-opt civil society should be appropriately included in the autocratic category.

Some scholars and international civil servants, lamenting the weakness of many developing country governments, have criticized the increase in donor funding for civil society that took place in the 1990s.[35] In this zero-sum view, developing country governments are weak because civil society is gaining greater capacity and access to external funding. Consequently, they argue, an even greater share of bilateral assistance should flow to developing country governments and multilateral agencies (that channel virtually all of their resources through national governments).

We believe this perspective misidentifies the problem. Strong government and civil society are mutually reinforcing and positively correlated. Consider the United States. It has one of the most active civil societies in the world—yet few would claim it has a weak government. The same relationship applies in the developing world. Benin, Costa Rica, Chile, Czech Republic, Ghana, Korea, Mauritius, Poland, Senegal, and Thailand are a few of the countries in the developing world that have vibrant civil societies and yet quite capable governments within the norms of their respective regions.

In our view, overly centralized and unaccountable governments are not the means to development. Rather, the corruption and patronage they tend to spawn are often a major impediment to effective development. A development strategy that simply provides them with more resources will not contribute to a solution. It will much more likely deepen the hole from which these countries will need to climb. Indeed, the vast majority of development funds that have been wasted are resources that flowed through national governments—no doubt contributing to international development's perceived poor track record. Further restricting the flow of development resources to national government channels and the exclusion of civil society would not only be of questionable developmental value, but it would also contribute toward suffocating a mechanism through which greater transparency could be introduced. In turn, so long as transparency is limited, private sector development will remain stunted. Strong, accountable government is critical to development. An active civil society, rather than undermining, is an essential and complementary ingredient to building and maintaining that accountability.

Bilateral Donor Coordination

By making it their policy to favor democracies in the allocation of development aid, bilateral donors would be providing a strong incentive for developing countries to undertake difficult political and economic reforms. For this strategy to work, developing countries making the most progress toward reform should benefit more. This would require donors to coordinate their activities at both the macroeconomic and project levels so that one of them doesn't rush in to fill in the gap left by another that has withheld support in response to financial malfeasance or political oppression. Historically, donors have in fact undermined one another's efforts in this way, often inadvertently, thereby weakening incentives for change. For example, French support for the authoritarian governments of Cameroon, Togo, and Burkina Faso in the early 1990s undercut efforts by the IFIs and bilateral donors alike to push them toward reform.[36]

Donor reform is therefore required both on conceptual and procedural levels. Conceptually, donors need to agree on what they are trying to achieve. Bilateral donors need to understand democracy's clear advantage in economic development. The Canadian International Development Agency, Swedish International Development Agency, European Union, and USAID have at least already explicitly listed democracy as an objective in their development strategies. Democracy is also identified as an integral component of development guidelines signed by donors and developing countries as part of the Organization of American States, the New Partnership for African Development, and the Cotonou Agreement between the European Union and the African, Caribbean, and Pacific (ACP) countries, among others. Furthermore, the European Bank for Reconstruction and Development's dual objectives of development *and* democracy are strongly supported across Europe.

The next stage of this process will involve moving past the rhetorical vision to implementing more cogent strategies for ensuring that both development and democratization objectives are complementary. The United States would appear to be the key actor in shaping such new norms. Because of its geo-strategic agenda, the United States is the donor country that historically has most frequently used its development resources in a way that has undermined democracy (as described in Chapter 4).[37] If the United States fully embraced a democracy-oriented development strategy, there is a good likelihood that it would gain conceptual traction among other key bilateral donors. With this framework in hand, bilateral donors could collectively agree on which countries qualify as democracies, which as democratizers, and which as autocracies. Obtaining such consensus and acting in a coordinated manner toward each category of country would go a long way toward creating a global incentive structure for reform.

Procedural coordination would be enhanced if bilateral donors could agree on guidelines for improving collective action. These may include methods for in-country coordination by geographic regions or development sectors so as to reduce overlap and competition. Donors should also agree to refrain from making up for aid that has been dropped by others for reasons of corruption or veering off the democratic path. And they should show greater discipline themselves in penalizing such behavior.

As for internal procedures, donors need to realize that a decision by one can affect the collective impact of all—and alter the way they assess staff performance. Volume of assistance should be discarded as a factor and replaced by *quality* of assistance, as measured by such variables as project sustainability, difficulty of operating environment, accountability for funds disbursed, institutional and human capacity gained, and improvements in social welfare.

Some have suggested that advocating improved donor coordination is akin to advocating a donor cartel.[38] This is a misguided comparison. Development assistance does not resemble a competitive market on either the supply or the demand side. Because donors have not consistently applied performance or accountability criteria in their selection of recipients, developing countries do not compete to attract "development investment." Donor decisions to fund a given country are frequently made on political or strategic grounds. And within recipient countries relatively few channels exist through which development resources can flow, leaving the national government with near monopoly power over where it goes. The effect is to further entrench unresponsive governments. With only one primary "buyer," coupled with donors' bureaucratically driven penchant for increasing loan volume, incentives to maintain accountability standards are weak. The result is the paradox of a dearth of funds for worthy development initiatives, many run by private development agencies and provincial governments, and an overabundance of money for certain central governments. Rather than creating a cartel, improving donor coordination is a matter of enhancing information sharing and standardizing basic rules of the game. This is an indispensable element of a well-functioning market and an antidote to monopolistic practices that reinforce unaccountable governance.

The problem of donor coordination is a commonly cited development challenge[39] and by discussing it here, we are simply acknowledging its importance. The main thrust of our argument is that making democracy the standard for providing assistance is the best way to influence procedural and institutional changes necessary for economic development. But that won't happen without donor cooperation.

Summary

We believe that democracy should be a central guiding criterion in determining preferences for U.S. development assistance. In our view, democracies hold fundamentally greater prospects for using foreign assistance effectively. Democracies, therefore, should be given top priority in the allocation of limited assistance resources. We urge the U.S. government, which by virtue of its economic and diplomatic muscle can shape the global-development political debate more than any other country, to adopt this stance.

The level of development assistance will not, on its own, eliminate poverty and propel all countries onto a developmental path. This will only occur through the creation of institutions that reward innovation, increase productivity, and enhance human capacity. In addition, domestic resources and private capital both dwarf official development funding. In view of this reality, all development assistance provided by the U.S. government should be evaluated by how well it creates incentives for institutional reform. Creating institutional checks and balances will foster more accountable government, strengthening both democracy and more productive development.

Pursuing an institution-led development strategy will first require establishing a consensus among key departments of the U.S. government. It will also require a more balanced approach to how the United States pursues its development agenda. Rather than relying nearly exclusively on the macroeconomic focus of the Department of Treasury for setting priorities with the multilateral financial institutions, sectors of the U.S. government that bring development expertise and emphasis should also be systematically involved. By putting more of its development aid into democratizing countries, the donor community would also be alerting the private sector to promising investment environments, further facilitating prospects for long-term growth there.

A democracy-oriented development strategy also calls for the United States to dramatically restrict its funding of autocratic governments—even in the face of apparent security or economic imperatives. Failing to do so hampers the overarching security goal of creating a global community of stable and prospering democratic states.

CHAPTER 7

Bringing Democracy to
the Center of Development

> In any society with autocratic governments, an autocrat with the same
> incentives as a roving bandit is bound to appear sooner or later. And as
> we should expect, the examples of confiscations, repudiated loans, de-
> based coinages, and inflated currencies perpetuated by monarchs and
> dictators over the course of history are beyond counting.
>
> **Mancur Olson**
> *Power and Prosperity*

Previous chapters have made the point that democratic, accountable political institutions are both an end in themselves and an effective means toward the separate goal of development. This chapter examines a series of
policy recommendations aimed at incorporating considerations of democracy and good governance more centrally into the development decision-
making of multilateral financial institutions. We contend that international
financial institutions (IFIs) ought to differentiate between democracies and
other governance regimes when entering into lending agreements and for-
mulating overall strategy. This is justified because of democracies' greater
political legitimacy as well as their generally superior development record.
The IFIs should also be willing to demonstrate greater flexibility in the implementation of their policies in young democracies when the repercussions of economic reform threaten to trigger a popular backlash.

Differential treatment would require a shift in the financial institutions' self-perception as purely technocratic organizations that focus solely on economic criteria and refuse to compromise their objectivity by delving into political considerations. We contend that this self-image is illusory. All development activities have inescapable political ramifications because they involve financial transfers and thus affect power relationships. Indeed, those ramifications are particularly acute in developing countries with nascent democratic institutions. We call on the IFIs to recognize this reality. Rather than taking a position of official indifference over how a country is governed, they should embrace and promote democracies. This makes all the more sense in that most of the assets of these international bodies are owned by industrialized democracies.

Set Democracy as an Objective in IFIs Charters

To ignore governance as a factor in policy decisions assumes that the type of political system through which development assistance is channeled makes no difference. From this perspective, development is purely an economic or technical phenomenon. The superficial attractiveness of maintaining such a separation is understandable. Keeping technical and political considerations distinct simplifies decision-making. Economic policymakers can focus on actions that enhance economic growth without worrying about noneconomic consequences. Taking political factors into consideration, however, opens the door to a clearer identification of the development challenges facing a particular transitional country. While a more complicated undertaking, it offers the potential to improve the effectiveness of macroeconomic policy and development objectives.

Historical Origins of the Separation of Political Institutions from Economic Policy

The technocratic approach employed by the IFIs can be explained by their origins. They were created by the world's bankers in the aftermath of World War II in order to create a stable international financial architecture to address the pressing challenges of that time. This included the reconstruction of Europe, the revitalization of the global economy by reducing the risks to foreign investment, the stabilization of exchange rates, and the promotion of international trade.[1] Raising living standards for the developing nations of the world was not an overt aim.

This technocratic emphasis was clearly reflected in the charters of the Bretton Woods institutions. Political considerations were explicitly prohibited in financial decision-making. For example, Article III, Section 5, paragraph (b) of the World Bank's charter states

The Bank shall make arrangements to ensure that the proceeds of any loan are used only for the purposes for which the loan was granted, with due attention to considerations of economy and efficiency and without regard to political or other noneconomic influences or considerations.

Article IV, Section 10 of the World Bank charter further clarifies that this political prohibition also applies to the consideration of regime type:

The Bank and its officers shall not interfere in the political affairs of any member; nor shall they be influenced in their decisions by the political character of the member or members concerned. Only economic considerations shall be relevant to their decisions, and these considerations shall be weighed impartially in order to achieve the purposes (of the Bank).

The designers went to great lengths to ensure that the institutions maintain a technocratic mind-set. Not only did they intend for these bodies to have an exclusive economic focus, they also clearly wanted to ensure that the world's bankers and economists maintained control of the new architecture. Article III, Section 2 of the World Bank's Articles of Agreement included the stipulation:

Each member shall deal with the Bank only through its Treasury, Central Bank, stabilization fund, or other similar fiscal agency, and the Bank shall deal with members only by or through the same agencies.

The ostensible goal of the IFIs' designers to compartmentalize economic policy from political considerations is laudable. Exposing economic decision-making to unchecked political pressures would make it vulnerable to manipulation. Furthermore, insulating economic policymaking from short-term political pressures has been widely recognized as important for long term, fundamentally sound policies. Indeed, this has been the rationale for creating autonomous central banks within national governments, including the U.S. Federal Reserve.

The global context in 1944 also had a direct influence on the political prohibition clause. At the time the World Bank and IMF charters were drafted, only ⅓ of the world's states were democracies. Of the World Bank's original 37 members, only 10 were democracies. Limiting the Bretton Woods institutions' activities to these democracies would have undermined the vision of creating a global economic body. The political-prohibition clause, in particular, was an outgrowth of this period and its emerging Cold War dynamics. Treasury Secretary Harry White, who along with John

Maynard Keynes was the main architect of the Bretton Woods system, believed that the Soviet Union must be included if the new structure were to be stable.[2] Despite his efforts, the Soviet Union declined membership. The political-prohibition clause, however, was retained. In short, given the focus on rebuilding the war-ravaged societies of Europe, the desire to create a global financial architecture that would stabilize the major economies and prevent a return to the Great Depression, and the prevailing geo-strategic realities of that era, considerations of democracy were a low priority in the creation of the first IFIs, even among the established democracies of that period.

Following the lead of the Bretton Woods charters and the strong influence of the World Bank, the regional multilateral banks that were subsequently set up by and large adopted similar organizing principles. Weighing noneconomic factors was expressly prohibited at the founding of the Inter-American, African, and Asian development banks in 1959, 1963, and 1965, respectively.

Evolution of Governance in IFI Policies

In the late 1960s, with post-World War II reconstruction largely completed, the World Bank, under the leadership of Robert McNamara, added poverty alleviation to macroeconomic stability as a primary objective of the Bank's mission. The World Bank's attention thus expanded to include health, nutrition, education, agriculture and rural development, population, and other poverty-related issues. Bank funding levels subsequently increased nine-fold between 1968 and 1978. After a decade of mixed results, however, the Bank began conditioning its loans on public-sector reform as part of its structural adjustment programs. This required reducing the number of civil servants, restructuring ministries, liquidating or privatizing public enterprises, and enacting legislative changes pertaining to labor regulations, investment, and taxation in order to foster an "enabling business environment."[3] By the late 1980s, poor governance was explicitly cited as a fundamental contributing factor to underdevelopment.[4] Over time, the Bank was drawn directly into projects supporting good governance, including civil-sector reform, legal reform, accountability systems for public funds, and establishing budget discipline (including the manner in which a country made its federal budget priorities).[5] In other words, the Bank had become heavily engaged in influencing the political landscape in the countries in which it was involved, even if it was not overtly attempting (or claiming that it was attempting) to do so.

In an effort to reconcile the Bank's expanding governance agenda with the prohibition against considering political factors in lending decisions,

Ibrahim Shihata, the long-time general counsel at the World Bank, issued an influential legal memorandum on the subject. The thrust of his position was that the Bank's involvement in the area of governance was justified on the grounds of economic efficiency.[6] That is, if an action were deemed necessary to meet the Bank's economic goals, then it was acceptable under the mandate. In this way, governance considerations were but the "logical last step in [the Bank's] gradually expanding involvement in policy reform."[7]

However, Shihata's interpretation of governance was highly qualified. Good governance was limited to maintaining "good order," by which he meant, "having a system based on abstract rules" (that is, the rule of law). The Bank's support for governance projects was justified in that a prerequisite to economic development was a "stable business environment" and "a modern state." Although he recognized there is a political economy facet of governance-related activities, he cited the *Compact Edition of the Oxford Encyclopedia's* narrow definition of political economy, "the art or practical science of managing the resources of a nation so as to increase its natural prosperity," to limit his interpretation to its economic dimensions.

Acknowledging development practitioners' experience that community participation was an indispensable element of successful development, Shihata noted, "This form of participation has been readily accepted as relevant to the success of the projects financed by the Bank . . . However, this should not lead the Bank to prescribe for a borrowing country any particular political system or form of government." Interestingly, he adds, "There may be extreme cases where the Bank staff reach the firm conclusion that compliance with rules relevant to Bank operations in a given community is not possible without a measure of popular participation in the making of such rules. In such cases, the Bank's concern with the issue of compliance may substantiate its pursuit in the policy dialogue with a given country of a form of popular participation in the making of such relevant rules taking into account the country's cultural values and its stage of development."[8]

Shihata thereby acknowledged the important role that governance plays in development. Furthermore, he interpreted this as falling within the Bank's mandate so long as it contributed to compliance and the Bank's goal of improving economic efficiency. Although he clearly intended to communicate a narrow interpretation of governance, his statement regarding "extreme cases" could easily have been used as a legal substantiation for supporting democratic participation in a score of repressive states mired in poverty. Yet the World Bank and the other IFIs have, thus far, chosen not to do so.

Nevertheless, the intertwining of economics and politics that takes place in every country has steadily pushed the IFIs to incorporate governance issues in their economic-development policymaking. The World

Bank, frustrated by the paralyzing effects of corruption and misgovernment on development in Africa in the 1980s, led the way with its approval of a staff paper on sound development management in 1991. That paper provided a framework for Bank lending for public sector reform in the 1990s.[9] From that point on, the Bank's views on development evolved rapidly toward a full embrace of governance themes as its 1997 World Development Report, *The State in a Changing World*, attests. In that same year (the very year Indonesia suffered its cataclysmic collapse), the World Bank created a Governance and Public Sector Reform unit to help strengthen its work on institutional reform and corruption. The Bank's early governance efforts largely focused on the economic sector—public expenditure analysis, tax policy, civil service reform, legal institutions, and the like. In 1999, it began conducting Institutional Governance Reviews of client countries aimed at tracing public-sector problems like poor delivery of services, corruption, and misguided economic policies to their governance roots in order to devise more effective institution-building programs.[10]

Starting in the late 1990s, the World Bank also began requiring a Poverty Reduction Strategy Paper (PRSP) from each prospective recipient government. The aim of this innovation was to initiate greater public participation in the review of new World Bank-funded projects, providing more opportunity to vet concerns and forge national ownership. While conceptually another step forward for the World Bank—long criticized for its closed decision-making process—in practice the quality of the PRSP process varies widely by country. Lacking formal guidelines, the procedures undertaken to meet the PRSP criterion are left up to the recipient governments. The end result is that the extensiveness of participation, comprehensiveness of deliberation, and seriousness with which public input is considered are largely proportional to the openness and representativeness of the national government. Those countries most in need of greater public involvement are typically left with the sketchiest PRSP process.

The IMF's consideration of governance has largely mirrored, though lagged, that of the World Bank. The political-prohibition clause was narrowly and for the most part noncontroversially applied from the Fund's establishment through the 1980s.[11] A former director of the IMF's Exchange and Trade Relations Department concisely summarized this view: "[The IMF] has not been established to give guidance on social and political priorities, nor has its voting system been designed to give it moral authority to oversee priorities of a noneconomic nature. Its functions have to be kept narrowly technical if it is to be effective in the exercise of its role as a promoter of the adjustment process. For this purpose, the Fund has to accept that the authorities of a country are the sole judges of its social and political priorities."[12]

The end of the Cold War and the growing recognition that the political situation in a member country was a dominant influence on its implementation of IMF agreements have led the Fund to increase its emphasis on governance issues since the mid-1990s. In 1996, the IMF was urged by its board of governors to "promote good governance in all its aspects including by ensuring the rule of law, improving the efficiency and accountability of the public sector, and tackling corruption, as essential elements of a framework within which economies can prosper."[13] Although expanding its focus on good governance, the board's injunction was restricted by the qualification that "the IMF's judgments should not be influenced by the nature of a political regime of a country . . . "[14] The IMF thus attempted to focus its governance efforts on those aspects that could have a significant macroeconomic impact.[15] In practical terms, this played out as giving more attention to reducing corruption—improving the management of public resources (through reforms of public sector institutions such as the central bank, the treasury, public enterprises, and the civil service) and supporting a transparent and stable economic and regulatory environment conducive to efficient private-sector activities (like pricing, trade, and banking systems). For example, to promote transparency the IMF has encouraged client countries to adopt manufacturing and accounting standards and corporate codes of conduct. Redressing corruption has increasingly become a condition of eligibility for IMF loans.[16]

Thus, the IFIs have made considerable conceptual and operational headway in linking good governance to development. They have come to see that merely streamlining government bureaucracy won't make for better government. The World Bank, in fact, has explicitly recognized the need for political competition and a greater voice for the citizenry in political decision-making to achieve good governance.[17] In other words, international lenders have walked up to the doorstep of the integration of political institutions and economics, yet they have been unable to step through. More than half a century after the creation of the Bretton Woods institutions, their charters remain virtually unaltered. And this despite the end of the Cold War, the global movement toward democracy, the accumulated experience of development effectiveness, and a shift in the principal aims of the World Bank.

The tension at these Bretton Woods institutions between promoting more effective development and overstepping their mandates' restrictions on considering a country's political system remains unresolved. It is as though after discovering a long-missing piece of a complex jigsaw puzzle, they are prevented from putting it into its proper place. Or, to use another metaphor, it is as if after groping in a dark cave for hours, they have found a flashlight with the switch covered by a safety lock. The effect of the charter prohibitions has been to preclude consideration of highly pertinent criteria to sound economic policymaking. Good governance entails institutional mechanisms that hold leaders accountable to their populations—in short, democratic institutions. In our view, until the IFIs find a solution to this impasse, their development initiatives will continue to be considerably less effective than they aim to be.

The news from regional multilateral development agencies is somewhat more encouraging. Historically, they have followed the World Bank's precedent on governance in both its conceptual and operational orientation. However, in recent years some of these regional organizations have begun to take the intellectual lead in the explicit, if gradual, recognition that democratic governance is central to development. In 1999, in an appendix on governance to the amended African Development Bank charter, democratic governance was cited as the desired goal for all member states. In the Cotonou Agreement between the members of the African, Caribbean, and Pacific Group of States and the European Commission in 2000, democracy was identified as both integral to sustainable development and reinforced by it. In 2001, the Organization of American States adopted a democracy charter explicitly affirming democratic government as the standard for relations between states in the hemisphere. Furthermore, the organization encouraged the Inter-American Development Bank, the World Bank, and all relevant international donor agencies to consider the promotion of democracy in their development decision-making. In 2002, the African Union endorsed the New Partnership for African Development guidelines for development that cite democratic governance as a criterion for future development assistance. The U.S. government's announcement of the MCA in 2002, in which only states deemed to be ruling justly would qualify for this new pot of development funding, was in keeping with this trend.

European Bank of Reconstruction and Development

One regional multilateral bank, however, stands out from the crowd for its unequivocal support of democracy: the European Bank of Reconstruction and Development (EBRD). Born in a vastly different era than the other multilateral development banks, the EBRD explicitly endorses the complementary goals of economic growth and democratization. In fact, the first line of the preamble of the Agreement that established it in 1990 captures this theme:

> The contracting parties, committed to the fundamental principles of multiparty democracy, the rule of law, respect for human rights, and market economics . . .

The significance of the political objective to the EBRD's mission is clearly declared in Article 1 (Purpose) of the Agreement:

In contributing to economic progress and reconstruction, the purpose of the Bank shall be to foster the transition toward open market-oriented economies and to promote private and entrepreneurial initiative in the Central and Eastern European countries committed to and applying the principles of multiparty democracy, pluralism and market economics.

This new institution, dedicated to the strengthening of democracy and market economics, represented a consensus in modern European societies about the relationship between the two.[18] Perhaps equally astoundingly in the slow-moving arena of multinational development lending, the EBRD was established just seven months after its conception.

Its commitment to the twin mandates of economic development and democracy remains strong some 15 years after its founding. It has been actively involved in ensuring that democratic processes advanced hand in hand with the transition to open-market economies in Poland, Hungary, the Czech Republic, Slovakia, Slovenia, as well as other states. And it continues to make commitment to political reform a central factor in its involvement in any given country.

Contrary to the fears of those who have argued against bringing political considerations into international lenders' decision-making, the EBRD has been financially profitable. By the close of 2003, it had disbursed loans totaling 22.7 billion euros in 27 countries, with commitments averaging nearly 4 billion euros a year from 2001 to 2003. It reported a profit of 378 million euros and reserves of nearly 1 billion euro at the end of 2003.[19] As some of the initial central European loan recipients have stabilized and gained unrestricted access to private capital markets, it has increasingly shifted its attention eastward and southward into the former Soviet Union.

Another distinctive characteristic of the EBRD is its interest in strengthening the private sector. Taking the view that a vibrant private sector is not only a primary engine for development but an important counterweight to uni-polar political power in a society, the EBRD actively seeks out and finances promising but cash-strapped private-sector projects, often in partnership with commercial banks, both as a way of defraying those banks' risk and of leveraging private-sector capital. In 2003, 72 percent of EBRD projects were in the private sector. It was widely considered the foremost vehicle for private-sector investment in Central and Eastern Europe and the former Soviet Union at the height of the post-communist transition.[20]

Moreover, unlike the World Bank or the IMF, it does not lend to governments to support macroeconomic policies. It lends solely for projects. A significant portion of its private-sector portfolio is targeted at small- and medium-sized enterprises. It made one-third of its loans to them in 2003, for example, compared with just 2 percent that the International Finance Corporation, the World Bank's private-sector lending arm, commits to this sector. It has both an economic and a political rationale for doing so. Small businesses generate quick economic payoffs, are the major source of new jobs, and are quick to adapt to economic reforms. Yet, in the absence of a free market legacy, they face tight financing constraints. By supporting them, the EBRD not only helps fill a sectoral gap in many post-communist countries that were dominated by large manufacturing, it enhances its goals of supporting decentralization and privatization in transition economies.[21] Targeting them also provides an opportunity for the EBRD to work through local financial intermediaries and thereby help develop the local financial system[22] needed to achieve self-sustainability. And lending to small business has only gained in credibility over the years as defaults have stayed close to zero.

Politically, by assisting in the creation of an entrepreneurial class of small business owners, and more broadly, by strengthening the middle class, historically a bulwark of democracy, such lending furthers the Bank's aims of promoting democratic governance.[23] As Horst Kohler, former EBRD president, once said, the emphasis on lending to small- and medium-sized enterprises "will offset colonization worries by building economic transition from the bottom up."[24]

The EBRD also distinguishes itself from other multilateral lenders—and from commercial ones, for that matter—by providing considerable technical advice to potential loan recipients so as to ensure sound business plans. As part of this assistance, it pays great attention to the state of rule of law in a country. The Bank explicitly frames its loans on the basis of international public law, including relevant treaty obligations and specific arbitration procedures. This is intended to raise a country's legal, environmental, health, and labor standards to the international level, reducing barriers for future international private investment.

The Bank also makes more loans than other international financial institutions for regional projects that can benefit from economies of scale. Otherwise put, it uses its position as a regional development bank to help break down resistance within the various recipient nations to a regional development strategy. It believes this approach is more effective in advancing public welfare goals like upgrading transportation, telecommunications and power systems, environmental protection, public health, financial market regulation, agricultural research, and law enforcement than could be achieved by lending solely on a country-by-country basis.

Although the EBRD monitors each recipient country's progress toward democracy, it isn't dogmatic about rewarding the winners and punishing the losers. This allows it more flexibility in addressing the uniqueness of each context, though such an approach also opens it to criticisms of inconsistency or fecklessness. The EBRD reports on democratic and human rights progress in a "country strategy paper" rather than on a project-by-project basis. And, rather than conducting its own assessments, with the risks of appearing to play favorites, it draws on the work of other organizations, especially the Council of Europe, the European Commission on Human Rights, and the Organization for Economic Cooperation and Development's Office for Democratic Institutions and Human Rights. Democratic progress is measured by the existence of [25]

- free elections;
- representative government in which the executive is accountable to the elected legislature;
- a government that acts in accordance with the constitution and the law, and that makes redress against its administrative decisions available;
- the separation of the state and political parties;
- the independence of the judiciary and equal protection under the law for all, including minorities;
- fair criminal procedures;
- freedom of speech, of the press, and of association, and the right of peaceful assembly;
- freedom of conscience and religion;
- freedom of movement;
- the right to private property; and,
- the right to form trade unions and to strike.

In scaling back lending to a country because of lack of progress toward democratic rule, the EBRD curtails support for public-sector projects before private-sector ones, for national before local ones, and for operational assistance before technical assistance. The EBRD contends that this approach enables it to respond meaningfully to setbacks while remaining engaged. Essentially, it views a country's depth of commitment to democracy as a guidepost, not a litmus test. Thus, it is willing to get involved in dictatorial regimes so long as it perceives a willingness to promote democratic change. This pragmatism gives it leeway to use both the carrot and the stick to nudge countries along the road to the rule of law. For example, the EBRD refused to allow Yugoslavia to become a member until 2001 (after it had democratized and the EBRD was satisfied that basic human rights were being respected). Slovenia, Croatia, and Macedonia—other fragments of the former Yugoslavia—joined in 1993. Similarly, in 2002, the EBRD sent an open letter to Turkmenistan objecting to its suppression of multiparty democracy and threatening to cease lending to it.[26] In 2004, the EBRD froze much of its lending to Uzbekistan for its failure to meet minimum democracy and human rights reforms.

As part of its strategy for building public support for reform and motivating reluctant governments, the EBRD undertakes cross-national surveys that compare the progress being made by countries in the region. In its annual *Transition Report*, it publishes the results of its Legal Indicator Survey of practicing attorneys in all 27 countries in the region,[27] analyzing the reforms—or lack thereof—that have been made in each. It also publishes an annual *Business Environment and Enterprise Performance Survey* for every country in the region, based on surveys of more than 4,000 firms in 22 countries and on reports of teams in all 27 who monitor local attitudes.

These surveys serve primarily as tools for assessing member countries' progress toward reform and for setting the EBRD's priorities for future aid. They also play an increasingly important role in measuring the business climate for investors, and are now frequently cited in business, policy, and academic circles.[28] In this way, the EBRD is providing an important public good while driving home incentives for continued reform.

Unlike the other development banks, which deal exclusively with the finance ministers of the member states, the EBRD also maintains ties with their foreign ministers and with international organizations like the Council of Europe and NATO, reflecting the importance it attaches to political development. In other words, getting the economic policies "right" is not distinct from getting a set of responsible political systems in place. The EBRD also distinguishes itself by its openness to public scrutiny; unlike the World Bank and the IMF, it reports the results of all its meetings, including those with recipient governments, and those of its staff with civic groups, local governments, labor unions, and other constituencies with a stake in development plans. Not only is this an exercise in participatory democracy, but it also reduces the risk that powerful individuals will exert undue influence on state policy.[29]

Although the EBRD wins plaudits from many quarters for its novel approach, it also has its share of detractors. Some assert that it is more focused on profit than on transitions to democracy.[30] Others claim that it has not been adequately stringent in applying its democracy mandate as a condition for assistance,[31] pointing out that it maintains a presence in less than fully democratic Belarus, and Turkmenistan. Others worry about the use of public funds to generate private gains and about the methods for choosing which private firms should get loans. Still others fret that by lending to the private sector, the EBRD is competing with commercial lenders and thereby slowing economic development.[32] Then there are those who question mixing politics and economics, and suggest that if the projects really are sound, they should be left to the commercial banks.[33] Some economists even argue a variant of the authoritarian-advantage view—that by delaying financing on political grounds also delays a country's transition to democracy.[34] Yet other criticisms focus on the Bank's management procedures. Because of its extensive review of the legal framework of a country and its efforts to reconcile post-communist legal structures with European standards, the EBRD is accused of being overly bureaucratic and inflexible. These critics argue it would be better to change one aspect of the law at a time and reward this engagement with infusions of capital, thereby moving the process along. The arduous loan review process and book-sized contracts are felt to deter many potential entrepreneurs.[35] Comparatively few criticisms have been made on financial grounds—with the notable exception of the losses the EBRD incurred in the 1998 Russian financial meltdown, in which the Bank lost $235 million in bad loans (out of a total exposure of $3 billion).[36]

For all of the carping, skepticism about the European Bank's overall effectiveness has largely subsided nearly 15 years after its formation.[37] At the 2002 Annual Meeting of the Bank by Paul O'Neill, then U.S. Treasury Secretary remarked: "I have come [here] because I think the EBRD has been an exceptionally effective tool for development and transition in the region. It is uniquely endowed with a mandate to support countries committed to and applying the principles of multiparty democracy, pluralism, and market economics."

The EBRD, then, has shown that a major multilateral lending institution can simultaneously support sound economic practices while advancing democratic political institutions. And it has done so in a region where neither democracy nor market economics had very deep roots.

Global Trends Toward Democracy
Let us not forget that the growing recognition of the importance of democratic political institutions has occurred during a period when there have been widespread shifts toward democracy around the world. Whereas less than one-third of the world's states were democracies in 1947, more than two-thirds were on a democratic path in the early twenty-first century, according to Freedom House's annual surveys. This trend is also reflected among World Bank shareholders. Although the relative share of World Bank assets owned by the United States has diminished to 17 percent from 38 percent in 1947, shares held by members of the Community of Democracies

now total 88.5 percent.[38] Nineteen of the 24 executive directors are from Community of Democracy members.

The global movement toward democracy has, understandably, had an impact on how individual states relate with the rest of the world. With the end of the Cold War the formerly taboo topic of regime type is commonly raised. Exemplifying this shift, several multilateral organizations have officially adopted declarations espousing democratic governance as the norm for their members. These include the African Union, the Caribbean Community, the Commonwealth, the Council of Europe, the New Economic Partnership for African Development, the Organization of American States and Summit of the Americas, the Organization for Security and Cooperation in Europe, and the United Nations Development Program.[39]

The growing emphasis on political factors in global bodies is paralleled by a similar trend within the private sector. CalPERS, the Californian public employees pension fund (and the largest pension fund in the United States), started weighing corporations' governance practices, their treatment of workers and their records on human rights as factors in its investment decisions in 2002. Ashmore Investment Management, considered one of the leading investment firms in emerging markets, cites its extensive weighting of political factors as a distinctive feature to its success.[40] Similarly, in 1997, the White House Apparel Industry Partnership (now the Fair Labor Association), representing major labels such as Phillip van Heusen, Levis-Strauss, Adidas, and Liz Claiborne, established a Code of Conduct setting minimum human rights and labor rights standards for all apparel firms with which they deal. Obviously, such a stance makes for good public relations as well as higher profits. Yet it is also another indication of the connection between democratic governance and stable development.

Recommendations

The growing recognition of this connection in both the public and private spheres shows how much the world has changed since 1947. Even so, while the IFIs have made some modifications to their operating procedures over the years, they are still functioning with a charter oriented to an earlier, less democratic era. To more effectively serve their developmental aims, we recommend that they amend their charters to

- Explicitly acknowledge the importance of political institutions to development.
- Make the pursuit of democracy a central institutional objective, along with economic stability and socioeconomic development, on the EBRD model.

- Establish formal linkages with member governments' foreign and development ministries.
- Reform internal lending structures and incentives with the aim of strengthening the middle class in democratizing societies. Among other actions, this would involve increasing the share of lending made to small- and medium-sized enterprises.
- Extend multilateral bank funding beyond the central government. Targeting private-sector firms, provincial government, and nonprofit organizations would enhance incentives for good performance while advancing broad-based economic development and democratization.

Do No Harm: Protecting Democracies in the Process of Development
Throughout this book we have argued that democratic, accountable political institutions are both an end in themselves and an effective means toward development. Establishing the tandem objectives of economic development and democratization as an organizing framework for international development agencies is a sensible strategy. Nonetheless, as the examples of Ecuador, Nigeria, and Bulgaria discussed in Chapter 5 underscore, inflexible approaches to development may at times unintentionally undermine the democratization process. This may lead to social hardship, disaffection with democracy, and unrest. Democratically elected reformist leaders might be forced out of office and replaced by politicians less committed to change. Efforts at socioeconomic development and poverty alleviation might be set back. Worse, popular disenchantment could create openings for unconstitutional seizures of power and a derailment of the democratic process altogether.

To avoid those dire outcomes, a mechanism for measuring the potential threat to democratic processes posed by certain development policies is urgently required. This would alert policymakers to the prospective negative fall-out of a policy and prompt its redirection or delay. Such a mechanism would compel development planners to recognize that their policies do not take place in a vacuum. Nor, with such a mechanism in place, could policymakers blithely assume that the political implications of development policies are neutral and thus not worth examining.

Democracy Impact Statements—Purpose
We therefore call on policymakers to adopt "democracy impact statements" to identify potential threats to nascent democratic movements and institutions in poor countries from the economic development policies they are considering.

This exercise would foster more democracy-friendly development policies by prompting systematic consideration of the impact on democracy from a proposed development strategy. Proposals deemed harmful to emerging democratic processes could be modified or rejected. This would bring greater consistency to policymakers' decision-making and send clearer signals to developing countries regarding legitimating standards of governance.

There is a compelling precedent for such a policy initiative: the environmental-impact statement. During the 1960s, it became increasingly apparent in the United States that government planners were overlooking the impacts public works projects like dams and highways were having on the environment. This neglect amounted to treating the environment as if it were worthless. Because no individual "owned" the environment, no one had a financial incentive to challenge government decisions or hold legislative or regulatory authorities accountable for them.

Part of the answer to government mismanagement of the environment was as simple as it was potent. The 1969 National Environmental Policy Act required the government to prepare an analysis of the likely impact of big construction projects before they were undertaken. The mandate suddenly made visible what had previously been invisible. Experts can argue whether environmental rules go too far or not far enough. But few dispute that the 1969 legislation successfully brought environmental pluses and minuses to the forefront of policymaking.

Democracy and the environment might seem a far-fetched analogy. But in fact they are analytical close cousins. Both are socially valuable. Both are classic public goods—once a well functioning democracy, like a clean environment, exists for anyone, it exists for everyone. Because neither is owned by private individuals, no one possesses a direct financial stake in taking proper care of these goods while pursuing their own interests.

The impact of decisions by the national governments or international organizations, like the World Bank or IMF, on democratic institutions and forces in poor countries can be as invisible as their impact on the environment. For example, Joseph Stiglitz has criticized programs imposed by the IMF on crisis-ridden countries not only because, he says, they produce appallingly bad economic results but also because they trample internal democratic forces, stripping domestic political movements of the room to set domestic policies.[41] Professor Stiglitz raises a provocative point. Policymakers should at least recognize that imposing economic policies, even if well designed to promote growth, could come at a steep price. The recognition would not suggest the IMF should close up shop. But it might set the IMF, the World Bank, and Western aid agencies to the task of mitigating the perverse political impacts of their pursuit of narrow economic objectives.

The World Bank has recognized the gist of this reality. Ibrahim Shihata, a former general counsel, notes that the World Bank's freedom to acquire relevant knowledge of "the political situation in its borrowing members and to gain insight as to the underlying social and cultural factors behind such a situation . . . is not only legitimate; it is essential for the Bank's ability to provide useful advice on policy reform in the economic and social sectors. Without it, the Bank's assessment of the feasibility and effects of this type of reform may be grossly distorted."[42]

Similarly, a World Bank report examining the effects of structural adjustment lending warned that the cost of failure was too great "to ignore the potential contribution of a better understanding of the reality of the political economy of adjustment."[43] The report suggested the need to be aware of the importance of the timing of reform measures, not only with regard to their political and economic vitality, but also in terms of their design and presentation. The same report suggested that it was important to identify the groups that benefit from adjustment and those adversely affected by it. Compensation measures could thus be appropriately targeted and could contribute to the political viability and economic efficiency of the program.[44] Therefore, as with the environment, the aim of a democracy impact statement would be to move democracy from being treated as an "externality," that is, an unaccounted-for by-product of an action, to a valued consideration in deciding whether a development policy should be pursued.

These similarities between democracy and the environment raise the prospect that democracy impact statements could play as constructive a role in protecting the latter as they have in the former. The idea is straightforward. We call for democracy impact statements to accompany all large economic development programs funded by IFIs and bilateral aid organizations. The impact statements would assess the likely impact on democratic forces and institutions within the recipient country. Democracy impact statements would not steer development policy in one direction or another any more than environmental impact statements predetermine whether any specific dam or other public works project should be built. They certainly would not favor one political party over another. Their focus would be specified: to identify potential impacts on democratic government—accountable, transparent government in which the rule of law prevails, power is shared, and leaders are chosen according to the freely expressed preferences of their compatriots. By doing so, they would also improve prospects for compliance with lending agreements as well as overall economic and developmental effectiveness. After all, there are compelling economic benefits to be gained by avoiding and mitigating social disruption and political instability.

How Realistic?

We concede that the analogy between environmental impact statements and democracy impact statements is not perfect. Public works projects create concrete, often quantifiable economic benefits while also doing identifiable, often quantifiable damage. A dam generates low-cost electricity and destroys cropland. The electricity and cropland often have readily estimated market values. Tracing the benefits and costs from increased electricity and decreased cropland is easier than tracing the benefits and costs of something as intangible as democracy.

Yet, however imperfect the analogy, it is not far-fetched. If environmental impact statements look at quantifiable costs and benefits, they must also take into account a phenomenon every bit as loosely defined as democracy —their social impact. Furthermore, environmental impact statements have moved well beyond the analysis of mere projects, such as isolated dam building. They have come to apply to entire programs or policies like electrification or public health infrastructure, an application known in the literature as "strategic socioeconomic assessment." Similarly, strategic assessments have been made of international trade agreements. At least one expert, Ralf Buckley, regards strategic environmental assessment as the single most important aspect of environmental analysis. The value of strategic assessment lies as much in the collection of information as in its subsequent use by various parties to the policy debate. This holds true for the protection of democracy as well as the environment.

Building on the experience of environmental impact statements and the social-analysis methods developed in the 1960s and 1970s,[45] the World Bank and other international development agencies began conducting social impact assessments in the 1990s. Social impact assessments seek to measure the impact of policy reforms on the well being of various social groups, notably the more vulnerable segments of society like the poor and the marginalized.[46] That requires a thorough analysis of the country's institutions and political context.[47] Social impact assessments are thus an attempt to identify risks to policy reform before it is implemented. Their value is as much in the asking of the questions as in the formulation of policy. They thus help prepare a society for bumps along the road of reform— the disruptive changes and social and economic costs that are incurred before the benefits become apparent.

Although the World Bank has been leading the effort to put this into effect, joint World Bank-IMF working groups have explored how poverty and social impact assessments can be used to benefit both institutions.[48] The expectation is that they will lead to more informed debate at the national level, play a role in setting the sequence of activities, and help identify ways to minimize the side effects. Some of the key lessons gained from these assessments are that they too often[49]

- Are undertaken too late to have any real influence on policymakers.
- Inadequately document their basic assumptions, reducing transparency.
- Play down the risks of implementing the policies being considered.
- Fail to identify the potential losers if reforms are carried out or, if they do identify them, fail to consider ways of alleviating their pain.
- Lack access to the information required to do a comprehensive analysis.
- Use flawed analytical models for assessing the distribution of benefits and other impacts of reforms.

The private sector, too, has been experimenting with social impact analysis—with positive results. Generally, it has looked back to see what has gone wrong, but even so, the assessments have shown how investment decisions based on purely economic considerations can reverberate through the social and cultural life of a community.

Consider the Isabel Timber Company. It conducted a social impact assessment of its logging operations in Isabel Province, Solomon Islands, in 1997. Relying on extensive interviews with villagers, the assessment documented the company's pattern of failure to comply with its contract, especially with provisions that it consult and negotiate with landowners about its logging operation and that it leave certain sites intact. The assessment also found that the company had created few jobs and, worse, had disrupted village life by setting up logging camps that had triggered all sorts of unintended consequences. For example, the company provided motorized canoes to slash travel times, which had the intended result of improving productivity—as well as the unintended outcome of enabling the men to buy more alcohol in the faraway capital. Traditional political authority was also undermined by market-based opportunities replacing reliance on the land, especially when the rewards of market behavior were unevenly distributed. The lesson of these findings was not that logging should be suspended, or should never have begun. Rather, had the political and socioeconomic consequences been flagged ahead of time, the impact could have been mitigated.

Democracy impact statements would require nothing qualitatively different than social impact assessments. In fact, the most probable reason they have not already been included alongside the poverty and social impact assessments now undertaken by the World Bank is the political prohibition clause of its charter.

What Would Democracy Impact Statements Entail?

The U.S. federal government, the World Bank, and private companies have long relied on the social sciences to assess impacts of their programs and policies, especially on disadvantaged segments of society.

Democracy impact statements would ask of policy analysts no more, no less. The goal would be to ensure that potentially damaging consequences on democracy are explicitly considered and incorporated into policy decisions. Toward that end, they would need to identify the impact of proposed policies on political institutions, evaluate consequences, and outline possible methods to mitigate adverse impacts prior to the actual implementation. There is no analytical reason why democracy impact statements cannot work just as well as environmental impact or social impact statements; indeed, they would include similar components.

Who Would Submit Democracy Impact Statements?
The answer to this question would be all major international governmental and intergovernmental agencies that finance development activities. This includes the World Bank, the IMF, other multilateral development institutions, and Western aid donors (for example, USAID, the European Union, the U.K.'s Department for International Development, and so forth). A democracy impact statement would be undertaken before any new major policy initiative would be launched. Each donor would also commission a biannual democracy impact statement to assess how the entirety of its programs was spurring or inhibiting democracy. The World Bank could do this by expanding its poverty and social impact assessments. The IMF might integrate democracy impact statements into existing biannual country reviews. A determination to conduct a democracy impact statement would be based on more than solely the dollar value of a project. Potential threats to democracy may be more a matter of timing or emphasis than funding. Consequently, a donor or a host government should retain the option of requesting a democracy impact statement for any new project to be undertaken.

Given the many context-specific factors influencing political developments in a society, most analysts preparing democracy impact statements would ideally be drawn from within the society under discussion. They would be complemented by some external participants to guard against bias, as well as to build on experience gained elsewhere. As with any social survey, to gather as complete a picture as possible, the perspectives of all segments of a population to be affected by the policy must be incorporated.

Aid agencies could choose to develop the capacity to undertake these assessments themselves. Alternately, they could turn to independent evaluators that would specialize in analyzing risks to democracy much as independent assessors of corporate and political risk have arisen to guide international investors. There are also now organizations that specialize in independent assessments of corporate performance, often under the banner of corporate social responsibility. Independent assessments would in most circumstances be viewed with more credibility. Moreover, this approach would reduce the potential political fallout to a bilateral relationship resulting from assessments that raise cautionary flags.

Historical Review

Any assessment needs context. A democracy impact statement would need to describe the recent evolution of democracy in a country and the challenges it faces, with particular attention to four elements:

- Competitiveness. How are national and provincial government leaders selected? Is the process competitive? Are opposition political parties allowed to organize, campaign, and criticize the government? How free are citizens to participate in the political process?
- Power Sharing. To what extent are the constitution's provisions of sharing power implemented? How autonomous and empowered are the executive, legislative, and judicial branches and federal, provincial, and local levels of government?
- Autonomy of Civil Service. How independent is the civil service from political pressures? Is advancement in the government bureaucracy contingent on one's political allegiances? Are public goods and services provided in a neutral and consistent manner? To what extent do adequate protections exist to enable anticorruption agencies or ombudsmen to operate effectively? Are government regulatory agencies sufficiently autonomous to oversee private sector adherence to federal disclosure, tax, and audit laws? To what extent is information publicly available about government budgetary allocations and expenditures?
- Political Participation. Do citizens have channels through which their interests and concerns can be voiced to political leaders in the executive and legislative branches as well as opposition parties? How free are the media to take stands that diverge from, or even criticize, those of the governing party? How engaged is the public in policy debates?

Description of Proposed Project or Policy

This section would summarize a proposed project's objectives, list the parties taking part (notably the funding institution, the government agencies, the civic groups, and the private-sector firms), break down the costs, and describe the activities involved. It would also say whether the project originated with the country's democratic government and, if not, say how consistent it was with that government's development strategy.

Impact of Proposed Project or Policy on Democratic Processes
This section would be the heart of the democracy impact statement. It would examine how the proposed policy or project would affect the current democratic dynamics described above. This analysis, though speculative, would be grounded in the country's recent history and that of other countries in the region. To the extent possible, it would attach ranges of probabilities to likely outcomes. Following the structure outlined above, it would consider how political competition, power-sharing, autonomy of accountability structures, and political participation would be enhanced or undermined by the proposed policy. More broadly, this section would seek to answer how the implementation of the development project would affect democratic reforms in the host country.

Some of the questions it would seek to answer are: How would the process of selecting a country's leaders and the balance of power shift under the proposed program? Would the policy affect the conduct of free, fair elections? Would the policy create resentments among those who lose out and, if so, what would be the political fallout? Would the policy affect the autonomy of civil servants, including officials of the central bank, regulatory agencies, and the judiciary? Would it encourage monopolies in key markets (say by promoting ill-prepared privatizations), or encourage competition and decentralization of political and economic power? Would the proposed policy encourage or discourage corruption? Would the policy bolster or undermine an independent press? Would the proposed policy draw people toward democratic reforms and institutions, or instead encourage political cynicism or disillusionment? Would the policy create social hardships triggering riots, perhaps leading to the overthrow of duly elected officials? And would the program make it easier or harder for ordinary citizens to pursue and protect their interests?

None of these questions would be easy to answer. However, the very process of considering them would provide an opportunity for national governments and international funding agencies to reassess how they can promote sound development policy while minimizing potential negative political repercussions. Indeed, the entire process is aimed at facilitating greater dialogue between international agencies and democracy proponents in order to sensitize policymakers to the potential harm to democracy that may result.

Alternatives to the Proposed Course of Action
This section of the democracy impact statement would examine a range of alternate actions that the government and donor agency could take to meet a project's objectives, and would assess the impact of each on democratic government. It would also spell out the political implications of doing nothing. This comparative process would provide an opportunity to highlight the relative strengths of the proposed policy and to consider appropriate ancillary measures that would mitigate the negative impact on the democratization process stemming from the proposed policy. For example, slowing the speed at which certain economic reforms are pursued may be less efficient but more stabilizing politically.

Of course, accommodating the concerns raised by a democracy impact statement would be a delicate matter for countries that have just started down the path to democracy and that have not yet internalized a commitment to power sharing. Nonetheless, it would at least provide an explicit opportunity to recognize these threats and make adjustments rather than proceeding blindly down the path of economic transition without a guide to the likely political and social consequences.

Monitoring and Evaluation
This section of the democracy impact statement would establish some benchmarks and measurement criteria that would enable the monitoring of democratic functions or processes that had been identified as potentially affected by the proposed policy. This would provide a module for the biannual monitoring reviews and end of project evaluations that would be undertaken by development agencies. Having identified key democratic functions to monitor, the process of measuring and documenting impacts on democracy ex-post policy implementation would expand the existing public database of democratic consequences from development. In the process, it would have the indirect benefit of sharpening the analytical skills for political–economy analysis within the broader international development community.

Challenges to Conducting Democracy Impact Statements
An increasing number of development thinkers and practitioners would likely agree that governance is central to developmental progress and therefore needs to be incorporated into the policymaking process. However, the practical challenges of adopting democracy impact statements can still be expected to generate skepticism.

A primary concern centers on the lack of verifiable data on which to base predictions of the democratic outcomes from certain courses of actions.

Causal relationships can, for the most part, only be inferred. Furthermore, in-depth case studies of political consequences resulting from development policies are relatively sparse. Although it is commonly understood that the curtailment of essential government services and provisions will lead to public disenchantment and possible unrest, the empirical basis for this assumption is largely undocumented. This, it could be argued, is a substantial difference from an environmental impact statement, which can draw on hard science and testable claims. Given the thinness of the existing database, therefore, it may be unreasonable to ask writers of a democracy impact statement to draw firm conclusions.

A comparable concern is whether sufficient analytical capacity exists to undertake democracy impact statements. There are numerous development experts and a growing cadre of democracy promotion practitioners. However, reflecting the compartmentalization of these fields, there are relatively few individuals who can undertake the hardheaded political economy analysis that would be required in a democracy impact statement.

These are important considerations. However, to some extent these arguments perpetuate a form of circular reasoning. The lack of data and qualified political-economy analysts is largely due to the fact that we have not been asking the questions. Once these issues are spotlighted as sufficiently important to be a matter of public policy, the quantitative and qualitative database will grow, as will the analytical capacity to use this data. Knowledge of a subject and the analytical tools to examine it follow one from the other. This is as true for the field of physics as social science. For example, interest in promoting democratization fostered the development of numerous indices of democracy over the last several decades. The more refined of these have been annualized and have, in turn, contributed greatly to our understanding of how democracy interacts with other phenomenon —a process that continues to evolve. The study of institutions is another example. The work of Douglass North, Mancur Olson, and others laid the conceptual groundwork of the importance of institutions to development. This then spawned a growing catalog of indices assessing various aspects of institutional strength. These indices have contributed enormously to the empirical analysis of these institutions and their relationship with various facets of political and economic development. Therefore, the lack of intranational political economy tools is not a determinative reason for not considering the implications of a development strategy on democracy.

The concern over the relative value of quantifiable versus qualitative data reflects a larger debate over the comparative usefulness of social science and physical science in analyzing a situation. To exclude qualitative data would be to omit from consideration an entire body of knowledge—

one that most individuals and organizations value in making decisions. From a practical standpoint, most of these battles have already been fought. With the introduction and implementation of social impact statements, the World Bank has already recognized the importance of qualitative social science insights to its decision-making.

The criticism of pursuing a course of action without a demonstrated causal relationship is a challenge to all public policy. Decisions must often be made contemporaneously without perfect information. This applies to issues involving the social as well as the physical sciences. Consider that the causal relationship between smoking and cancer is still a matter of some dispute. Similarly, despite the increasingly widespread acknowledgement of a link, the connection between CO_2 emissions and global warming remains unproven in the minds of some. The risk of inaction in such instances becomes greater than the cost of taking corrective action. In the case of democracy impact statements, examples of economic strain leading to social unrest and political upheaval are sufficiently common to warrant further study. In the process, potentially egregious courses of action can be avoided. As the relationship becomes better understood, the democracy impact statements can be refined accordingly.

Another concern about the democracy impact statement is that it might undermine sound economic policy. On the one hand, this perspective reflects the traditional view that development is solely a technical process. A more nuanced view is that although politics do matter, if these are directly taken into consideration, then the difficult steps required to pursue sound macroeconomic policy will be more easily put off. Another variant of this concern is that the democracy impact statements could be used as an instrument by international actors to pursue their geo-strategic interests.

These criticisms all have some merit and must be factored into how a democracy impact statement would be implemented. The intent of the democracy impact statement is not to subvert sound—and difficult—development policies. IFIs should continue to promote those policies they believe are conducive to development. The democracy impact statement, however, can lead to more informed decisions—thereby allowing for a better weighting of costs and benefits. The upshot may be that the same macroeconomic policy goals would be pursued, though perhaps with modifications. This may involve adjusting the timing for certain provisions. It may also involve strengthening the social safety net that is built into a development policy so as to soften the negative political impact. In short, the intended outcome of the democracy impact statement is not to dilute sound economic policy but to interject a greater degree of flexibility when the costs to democracy and good governance may be substantial. This would require greater customization and creativity in development packages.

The criticism that democracy impact statements would allow greater room for geo-strategic string-pulling begs the question, are they valuable in themselves? Development decisions have frequently been an extension of a country's foreign policy. Although this has lessened with the termination of the Cold War, these tensions are again ascendant as the global threat of terrorism grows. Our view is that donor governments will find ways of rewarding developing country allies, if this is their aim, with or without the adoption of democracy impact statements. As we suggested in Chapter 6, this practice is best acknowledged for what it is—a security waiver—and kept separate from development allocations. This will avoid sending mixed signals and incentives for best development practices.

Another key question regarding the implementation of democracy impact statements pertains to preparation time. Given the long lead times often required before IFIs can approve a project, will undertaking a democracy impact statement delay the process even further? We do not foresee this as a major problem. The compilation of a democracy impact statement shouldn't be an unduly lengthy process; the World Bank takes about five weeks on average to complete a poverty and social impact assessment.[50] A democracy impact statement could be undertaken contemporaneously.

A final concern we will mention is "mission creep." Over recent years, staff from the World Bank have expressed concern that its mandates (and those of other multilateral development banks) have become so broad as to be unmanageable.[51] In addition to macroeconomic considerations, the multilateral banks are addressing infrastructure, environmental, gender, labor, and legal criteria among others. Wouldn't adding democracy to the mix be just one more distraction from their core aim of promoting economic stability?

The answer is no. As we have contended throughout this book, democracy and good governance are not simply additional developmental objectives. Rather, the quality of governance is a prism through which all development resources and efforts flow. If a government system is more accountable and transparent, and if it adheres to a system of rule of law, it is more likely to generate positive development outcomes. Therefore, the democratic implications of development initiatives should be viewed as central rather than ancillary to the functions of the multilateral development agencies. Amending the charters of the IFIs to make democracy a dual objective with development would allow them to frankly acknowledge the importance of accountable representative government to development.

The IFIs would then be able to adapt their development efforts to this reality rather than constantly trying to work around it.

Summary

There is a growing recognition that democracy and good governance matter to development. International agencies that finance development need to adopt their charters and practices so as to reflect this reality. Rather than maintaining the illusion of a clear distinction between politics and economics, they should explicitly recognize their linkage. In this way, democracy would be pulled from its current marginal position in development policy to a central role. This approach would model the path taken by the only multilateral development bank established in the post-Cold War era—the EBRD. It has shown that simultaneously pursuing economic growth and democracy objectives is feasible and mutually reinforcing. Not only has the EBRD fostered development in Central Europe and the former Soviet Union, it has done so in a profitable manner. The fears of many economists that taking political factors into consideration would undermine economic principles have simply not been borne out.

Meanwhile, to guard against unintended negative consequences on democracy from compartmentalized development policies, we call for the implementation of democracy impact statements with every major internationally financed development initiative. This would force multilateral and bilateral aid organizations to ponder otherwise unanticipated political reverberations of their decisions and give opportunities for greater flexibility in development policymaking. This analysis would build on the experience of environmental impact and social impact assessments to consider democratic implications of development policies. In the process, it would void the current implicit assumption that all development plans have neutral political ramifications. Although proactively assessing political outcomes of development policies would not be easy, it would provide an early warning system to potential serious political repercussions. In the process, it would further stimulate relevant data collection and political economy analysis that would deepen the understanding of how democracy and development interact, leading to more informed policy actions.

CHAPTER 8
The Great Race

The policy of placing stability above all else can only create greater instability.

Dr. Jiang Yanyong
Chinese medical doctor, Communist Party member, and folk hero[1]

In an era of transformational global changes—trade, communications, mi-
gration, epidemics, global warming, and terrorism—that are affecting the
lives of every person on the planet, one epic movement has largely escaped
notice: global democracy. Today, nearly seven of 10 countries in the world,
representing every region, are on a democratic path. Their number edges
upward each year despite setbacks. Transitions to democracy, which not so
long ago were exceedingly rare, are now viewed as almost commonplace.
This trend toward democracy is astonishing; during our lifetimes democracy has reached a majority of the human race for the first time in history.
This marks a dramatic reversal from the reality of just 15 years ago when
autocratic governance was the solid norm. The transformation is all the
more remarkable in that it came on the heels of three decades of democratic stagnation following World War II.

Despite this rapid turnabout in governance norms, certain development
models remain frozen in a Cold War mindset. Many mainstream foreign
policy experts still believe authoritarian governments can be counted on to
do a better job of promoting economic development and international security than can democracies. International financial institutions maintain
legal provisions that bar them from considering how the national leaders

with whom they are dealing came to power. Levels and terms of development assistance targeted to countries with democratic leaders are no greater than for states where leaders are self-appointed and rely on repression to stay in power. Fears that democratization in poor countries will lead to ethnic conflict abound. International support for democracy in the developing world remains tentative. The upshot is that the lack of appreciation for the historical moment in which we live undermines prospects for democratic consolidation around the globe.

In some ways, this lukewarm attitude should come as little surprise. Reservations have dogged the spread of democracy at nearly every historical juncture of its evolution. The British treated as comical the notion that economically backward American revolutionaries could govern themselves. The European elite long regarded the concept of one person, one vote as incomprehensible before democracy took hold there. The fight for women's suffrage was marked by ridicule of women's capacity for political discernment. Doubts over African-Americans' fitness to participate as equals and the divisiveness this would bring long delayed their participation in the political process in the United States. Cultural values incompatible with democracy were often cited as irreconcilable obstacles to democratization in Asia, Africa, and the former Eastern bloc. The arguments trotted out by democracy skeptics on why certain populations are unfit for self-governance have remained remarkably consistent over the years, even as the context of the debate has shifted. Today, skepticism over whether citizens in poor countries are capable of governing themselves remains high.

Often overlooked in this debate is that those who promote an authoritarian-led development strategy rely on an idealized image of authoritarian rule. They see autocrats as technically competent, efficient, supportive of the private sector, willing to mobilize society's resources in the public interest, and capable of enforcing a market-enhancing rule of law. In effect, they are pinning the hopes for progress in the developing world on the emergence of a series of benign dictators, preferably with advanced degrees in economics. In fact, such leaders are rare. Moreover, human nature being what it is, deference by international policy makers to even the best-intentioned of autocrats is far more likely to breed among them arrogance and self-indulgence rather than magnanimity and concern for the common good. Simply put, relying on enlightened autocrats is not a viable model for systematically promoting development.

We should discard the authoritarian-led development model. It not only misjudges human nature, it also ignores historical reality. Autocracies, on average, fail to generate development as rapidly and broadly as do democracies. And the cases in which authoritarian governments have developed economically and then made the transition to democracy are exceedingly few. More commonly, their monopolistic nature hampers economic development. Their reliance on a narrow base of support runs contrary to the qualities of shared power and a broad distribution of the fruits of growth that characterize countries that have sustained rapid development over time. Therefore, the notion that delaying democracy until a country has developed economically is a bit like putting off changing a car's three flat tires until it reaches the top of the mountain. Similarly, the argument that deferring democracy, in fact, enhances a country's long-term prospects for a more sustained democracy ring hollow when held up to empirical light. Experience shows, rather, that the far more likely result is the perpetuation of poverty, repression, and conflict. Although the process of democratization is likely to be bumpy, that is an insufficient rationale to discourage it. Prospects for development, stability, and sustained democracy are all greater in countries that have embarked on the path of democratic reform than in countries that remain on the authoritarian road.

The Triad of Challenges
Policy toward the developing world should focus on addressing the three key roadblocks to development: poverty, conflict, and autocratic government. Democracy addresses each. Democracies and countries on the path to democracy have markedly better track records in alleviating poverty. They have also been less likely to engage in conflict—a pattern that has solidified in the 1990s, with the number of conflicts declining as the number of democracies has increased. And finally, by establishing institutions of legitimate governance and creating an environment of openness, democracies promote the values of individual initiative, tolerance, civic-mindedness, and commitment to the rule of law that can build social cohesion in formerly autocratic nations after years of government repression and omnipresence have bred fear and distrust.

Because democracy is key to overcoming the three roadblocks that confront the developing world, we argue that the United States should make progress toward democracy the overarching goal of its foreign policy toward these regions. Relations with democracies and countries on the path to democracy should differ fundamentally from relations with governments that lack legitimacy in representing their nations. Security pacts with the latter group should be restricted, time-limited, and more realistic about the long-term political costs they entail. Meanwhile, preferential support for development assistance and debt relief should be provided to democracies to send clear signals to reformers and tyrants alike. This will serve as both recognition that those resources will be more effectively used and as a clear incentive for political reform. Similarly, assistance to democracies should be guided by a greater degree of flexibility, recognizing that leaders in these countries are accountable to their populations and have a mandate to be responsive to their priorities. Such a stance will help fledgling members of the democratic community to meet their material aspirations as well as sustaining domestic commitment for institutional reforms. Their success, in turn, will contribute to a more stable and prosperous world.

We should clarify that we are not advocating the use of military force to "bring democracy" to the rest of the world. To have credibility and sustainability, democracy should emerge from within a society. The United States and other leading democracies, however, can and should encourage these internal forces by ensuring that an external environment conducive to reforms exists.

Toward a New Approach

Let's remember that development assistance makes up only a small share of the capital that moves through most developing-country economies. Even so, it plays a vital role beyond just financing the construction of dams and highways and the like. If targeted to countries that are seriously undertaking reforms, it acts as a catalyst to shake up dysfunctional public and financial institutions. As a result, all investments made in these economies become more productive. Leaders who are benefiting from monopolistic and unaccountable systems, however, have little incentive to pursue such reforms on their own. The international community can better leverage its development assistance to stimulate reform, therefore, if it sheds its neutralist stance and reward regimes that embrace democracy.

One reason for this neutralism is legal; the multilateral agencies are prohibited from considering a client country's political orientation. But as the full impact of democratic government on economic development becomes clearer, this constraint becomes more and more untenable. Evidence from countries across the globe backs up what development practitioners have long known from firsthand observation: Greater levels of public participation in the development process contribute to more successful development performance. We therefore call for the removal from agency charters any stricture against a firm tilt toward democracies. In its stead provisions that stipulate a preference for democratic governance, notably institutions that share power, transparency, and popular participation should be inserted. Such an amendment would in no way signal a retreat from sound macroeconomic policy. It would, however, recognize that the accountability of the government structures through which development resources are channeled makes a major difference in the outcomes that can be expected.

The World Bank, the IMF, and various agencies of the United Nations have taken steps in the right direction in recent years. They have been talking more openly about the importance of good governance, have undertaken projects aimed at bolstering it, and have delayed funding to projects deemed tainted by corruption. Commendable though these actions are, they are insufficient so long as the prospects of an authoritarian government receiving development financing are as great as those of a democracy. Moreover, they sidestep the fundamental reality that a government leadership's commitment to the rule of law is intrinsically linked to the legitimacy of the manner in which it came to power.

Some policymakers at the IFIs will reason that funding decisions should be made solely on the basis of economic criteria. However, the allocation of resources in a society is fundamentally a political decision. All the more so when 93 percent of all development assistance is channeled through central governments. How representative that government is, whose interests are considered, and how priorities are determined all influence how those resources are going to be used.

The importance of political institutions to economic development is a reality that a number of eminent development economists have emphasized, if at times late in their careers. For example, Albert Hirschman acknowledged that his growth model had not adequately considered noneconomic implications. "Had I done so I might have inquired into the political consequences and prerequisites of the process . . . This matter was later investigated in my article, 'The Tolerance for Income Inequality in the Course of Economic Development,' but only after the antagonistic potential of the development process had led to civil wars and various other disasters. Along with my fellow pioneers, I thus stand convicted of not having paid enough attention to the political implications of the economic development theories we propounded."[2] Having worked on the reconstruction of France and Italy in the aftermath of World War II as part of the Marshall Plan, Hirschman noted, "Orthodox policy prescriptions for the disrupted postwar economies of Western Europe—stop the inflation and get the exchange rate right—were often politically naïve, socially explosive, and economically counterproductive from any longer-run point of view."[3] As Hirschman's own economic growth model involved persistent back and forth iterations around an idealized equilibrium (thus constantly creating winners and losers), he expressed admiration for the genius of democratic systems' ability to reconcile multiple social objectives.[4]

Similarly, Walt Rostow, author of *The Process of Economic Growth*, felt economic growth should be viewed as simply one manifestation of a society's total performance. Consequently, noneconomic dimensions had to be taken into account. He was explicit about the crucial role of politics in the early phases of modernization. Specifically, he argued that a coalition of competing interests was at play—the military, politicians, merchants, professionals, and intellectuals—that could pull a newly independent country, that by definition was in a fragile condition, in any number of divergent directions, from external aggression in search of national aggrandizement, to dictatorship, to a democratic path of economic, social, and political modernization. He therefore implored domestic and international actors to pay particular attention to the balance of power within this governing coalition.[5]

Our review of the dynamics of international development assistance indicates that aid is not an unmitigated good, particularly in terms of its impact on democracy. Enacting sustainable reforms in any society requires building a broad enough coalition of support to ensure that multiple interests are addressed and that a policy will be continued even when a change in government administration occurs. This takes time and diplomacy, both of which will vary by country. By focusing solely on macroeconomic targets with pre-determined timeframes—and ignoring the social and political ramifications—international players can inadvertently undercut the effort to instill reformist ideals in that coalition of interests. Such a course makes it more likely that political leaders who champion reform will be voted out of office prematurely or that the entire democratic process will be jettisoned.

To avoid this outcome, we advocate the adoption of democracy impact statements. These assessments, to be undertaken by all major international development actors, would be mechanisms by which the political implications of a policy can be systematically considered. Building on the experience of environmental impact statements and social impact assessments, they would aim to raise awareness of potential risks before an action is undertaken. The objective of democracy impact statements would not be intended to block development initiatives but to weigh how their implementation and the distribution of their benefits would affect the strength of a society's democratic institutions.

To fortify incentives for good performance, international development actors should expand the institutional channels through which they are working. In addition to the central government, provincial administrations should be direct recipients of international assistance. After all, the effectiveness of public authorities across regions varies greatly, and targeting relatively greater levels of assistance to provincial leaders who are most responsive to the interests of their populations will improve the efficiency of the finite foreign-assistance resources available. Widening private sector and nongovernmental organizations channels for aid will have similar effects.

Favoring democracies in development decision-making does not mean writing them a blank check. Sound macroeconomic and development policies need to be applied. Moreover, corruption trumps democracy's developmental advantage and therefore should not be indirectly endorsed just because a country is a democracy. One of democracy's most powerful development-enhancing assets is its self-corrective capacity. For this to come into play, democratic societies must see the risks they face if they pursue unsustainable policy choices like tolerating corruption, running persistently high budget deficits, subsidizing unviable state owned enterprises, or altering a previously negotiated rate structure for private utility suppliers. The mere consciousness of these risks can persuade leaders and voting publics to change course. Through this process of trial and error, innovative and balanced strategies can be fashioned.

If a developing country is not on the path to democracy, then development assistance should be restricted. Its government should not automatically qualify as the custodian of international development resources. Only initiatives considered of utmost importance to the country's citizens or to the broader international community, like responding to a humanitarian crisis, fighting AIDS, or launching a global vaccination campaign, would merit support. And in those cases, resources would be channeled primarily through nongovernmental bodies or through government agencies subject to external oversight. This would increase the probability that the funding would reach the intended populations and lessen the likelihood it would be used to prop up an unaccountable government.

The argument for targeting aid to democracies or democratizers boils down to this. First, international development assistance falls far short of need, so giving aid to autocracies subtracts from the amount of aid given to the poor in democracies. Second, the poor living in democracies are no less worthy of help than are the poor living in autocracies. Third, aid provided to democracies is far more likely to reach those who need it and does far more good—cutting poverty and promoting growth—than does aid provided to autocracies. Fourth, giving preference to democracies in development policymaking creates ongoing incentives to reform for both fledging democracies and closed political systems. The inescapable implication is that donors should shower their aid where it can do real good—on democracies and democratizers.

On the other hand, funding for the purpose of building institutions of shared power could flow unimpeded to autocratic governments, though these are likely to be the activities in which they would be least interested. They could be spent to help develop the legislative branch as a counterweight to the chief executive's power, to foster the separation of party from state financing, and to establish the independence of the civil service, to name a few examples.

Similarly, financial aid could be used to support the creation of laws and practices to bolster the private sector, to protect legal institutions from political influences, and to encourage an active civil society and a free press. The funding of such initiatives would facilitate more rapid and broad-based development in these countries, lowering the risk that they would fall victim to the humanitarian and economic catastrophes to which they are so susceptible, while at the same time helping to lay the foundations of a democratic society.

Implicit in all of our recommendations is a call for a conceptual shift by policymakers that is potentially more profound than any specific policy change that we have proposed. Relations between states should be qualified on whether or not they are democratic. International legitimacy in the twenty-first century should be conferred only on those leaders that are the genuine representatives of their societies. How the world's leading democracies approach alleviating poverty and advancing development is one reflection of this philosophy. We argue that the global community should as a matter of policy view democratic governance as the norm and should treat any funding for dictatorships as deviations from that norm. The adoption of such a protocol in the charters of the institutions it has created to foster development would go a long way toward creating a new mindset —both in the industrialized and developing worlds. It would reinforce the emerging standard that leaders must come to power through representative and competitive political processes, and must accommodate a free press and institutional checks against abuse of power if they wish to be accorded the full legitimacy of sovereign heads of state.

In other words, addressing global poverty and development requires more than new policies from the world's aid agencies. It entails a shift in the norms of relations between states.

A Democratic Vision Far Closer Than Realized

The recognition that the vast majority of states today are on a democratic path opens up a once almost unimaginable possibility—of a world rid, at last, of dictators. In *Breaking the Real Axis of Evil: How to Oust the World's Last Dictators by 2025*, former U.S. Ambassador Mark Palmer sets a target date for that goal. More pertinent than any specific proposals it offers, this work is significant for helping to shape the vision of a world that is very different than the one we have known. It is a future that may be far closer to reality than most realize. As democracy becomes more and more recognized as the norm, expectations of even people in closed political systems will change, leading to greater scrutiny of age-old practices of transferring power through families or ruling elites, thereby hastening autocracy's demise. Given democracies' averseness to armed conflict, a new era of universal peace might actually become a reality.

Idealistic? Yes. But realistic, too—since experience has shown that democracies do the best job of systematically reducing causes of interstate and civil conflict. Although tensions between competing groups in democracies surely continue to exist, they are channeled into processes of negotiated settlement. Therefore, the advancement of democracy is very much in the global community's security interests.

The prospect of a world governed by democracies within the foreseeable future provides a strategic framework for the foreign policies of the United States and other democracies. The new guiding principle would be whether a given course of action advanced the cause of an autocracy-free world or detracted from it. Justifying dictatorships as a "necessary evil" would no longer be a respectable option. The inevitable temptation to temporarily resist democratization in lieu of an alternate security or economic interest would be resisted. By so doing, the short- and long-term costs of such relationships would correctly be recognized as undercutting the goal of a world governed on the principles of democracy and the rule of law. The credibility, and therefore effectiveness, of a policy advancing these global norms would, of course, depend on its consistent application. Perpetuating notions of an authoritarian advantage in global development—in addition to being bad development policy—would undermine this strategic vision. Should the United States commit itself to this democracy-centered strategy, it would be compelled to recognize that one of the greatest obstacles to its realization is none other than itself. The financial, political, and military assistance that Washington has given to autocratic governments over the decades, even after the Cold War ended, has provided tangible sustenance to these regimes. And given their proclivity to conflict, support for terrorism, and proliferation of banned weapons, the long-term effect of this assistance has been to weaken U.S. security. Furthermore, with the prospect of international terrorists gaining access to weapons of mass destruction, the distinction between short- and long-term costs has largely dissolved.

Selective U.S. support for strategic autocratic allies has simultaneously muddied the waters of what constitutes legitimate leadership. Withdrawing that support would send an unambiguous message to such rulers that their days are numbered and they should begin planning their transitions from power so as to ensure themselves a soft landing. Pursuing a clear democracy-centered foreign policy would require substantial reconciliation of current practices and priorities among the Departments of State, Defense, Treasury, and CIA, among others. This will only occur with an unmistakable and consistent commitment on the part of successive presidents. Demonstrating such commitment will involve far more than simply increasing the frequency of references to democracy in presidential oratory.

Unfortunately, achieving a global community of democracies is not foreordained. As weapons of mass destruction proliferate, terrorism and war, the offspring of autocracy, will have ever-greater potential to wreak havoc on the human family. And the autocratic governments themselves, unable to meet the basic needs of their citizens and coming under mounting pressure to loosen their grip on power, will face increased temptation to redirect responsibility for their societies' shortcomings onto external influences, heightening the risk of regional and even global instability. The economic costs of such disruption would be great, reversing decades of progress in the campaign against poverty. We sound this alarm not to demoralize readers but to make an urgent point: casting democracy and national security as competing priorities, always a dubious proposition, has become a clear and present danger to world peace and prosperity.

Even leaving aside the security dimension, the democratic gains of the past two decades cannot be taken for granted. As we have seen, new democracies are at risk during times of economic stagnation. Stresses to the global system—be they economic, political, or physical—could likewise reverse recent democratic gains. Indeed, such retrenchments followed previous episodes of democratic advance over the past century. As Ted Gurr, Keith Jaggers, and Will Moore observed of the aftermath of WWI when democracy in Europe seemed to be on the ascendant, "However, a more effective and powerful form of autocracy emerged out of the Russian Revolution, one which provided an attractive model for many other rulers, especially those of new African and Asian states, who wanted to build national power without sacrificing their autonomy to the demands of factious citizens."[6] At just the moment in history when democracy is on the march everywhere, autocracy could make a comeback. And the longer that pockets of it survive, the greater the chance that it will regain lost ground.

We are thus in a great race. Can the world democratize, creating a sustainable platform for economic development and the peaceful resolution of differences? Or will the persistence of autocratic governments into the era of accessible weapons of mass destruction give those who thrive on instability the upper hand? The policies we adopt for supporting democracy and economic development will help decide that momentous question.

APPENDIX **A**
Country Listings by Polity IV Democracy Level in 2003[1]

[1]Countries scored in the top tier (i.e. 8 to 10) are categorized as democracies; those receiving the lowest ratings (between 0 and 2) are classified as autocracies. Afghanistan, Bosnia, Burundi, Ivory Coast, Democratic Republic of Congo, Iraq, Lebanon, Libaria, and Somalia were not assigned a democracy score in 2003 because of war or the presence of foreign forces.

0	1	2	3	4	5	6	7	8	9	10
Azerbaijan	Algeria	Burkina Faso	Cambodia	Comoros	Armenia	Bangladesh	Albania	Argentina	Bulgaria	Australia
Bahrain	Angola	Jordan	Djibouti	Iran	Georgia	Benin	Colombia	Bolivia	Botswana	Austria
Belarus	Cameroon	Singapore	Ethiopia	Malaysia	Sierra Leone	East Timor	Croatia	Brazil	Chile	Belgium
Bhutan	C.A.R.		Tanzania	Niger		Ecuador	El Salvador	Dom. Rep	France	Canada
China	Chad		Zambia	Nigeria		Fiji	Estonia	Guatemala	India	Costa Rica
Rep. of Congo	Guinea					Guyana	Ghana	Indonesia	Jamaica	Cyprus
Cuba	Haiti					Mali	Honduras	Kenya	Macedonia	Czech Rep.
Egypt	Nepal					Mozambique	Madagascar	Latvia	Panama	Denmark
Eq. Guinea	Kyrgyz Rep.					Namibia	Malawi	Lesotho	Peru	Finland
Guinea-Bissau	Tajikistan					Serbia	Russia	Mexico	S. Africa	Germany
Eritrea	Togo					Venezuela	Sri Lanka	Moldova	Slovak Rep.	Great Britain
Gabon	Tunisia						Ukraine	Nicaragua	Taiwan	Greece
Gambia	Yemen						Yugoslavia	Paraguay	Thailand	Hungary
Kuwait								Philippines		Iceland
Lao PDR								Romania		Ireland
Libya								S. Korea		Israel
Mauritania								Senegal		Italy
Morocco								Turkey		Lithuania
Myanmar										Japan
N. Korea										Mauritius
Oman										Mongolia
Pakistan										Netherlands
Qatar										New Zealand
Rwanda										Norway
Saudi Arabia										P. N. Guinea
Sudan										Poland
Swaziland										Portugal
Syria										Spain
Turkmenistan										Slovenia
U.A.E.										Sweden
Uganda										Switzerland
Uzbekistan										Trinidad
Vietnam										Uruguay
Zimbabwe										USA

Freedom Scores in 2003[2]

---

[2]Countries that score in the 11 to 14 range are deemed "free," those between 2 and 5 are considered "not free," and nations in the 6 to 10 range are "partly free."

2
Burma
Cuba
Iraq
Libya
N. Korea
Saudi Arabia
Sudan
Syria
Turkmenistan

3
China
Eq. Guinea
Eritrea
Laos
Somalia
Uzbekistan
Vietnam

4
Afghanistan
Belarus
Cameroon
Congo*
Cote d'Ivoire
Egypt
Haiti
Iran
Liberia
Rwanda
Qatar
Zimbabwe

5
Algeria
Angola
Azerbaijan
Bhutan
Brunei
Burundi
Cambodia
Chad
Guinea
Jordan
Kazakhstan
Kyrgyzstan
Lebanon
Maldives
Oman
Pakistan
Swaziland
Tajikistan
Togo
Tunisia
U.A.E.
Yemen

6
Bahrain
C.A.R.
Congo†
Ethiopia
Malaysia
Mauritania
Morocco
Russia
Uganda

7
Comoros
Djibouti
Gabon
Guinea-Bissau
Kuwait
Nigeria
Singapore

8
Armenia
Bangladesh
Bosnia
Burkina Faso
Colombia
Gambia
Georgia
Guatemala
Kenya
Malawi
Nepal
Niger
Sierra Leone
Tonga
Ukraine
Zambia

9
Fiji
Indonesia
Madagascar
Moldova
Mozambique
Paraguay
Sri Lanka
Tanzania
Turkey
Venezuela

10
Albania
Antigua &
Barbuda
Argentina
E. Timor
Ecuador
Honduras
Macedonia
Nicaragua
Seychelles
Solomon Is.
Trinidad

11
Benin
Bolivia
Brazil
El Salvador
Ghana
India
Jamaica
Lesotho
Mali
Namibia
P.N. Guinea
Peru
Philippines
Senegal
Thailand
Yugoslavia

12
Botswana
Croatia
Dom. Rep.
Guyana
Israel
Mexico
Mongolia
Romania
Samoa
S. Korea
Taiwan

13
Belize
Bulgaria
Cape Verde
Chile
Costa Rica
Czech Rep.
Estonia
Greece
Grenada
Hungary
Japan
Latvia
Lithuania
Mauritius
Monaco
Micronesia
Nauru
Panama
Palau
Poland
Sao T. & P.‡
Slovak Rep.
S. Africa
St. Kitts
St. Lucia
St. Vincent
Suriname
Vanuatu

14
Andorra
Australia
Austria
Bahamas
Barbados
Belgium
Canada
Cyprus
Denmark
Dominica
Finland
France
Germany
Great Britain
Iceland
Ireland
Italy
Kiribati
Liechtenstein
Luxembourg
Malta
Marshall Is.
Netherlands
New Zealand
Norway
Portugal
San Marino
Slovenia
Spain.

14 (cont'd)
Sweden
Switzerland
Tuvalu
Uruguay
United States

* Democratic Republic of Congo
† Republic of Congo
‡ Sao Tome and Principe

List of Low-Income Democracies Since 1960[3]

Latin America

Belize	1982–1986*
Bolivia	1982–
Colombia	1972–1987*
Costa Rica	1960–1965*
Dominica	1978–1983*
Dominican Republic	1963, 1972–1973, 1978–1992, 1996–1999*
Ecuador	1979–1999
Grenada	1977–1978, 1985*
Guatemala	1972–1973, 1996–
Guyana	1972, 1993–
Honduras	1982, 1984–1992, 1997–1998
Jamaica	1960–1965*, 1980–1988*
Nicaragua	1995–
Peru	1990–1991
El Salvador	1972–1975, 1997–
Suriname	1975–1979, 1988, 2000–
St. Lucia	1982–1983*
St. Vincent	1979–1987*

Central Europe

Bulgaria	1990–
Romania	1996–
Turkey	1961–1970, 1973–1975*

Former Soviet Union

Belarus	1994
Latvia	1993–1995*

---

[3]List is combined from countries qualifying under Polity or Freedom House criteria. For Polity, countries are classified democracies if in a given year they score 8 to 10 on the 0 to 10 democracy scale. Using the Freedom House Index, democracies are categorized as those with (inverted) political rights and civil liberties sums of 11 or more (that is, "Free") on the inverted 2 to 14 point scale. Note that Freedom House listings begin in 1972. Polity excludes countries with populations below 500,000. Economic data is drawn from World Development Indicators, 2003. Low-Income is defined as GDP/per capita (constant 1995 $) <$2,000.

| Lithuania | 1993–1999* |
| Moldova | 2001– |

Sub-Saharan Africa

Benin	1991–
Burkina Faso	1978–1979
Botswana	1973–1983*
Cape Verde	1991–
Gambia	1966–1993
Ghana	1980–1981, 2000–
Lesotho	1966–1969, 1993–1997
Madagascar	1992–1997
Malawi	1994–1998
Mali	1992–1993, 1995–1996, 2000–
Mauritius	1968–1984*
Namibia	1990–1992*
Niger	1992–1995
Nigeria	1960–1965, 1979–1983
Sao Tome	1991–
Senegal	2000–
Sudan	1965–1968, 1986–1988
Zambia	1991–1992

South Asia

Bangladesh	1972–1973, 1991–1992
India	1960–
Nepal	1991–1992
Pakistan	1973–1976, 1988–1996
Sri Lanka	1970–1982

East Asia

Fiji	1970–1972*
Indonesia	1999–
Kiribati	1978–
Malaysia	1960–1968, 1972–1973
Marshall Islands	1991–
Micronesia	1991–1999
Mongolia	1991–
Papua New Guinea	1975–
Philippines	1987–
Samoa	1989–
Solomon Islands	1978–1999
South Korea	1960
Thailand	1975, 1989–1990*
Vanuatu	1980–1982, 1989–

*Asterisks represent countries that grew beyond $2,000 per capita income level.

Autocratic Recipients of U.S. Military or Economic Funding Above the Decade Median Levels of Per Capita Assistance, 1950 to 2000

Country	Years of Military Assistance	Years of Economic Assistance
Afghanistan		1956–1959, 1961–1969, 1972–1973, 1975, 1977, 1989
Algeria	1981–1989	1963–1966
Angola	1996	1992–2000
Argentina	1966–1969, 1971–1972, 1976	
Armenia		1996–1997
Azerbaijan		1994, 1998–2000
Bahrain	1992–2000	1977
Bangladesh		1975–1979
Belarus		1996
Benin		1972, 1974
Bolivia	1961–1977, 1979	1956–1980
Bosnia & Herzegovina		1994–1995
Brazil	1966–1967, 1974–1976	1964–1968, 1970
Burkina Faso		1974–1975, 1980–1981, 1985–1986
Burundi	1991	1990–1994
Cambodia	1956–1957, 1960–1962, 1970–1975	1955–1963, 1971–1975, 1980, 1993–2000
Cameroon	1978, 1981–1985, 1991	1962, 1978–1979, 1985, 1987, 1989
C.A.R.	1987, 1990–1992	
Chad	1983–1991	1974, 1977–1979, 1984–1988, 1990–1992

Country	Years of Military Assistance	Years of Economic Assistance
Chile	1973–1974	1975–1977
Dem. Rep. of Congo	1965, 1971, 1973, 1976–1986, 1990	1961–1968, 1977, 1979
Republic of Congo		1971
Columbia		1956
Comoros		1984, 1986–1989
Croatia	1997–1998	1994–1996, 1998
Djibouti	1982–1998	1978–1993, 1995
Dominican Republic	1966–1970, 1975–1977	1966–1969, 1970–1977
Ecuador	1961–1962, 1964–1967, 1976–1978	1961–1967, 1972–1973
Egypt	1979, 1981–2000	1955–1956, 1959–1965, 1975–2000
Equatorial Guinea	1983–1992	1981–1986, 1988–1992
El Salvador	1962–1963, 1975	1957, 1962–1963, 1972, 1974, 1976–1978
Eritrea	1994–1999	1994–2000
Ethiopia	1961–1962, 1965–1975	1961, 1966, 1993–1994
Gabon	1976–1978, 1981–1985, 1990–1993	1963–1968, 1979, 1990–1995
Gambia	1994	1994–2000
Ghana		1961–1962, 1966–1968, 1972–1973, 1976–1977, 1991–1994
Greece	1967–1973	
Guatemala	1962, 1964, 1975–1976	1955–1965, 1975–1979, 1983, 1985
Guinea	1984–1987, 1990–1991	1962–1966, 1968–1969, 1971, 1974–1976, 1978–1979, 1986, 1988–2000
Guinea-Bissau	1986–1993	1975, 1977–1979, 1981–1986, 1988–1993
Guyana		1980, 1986–1991
Haiti	1984, 1986, 1991	1955–1963, 1973–1989, 1991–1993, 2000
Honduras	1962, 1965–1967, 1975–1980	1954–1980
Hungary		1957
Indonesia	1976–1978, 1980–1985, 1991	1969–1973, 1978–1979
Iran	1956–1969	1955–1963
Iraq	1955, 1957–1958, 1997, 2000	1957, 1964
Ivory Coast	1991, 1998	1964
Jordan	1958, 1960–1967, 1969, 1971–2000	1957–2000
Kazakhstan	1997–2000	1994–1995, 1999–2000

Country	Years of Military Assistance	Years of Economic Assistance
Kenya	1975–1989	1975, 1977–1986, 1989, 1993, 1999–2000
Kyrgyzstan	1997–2000	1993–1996, 1998–2000
Laos	1960–1967, 1975, 1993, 1996	1960–1975
Lebanon	1993, 1995–2000	1992–1993, 1995, 1997–2000
Lesotho	1991	1970–1971, 1973–1992
Liberia	1961–1962, 1964–1969, 1970–1972, 1975–1986, 1996	1951–1996
Libya	1960–1968	1952–1964, 1969
Malawi	1985, 1990	1968, 1973–1974, 1985–1986, 1988–1993
Mali		1973–1975, 1977–1979, 1984–1986, 1988–1990
Mauritania	1986–1988	1971, 1974–1991, 1993
Mauritius	1985	
Mexico	1990, 1992	1950, 1964
Morocco	1961–1962, 1965, 1967, 1969, 1971–1993, 1999–2000	1957–1973, 1975–1979, 1981–1982, 1984–1989, 1991–1993
Mozambique		1979, 1985, 1987–1993
Myanmar (Burma)		1962
Nepal		1960, 1963, 1965–1966, 1970, 1973
Nicaragua	1960, 1962–1969, 1970–1976	1952–1976, 1978–1981
Niger	1981–1988, 1990	1974–1979, 1981–1990
North Korea		1998–2000
Oman	1980–1986, 1990–1993, 1998–2000	1980, 1982–1989, 1992
Pakistan	1958–1961, 1970–1973, 1983–1987	1958–1961, 1969–1971, 1977, 1980, 1982–1992
Panama	1975–1977, 1979, 1982–1987	1952–1954, 1968–1987, 1990–1992
Paraguay	1963–1973, 1974–1976	1952, 1954, 1955–1976, 1979
Peru	1974–1977	1970, 1972, 1976, 1977, 1992
Philippines	1972–1985	1972–1979, 1985
Poland		1957, 1958
Portugal	1951–1953, 1959–1964	
Rwanda	1981, 1993–1994, 1996	1979, 1985, 1991–2000
Saudi Arabia	1957–1964, 1966–1968, 1971	1958
Senegal	1962, 1977, 1984–1988, 1990–1993, 1997–1999	1964, 1967, 1974–1975, 1977–1992, 1994–1995, 1997–1999

Country	Years of Military Assistance	Years of Economic Assistance
Sierra Leone	1985–1986, 1990–1991	1967, 1975–1979, 1981–1982, 1986–1987, 1989–1990, 1992–1994, 1997
Singapore	1968–1969	
Somalia	1980–1988, 1993	1978–1979, 1980–1989, 1992–1994
South Korea	1955–1959, 1961–1962, 1972–1986	1950–1959, 1961–1962, 1972–1973, 1976–1978
Spain	1954, 1956, 1957, 1960–1964, 1966–1967, 1970–1973	
Sudan	1980–1984	1959–1960, 1979–1984, 1994, 1999
Swaziland	1991–1993, 1997–2000	1973–1995
Syria		1960–1962, 1975–1979
Taiwan	1951–1978	1951–1966, 1971
Tajikistan		1993–1994, 1999–2000
Tanzania		1975–1979, 1987
Thailand	1951–1952, 1954–1955, 1960–1967, 1973, 1976–1977	1955–1959, 1962, 1966–1968
Togo	1990–1991, 1997–2000	1962, 1964, 1966, 1975–1979, 1981–1982, 1984–1993
Tunisia	1961–1962, 1967–1993, 1995–2000	1959–1981, 1985–1992
Turkey	1971–1972, 1980–1982	1971–1972, 1980–1982
Turkmenistan		1993, 1994, 1996
Uganda	1996–1998	1991–1995, 1998–2000
Uruguay	1973–1976	1973, 1975
Uzbekistan	1998–2000	
Venezuela	1957	
Yemen	1982–1988	1982–1990, 1998, 2000
Yugoslavia	1953–1957	1953–1959, 1960–1966, 1993, 1999
Zambia		1977–1979, 1980–1988, 1990
Zimbabwe	1991, 1993	1989–1994

Notes

Prologue

1. See, for example, Kaplan, Robert, 2001, "Looking the World in the Eye," *Atlantic Monthly*, vol. 288 (5): pp.68–82;" Kaplan, Robert, 1997, "Was Democracy Just a Moment?" *Atlantic Monthly*, vol. 280 (6): pp. 55–80; Zakaria, Fareed, 2003, *The Future of Freedom: Illiberal Democracy at Home and Abroad*; Chua, Amy, 2003, *World on Fire: How Exporting Free Market Democracy Breeds Ethnic Hatred and Global Instability*.

Chapter 1

1. Richmond, Roaldus, ed., "A Yankee Businessman in New Hampshire," *American Life Histories: Manuscripts from the Federal Writers' Project, 1936–1940*.
2. Central Intelligence Agency, *The World Factbook*. Official estimates put this figure at 59 million. Xinhuanet News Agency, "China: Major Improvements in Standard of Living in Past Five Years."
3. Kohli, Atul, *Democracy and Discontent: India's Growing Crisis of Governability*.
4. We use the terms authoritarian and autocratic synonymously. This represents a broad category of governance systems (for example, fascist, communist, monarchial, military-led, neo-patrimonial) in which the institutions of representative and accountable governance are sharply limited. Chief executives are selected in closed or noncompetitive political processes. Institutions for popular participation are nonexistent or marginalized. Once in office, executives in these systems face few institutional checks or balances. (Belarus, Cuba, North Korea, and Zimbabwe are examples of countries that fall into this category).
5. World Bank, *The East Asian Miracle: Economic Growth and Public Policy*.
6. Quibria, M.G., "Growth and Poverty: Lessons from the East Asian Miracle Revisited."
7. Dornbusch, Rudiger, and Sebastian Edwards, "Macroeconomic Populism."
8. Kaplan, Robert, "Was Democracy Just for a Moment?," "The Coming Anarchy."
9. Snyder, Jack, *From Voting to Violence: Democratization and Nationalist Conflict*.
10. Chua, Amy, *World on Fire: How Exporting Free Market Democracy Breeds Ethnic Hatred and Global Instability*.
11. Some may think to include Thailand here. However, it started down the path to democracy at a much earlier stage than the others (that is, with a per capita income of $700) and therefore does not really fit this pattern.
12. As with most economic figures presented in this book, this is drawn from the World Bank's *World Development Indicators, 2003* dataset, (1995 US$).
13. For example, according to the UNDP, the percentage of people living on less than $1 a day in Bolivia has increased from 7.1 to 29.4 percent from 1998 to 2001; in Colombia the percentage has risen from 7.4 to 11 percent and in Venezuela from 11.8 to 18.7 percent.
14. For example, Chavez challenged the "excessive autonomy" of municipal and state governments, public universities, the Central Bank, and the state-run oil company. The new constitution approved by a constituent assembly aimed to correct this situation by giving the

251

executive branch the power of "coordination," thus facilitating more extensive central government involvement in all of these spheres. Ellner, Steve, "The Radical Potential of Chavismo in Venezuela: The First Year-and-a Half in Power."

15. British Broadcasting Corporation, "Venezuela's Chavez Says He Will Stay in Power Until 2021."

16. They were later ordered released by an appeals court—taking exile in neighboring countries.

17. Inter-American Dialogue, "The Troubled Americas;" Lozada, Carlos, "Is Latin America Running Out of Chances;" Ellner, Steve, "The Radical Potential of Chavismo in Venezuela: The First Year-and-a Half in Power."

18. We operationalize this more explicitly in Chapter 2 for the empirical analysis we undertake. Meanwhile, a more complete articulation of democratic principles and values can be found in the Warsaw Declaration of the Community of Democracies at its inaugural convening in 2000.

19. Zakaria, Fareed, *The Future of Freedom.* See also Carothers, Thomas, "Zakaria's Complaint."

20. Przeworski, Adam, Michael Alvarez, Jose Antonio Cheibub, and Fernando Limongi, *Democracy and Development: Political Institutions and Well-Being in the World, 1950–1990.*

21. Freedom House, *Freedom in the World: The Annual Survey of Political Rights and Civil Liberties, 2001–2002.*

22. Figure 1.1 is based on data from the Polity IV index that assesses annual democracy scores for every country with a population over 500,000 based on their establishment of institutions for the selection of their political leaders, opportunities for popular participation in the political process, and checks on the chief executive. See Gurr, Ted Robert, Keith Jaggers, and Will Moore, "The Transformation of the Western State: The Growth of Democracy, Autocracy, and State Power since 1800;" Jaggers, Keith and Ted Robert Gurr, "Tracking Democracy's Third Wave with the Polity III Data;" Marshall, Monty and Keith Jaggers, "Polity IV Project: Codebook." Using the Freedom House index (which includes countries with populations under 500,000) the crossover point to majority status for democracies is even more distinct.

23. Marshall, Monty, and Ted Robert Gurr, "Peace and Conflict 2003: A Global Survey of Armed Conflicts, Self-Determination Movements, and Democracy."

24. Olson, Mancur, "Dictatorship, Democracy, and Development;" Olson, Mancur, "The New Institutional Economics: The Collective Choice Approach to Economic Development."

25. Based on data from annual United Nations Development Program (UNDP) Human Development Reports.

26. Lagos, Marta, "A Road With No Return?;" Bratton, Michael, et al. "Afrobarometer Round 2: Compendium of Comparative Results from a 15-Country Survey."

27. Campos, Jose Edgardo, and Hilton Root, *The Key to the Asian Miracle: Making Shared Growth Credible.*

28. O'Donnell, Guillermo, *Modernization and Bureaucratic-Authoritarianism: Studies in South American Politics.* It should be noted that while Samuel Huntington advocated the authoritarian advantage perspective, he distinguished himself by never claiming that authoritarian governments would then inevitably transition to democracy.

29. Business Line, "India: Democracy and Sustainable Growth."

30. Sosnowski, Saul, and Roxana Patino, eds., *Una Cultura para la Democracia en America Latina.*

31. That is, a shrinkage in annual GDP/capita of 10 percent or more.

32. Sen, Amartya, "Food and Freedom."

33. Reiter, Dan, and Allan Stam, "Democracy, War Initiation, and Victory."

34. Collier, Paul, "Conflict and Development."

35. Chile under Pinochet is frequently included in this category. However, despite experiencing positive growth in most years of his rule, due to two periods of acute contraction, it was only toward the end of Pinochet's 17 years of power that Chile sustained a per capita income level above what it had in 1973.

36. Pei, Minxin, "China's Governance Crisis."

37. Lanyi, Anthony (ed.), 2004, *The Corruption Nexus and the People's Republic of China.*

38. Pei, 2002b.

39. Pei, Minxin, "Beijing Drama: China's Governance Crisis and Bush's New Challenge."
40. China acknowledged in 2002 that it had overstated its growth figures in the 1990s. Nonetheless, China's 7.7 percent rate of annual per capita growth is still outstanding.
41. Bhalla, A.S., "Recent Economic Reforms in China and India."
42. Recall, an estimated 30 million people are thought to have perished in the 1959–1961 famine in China associated with the Great Leap Forward. It was also during this period that China suffered a 30 percent contraction in GDP. The Cultural Revolution of the mid 1960s was also a period of great hardship for China.
43. Bhalla, 1995.

Chapter 2

1. We use the terms authoritarian and autocratic interchangeably to capture those governance systems characterized by the monopolization of the mechanisms of political power and substantial limits to popular participation in political life including freedoms of speech, press, and association. Democracies, in contrast, derive political authority from their citizenry. They are typified by institutions fostering shared power, competitive selection of the head of state, and basic political rights and civil liberties that enable popular participation in the political process. For a comparative listing of states by political system, please see Appendices A and B. For the 0 to 10 Polity democracy scale (Appendix A), we consider countries with scores of 8 to 10 as democracies. Countries with scores from 0 to 2 are categorized as authoritarian. Using the (inverted) 2 to 14 point Freedom House index (Appendix B), countries classified as "free" (that is, in the 11 to 14 range on the scale) are treated as democracies and nations categorized as "not free" (between 2 to 5) are considered autocratic.
2. Lipset, Seymour Martin, "Some Social Requisites of Democracy: Economic Development and Political Legitimacy;" Lipset, Seymour Martin, *Political Man: The Social Bases of Politics.*
3. See also Lerner, David, *The Passing of Traditional Society.*
4. Galenson, Walter, *Labor and Economic Development*; de Schweinitz, Karl, Jr., "Industrialization, Labor Controls, and Democracy;" La Palombara, Joseph, *Bureaucracy and Political Development.* An important early critique of modernization theory was Guillermo O'Donnell's, *Modernization and Bureaucratic-Authoritarianism: Studies in South American Politics.*
5. Huntington, Samuel, *Political Order in Changing Societies.*
6. It was the occupation of Japan by the United States that resulted in the rewriting of Japan's feudal land laws as well as the reform of numerous economic, legal, and social institutions that positioned Japan for its accelerated post-WWII development.
7. Huntington, *Political Order in Changing Societies*; Koo, Anthony, *The Role of Land Reform in Economic Development: A Case Study of Taiwan*; Haggard, Stephan and Robert R. Kaufman, *The Political Economy of Democratic Transitions.*
8. Huntington, Samuel and Joan Nelson, *No Easy Choice: Political Participation in Developing Countries.*
9. Kohli, *Democracy and Discontent: India's Growing Crisis of Governability.* Bhagwati used the term "cruel dilemma" 25 years earlier, Bhagwati, Jagdish, *The Economics of Underdeveloped Countries.*
10. Kaplan, "Was Democracy Just for a Moment?;" Kaplan, "Looking the World in the Eye;" Zakaria, *The Future of Freedom.*
11. Quibria, "Growth and Poverty: Lessons from the East Asian Miracle Revisited."
12. Barro, Robert J., "Don't Bank on Democracy in Afghanistan;" Barro, Robert, *Determinants of Economic Growth: A Cross-Country Empirical Study.*
13. Numerous personal interactions by authors. Also, see references in Przeworski et al., *Democracy and Development: Political Institutions and Well-Being in the World, 1950–1990*; Carothers, Thomas, *Aiding Democracy Abroad: The Learning Curve* (p. 277).
14. Mahatir, Mohammad and Ishihara Shintaro, *The Asia That Can Say No*; Mahbubani, Kishore, "The Dangers of Decadence: What the Rest Can Teach the West;" Nam, Tae Yul, "Singapore's One-Party System: Its Relationship to Democracy and Political Stability."
15. Dornbush and Edwards, "Marcoeconomic Populism."

16. It bears noting that democracy scholars have long argued that the absence of finality is actually a strength of democracies. It guarantees "losers" in a particular debate that their interests need not be perpetually sidelined. The minority in any given vote maintains the option of raising awareness and rallying public opinion in support of their position. This flexibility, in turn, gives democracies the capacity to adapt as new information or experience comes to light.

17. Mansfield, Edward, and Jack Snyder, "Democratization and the Danger of War."

18. Snyder, Jack, *From Voting to Violence: Democratization and Nationalist Conflict*.

19. Przeworski, Adam, and Fernando Limongi, "Political Regimes and Economic Growth," *Journal of Economic Perceptions*; Alesina, Alberto and Roberto Perotti, "The Political Economy of Growth: A Critical Survey of the Literature;" Inkeles, Alex and Larry Sirowy, "The Effects of Democracy on Economic Growth and Inequality: A Review;" Burkhart, Ross and Michael Lewis-Beck, "Comparative Democracy: The Economic Development Thesis;" Helliwell, John, "Empirical Linkages Between Democracy and Economic Growth."

20. Gurr et al., "The Transformation of the Western State: The Growth of Democracy, Autocracy, and State Power since 1800;" Jaggers and Gurr, "Tracking Democracy's Third Wave with the Polity III Data;" Marshall and Jaggers, "Polity IV Project: Codebook." The Polity democracy score measures the institutional features of political competition and participation—the core components of established definitions of democracy (Dahl 1998, 1989, 1971). The 0 to 10 rating assigned to each country for each year since 1800 aggregates measures of checks on the chief executive, competitiveness and openness of executive selection, and mechanisms for popular participation. States with a score of eight or more are considered democracies. Nondemocracies are all countries that fall below this threshold of democracy (i.e., countries with scores between 0 and 7 on the Polity democracy scale). As a subset of nondemocracies, autocratic governments are those that have democracy scores of 0 to 2. Naturally, democracy is a far more complex system of relationships than can be neatly synthesized into a single number. However, this categorization does aid analysis by allowing di- and trichotomous comparisons that we use for illustrative purposes throughout this book. We recognize, however, that there are broad ranges of regime types exhibiting varying degrees of democratic institutional capacity. Countries do not become democracies overnight. Therefore, the scaled nature of this and other continuum measures of democracy also provide flexibility when assessing increments in progress. Another commonly employed scaled measure is Freedom House's *Annual Survey of Freedom*. This dataset generates annual (since 1972) "freedom" scores (that, when inverted, scale from 2 to 14) for every country in the world based on its adherence to a broad range of political rights and civil liberties. Freedom House classifies countries into free, partly free, and not free categories. Although most of the results presented in our discussion are based on the Polity data (which covers a longer time span and is more methodologically rigorous), the findings are similar to those found using the Freedom House Index. The 0.91 correlation between the two democracy indices indicates a very strong degree of overlap.

21. We use median levels throughout this book to reflect "typical" outcomes and avoid the skewed results that can be generated when relying on mean measurements due to exceptionally strong or weak performances of a few countries. Given its more representative nature, medians are also a more relevant measure when considering policy implications.

22. Although a difference may not seem remarkable, as with the interest earned from a savings account, a one percentage point difference is substantial. A country with a per capita income of $1,000 growing at a rate of 2 percent per year will have increased its income in 20 years by nearly 50 percent, or to $1,500, compared to the $1,200 income level for a country growing at 1 percent per year.

23. Przeworski et al., *Democracy and Development: Political Institutions and Well-Being in the World, 1950–1990*; Gourevitch, Peter, "Democracy and Economic Policy: Elective Affinities and Circumstantial Conjunctures;" Barro *Determinants of Economic Growth: A Cross-Country Empirical Study*.

24. Given that the vast majority of low-income countries are not democracies, there is a tendency to overlook the existence of this sub-group altogether. In fact, there have been 34 low-income democracies at some point in time during the 1960 to 2002 time span according to

the Polity democracy index. Using the Freedom House Index, which includes countries with populations below 500,000, there have been 47 low-income democracies. For a full list of these countries, please see Appendix C.

25. This compares countries with per capita incomes below $4,000. Using the under-$2,000 categorization, the difference is 26 percent vs. 8 percent.

26. Correspondence with Barbo Hexeberg, Development Data Group, World Bank, September 2002.

27. Indeed, it bears keeping in mind that the United States' economic history is characterized by its steadiness rather than its speed. The United States has averaged per capita growth of 2.2 percent over the course of its history.

28. Comparing countries with per capita GDPs below $2,000 and $1,000 yields similar differences (4 percent vs. 1.7 percent)

29. Measured by dividing the standard deviation by the mean of a sample. Consider two countries that both averaged per capita growth of 2 percent per year over 10 years. If one has a standard deviation of five (generating a coefficient of variation of 2.5), while the other has a standard deviation of seven (a coefficient of variation of 3.5), we can say the latter experienced relatively greater volatility.

30. These results are consistent with Quinn, Dennis P., and John T. Woolley, "Democracy and National Economic Performance: The Preference for Stability."

31. Mellor, John, and Sarah Gavian, "Famine: Causes, Prevention, and Relief;" Cuny, Frederick, *Disasters and Development.*

32. Olson, "Dictatorship, Democracy, and Development;" Olson, "The New Institutional Economics: The Collective Choice Approach to Economic Development."

33. United Nations Development Program, *Arab Human Development Report 2002: Creating Opportunities for Future Generations.*

34. Although the graphs depict differences for countries with GDP per capita below $2,000, comparable divergences are observed among a sample of nations with GDPs per capitas below $1,000.

35. Recalling our discussion of missing economic growth observations, data on infant mortality rates (IMR) are much more readily available. Although autocracies still report a greater proportion of missing to available data, the levels are much lower. Six percent of developing country autocratic IMR data points are missing from 1960 to 2001. In comparison, no democracies are missing this data. Thus, IMR rates may not only be more valid but also more reliable measures of development.

36. See also Zweifel, Thomas and Patricio Navia, "Democracy, Dictatorship, and Infant Mortality: Navia, Patricio and Thomas Zweifel, Democracy, Dictatorship, and Infant Mortality Revisited."

37. Putnam, Robert, *Making Democracy Work: Civic Traditions in Modern Italy.*

38. Narayan, Deepa, "Focus on People's Participation: Evidence from 121 Rural Water Projects."

39. Isham, Jonathan, Daniel Kaufmann, and Lant Pritchett, "Civil Liberties, Democracy, and the Performance of Government Projects."

40. Sen, "Food and Freedom."

41. Wittman, Donald, *The Myth of Democratic Failure: Why Political Institutions are Efficient;* Wittman, Donald, "Why Democracies Produce Efficient Results."

42. Murrell, Peter, "Missed Policy Opportunities during Mongolian Privatization: Should Aid Target Policy Research Institutions?"

43. Kornai, Janus, "Resource-Constrained Versus Demand-Constrained Systems."

44. The 2001 Nobel Prize for Economics was awarded to George Akerlof, A. Michael Spence, and Joseph Stiglitz for their work in examining the economic implications from asymmetric information.

45. Schumpeter, Joseph, *Capitalism, Socialism, and Democracy.*

46. This study focused on the phenomenon of 'state capture'—the capacity of oligarchs to manipulate public policy formulation and the legal environment to their own advantage by providing illicit gains to public officials. This is in contrast to the traditional conception of corruption whereby public officials extract bribes for the exclusive benefit of politicians and bureaucrats. Hellman, Joel, Geraint Jones, and Daniel Kaufmann, "Seize the State, Seize the Day."

47. Olson, "Dictatorship, Democracy, and Development."
48. Lanyi, Anthony, and Young Lee, "Governance Aspects of the East Asian Crisis."
49. Haggard, Stephan, *The Political Economy of the East Asian Financial Crisis*.
50. See also Pei, Minxin, and Merrit Lyon, "Bullish on New Democracies: Research Notes on Multinationals and the Third Wave;" Przeworski, Adam, Michael Alvarez, Jose Antonia Cheibub, and Fermando Limongi, "What Makes Democracies Endure?"
51. Ahmed, Rashmee, "India Beats China as Business Destination."
52. East Asian Tigers include Hong Kong, Indonesia, Malaysia, Singapore, South Korea, Taiwan, and Thailand.
53. Today, record levels of agricultural subsidies in the West greatly limit the extent to which developing countries can follow the example of the East Asian Tigers and maximize their comparative advantage (agriculture and textiles) in the global economic structure.
54. Pei, Minxin, "The Puzzle of East Asian Exceptionalism."
55. North, Douglass, *Institutions, Institutional Change, and Economic Performance*.
56. Kaminsky, Graciela, and Carmen Reinhart, "On Crises, Contagion, and Confusion."
57. Asian values commonly seen as contributing to the region's economic growth include: respect for authority, strong families, reverence for education, hard work, frugality, teamwork, and a balance between the individual's interests and those of society.
58. Campos, Jose Edgardo, and Hilton L. Root, *The Key to the East Asian Miracle: Making Shared Growth Credible*; Root, Hilton L., and Nahalel Nellis, "The Compulsion of Patronage: Political Sources of Information Asymmetry and Risk in Developing Country Economies."
59. Collier, Paul, "Ethnic Diversity: An Economic Analysis."
60. Young, Alwyn, "Lessons from the East Asian NICs: A Contrarian View;" Krugman, Paul, "The Myth of East Asia's Miracle."
61. Harper, T. N, "'Asian Values' and Southeast Asian Histories [Review Article]."
62. Campos and Root, *The Key to the Asian Miracle: Making Shared Growth Credible*; Bueno de Mesquita, Bruce and Hilton Root, "When Bad Economics is Good Politics."
63. As calculated from Freedom House's *Annual Survey of Press Freedom*.
64. Gross national savings as a percentage of GDP, based on World Development Indicators 2002 data.
65. Between 1958 and 1961, China had experienced one of the worst famines in history with up to 30 million people perishing.
66. Owens, Edgar, *The Future of Freedom in the Developing World: Economic Development As Political Reform*; Owens, Edgar, and Robert Shaw, *Development Reconsidered: Bridging the Gap Between Government and People*.
67. Pei, Minxin, "Is China Democratizing?"
68. In 1995 U.S. dollars.
69. Young, Alwyn, "Gold Into Base Metals: Productivity Growth in the People's Republic of China during the Reform Period."
70. Woo, Wing Thye, "The Real Reasons for China's Growth."
71. Jefferson, Gary, Thomas Rawski, Wang Li, and Zheng Yuxin, "Ownership, Productivity Change, and Financial Performance in Chinese Industry."
72. Hu, Baiding, and Michael McAleer. "Input-Output Structure and Growth in China."
73. Sen, Amartya, "Human Rights and Asian Values."
74. Clague, *Institutions and Economic Development: Growth and Governance in Less-Developed and Post-Socialist Countries*.
75. North, Douglass, *Institutions, Institutional Change, and Economic Performance*.
76. Shihata, Ibrahim, *The World Bank in a Changing World: Selected Essays*.
77. Knack, Stephen, and Phillip Keefer, "Institutions and Economic Performance: Cross-Country Tests Using Alternative Institutional Measures;" Clague, *Institutions and Economic Development: Growth and Governance in Less-Developed and Post-Socialist Countries*.
78. Olson, Mancur, Naveen Sarna, and Anand Swamy, "Governance and Growth: A Simple Hypothesis Explaining Cross-Country Differences in Productivity Growth."
79. Keefer, Phillip, and Stephen Knack, "Why Don't Poor Countries Catch Up?: A Cross-National Test of an Institutional Explanation;" Rodrik, Dani, "Institutions for High-Quality Growth: What They Are and How to Acquire Them."
80. Kaufmann, Daniel, Aart Kraay, Massimo Mastruzzi, "Governance Matters III: Governance Indicators for 1996–2002;" Kaufmann, Daniel, Aart Kraay, and Pablo Zoido-Lobaton, "Governance Matters;" "Governance Matters II: Updated Indicators for 2000–01."

81. Siegle, Joseph, *Democratization and Economic Growth: The Contribution of Accountability Institutions.*

82. Siegle, *Democratization and Economic Growth: The Contribution of Accountability Institutions.* This index is comprised of five different institutional dimensions of accountability: checks on the chief executive, autonomy and efficiency of the civil service, independence of the private sector, rule of law, and press freedom/civil liberties.

83. Our focus on institutions is not intended to discount the importance of other factors affecting development progress. Structural characteristics of a society, including inequality, geographic location, and climate are all important influences. Similarly, leadership matters greatly—and no doubt partly explain the exceptions that dot the historical experience of the relationship between democracy and development. We have focused on institutions since they represent certain general societal norms, are sufficiently durable to merit cross-national analysis, yet are amenable to change.

84. Siegle, *Democratization and Economic Growth: The Contribution of Accountability Institutions*; Kaufmann et al., "Governance Matters;" Kaufmann and Kray, "Governance Indicators, Aid Allocation, and the Millennium Challenge Account."

Chapter 3

1. Perhaps most brazenly, Izzat Ibrahim, vice chairman of Iraq's Revolutionary Command Council, deemed the October 2002 referendum giving Saddam Hussein 100 percent support, " . . . a unique manifestation of democracy superior to all other forms of democracy . . . "

2. Recall from Chapter 2 that the Polity democracy index measures institutional features of political competition and participation from which it assigns an annual democracy score of 0 to 10 for each country with a population over 500,000. Marshall, Monty and Keith Jaggers, "Polity IV Project: Codebook;" Jaggers, Keith and Ted Robert Gurr, "Tracking Democracy's Third Wave with the Polity III Data; Gurr et al., "The Transformation of the Western State: The Growth of Democracy, Autocracy, and State Power since 1800."

3. This time period captures the contemporary democratization phenomenon, absent the lagging southern European democratizers. This categorization of democratizers excludes countries that were already in the top tier of the democracy scale (i.e., in the 8 to 10 range) prior to making further democratic advances. Naturally, this list changes from year to year. A few of the countries in the 2002 listing no longer qualify, while others could be included. Taking these additions and subtractions into account, however, does not alter the aggregate characteristics associated with this group of countries. Rather the statistical relationships we highlight in this chapter remain consistent from year to year.

4. By contrast, there are five countries that have realized outright declines in their democracy scores over this timeframe (i.e., Colombia, Gambia, Malaysia, Venezuela, and Zimbabwe).

5. Based on changes in democracy score since 1977 (or independence if more recent). Only countries with populations greater than 500,000 are considered. Otherwise, Antigua & Barbuda, Bahamas, Cape Verde, Dominica, Grenada, Kiribati, Malta, Samoa, Sao Tome & Principe, Seychelles, St. Kitts & Nevis, St. Lucia, and Suriname could be included.

6. Retaining the same democracy score for five consecutive years is a simple proxy for absence of democratic progress. It could be argued, however, that consistency in the maintenance of democratic institutions at a middling level after years of authoritarian rule is actually a sign of success. As a society establishes relatively more democratic norms, the likelihood of reversion recedes. From this view, the interim plateau allows for the establishment of basic attitudes and expectations of political competition and participation. This may then represent a foundation for further democratic advances and consolidation.

7. This excludes countries backtracking *within* the top tier (that is, 8 to 10) of the democracy scale.

8. This pattern adds further caution to generalizations of a firm democracy–income level relationship, as discussed in the previous section.

9. Although outside the time period we are considering, Peru also collapsed in 1968 after a 34-year period of hovering at a middling level of democratic institutionalization.

10. Defined as a three-year average GDP per capita growth rate of less than 1 percent, based on WDI 2003 data.

11. Przeworski et al., *Democracy and Development: Political Institutions and Well-Being in the World, 1950–1990.*

12. Countries that reinitiated their democratization efforts following a collapse include Algeria, Armenia, Burkina Faso, Cambodia, Croatia, Fiji, Ghana, Guatemala, Guinea-Bissau, Guyana, Niger, Nigeria, Sierra Leone, Tajikistan, and Yugoslavia.

13. Specifically, there were 859 instances of democratizers with annual per capita incomes below $4,000 experiencing a three-year average of stagnant per capita growth since 1977. Of these, only 42 resulted in democratic backtracking. The same rate holds for democratizers with per capita incomes below $2,000.

14. Przeworski et al., *Democracy and Development: Political Institutions and Well-Being in the World, 1950–1990.*

15. Argentina also backtracked in 1989 when, upon taking office, President Carlos Menem frequently bypassed the legislature and ruled by presidential decree. Its per capita income at that time was $6,000. All figures are from WDI 2003, which uses 1995 US$ as the base.

16. Although countries with GDP's/per capita below $2,000 comprise 73 percent of democratizers, they represent 79 percent of backtrackers.

17. Turkey, Slovak Republic, Algeria, Pakistan, and Fiji, respectively. Further diminishing the importance of per capita income in democratic reversals, the median income of countries that have regressed from democracy during economic stagnation is not appreciably different than the respective averages for the three most affected regions.

18. Haggard, Stephan and Robert Kaufman, *The Political Economy of Democratic Transitions.*

19. Grichtchenko, Jane and A. A. Gritsanov, "The Local Political Elite in the Democratic Transformation of Belarus."

20. Kalinovsky, Valery, "Socialist-Style Belarus in Worsening Economic Straits;" Dabrowski, Marek and Rafat Antczak, "Economic Transition in Russia, Ukraine, and Belarus: A Comparative Perspective."

21. Halperin, Morton H. and Mirna Galic, eds., *Protecting Democracy: International Responses.*

22. Typically considered to require multiple transfers of power between competing political parties through democratic processes.

23. The differences in median levels between the two groups are statistically significant at the 1 percent level of confidence for the Latin America, Africa, and overall comparisons; the difference for the former Soviet Union sample is significant at the 10 percent level of confidence.

24. These differences are statistically significant to the 1 percent level of confidence in the Latin American, African, and full democratizer samples. The former Soviet Union difference is not significant due to the limited number of observations and wide variance.

25. These differences in debt service levels are robustly significant in multivariate analysis distinguishing stagnant backtrackers.

Chapter 4

1. The conflict patterns we reference in this chapter apply to both internal and interstate wars unless otherwise specified. Given the predominance of civil conflicts in recent decades, references to conflicts during this period can be assumed to apply to internal wars.

2. Collier, Paul, et al., *Breaking the Conflict Trap: Civil War and Development Policy.*

3. Marshall, Monty, and Ted Robert Gurr, *Peace and Conflict 2003: A Global Survey of Armed Conflicts, Self-Determination Movements, and Democracy.*

4. Collier, Paul, "Economic Causes of Civil Conflict and their Implications for Policy."

5. Collier, Paul, "Conflict and Development."

6. Ibid.

7. That is, countries with per capita GDPs below $2000. Similar observations are seen using the under $4,000, $1,000, or $500 categorizations.

8. Episodes of armed conflict resulting in 1,000 or more directly related deaths in a given year, based on data compiled by the Center for Systemic Peace's Major Episodes of Political Violence dataset. The unit of observation is a country-year (that is, was a country experiencing an armed conflict in a given year?); "Assessing the Societal and Systematic Impact of Warfare: Coding Guidelines;" Marshall, Monty , "Measuring the Societal Impact of War."

9. Marshall, Monty and Ted Robert Gurr, "Peace and Conflict 2003: A Global Survey of Armed Conflicts, Self-Determination Movements, and Democracy;" Gurr, Ted Robert, Monty Marshall, and Deepa Khosla, *Peace and Conflict 2001: A Global Survey of Armed Conflicts, Self-Determination Movements, and Democracy.*

10. Marshall, Monty, "Measuring the Societal Impact of War."
11. Marshall, Monty, and Ted Robert Gurr, "Peace and Conflict 2003: A Global Survey of Armed Conflicts, Self-Determination Movements, and Democracy."
12. Rousseau, David, et al., "Assessing the Dyadic Nature of the Democratic Peace 1918–1988."
13. Reiter, Dan, and Allan Stam, "Democracy, War Initiation, and Victory." This is attributed to democratic leaders, recognizing they need to maintain the support of their citizenry, being more cautious about entering into conflict unless they are confident they can win quickly and with minimal casualties. Moreover, the armed forces in democracies are more highly motivated and are better able to conduct successful operations when called upon to do so. See also Reiter and Stam, *Democracies at War*.
14. Oneal, John, and Bruce Russett, *Triangulating Peace: Democracy, Interdependence, and International Organizations.*
15. Ibid.
16. Hegre, Havard, et al., "Toward a Democratic Civil Peace? Democracy, Political Change, and Civil War, 1816–1992."
17. Gurr, Ted Robert, Monty Marshall, and Deepa Khosla, *Peace and Conflict 2001: A Global Survey of Armed Conflicts, Self-Determination Movements, and Democracy.*
18. Collier, Paul, "Ethnic Diversity: An Economic Analysis.
19. Esty, Daniel, et al., "The State Failure Project: Phase II Findings."
20. Ibid.
21. Based on data from United Nations High Commissioner for Refugees Annual Surveys, 1980 to 2003 and Center for Systemic Peace.
22. Recall that we are categorizing as autocracies all those countries with democracies scores below three on the 0 to 10 point Polity Index.
23. Sierra Leone had a democracy score of five on Polity's 0 to 10 scale, in 1999.
24. Owen, John, "How Liberalism Produces Democratic Peace."
25. Braumoller, Bear, "Deadly Doves: Liberal Nationalism and the Democratic Peace in the Soviet Successor States."
26. Rousseau, David, et al., "Assessing the Dyadic Nature of the Democratic Peace 1918–1988."
27. Owen, John, "How Liberalism Produces Democratic Peace."
28. See, for example, Farber, Henry and Joanne Gowa, "Polities and Peace;" Layne, Christopher, "Kant or Cant: The Myth of the Democratic Peace."
29. These cases are disputed on the grounds that they were either monarchies or fell below the standards of democracy for their times (see Owen, 1994). The India–Pakistan conflict in 1999 is generally accepted as an exception even though many of those engaged from the Pakistani side were Islamic guerillas and not Pakistani troops (Oneal and Russett, 2001).
30. Farber, Henry, and Joanne Gowa, "Polities and Peace."
31. Oneal, John, and Bruce Russett, *Triangulating Peace: Democracy, Interdependence, and International Organizations.*
32. Ibid.
33. Director of Central Intelligence, "Unclassified Report to Congress on the Acquisition of Technology Relating to Weapons of Mass Destruction and Advanced Conventional Munitions, 1 January through 30 June 2002."
34. Mansfield, Edward, and Jack Snyder, "Democratization and the Danger of War;" Snyder, Jack, *From Voting to Violence: Democratization and Nationalist Conflict*; Huntington, Samuel, *Political Order in Changing Societies*; Kaplan, Robert, "Was Democracy Just for a Moment?"
35. Marshall, Monty, "Authority, Opportunity, and Outbreaks of Violent Societal Conflicts 1955–1999."
36. Mansfield, Edward and Jack Snyder, "Democratization and the Danger of War;" Snyder, Jack, *From Voting to Violence: Democratization and Nationalist Conflict.*
37. As discussed in Chapter 3, democratizers are defined as any country that experienced at least a one point advance in their Polity democracy rating from 1977–2002. Periods of democratization are those years in which this advance was maintained above the level at which it was initiated.
38. Marshall, Monty, and Ted Robert Gurr, "Peace and Conflict 2003: A Global Survey of Armed Conflicts, Self-Determination Movements, and Democracy," identify Africa, central Asia, and the Caucuses as the leading global trouble spots.

39. Recognizing that conflicts vary greatly in their level of societal devastation, the Center for Systemic Peace provides a 0 to 10 ranking of conflict magnitude for each conflict in its listing. For a description of scale and list of countries and magnitude of conflicts, see Center for Systemic Peace, "Assessing the Societal and Systemic Impact of Warfare: Coding Guidelines;" see also Marshall, Monty, "Measuring the Societal Impact of War."

40. Rousseau, David, "Democratization and International Conflict;" Thompson, William, and Richard Tucker, "A Tale of Two Democratic Peace Critiques;" Oneal, John, and Bruce Russett, *Triangulating Peace: Democracy, Interdependence, and International Organizations*; Oneal, John, and Bruce Russett, "The Classic Liberals Were Right: Democracy, Interdependence, and Conflict, 1950–1985."

41. Oneal, John, and Bruce Russett, *Triangulating Peace: Democracy, Interdependence, and International Organizations*.

42. Mansfeld and Snyder's findings that, based on the 1811 to 1980 period, democratization is associated with conflict have been criticized for conflating democratization and autocratization. When democratization is examined separately, no relationship between democratization and war is observed. Thompson, William, and Richard Tucker, "A Tale of Two Democratic Peace Critiques."

43. Hegre, Havard, et al., "Toward a Democratic Civil Peace? Democracy, Political Change, and Civil War, 1816–1992."

44. Some estimates range as high as 70,000. Abuza, Zachary, "Tentacles of Terror: al-Qaeda's Southeast Asian Network."

45. All references to terrorism refer to international terrorism—the purposeful and indiscriminate use of deadly violence against civilians to cause societal panic and instability in the attempt to achieve a political aim.

46. Staub, Ervin, "Notes on Cultures of Violence, Cultures of Caring and Peace, and the Fulfillment of Basic Needs."

47. Amin, Galal, *Whatever Happened to the Egyptians?: Changes in Egyptian Society from 1950 to the Present*; Ibrahim, Said Eddin, "Egypt's Islamic Militants."

48. Staub, Ervin, "Notes on Cultures of Violence, Cultures of Caring and Peace, and the Fulfillment of Basic Needs."

49. Staub, Ervin, "Notes on Cultures of Violence, Cultures of Caring and Peace, and the Fulfillment of Basic Needs;" Abuza, Zachary, "Tentacles of Terror: al-Qaeda's Southeast Asian Network."

50. Notably, those totalitarians that are so repressive that they even dominate the religious institutions in society are not sources of nonstate terrorism.

51. Stacher, Joshua, "Post-Islamist Rumblings in Egypt: The Emergence of the Wasat Party."

52. Staub, Ervin, "Notes on Cultures of Violence, Cultures of Caring and Peace, and the Fulfillment of Basic Needs."

53. Rugh, William, "Arab Education: Tradition, Growth, and Reform."

54. Cordesman, Anthony, "Islamic Extremism in Saudi Arabia and the Attack on Al Khobar."

55. Qutb, in turn, was influenced by Ibn Taymiyya, a fourteenth century cleric who advanced a violent view of Islam in response to Mongol attacks on Baghdad. Watson, Peter, "The Fundamentalist Challenge."

56. Berman, Paul, "The Philosopher of Islamic Terror."

57. Ibid.

58. Jones, David Martin, "Out of Bali: Cybercaliphate Rising."

59. Berman, Paul, "The Philosopher of Islamic Terror."

60. Many of the details on the influence of Farag are drawn from Hashim, Ahmed, "The World According to Usama Bin Laden."

61. Berman, Paul, "The Philosopher of Islamic Terror."

62. The details on Saudi financing of Islamic fundamentalism draws heavily from Alexiev, Alex, "The Pakistani Time Bomb;" Alexiev, Alex, "The End of an Alliance."

63. Abuza, "Tentacles of Terror: al-Qaeda's Southeast Asian Network."

64. Berman, Paul , "The Philosopher of Islamic Terror."

65. Ibid.

66. Hashim, Ahmed, "The World According to Usama Bin Laden. al-Qaeda's modus operandi is to align itself with local militant groups with country-specific grievances so as to increase its reach and influence. Although not formally subsumed into al-Qaeda, they work closely with

it, immediately giving al-Qaeda access to an in-country organizational network. In return, al-Qaeda shares intelligence, money, equipment, and recruitment (Abuza, 2002).

67. Kingstone, Heidi, "Trouble in the House of Saud."
68. The global rate was 2 percent, by comparison.
69. For perspective, per capita income in Saudi Arabia is still triple the regional median of $1,632.
70. Based on data from WDI, 2002.
71. Kingstone, Heidi, "Trouble in the House of Saud."
72. Cordesman, Anthony, "Islamic Extremism in Saudi Arabia and the Attack on Al Khobar."
73. Oxford Analytica, "Saudi Arabia."
74. Ibrahim, Youssef, "The Mideast Threat That's Hard to Define."
75. Oxford Analytica, "Saudi Arabia."
76. Shuster, Mike, "Wahhabism is on the Decline in Saudi Arabia."
77. Median levels from 1980 to 2000 based on WDI 2002.
78. Amin, Galal, *Whatever Happened to the Egyptians?: Changes in Egyptian Society from 1950 to the Present.*
79. Alterman, Jon, "Egypt: Stable but for How Long?;" Cohn, Martin Regg, "Peaceful Islamists Making Gains 'The Only Solution.'"
80. Ottaway, Marina, *Democracy Challenged: The Rise of Semi-Authoritarianism.*
81. Carapicco, Sheila, "Foreign Aid for Promoting Democracy in the Arab World.
82. Alterman, Jon, "Egypt: Stable, but for How Long?"
83. Ibid.
84. Hashim, Ahmed, "al-Qaeda's Origins, Structure, Goals, Grand Strategy, and Operational Art."
85. Cohn, Martin Regg, "Peaceful Islamists Making Gains 'The Only Solution.'"
86. Ibid.
87. Khan, Akhter Hammed, *Rural Development in Pakistan.*
88. Alexiev, Alex, "The Pakistani Time Bomb."
89. Malik, Iftikhar, "Military Coup in Pakistan: Business as Usual or Democracy on Hold!;" Zaman, Muhammad Qasim, "Sectarianism in Pakistan: The Radicalization of Shi'i and Sunni Identities."
90. Ibid.
91. Alarmed by this show of force, the government backed down.
92. Zaman, Muhammad Qasim, "Sectarianism in Pakistan: The Radicalization of Shi'a and Sunni Identities."
93. Ibid.
94. Alexiev, Alex, "The End of an Alliance."
95. Malik, Iftikhar, "Military Coup in Pakistan: Business as Usual or Democracy on Hold!"
96. Jilani, Amina, "On the Low Road;" Hussain, Irfan, "Intolerable Intolerance."
97. Alexiev, Alex, "The Pakistani Time Bomb."
98. This was accomplished, among other things, when 29 amendments to the constitution were made during a single day. Nazir, Javed, "Religious Parties Imperil Pakistan."
99. Alexiev, Alex, "The Pakistani Time Bomb."
100. We underscore here our characterization of democracy as involving mechanisms for shared power, civic participation, and a free press—and not solely the holding of elections.
101. Golden, Tim, Desmond Butler, and Don Van Natta, "As Europe Hunts for Terrorists, the Hunted Press Advantages."
102. Wilkinson, Paul, *Terrorism Versus Democracy: The Liberal State Response.*
103. Countries that received total per capita military or economic assistance from the United States that exceeded the respective decade median levels allocated.
104. Military aid is calculated as the total level of funding from the four major military assistance programs: Foreign Military Financing (FMF), Military Assistance Program (MAP), MAP Merger Funds, and International Military Education and Training (IMET). Based on data compiled from Department of Defense, 2001. Fiscal Year Series (as of September 30, 2000), published by Deputy for Financial Management Comptroller, Department of Defense-Security Assistance Agency.
105. Considers only countries with per capita GDPs below $4000.

106. Economic assistance data cover loan and grant commitments for (nonsecurity related) Economic Support Fund (ESF) and Development Assistance (DA) accounts. U.S. Agency for International Development (USAID), 2002; U.S. Overseas Loans and Grants-and Assistance from International Organizations, Obligations and Loan Authorizations July 1, 1945-September 30, 2000. (Statistical Annex I to the Annual Development Coordination Committee Report to Congress).

107. As our economic data only covers the period from 1960 to 2000, consideration of economic impacts is limited to this time period.

108. Among a sample of countries with per capita incomes below $4,000.

109. Wars are defined as incidents of 1,000 directly related deaths from armed conflict in a given year. Magnitude of conflict assesses the level of societal devastation caused by war. For a description of the 0 to 10 scale and a list of conflicts and their magnitudes, see Center for Systemic Peace, "Assessing the Societal and Systemic Impact of Warfare: Coding Guidelines;" see also Marshall, Monty, "Measuring the Societal Impact of War."

110. See Esty et al., 1999. Income levels are proxied by infant mortality rate. Goldstone et al., 2000.

111. Collier et al., *Breaking the Conflict Trap: Civil War and Development Policy.*

112. In multivariate analysis, the relationship with regard to magnitude of conflict holds for 20 years out; for frequency of conflict, this remains significant 10 years after the assistance was provided.

113. Among countries with per capita incomes below $4,000.

114. As per multivariate regressions. The same pattern applies when measuring magnitude of conflict.

115. Again, we limit the review to countries with per capita incomes below $4,000 to provide a basis of comparison.

116. As with the other relationships cited, this controls for trade and income level.

117. Marshall, Monty, "Measuring the Societal Impact of War."

118. This pattern does not consider the 30 or so cases where through support to coups, rigged elections, or the discrediting of democratic parties the United States has directly undercut the emergence of democratic government.

119. The relationship also holds for 15 years under certain configurations.

120. This applies for low-income (i.e., under $2,000 or $4,000 GDP/per capita) as well as a full sample of countries.

121. The unit of measure is a t-score, which is simply a standardized summary indicator of the level of significance in the relationship between the level of democracy and the respective recipient category in a simple statistical analysis controlling for income. A t-score of 2.0 or more indicates a confidence level of 95 percent or more that the measured relationship is not occurring by chance.

122. In addition to the list of top autocratic recipients of U.S. economic assistance mentioned earlier, some of the other cases that contribute to this inauspicious pattern include Morocco, Tunisia, Angola, Burundi, Burkina Faso, Bhutan, Cameroon, Algeria, Gabon, Myanmar, Mauritania, Rwanda, Chad, Togo, and the Democratic Republic of Congo.

123. Naturally, as with earlier chapters, this analysis must be couched in the limitations of the quality and completeness of data available. Nonetheless, the consistency of the patterns observed, rather than any one particular result, is what is most noteworthy.

Chapter 5

1. For an insider's synthesis of Russia's economic transition, see Stiglitz, Joseph, "The Insider: What I Learned at the World Economic Crisis."

2. Based on figures from the Central Bank of the Russian Federation.

3. For example, bidding sessions would be convened in remote provinces where transportation routes could be blocked except for the designated purchaser.

4. Institute of Economics, Moscow and the Center for the Study of International Economic Relations, "The Problem of Capital Flight from Russia."

5. Buiter, Willem, and Ivan Szegvari, "Capital Flight and Capital Outflows from Russia: Symptom, Cause, and Cure."

6. WDI, 2002.

7. Milanovic, Branko, "Explaining the Increase in Inequality during the Transition."

8. World Health Organization, "Health Summary Measures: Russian Federation."
9. Goldgeier, James, and Michael McFaul, *Power and Purpose: U.S. Policy Toward Russia After the Cold War.*
10. Ibid.
11. Maass, Peter, "Yeltsin Suspends Top Court."
12. Machiavelli, Niccolo, *The Prince and the Discourses.*
13. Robinson, Anthony, "Survey of Bulgaria."
14. Dempsey, Judy, "Industry Man in a Hurry."
15. Minassian, Garabed, "Bulgaria and the International Monetary Fund."
16. Dempsey, Judy, "Wayward Bulgaria Returns to Path of Reform."
17. Minassian, Garabed, "Bulgaria and the International Monetary Fund."
18. Stephen, Chris, "Bulgarians Savour Aroma of Victory: In a Sofia Coffee Shop, Chris Stephen Finds Democrats Ready to Suffer for a Free Market."
19. Ganev, Venelin, "Bulgaria's Symphony of Hope."
20. Bell, John, "Democratization and Political Participation in 'Post-Communist' Bulgaria."
21. Ganev, "Bulgaria's Symphony of Hope."
22. Upon returning to power, the UDF oversaw vigorous reforms and a rebound in growth. In 2001, they surprisingly lost a parliamentary election to the long-exiled heir to the Bulgarian monarchy, Simeon Saxe-Coburg-Gotha, and his new Coalition National Movement. Most observers attribute this to Simeon's celebrity. However, concerns over the social costs of economic reform and a belief among the public that the UDF was becoming too powerful were also factors. Simeon has largely continued the UDF's economic reform agenda.
23. Brown, Stephen, "Authoritarian Leaders and Multiparty Elections in Africa: How Foreign Donors Help to Keep Kenya's Daniel arap Moi in Power."
24. KANU was finally dislodged in the December 2002 elections, after Moi's retirement, sparking an upsurge of development activity.
25. Bueno de Mesquita, Bruce and Hilton Root, "The Political Roots of Poverty: The Economic Logic of Autocracy."
26. Considered Latin America's third most inequitable. Lucero, Jose Antonio, "Crisis and Contention in Ecuador."
27. Viewed as a guise to remove a populist leader who challenged the elite interests in Congress.
28. Newsome, Justine, "Investors Still Jittery over Ecuador's Continuing Economic Crisis."
29. Sancisi, Juan Salazar, "Ecuador Undergoes Big Change for Sustainable Growth."
30. Newsome, Justine, "Ecuador Relaunches Telecoms Sell-Off."
31. Saavedra, Luis, and Barbara Fraser, "Solidarity Voucher Called A Ploy to Exclude the Poor."
32. Newsome, Justine, "Investors Still Jittery over Ecuador's Continuing Economic Crises."
33. A value equivalent to roughly $1/7$ of Ecuador's GDP.
34. Hall, Kevin, "Ecuador Readies Export Boost."
35. Cable News Network, "Ecuador Launches Tough Economic Plan;" Associated Press, "Anti-government Protests Leave Three Dead in Ecuador."
36. Smith, Elliot Blair, "Ecuador's Finances Unravel The Plan: Raise Taxes, Slash Outlays."
37. Lucero, Jose Antonio, "Crisis and Contention in Ecuador."
38. Bonilla, Adrian, "Ecuador."
39. Lucero, Jose Antonio, "Crisis and Contention in Ecuador."
40. Newport, Samantha, "Did the IMF Drop the Ball in Ecuador?"
41. IMF, "Ecuador Signs Letter of Intent with IMF."
42. Patino, Maria Laura, "Lessons from the Financial Crisis in Ecuador in 1999."
43. Newport, Samantha, "Did the IMF Drop the Ball in Ecuador?"
44. Euromoney, "U.S. Dollar Becomes Ecuador's Currency," October 2000.
45. Newport, Samantha, "Did the IMF Drop the Ball in Ecuador?"
46. IMF, "IMF, World Bank, IDB, and CAF Prepared to Support Ecuador."
47. International Center for Not-for-Profit Law, "The Tax Treatment of Nongovernmental Organizations: A Survey of Best Practices from Around the World."
48. World Bank, "Handbook on Good Practices for Laws Relating to Non-Governmental Organizations."
49. International Center for Not-for-Profit Law, "Tax Preferences for Nongovernmental Organizations;" International Center for Not-for-Profit Law, *Survey of Tax Laws Affecting Non-Governmental Organizations in Central and Eastern Europe.*

50. Carapico, Sheila, "Foreign Aid for Promoting Democracy in the Arab World;" World Bank. 1997, "Handbook on Good Practices for Laws Relating to Non-Governmental Organizations."
51. Scott, James, *Seeing Like a State: How Certain Schemes to Improve the Human Condition Have Failed.*
52. Stiglitz, Joseph, *Globalization and Its Discontents.*
53. Balcerowicz, Leszek, "Understanding Postcommunist Transitions." Cuny has noted a similar phenomenon with regard to natural catastrophes. In the aftermath of such arresting events, societies share a collective belief that change is needed and are willing to abandon old ways of doing things. Cuny, Frederick, *Disasters and Development.*
54. Recall from our discussion in Chapter 3 that $1/2$ of all democratic backtracking occurs in the initial three years of the democratization process.
55. Pei, Minxin, and Merrit Lyon, "Bullish on New Democracies: Research Notes on Multinationals and the Third Wave."
56. Based on World Development Indicators, 2003, and Polity data.
57. Awoniyi, Ola, "Nigerians to 'Get Back to Business' after Speaker Row."
58. Holman, Michael, and William Wallis, "Nigerian President Relents on Close IMF Supervision."
59. Cunliffe-Jones, Peter, "Obasanjo Promises Nigerians Better Times on 100th Day in Office."
60. Africa News, "What IMF Told Obasanjo."
61. Holman, Michael, and William Wallis, "Nigerian President Relents on Close IMF Supervision."
62. Kendall, Sue, "World Bank Hosts Aid Meeting for Nigeria."
63. IMF, "IMF Approves Stand-By Credit for Nigeria."
64. Ibid.
65. Africa News, "Nigeria Shelves Plans to Privatize State Oil Interests." Despite being a major oil producer, Nigerians must often wait in long lines for gasoline due to lack of refinery capacity.
66. Ibid.
67. Wallis, William, "One Step Forward, Then One Step Back."
68. Komolafe, Funmi, "Labor: Let's Create Wealth, Not Manage Poverty—Oshiomhole."
69. This Day, "Sh!! . . . The Bank is Talking."
70. Goldman, Antony, and William Wallis, "Gambling with the Future: Confidence in the Country's Ability to Implement Much-Needed Reform is Waning."
71. Wallis, William, "One Step Forward, Then One Step Back."
72. Ibid.
73. Wallis, William, "I Know that We're Moving . . . That We're Improving: Interview with the President."
74. Goldman, Antony and William Wallis, "Gambling with the Future: Confidence in the Country's Ability to Implement Much-Needed Reform is Waning."
75. Ibid.
76. Recall that autocracies are countries with democracy scores of 0 to 2 on Polity's eleven-point scale. By using this dichotomization, which excludes countries with intermediate levels of democratic institutions, we are able to compare two distinct governance categories. The lack of aid differentiation that emerges, therefore, is all the more revealing.
77. Controlling for income level and other factors in a sample of all countries with per capita incomes below $4,000 for the 1960 to 2000 time period finds level of democracy to be insignificantly associated with ODA as a percentage of GDP.
78. As derived from WDI 2003 and Polity data.
79. Organisation for Economic Cooperation and Development (OECD), "Geographic Distribution of Financial Flows to Aid Recipients: 1996–2000."
80. Department for International Development, Statistics on International Development 1997/98—2001/02.
81. Organisation for Economic Cooperation and Development (OECD), "Geographic Distribution of Financial Flows to Aid Recipients: 1996–2000."
82. The Economist, "Co-prosperity by Peaceful Means."
83. In fact, few donors are explicit about the factors they weigh when allocating development assistance. This ambiguity allows them the flexibility to make funding decisions on a case-by-case (that is, strategic) basis. If implemented as designed, the Millennium Challenge Account

would be precedent-setting for favoring countries that are determined to "rule justly," something we discuss in more depth in Chapter 6.

84. German, Tony, and Judith Randel, "Never Richer, Never Meaner."
85. Cuny, Frederick, *Disasters and Development.*
86. WDI 2002; World Bank, "Addressing the Social Impact of the Crisis in Indonesia: A Background Note for the 1998 Consultative Group on Indonesia;" Xinhua News Agency, "Indonesia's Capital Flight Reaches $32 Billion."
87. World Bank, "Addressing the Social Impact of the Crisis in Indonesia: A Background Note for the 1998 Consultative Group on Indonesia."
88. The exact figure is difficult to ascertain given the many hundreds of companies and foundations owned by the family. Winters, Jeffrey, "Some Comments on Soeharto's Wealth and Trying to Track It."
89. World Bank, "Memorandum to the Executive Directors and the President, Operations Evaluation Department, Indonesia: Country Assistance Note."
90. Asian Development Bank, "Country Assistance Strategy: Indonesia."
91. Schwarz, Adam, ed., *A Nation in Waiting: Indonesia's Search for Stability.*
92. Ibid.
93. Ibid.
94. Schwarz, *A Nation in Waiting: Indonesia's Search for Stability.*
95. Ibid.
96. Ibid.
97. Winters, Jeffrey, *Structural Power and Investor Mobility: Capital Control and State Policy in Indonesia, 1965–1990.*
98. Schwarz, *A Nation in Waiting: Indonesia's Search for Stability.*
99. Haggard, Stephan, *The Political Economy of the Asian Financial Crisis.*
100. Ibid.
101. Based on WDI 2002.
102. World Bank, "Memorandum to the Executive Directors and the President, Operations Evaluation Department, Indonesia: Country Assistance Note."
103. ECA Watch, "Publicly Guaranteed Corruption: Corrupt Power Plants and the Responsibility of Export Credit Agencies in Indonesia."
104. Waldman, Peter, and Jay Solomon, "Wasted Energy: How U.S. Companies and Soeharto's Circle Electrified Indonesia."
105. World Bank, "Memorandum to the Executive Directors and the President, Operations Evaluation Department, Indonesia: Country Assistance Note."
106. Ibid.
107. Ibid.
108. Ibid.
109. Ibid.
110. Winters, Jeffrey, "World Bank Must Face the Corruption Music."
111. Sanger, David, "World Bank Beats Breast for Failures in Indonesia;" for a review of the institutional soul-searching and internal reforms undertaken by the World Bank in the wake of its Indonesian experience, see Mallaby, Sebastian, *The World's Banker.*
112. World Bank, "Memorandum to the Executive Directors and the President, Operations Evaluation Department, Indonesia: Country Assistance Note."
113. World Bank, "Indonesia, Country Assistance Strategy—Progress Report."
114. World Bank, "Memorandum to the Executive Directors and the President, Operations Evaluation Department, Indonesia: Country Assistance Note."
115. Asiamoney, "IMF and Indonesia: A Rocky Relationship."
116. Ibid.
117. Ibid.
118. Haggard, Stephan, *The Political Economy of the Asian Financial Crisis*; Asiamoney, "IMF and Indonesia: A Rocky Relationship."
119. Handley, Paul, "Can Indonesia Survive Soeharto?"
120. WDI 2003.
121. Easterly, William, *The Elusive Quest for Growth: Economists' Adventures and Misadventures in the Tropics.*
122. Using the International Country Risk Guide index.

123. Includes both International Bank for Reconstruction and Development (IBRD) and International Development Association (IDA) funding, World Bank Annual Reports 1998–2001.
124. USAID, "Remarks to Interaction Forum by USAID Administrator Andrew S. Natsios."
125. Imperato, Pascal James, *Mali: A Search for Direction.*
126. Larson, Adam, "Democratic Influences on Structural Adjustment in Mali."
127. U.S. Department of State, "Background Note: Mali."
128. Press, Robert, "Economic Woes Shake Mali's Democracy."
129. Ibid.
130. British Broadcasting Company (BBC), "President Konare Discusses Economy, Effect of CFA Franc Devaluation."
131. Key donors included Canada, France, Germany, Japan, the Netherlands, the United States, the European Union, and the World Bank.
132. BBC, "New President Gives Inaugural Address; Says He Will Not Be 'Peddler of Illusions."
133. Part of the West African CFA regional devaluation.
134. Press, Robert, "Economic Woes Shake Mali's Democracy."
135. Ibid.
136. Ibid.
137. IMF, "IMF Approves Three-Year Loan for Mali Under the ESAF."
138. All socio-economic figures referenced in this paragraph are drawn from WDI 2003.
139. Seeley, Jennifer, "A Political Analysis of Decentralization: Co-opting the Tuareg Threat in Mali."
140. Smith, Zeric Kay, "Mali's Decade of Democracy."
141. French, Howard,"Mali's Slips Reflect Stumbling African Democracy."
142. Agence France Press, "Mali Returns to Calm After Violence Mars Polls."
143. Smith, "Mali's Decade of Democracy."
144. The World Bank, "Mali Qualifies for HIPC Debt Relief Totaling $870 Million."
145. Bratton, Michael et al., "Popular Perceptions of Good Governance in Mali."

Chapter 6

1. Shapiro, Isaac, "Trends in U.S. Development Aid and the Current Budget Debate."
2. USAID, "Foreign Aid in the National Interest: Promoting Freedom, Security, and Opportunity."
3. U.S. development assistance refers broadly to international development, humanitarian assistance, and Economic Support Fund resources provided by the U.S. government for the promotion of economic and social well being. It excludes military and political assistance as well funding explicitly committed for the promotion of democracy.
4. International Monetary Fund, World Economic Outlook: Trade and Finance.
5. Meltzer Commission Report, Report of the International Financial Institution Advisory Commission.
6. International Monetary Fund, World Economic Outlook: Trade and Finance.
7. Congress only allocated $1 billion for the MCA in FY04—the first year of the initiative. This compares to the $3 billion President Bush called for initially and the $1.3 billion requested in his budget submission to Congress.
8. Kaufmann, Daniel, and Aart Kray, "Governance Indicators, Aid Allocation, and the Millennium Challenge Account;" Radelet, Steven, *Challenging Foreign Aid: A Policymaker's Guide to the Millennium Challenge Account*; Palley, Thomas, "The Millennium Challenge Account: Elevating the Significance of Democracy as a Qualifying Criterion;" Braindard, Lael et al., *The Other War: Global Poverty and the Millennium Challenge Account.*
9. These criteria are largely economic in orientation. They are based on factors such as contract enforcement capacity, protection from expropriation, and property rights protection.
10. Ideally, the democracy criterion would be based on a compilation of both the Polity and Freedom House indices. This would reduce the chances that countries are excluded on methodological quirks. It would also diffuse charges of bias.
11. *Final Warsaw Declaration: Toward a Community of Democracies*, 2000.

12. The five are Bahrain, Colombia, Ecuador, Morocco, and Venezuela.

13. For another perspective on how this might be put into practice, see Palley, Thomas, "Linking the Community of Democracies with the Millennium Challenge Account: A Case of Win-Win."

14. These are Chile, Czech Republic, India, Mali, Mexico, Poland, Portugal, South Africa, South Korea, and the United States.

15. These are Algeria, Armenia, Azerbaijan, Egypt, Georgia, Haiti, Kuwait, Madagascar, Qatar, Tunisia, Ukraine, and Yemen.

16. Meanwhile, democracy promotion initiatives could still be directed to these countries. In this way, avenues by which reformers could be assisted would not be completely cut off.

17. For a summary see Easterly, William, "How Did Heavily Indebted Poor Countries Become Heavily Indebted? Reviewing Two Decades of Debt Relief."

18. Easterly, William, *The Elusive Quest for Growth: Economists' Adventures and Misadventures in the Tropics.*

19. Based on data from WDI 2003 and Polity.

20. See also Kremer, Michael and Seema Jayachandran, "Odious Debt."

21. Pei, Minxin and Merrit Lyon, "Bullish on New Democracies: Research Notes on Multinationals and the Third Wave."

22. In practical terms, development assistance would need to be curtailed in line with the increased capital market access these lower-middle income developing countries can be expected to have. Under such circumstances, donor assistance should be in the form of technical assistance or targeted to specific activities or regions so as to ensure it is not hindering the development of capital markets.

23. Starr, Harvey, "Democratic Dominoes: Diffusion Approaches to the Spread of Democracy in the International System."

24. The Meltzer Commission Report recommended several derivatives of this approach including performance-based grants and institutional reform loans.

25. Stiglitz, Joseph, *Globalization and Its Discontents.*

26. Although initially created for Poland and Hungary, these unique private-public partnerships were subsequently expanded for eight other eastern European and former Soviet Union countries.

27. The other two are to promote the development of a free market economic system and a prohibition for any support to communist parties or the security forces of Warsaw Pact countries.

28. Birkelund, John P., "The Unheralded Success of American Enterprise Funds."

29. Ibid.

30. Although several less senior interagency working groups currently exist, they do not have the authority to influence the Treasury Department's policy stances.

31. Collier, Paul, *Living Down the Past: How Europe Can Help Africa Grow.*

32. The rationale is that even though the United States may not agree with the orientation of a political leadership, by remaining engaged with this government—economically, diplomatically, and military—greater leverage will be maintained to influence its actions in a positive manner.

33. Recall that semi-authoritarian governments are those that exhibit some of the rituals of a democratic society including a limited degree of civil society, free press, and opposition party activity—though the prospect of the ruling party sharing power is never seriously in question. See Ottoway, Marina, *Democracy Challenged: The Rise of Semi-Authoritarianism.*

34. See for example, Carapico, Sheila, "Foreign Aid for Promoting Democracy in the Arab World."

35. For a summary of this debate, see van de Walle, Nicolas, "The International Community and the Poorest Economies."

36. van de Walle, Nicolas, "The International Community and the Poorest Economies."

37. To be sure, other donors, particularly France and Japan, also have considerable progress to make in this regard.

38. Easterly, William, "The Cartel of Good Intentions."

39. OECD, *Shaping the 21st Century: Contribution of Development Cooperation.*

Chapter 7

1. For a concise summary of the histories of the World Bank and IMF see, Krueger, Anne, "Whither the World Bank and the IMF?"
2. Boughton, J., "Harry Dexter White and the International Monetary Fund;" Marquette, Heather, "Corruption, Democracy and the World Bank."
3. Shihata, Ibrahim, "The World Bank and Governance Issues in its Borrowing Members."
4. World Bank, "Sub-Saharan Africa—From Crisis to Sustainable Growth. A Long Term Perspective Study."
5. Shihata, Ibrahim, "The World Bank and Governance Issues in its Borrowing Members."
6. Ibid.
7. Ibid.
8. Ibid.
9. World Bank, "Governance and Development."
10. The Institutional Governance Review for Bolivia, for example, candidly states that the underlying causes of poor public administration have to do with "the dynamics of politics." It goes on to cite weaknesses in the political and bureaucratic structures as the key causes of patronage and clientelism. "Citizen Voice" is highlighted as a way of increasing public oversight of government administration. World Bank, "Bolivia: From Patronage to Professional State."
11. Gold, Joseph, "Political Considerations Are Prohibited by Articles of Agreement When the Fund Considers Requests for Use of Resources."
12. Finch, C. David, "Adjustment Policies and Conditionality."
13. IMF, "Partnership for Sustainable Growth."
14. IMF, "The Role of the IMF in Governance Issues: Guidance Note."
15. IMF, "The IMF's Approach to Promoting Good Governance and Combating Corruption—A Guide;" IMF, "The Role of the IMF in Governance Issues: Guidance Note."
16. IMF, "The IMF's Approach to Promoting Good Governance and Combating Corruption—A Guide."
17. See for example, World Bank, "Bolivia: From Patronage to a Professional State;" World Bank, "Institutional and Governance Reviews—a New Type of Economic and Sector Work."
18. Weber, Steven, "Origins of the European Bank for Reconstruction and Development."
19. European Bank for Reconstruction and Development (EBRD), *Annual Reports 1999–2003*.
20. Newburg, Andre, "The EBRD: A New-Age Financial Institution."
21. EBRD. *Agreement Establishing the EBRD.*
22. The EBRD works closely with national foreign investment advisory councils. By maintaining horizontal links with the business community, the EBRD feels it can affect the transition process not only through its projects but also by positively influencing the investment climate.
23. Weber, Steven, "Origins of the European Bank for Reconstruction and Development."
24. Milner, Mark, "The Master Rebuilder."
25. EBRD, "Procedures to Implement the Political Aspects of the Mandate of the European Bank for Reconstruction and Development."
26. Lemierre, Jean, *"Letter to Turmenistan's President;"* Roper, Steven and Lilian Barria, "Policy Preferences Among Multilateral Development Banks: Explaining Differences Between the IDB and the EBRD."
27. To improve the diagnostic effectiveness of these surveys, some respondents have suggested making the surveys more specific. Better to ask, "What are the specific shortcomings of a particular law?" rather than ask for a 1 to 5 score on the effectiveness of that law.
28. Kaufmann, Daniel, Aart Kraay, and Pablo Zoido-Lobaton, "Governance Matters, II: Updated Indicators for 2000–01."
29. *The Economist*, "Giving it the BERD."
30. Ibid.
31. Milner, Mark, "The Master Rebuilder."
32. Wagstyl, Stefan, "A Decade of Reform in Eastern Europe: The EBRD's problems are well documented but the Bank now has a valuable role."
33. Milner, Mark, correspondence, April 3, 2002.
34. Farsian, Behzad, "The EBRD—Living Up to Its Promise?"
35. Hewko, John, "Foreign Direct Investment: Does the Rule of Law Matter?"

36. EBRD, *Annual Reports 1999–2001.*
37. Wagstyl, Stefan, "A Decade of Reform in Eastern Europe: The EBRD's problems are well documented but the Bank now has a valuable role."
38. Approval of 80 percent of shareholders is required to amend the Bank's Articles of Agreement.
39. Herman, Robert, and Theodore Piccone, eds., *Defending Democracy: A Global Survey of Foreign Policy Trends 1992–2002.*
40. Global Investor, "Emerging Markets Debt Winner: Ashmore Investment Management."
41. Stiglitz, Joseph, *Globalization and Its Discontents*; Stiglitz, Joseph, "What I Learned At the World Economic Crisis. The Insider."
42. Shihata, Ibrahim, *The World Bank in a Changing World.*
43. World Bank, "Adjustment Policies for Sustainable Growth."
44. World Bank, 1990; Shihata 1991.
45. See Cernea, Michael, ed., *Putting People First: Sociological Variables in Rural Development.*
46. World Bank. "A User's Guide to Poverty and Social Impact Analysis."
47. World Bank. "Social Assessment: The Facets and Phases of Social Assessment."
48. IMF, "Social Impact Analysis of Economic Policies: A Factsheet."
49. World Bank, "A User's Guide to Poverty and Social Impact Analysis;" World Bank, "A User's Guide to Poverty and Social Impact Analysis."
50. World Bank, "Social Assessment: The Facets and Phases of Social Assessment."
51. See, for example, Einhorn, Jessica, "The World Bank's Mission Creep."

Chapter 8

1. Considered a national hero for exposing the true severity of the SARS crisis in China in 2003 that government officials were concealing. In a letter to the Chinese Communist Party leadership in 2004 he called for a reappraisal of the 1989 Tiananmen Square pro-democracy protests as a patriotic movement and that the errors committed by the party in the handling of these protests be acknowledged. The retired military physician was subsequently jailed and held in isolation for two months.
2. Hirschman, Albert O., "A Dissenter's Confession: 'The Strategy of Economic Development' Revisited."
3. Ibid.
4. Ibid.
5. Rostow, Walt Whitman, "Development: The Political Economy of the Marshallian Long Period."
6. Gurr, Ted Robert, Keith Jaggers, and Will Moore, "The Transformation of the Western State: The Growth of Democracy, Autocracy, and State Power since 1800."

Bibliography

Abuza, Zachary. 2002. "Tentacles of Terror: Al-Qaeda's Southeast Asian Network." *Contemporary Southeast Asia* 24 (3): pp. 427–465.

Africa News. 1999. "What IMF Told Obasanjo." *Africa News*, May 13.

_____. 2002. "Nigeria Shelves Plans to Privatize State Oil Interests." *Africa News*, October 18.

Agence France Press. 1997. "Mali Returns to Calm After Violence Mars Polls." *Agence France Presse*, July 21.

Ahmed, Rashmee. 2002. "India Beats China as Business Destination." *The Times of India*, April 25.

Alesina, Alberto and Roberto Perotti. 1994. "The Political Economy of Growth: A Critical Survey of the Literature." *The World Bank Economic Review* 8 (3): pp. 351–371.

Alexiev, Alex. 2002. "The End of an Alliance." *The National Review Online*, November 26.

_____. 2003. "The Pakistani Time Bomb." *Commentary* 115 (3): pp. 46–52.

Alterman, Jon. 2000. "Egypt: Stable but for How Long?." *The Washington Quarterly* 23 (4): pp. 107–118.

Amin, Galal. 2000. *Whatever Happened to the Egyptians?: Changes in Egyptian Society from 1950 to the Present.* Cairo: The American University in Cairo Press.

Asiamoney. 1998. "IMF and Indonesia: A Rocky Relationship." *Asiamoney* 9 (9), November.

Asian Development Bank. 2000. "Country Assistance Strategy: Indonesia." March.

Associated Press. 1998. "Anti-government Protests Leave Three Dead in Ecuador." *Associated Press*, October 1.

Awoniyi, Ola. 1999. "Nigerians to 'Get Back to Business' after Speaker Row." *Agence France Presse*, July 23.

Balcerowicz, Leszek. 1995. "Understanding Postcommunist Transitions." *Economic Reform and Democracy*. Edited by Larry Diamond and Marc Plattner. Baltimore, MD: The Johns Hopkins University Press.

Barro, Robert. 1997. *Determinants of Economic Growth: A Cross-Country Empirical Study.* Cambridge: MIT Press.

_____. 2002. "Don't Bank on Democracy in Afghanistan." *Business Week*, January 21.

Bell, John. 1997. "Democratization and Political Participation in 'Post-Communist' Bulgaria." *Politics, Power, and the Struggle for Democracy in South-East Europe.* Edited by Karen Dawisha and Bruce Parrott. Cambridge: Cambridge University Press.

Berman, Paul. 2003. "The Philosopher of Islamic Terror." *The New York Times Magazine*, March 23.

Bhagwati, Jagdish. 1966. *The Economics of Underdeveloped Countries.* London: Weidenfeld & Nicholson.

Bhalla, A.S. 1995. "Recent Economic Reforms in China and India." *Asian Survey* 35 (6): pp. 555–572.

Birkelund, John P. 2001. "The Unheralded Success of American Enterprise Funds." *Foreign Affairs* 80 (5): pp. 14–20.

Bonilla, Adrian. 2001. "Ecuador." *The Crisis of Democratic Governance in the Andes.* Edited by Cynthia Arnson. Washington, DC: Woodrow Wilson International Center for Scholars, Latin America Program.

Boughton, James M. 1998. "Harry Dexter White and the International Monetary Fund." *Finance and Development* 35 (3).

Bratton, Michael, Carolyn Logan, Wonbin Cho, and Paloma Bauer, 2004. "Afrobarometer Round 2: Compendium of Comparative Results from a 15-Country Survey," Afrobarometer Working Paper #24, East Lansing, MI: Department of Political Science, Michigan State University.

Braumoller, Bear. 1997. "Deadly Doves: Liberal Nationalism and the Democratic Peace in the Soviet Successor States." *International Studies Quarterly* 41 (3): pp. 375–402.

Braindard, Lael, Carol Graham, Nigle Purvis, Steven Radelet, and Gayle E. Smith. 2003. *The Other War: Global Poverty and the Millennium Challenge Account.* Washington, DC: Brookings Institution Press.

British Broadcasting Company. 1994. "President Konare Discusses Economy, Effect of CFA Franc Devaluation." *British Broadcasting Corporation*, November 26.

———. 1999. "New President Gives Inaugural Address; Says He Will Not be 'Peddler of Illusions'." *British Broadcasting Corporation*, June 12.

———. 2003. "Venezuela's Chavez Says He Will Stay in Power Until 2021." BBC Monitoring Latin America-Political, April 14.

Brown, Stephen. 2001. "Authoritarian Leaders and Multiparty Elections in Africa: How Foreign Donors Help to Keep Kenya's Daniel arap Moi in Power." *Third World Quarterly* 22 (5): pp. 725–739.

Bueno de Mesquita, Bruce and Hilton Root, eds. 2000. *Governing for Prosperity.* New Haven, CT: Yale University Press.

Bueno de Mesquita, Bruce and Hilton Root. 2002. "The Political Roots of Poverty: The Economic Logic of Autocracy." *The National Interest*, Summer 2002 (68): pp. 27–37.

Buiter, Willem and Ivan Szegvari. 2002. "Capital Flight and Capital Outflows from Russia: Symptom, Cause, and Cure." European Bank of Reconstruction and Development, Working Paper No. 73.

Burkhart, Ross and Michael Lewis-Beck. 1994. "Comparative Democracy: The Economic Development Thesis." *American Political Science Review* 88 (4): pp. 903–910.

Business Line. 2000. "India: Democracy and Sustainable Growth." *Business Line*, March 25.

Cable News Network. 1999. "Ecuador Launches Tough Economic Plan." *Cable News Network*, March 11.

Callaghy, Thomas. 1995. "Africa Back to the Future?" *Economic Reform and Democracy*. Edited by Larry Diamond and Marc Plattner. Baltimore: Johns Hopkins University Press. 1995.

Campos, Jose Edgardo, and Hilton Root. 1996. *The Key to the Asian Miracle: Making Shared Growth Credible.* Washington, DC: The Brookings Institution.

Carapico, Sheila. 2002. "Foreign Aid for Promoting Democracy in the Arab World." *Middle East Journal* 56 (3): pp. 379–395.

Carothers, Thomas. 1999. *Aiding Democracy Abroad: The Learning Curve.* Washington, DC: Carnegie Endowment for International Peace.

———. "Zakaria's Complaint." *The National Interest*, (72):pp. 137–143.

Center for Systemic Peace. "Assessing the Societal and Systematic Impact of Warfare: Coding Guidelines." http://members.aol.com/cspmgm/warcode.htm.

Central Intelligence Agency. 2002. *The World Factbook.* Washington, DC: Brasseys, Inc. 2002.

———. "Unclassified Report to Congress on the Acquisition of Technology Relating to Weapons of Mass Destruction and Advanced Conventional Munitions, 1 January through 30 June 2003." www.cia.gov/cia/reports/721_reports/jan_jun2003.html.

Cernea, Michael, ed. 1991. *Putting People First: Sociological Variables in Rural Development*, 2nd ed. Oxford: Oxford University Press for the World Bank.

Chang, Gordon. 2001. *The Coming Collapse of China.* New York: Random House.

Chua, Amy. 2003. *World on Fire: How Exporting Free Market Democracy Breeds Ethnic Hatred and Global Instability.* New York: Doubleday.

Clague, Christopher, ed. 1997. *Institutions and Economic Development: Growth and Governance in Less-Developed and Post-Socialist Countries.* Baltimore, MD: Johns Hopkins University Press.

Cohn, Martin Regg. 2003. "Peaceful Islamists Making Gains 'The Only Solution,'" *Toronto Star*, May 4.

Collier, Paul. 1998. *Living Down the Past: How Europe Can Help Africa Grow.* London: Institute of Economic Affairs, Studies in Trade and Development.

———. 2000. "Economic Causes of Civil Conflict and their Implications for Policy." World Bank, Development Research Group, June 15.

———. 2001a. "Ethnic Diversity: An Economic Analysis." *Economic Policy* 16 (32): pp. 127–166.

———. 2001b. "Conflict and Development." World Bank, Development Research Group, November 2001.

Collier, Paul, Lani Elliott, Havard Hegre, Anke Hoeffler, Marta Reynal-Querol, and Nicholas Sambanis. 2003. *Breaking the Conflict Trap: Civil War and Development Policy.* Washington, DC: The World Bank and Oxford University Press.

Community of Democracies. 2000. "Final Warsaw Declaration: Toward a Community of Democracies." From inaugural meeting of the Community of Democracies, June 27, 2000.

Cordesman, Anthony. 2001. "Islamic Extremism in Saudi Arabia and the Attack on Al Khobar." Draft Paper for discussion, Center for Strategic and International Studies.

Cray, Charlie. 2001. "Dubious Development: The World Bank's Foray into Private Sector Investment." *Multinational Monitor* 22 (9): pp. 20–26.

Cunliffe-Jones, Peter. 1999. "Obasanjo Promises Nigerians Better Times on 100th Day in Office." *Agence France Presse*, September 5.

Cuny, Frederick. 1983. *Disasters and Development.* Cambridge: Oxford University Press.

Dabrowski, Marek and Rafat Antczak. 1996. "Economic Transition in Russia, Ukraine, and Belarus: A Comparative Perspective." Chapter 3 in *Economic Transition in Russia and the New States of Eurasia,* Edited by Martlomiej Kaminski. 1996. *Economic Transition in Russia and the New States of Eurasia.* Armonk, NY: ME Sharpe.

Dahl, Robert. 1971. *Polyarchy: Participation and Opposition.* New Haven, CT: Yale University Press.

———. 1989. *Democracy and Its Critics.* New Haven, CT: Yale University Press.

———. 1998. *On Democracy.* New Haven, CT: Yale University Press.

Dempsey, Judy. 1991. "Industry Man in a Hurry." *Financial Times* May 17.

———. 1992. "Wayward Bulgaria Returns to Path of Reform." *Financial Times*, April 9.

Department for International Development. 2002. *Statistics on International Development 1997/98–2001/02.* London: DfID.

de Schweinitz, Karl, Jr. 1959. "Industrialization, Labor Controls, and Democracy." *Economic Development and Cultural Change* 7 (4).

Dornbusch, Rudiger and Sebastian Edwards. 1990. "Marcoeconomic Populism." *Journal of Development Economics* 32 (2): pp. 247–277.

Easterly, William. 2002a. *The Elusive Quest for Growth: Economists' Adventures and Misadventures in the Tropics.* Cambridge, MA: MIT Press.

———. 2002b. "The Cartel of Good Intentions." *Foreign Policy* 131: pp. 40–49.

———. 2002c. "How Did Heavily Indebted Poor Countries Become Heavily Indebted? Reviewing Two Decades of Debt Relief." *World Development* 30 (10): pp. 1677–1697.

The Economist. 1989. "Co-prosperity by Peaceful Means." *The Economist*, June 17.

———. 1991. "Bulgaria: Spoilt for Choice." *The Economist*, October 5.

———. 2001. "Giving it the BERD." *The Economist*, April 28.

———. 2003. The Economist Intelligence Unit; Country Reports, "China Country Report."

Einhorn, Jessica. 2001. "The World Bank's Mission Creep." *Foreign Affairs* 80 (5): pp. 22–35.

Ellner, Steve. 2001. "The Radical Potential of Chavismo in Venezuela: The First Year-and-a Half in Power." *Latin American Perspectives* 28 (5): pp. 5–32.

Esty, Daniel, Jack Goldstone, Ted Robert Gurr, Barbara Harff, Pamela Surko, Alan Unger, and Robert Chen. 1999. "The State Failure Project: Phase II Findings." *Environmental Change & Security Project Report*, Summer 1999 (5).

Euromoney. 2000. "U.S. Dollar Becomes Ecuador's Currency." October.

European Bank for Reconstruction and Development. 1990. *Agreement Establishing the EBRD.* Article 11, paragraph 2 (ii).

———. 1991. "Procedures to Implement the Political Aspects of the Mandate of the European Bank for Reconstruction and Development." From memorandum approved by EBRD, Board of Directors, 1991.

_____. 1999–2003. *Annual Reports 1999–2003*. London: European Bank for Reconstruction and Development.

Export Credit, Finance and Insurance Agencies Watch. 2000. "Publicly Guaranteed Corruption: Corrupt Power Plants and the Responsibility of Export Credit Agencies in Indonesia." *ECA Watch*. International NGO Campaign on Export Credit Agencies, 2000.

Farber, Henry and Joanne Gowa. 1995. "Polities and Peace." *International Security* 20 (2): pp. 123–145.

Farsian, Behzad. 2001. "The EBRD—Living Up to Its Promise?." *Metal Bulletin Monthly*, July.

Freedom House, 2003. *Freedom in the World: The Annual Survey of Political Rights and Civil Liberties, 2001–2002*. New York: Freedom House.

French, Howard. 1997. "Mali's Slips Reflect Stumbling African Democracy." *New York Times*, September 7.

Galenson, Walter. 1959. *Labor and Economic Development*. New York: Wiley.

Gallagher, Mary. 2002. "Reform and Openness: Why China's Economic Reforms Have Delayed Democracy." *World Politics* 53 (3): pp. 338–372.

Ganev, Venelin. 1997. "Bulgaria's Symphony of Hope." *Journal of Democracy* 8 (4): pp. 125–139.

German, Tony and Judith Randel. 2002. "Never Richer, Never Meaner." *The Reality of Aid 2002*. Edited by Tony German, Judith Randel, and Deborah Ewing. Ibon Foundation, January.

Global Investor. 2002. "Emerging Markets Debt Winner: Ashmore Investment Management." *Global Investor*, No. 149, February.

Gold, Joseph. 1983. "Political Considerations Are Prohibited by Articles of Agreement When the Fund Considers Requests for use of Resources." IMF Survey, May 23, 1983, pp. 146–148.

Goldman, Antony and William Wallis. 2002. "Gambling with the Future: Confidence in the Country's Ability to Implement Much-Needed Reform is Waning." *Financial Times*, April 9.

Goldstone, Jack, Ted Robert Gurr, Barbara Harff, Marc Levy, Monty Marshall, Robert Bates, David Epstein, Colin Kahl, Pamela Surko, John Ulfeder, and Alan Unger. 2000. *State Failure Task Force Report: Phase III Findings*. McLean, VA: Science Applications International Corporation (SAIC).

Gourevitch, Peter. 1993. "Democracy and Economic Policy: Elective Affinities and Circumstantial Conjunctures." *World Development* 21 (8): pp. 1271–1280.

Grichtchenko, Jane M. and A.A. Gritsanov. 1995. "The Local Political Elite in the Democratic Transformation of Belarus." *The Annals of the American Academy* 540: pp. 118–125.

Gurr, Ted Robert, Keith Jaggers, and Will Moore. 1990. "The Transformation of the Western State: The Growth of Democracy, Autocracy, and State Power since 1800." *Studies in Comparative International Development* 25 (1): pp. 73–108.

Gurr, Ted Robert, Monty G. Marshall, and Deepa Khosla. 2001. *Peace and Conflict 2001: A Global Survey of Armed Conflicts, Self-Determination Movements, and Democracy*. College Park: Center for International Development and Conflict Management.

Gurr, Ted Robert and Monty G. Marshall. 2003. *Peace and Conflict 2003: A Global Survey of Armed Conflicts, Self-Determination Movements, and Democracy*. Center for International Development and Conflict Management, Department of Government and Politics: University of Maryland, February 11.

Haggard, Stephan. 2000. *The Political Economy of the Asian Financial Crisis*. Washington, DC: Institute for International Economics.

Haggard, Stephan and Robert R. Kaufman. 1995. *The Political Economy of Democratic Transitions*. Princeton, NJ: Princeton University Press.

Hall, Kevin. 1999. "Ecuador Readies Export Boost." *Journal of Commerce*, March 15.

Halperin, Morton H. and Mirna Galic, eds. 2004. *Protecting Democracy: International Responses*. Lanham: Lexington Books.

Handley, Paul. 1998. "Can Indonesia Survive Soeharto?" *Institutional Investor* 32 (2): p. 73.

Harper, T.N. 1997. "'Asian Values' and Southeast Asian Histories [Review Article]." *Historical Journal* 40 (2): p. 507.

Hashim, Ahmed. 2001. "The World According to Usama Bin Laden." *Naval War College Review* LIV (4): pp. 11–35.

_____. 2002. "Al-Qaeda's Origins, Structure, Goals, Grand Strategy, and Operational Art." Presentation in Washington, DC, March 28.

Hegre, Havard, Tanja Ellingsen, Scott Gates, and Nils Petter Gleditsch. 2001. "Toward a Democratic Civil Peace? Democracy, Political Change, and Civil War, 1816–1992." *American Political Science Review* 95 (1): pp. 33–48.

Helliwell, John. 1994. "Empirical Linkages between Democracy and Economic Growth." *British Journal of Political Science* 24: pp. 225–248.

Hellman, Joel, Geraint Jones, and Daniel Kaufmann. 2000. "Seize the State, Seize the Day: State Capture, Corruption, and Influence in Transition." The World Bank Policy Research Working Paper No. 2444.

Herman, Robert and Theodore Piccone (eds). 2002. *Defending Democracy: A Global Survey of Foreign Policy Trends 1992–2002*. Washington, DC: Democracy Coalition Project.

Hewko, John. 2002. "Foreign Direct Investment: Does the Rule of Law Matter?" Carnegie Endowment for International Peace, Rule of Law Series, Working Paper No. 26.

Hirschman, Albert O. 1984. "A Dissenter's Confession: 'The Strategy of Economic Development' Revisited." *Pioneers in Development*. Edited by Gerald Meier and Dudley Seers. Oxford: Oxford Unifersity Press.

Holman, Michael and William Wallis. 1999. "Nigerian President Relents on Close IMF Supervision." *Financial Times*, October 16.

Hu, Baiding and Michael AcAleer. 2003. "Input-Output Structure and Growth in China." CIRJE-F-209 Discussion Paper, University of Western Australia.

Huntington, Samuel. 1968. *Political Order in Changing Societies*. New Haven, CT: Yale University Press.

_____. 1991. *The Third Wave: Democratization in the Late Twentieth Century*. Norman: University of Oklahoma Press.

Huntington, Samuel and Joan Nelson. 1976. *No Easy Choice: Political Participation in Developing Countries*. Cambridge: Harvard University Press.

Hussain, Irfan. 2000. "Intolerable Intolerance." *Dawn*, October 21, 2000 in Malik 2001.

Ibrahim, Saad Eddin. 1987. "Egypt's Islamic Militants." *Arab Society: Social Science Perspectives*. Edited by N. Hopkins and Saad Eddin Ibrahim. Cairo: The American University in Cairo Press.

Ibrahim, Youssef. 2002. "The Mideast Threat That's Hard to Define." *The Washington Post*, August 11.

Inkeles, Alex and Larry Sirowy. 1991. "The Effects of Democracy on Economic Growth and Inequality: A Review." *On Measuring Democracy: Its Consequences and Concomitants*. Edited by Alex Inkeles. New Brunswick, NJ: Transaction Publishers.

Imperato, Pascal James. 1989. *Mali: A Search for Direction*. Boulder, CO: Westview Press.

Institute of Economics, Moscow and the Center for the Study of International Economic Relations. 1998. "The Problem of Capital Flight from Russia." Final report from project undertaken by the University of Western Ontario, Canada, September 10.

Inter-American Dialogue. 2003. "The Troubled Americas." Inter-American Dialogue Policy Report 2003, Sol M. Linowitz Forum, (February 2003).

International Center for Not-for-Profit Law. 1997. "Handbook on Good Practices for Laws Relating to Non-Governmental Organizations." Discussion Draft prepared for the World Bank.

_____. 1998. "The Tax Treatment of Nongovernmental Organizations: A Survey of Best Practices from Around the World." Working Paper.

_____. 2000. "Tax Preferences for Nongovernmental Organizations." *International Journal of Not-for-Profit Law* 3 (3); International Center for Not-for-Profit Law. 2002. *Survey of Tax Laws Affecting Non-Governmental Organizations in Central and Eastern Europe*. Washington, DC: International Center for Not-for-Profit-Law.

International Monetary Fund. 1995. IMF Press Release No. 96/22, "IMF Approves Three-Year Loan for Mali Under the ESAF," April 12.

_____. 1999. IMF Press Release No. 9964, "Ecuador Signs Letter of Intent with IMF," September 30.

_____. 2000a. IMF Press Release No. 00/14, "IMF, World Bank, IDB, and CAF Prepared to Support Ecuador," March 9.

_____. 2000b. IMF Press Release No. 00/47, "IMF Approves Stand-By Credit for Nigeria," August 4.

_____. 2001. "Social Impact Analysis of Economic Policies: A Factsheet." International Monetary Fund, August.

_____. 2002. *World Economic Outlook: Trade and Finance* (September 2002). Washington, DC: International Monetary Fund.

Isham, Jonathan, Daniel Kaufmann, and Lant Pritchett. 1997. "Civil Liberties, Democracy, and the Performance of Government Projects." *The World Bank Economic Review* 11 (2): pp. 219–242.

Jaggers, Keith and Ted Robert Gurr. 1995. "Tracking Democracy's Third Wave with the Polity III Data." *Journal of Peace Research* 32 (4): pp. 469–483.

Jefferson, Gary, Thomas Rawski, Wang Li, and Zheng Yuxin. 2000. "Ownership, Productivity Change, and Financial Performance in Chinese Industry." *Journal of Comparative Economics* 28 (4).

Jilani, Amina, 1999. "On the Low Road." *Dawn Magazine*, October.

Jones, David Martin. 2003. "Out of Bali: Cybercaliphate Rising." *The National Interest*, Spring 2003 (71): pp. 75–86.

Kalinovsky, Valery. "Socialist-style Belarus in Worsening Economic Straits." *Agence France Presse*, February 16.

Kaminsky, Graciela and Carmen Reinhart. 2000. "On Crises, Contagion, and Confusion." *Journal of International Economics*, Supplement Vol. 51 (1): pp. 145–169.

Kaplan, Robert. 1994. "The Coming Anarchy." *The Atlantic Monthly* 273 (2): pp.44–76.

_____. 1997. "Was Democracy Just for a Moment?." *The Atlantic Monthly* 280 (6): pp. 55–80.

_____. 2001. "Looking the World in the Eye." *The Atlantic Monthly* 288 (5): pp.68–82.

Kaufmann, Daniel, Aart Kraay, and Pablo Zoido-Lobaton. 1999. "Governance Matters." Washington, DC: The World Bank.

_____. 2002. "Governance Matters, II: Updated Indicators for 2000–01." The World Bank Washington, DC

Kaufmann, Daniel and Aart Kraay. 2002. "Governance Indicators, Aid Allocation, and the Millennium Challenge Account." Draft Paper (December), World Bank.

Kaufmann, Daniel, Aart Kraay, and Massimo Mastruzzi. 2003. "Governance Matters III: Governance Indicators for 1996–2002.

Keefer, Phillip and Stephen Knack. 1997. "Why Don't Poor Countries Catch Up?: A Cross-National Test of an Institutional Explanation." *Economic Inquiry* 35: pp. 590–602.

Kendall, Sue. 1999. "World Bank Hosts Aid Meeting for Nigeria." *Agence France Presse*, April 9.

Kingstone, Heidi. 2003. "Trouble in the House of Saud." *The Jerusalem Report*, January 13.

Khan, Akhter Hammed. 1985. *Rural Development in Pakistan*. Lahore: Vanguard Books.

Knack, Stephen and Phillip Keefer. 1995. "Institutions and Economic Performance: Cross-Country Tests Using Alternative Institutional Measures." *Economics and Politics* Vol. 7 (November): pp. 207–227.

Kohli, Atul. 1990. *Democracy and Discontent: India's Growing Crisis of Governability*. Cambridge: Cambridge University Press.

Komolafe, Funmi. 2002. "Labor: Let's Create Wealth, Not Manage Poverty—Oshiomhole." *Vanguard*, December 5.

Koo, Anthony. 1970. *The Role of Land Reform in Economic Development: A Case Study of Taiwan.*

Kornai, Janus. 1979. "Resource-Constrained Versus Demand-Constrained Systems." *Econometrica* 47 (4): pp. 801–820.

Kremer, Michael and Seema Jayachandran. 2002. "Odious Debt." National Bureau of Economic Research Working Paper No. W8953. Cambridge: National Bureau of Economic Research.

Krueger, Anne. 1998. "Whither the World Bank and the IMF?." *Journal of Economic Literature* 36 (4): pp. 1983–2021.

Krugman, Paul. 1994. "The Myth of East Asia's Miracle." *Foreign Affairs* 73 (6): pp. 62–78.

Lagos, Marta. 2003. "A Road with No Return?" *Journal of Democracy* 14 (2): pp. 163–173.

La Palombara, Joseph. 1963. *Bureaucracy and Political Development*. Princeton, NJ: Princeton University Press.

Lanyi, Anthony and Young Lee. 2003. "The Role of Governance Failures in the East Asian Financial Crisis." *Market-Augmenting Government: The Institutional Foundations for Prosperity*. Edited by Omar Azfar and Charles A. Cadwell. 2003 Ann Arbor: University of Michigan Press.

Lanyi, Anthony (ed). 2004. *The Corruption Nexus and The People's Republic of China: Current Thinking on Causes and Consequences.* College Park, MD: the Center for Institutional reform and the Informal Sector at the University of Maryland.

Larson, Adam. 2002. "Democratic Influences on Structural Adjustment in Mali." Rice University.

Layne, Christopher. 1994. "Kant or Cant: The Myth of the Democratic Peace." *International Security* 19 (2): pp. 5–49.

Lerner, David. 1958. *The Passing of Traditional Society.* Glencoe, Illinois: The Free Press.

Lipset, Seymour Martin. 1959. "Some Social Requisites of Democracy: Economic Development and Political Legitimacy." *The American Political Science Review* 53 (3): pp. 69–105.

_____. 1960. *Political Man: The Social Bases of Politics.* Garden City: Doubleday.

Lozada, Carlos. 2003. "Is Latin America Running Out of Chances." *Foreign Policy* March/April 2003 (135): pp. 18–28.

Lucero, Jose Antonio. 2001. "Crisis and Contention in Ecuador." *Journal of Democracy* 12 (2): pp. 53–73.

Maass, Peter. "Yeltsin Suspends Top Court." *The Washington Post*, October 8.

Mahatir, Mohammad and Ishihara Shintaro. 1995. *The Asia That Can Say No.* New York: Kondansha International.

Mahbubani, Kishore. 1992. "The Dangers of Decadence: What the Rest Can Teach the West." *Foreign Affairs* 72 (4): pp. 10–14.

Mallaby, Sebastian. 2004. *The World's Banker.* New York: Penguin.

Malik, Iftikhar. 2001. "Military Coup in Pakistan: Business as Usual or Democracy on Hold!" *The Round Table* 360: pp. 357–377.

Mansfield, Edward and Jack Snyder. 1995. "Democratization and the Danger of War." *International Security* 20 (1): pp. 5–38.

Marquette, Heather. 2000. "Corruption, Democracy and the World Bank." Paper for the Political Studies Association-UK 50th Annual Conference, London. April 10–13, 2000.

Marshall, Monty and Keith Jaggers. 2000. "Polity IV Project: Codebook." Center for International Development and Conflict Management, University of Maryland, College Park.

Marshall, Monty. 2000. "Authority, Opportunity, and Outbreaks of Violent Societal Conflicts 1955–1999." Center for International Development and Conflict Management, University of Maryland, College Park.

_____. 2002. "Measuring the Societal Impact of War." *From Reaction to Conflict Prevention: Opportunities for the UN System.* Edited by Fen Osler Hampson and David Malone. Boulder, CO: Lynne Rienner Publishers.

Mellor, John and Sarah Gavian. 1987. "Famine: Causes, Prevention, and Relief." *Science* 235 (4788): pp. 539–545.

Meltzer Commission Report. 2000. Report of the International Financial Institution Advisory Commission (The Meltzer Commission), to the U.S. Congress, March.

Milanovic, Branko. 1999. "Explaining the Increase in Inequality during the Transition." *Economics of Transition* 7 (2): pp. 299–341.

Milner, Mark. 1999. "The Master Rebuilder." *The Guardian*, November 6.

Minassian, Garabed. 2001. "Bulgaria and the International Monetary Fund." *Russian and East European Finance & Trade* 37 (2): pp. 7–35.

Murrell, Peter. 1997. "Missed Policy Opportunities during Mongolian Privatization: Should Aid Target Policy Research Institutions?." *Institutions and Economic Development: Growth and Governance in Less-Developed and Post-Socialist Countries.* Edited by Christopher Clague. 1997. Baltimore, MD: John Hopkins University Press.

Nam, Tae Yul. 1970. "Singapore's One-Party System: Its Relationship to Democracy and Political Stability." *Pacific Affairs* 42 (4): pp. 465–480.

Narayan, Deepa. 1997. "Focus on People's Participation: Evidence from 121 Rural Water Projects." *Institutions and Economic Development: Growth and Governance in Less-Developed and Post-Socialist Countries.* Edited by Christopher Clague. Baltimore, MD: John Hopkins University Press.

Navia, Patricio and Thomas Zweifel. "Democracy, Dictatorship, and Infant Mortality Revisited." *Journal of Democracy,* 14 (3): pp. 90–103.

Nazir, Javed. 2003. "Religious Parties Imperil Pakistan." *The Detroit News*, January 28.

Newburg, Andre. 1995. "The EBRD: A New-Age Financial Institution." *Butterworths Journal of International Banking and Financial Law* 10 (6): pp. 251–252.

Newport, Samantha. 2000. "Did the IMF Drop the Ball in Ecuador?" *Businessweek Online* (International Edition), January 24.

Newsome, Justine. 1998. "Ecuador Relaunches Telecoms Sell-Off." August 14.

_____. 1999. "Investors Still Jittery over Ecuador's Continuing Economic Crisis." *Financial Times*, January 6, 1999.

North, Douglass. 1990. *Institutions, Institutional Change, and Economic Performance.* Cambridge: Cambridge University Press.

O'Donnell, Guillermo. 1973. *Modernization and Bureaucratic-Authoritarianism: Studies in South American Politics.* Berkeley: Institute of International Studies, University of California.

_____. 2000. *Power and Prosperity: Outgrowing Communist and Capitalist Dictatorships.* New York: Basic Books.

Olson, Mancur. 1993. "Dictatorship, Democracy, and Development." *American Political Science Review* 87 (3): pp. 567–576.

_____. 1997. "The New Institutional Economics: The Collective Choice Approach to Economic Development." *Institutions and Economic Development: Growth and Governance in Less-Developed and Post-Socialist Countries.* Edited by Christopher Clague. 1997. Baltimore, MD: Johns Hopkins University.

_____. 2000. *Power and Prosperity: Outgrowing Communist and Capitalist Dictatorships.* New York: Basic Books.

Olson, Mancur, Naveen Sarna, and Anand Swamy. 1998. "Governance and Growth: A Simply Hypothesis Explaining Cross-Country Differences in Productivity Growth." Institutional Reform and the Informal Sector Working Paper No. 218, University of Maryland, College Park.

Oneal, John and Bruce Russett. 1997. "The Classic Liberals Were Right: Democracy, Interdependence, and Conflict, 1950–1985." *International Studies Quarterly* 41 (2): pp.267–94.

_____. 2001. *Triangulating Peace: Democracy, Interdependence, and International Organizations.* Chapter 4, WW Norton & Co., January.

Organisation for Economic Cooperation and Development. 1996. "Shaping the 21st Century: Contribution of Development Co-operation." Development Assistance Committee, Paris.

_____. 2002. "Geographic Distribution of Financial Flows to Aid Recipients: 1996–2000." Organization for Economic Cooperation and Development.

Ottaway, Marina. 2002. *Democracy Challenged: The Rise of Semi-Authoritarianism.* Washington, DC: Carnegie Endowment for International Peace.

Owens, Edgar. 1987. *The Future of Freedom in the Developing World: Economic Development As Political Reform.* New York: Pergamon Press.

Owens, Edgar and Robert Shaw. 1972. *Development Reconsidered: Bridging the Gap Between Government and People.* Lexington, Mass: DC Heath and Company.

Owen, John. 1994. "How Liberalism Produces Democratic Peace." *International Security* 19 (2): pp. 87–125.

Oxford Analytica. 2002a. "Saudi Arabia." *Oxford Analytica*, Daily Brief, August 9.

_____. 2002b. "China: Growth Potential." *Oxford Analytica*, Daily Brief, October 10.

Palley, Thomas. 2003a. "The Millennium Challenge Account: Elevating the Significance of Democracy as a Qualifying Criterion." Discussion Paper. Open Society Institute.

_____. 2003b. "Linking the Community of Democracies with the Millennium Challenge Account: A Case of Win-Win." Open Society Institute discussion paper.

Palmer, Mark. 2003. *Breaking the Real Axis of Evil: How to Oust the World's Last Dictators by 2025.* Lanham, MD: Rowman & Littlefield Publishers, Inc.

Patino, Maria Laura. 2001. "Lessons from the Financial Crisis in Ecuador in 1999." *Journal of International Banking Regulation* 3 (1): pp. 589–624.

Pei, Minxin. 1995. "The Puzzle of East Asian Exceptionalism." *Economic Reform and Democracy.* Edited by Larry Diamond and Marc Plattner. 1995. Baltimore, MD: The Johns Hopkins University Press.

_____. 1998. "Is China Democratizing?" *Foreign Affairs* 77 (1): pp. 68–82.

_____. 2002a. "Beijing Drama: China's Governance Crisis and Bush's New Challenge." Carnegie Endowment for International Peace, Policy Brief No. 21.

_____. 2002b. "China's Governance Crisis." *Foreign Affairs* 81 (5): pp. 96–109.

Pei, Minxin and Merrit Lyon. 2002. "Bullish on New Democracies: Research Notes on Multinationals and the Third Wave." The National Interest, No. 70 (Winter 2002/2003): pp. 79–87.

Political Risk Services. 2002. International Country Risk Guide, annual ratings 1982–2002.

Press, Robert. 1994. "Economic Woes Shake Mali's Democracy." *Christian Science Monitor*, March 14.

Przeworski, Adam and Fernando Limongi. 1993. "Political Regimes and Economic Growth." *Journal of Economic Perceptions* 7 (3): p. 51.

Przeworski, Adam, Michael Alvarez, Jose Antonia Cheibub, and Fermando Limongi. 1996. "What Makes Democracies Endure?." *Journal of Democracy* 7: pp. 39–55.

_____. 2000. *Democracy and Development: Political Institutions and Well-Being in the World, 1950–1990.* Cambridge: Cambridge University Press.

Putnam, Robert. 1993. *Making Democracy Work: Civic Traditions in Modern Italy.* Princeton: Princeton University Press.

Quibria, M.G. 2002. "Growth and Poverty: Lessons from the East Asian Miracle Revisited." Asian Development Bank, Working Paper No. 33.

Quinn, Dennis P. and John T. Woolley. 2001. "Democracy and National Economic Performance: The Preference for Stability." *American Journal of Political Science* Vol. 45 (3): pp. 634–657.

Radelet, Steven. 2003. *Challenging Foreign Aid: A Policymaker's Guide to the Millennium Challenge Account.* Washington, DC: Center for Global Development.

_____. 2002. "Qualifying for the Millennium Challenge Account (draft)," December 13, 2002, Washington, DC: Center for Global Development.

Reinhart, Carmen M. 1999. "Capital Flows and Contagion: Causes, Consequences, and Policy Responses." A presentation before International Monetary Fund. School of Public Affairs, University of Maryland. March. www.puaf.umd.edu/courses/econ741/kflow.pdf.

Reiter, Dan and Allan Stam. 1998. "Democracy, War Initiation, and Victory." *The American Political Science Review* 92 (2): pp. 377–391.

_____. 2002. *Democracies at War.* Princeton, NJ: Princeton University Press.

Richmond, Roaldus, ed. "A Yankee Businessman in New Hampshire." *American Life Histories: Manuscripts from the Federal Writers' Project, 1936–1940.* Washington, DC: Library of Congress' American Memory Collection.

Robinson, Anthony. 1993. "Survey of Bulgaria." *Financial Times*, May 5.

Rodrik, Dani. 1999. "Institutions for High-Quality Growth: What They Are and How to Acquire Them." Paper prepared for the International Monetary Fund Conference on Second-Generation Reforms, Washington, DC. November 8–9.

Root, Hilton L. and Nahalel Nellis. 2000. "The Compulsion of Patronage: Political Sources of Information Asymmetry and Risk in Developing Country Economies." *Governing for Prosperity.* Edited by Bruce Bueno de Mesquita and Hilton L. Root. New Haven, CT: Yale University Press.

Rostow, Walt Whitman. 1984. "Development: The Political Economy of the Marshallian Long Period." *Pioneers in Development.* Edited by Gerald Meier and Dudley Seers. Oxford: Oxford University Press.

Rousseau, David. 2001. "Democratization and International Conflict." In *Domestic Institutions, International Norms, and the Evolution of International Conflict.* (Draft).

Rousseau, David, Christopher Gelpi, Dan Reiter, Paul Huth. 1996. "Assessing the Dyadic Nature of the Democratic Peace 1918–1988." *The American Political Science Review* 90 (3): pp. 512–534.

Rugh, William. 2002. "Arab Education: Tradition, Growth, and Reform." *Middle East Journal* 56 (3): pp. 379–395.

Saavedra, Luis and Barbara Fraser. 1998. "Solidarity Voucher Called A Ploy to Exclude the Poor." *National Catholic Reporter,* December 25.

Sancisi, Juan Salazar. 1999. "Ecuador Undergoes Big Change for Sustainable Growth." *Mainichi Daily News,* August 10, 1999.

Sanger, David. 1999. "World Bank Beats Breast for Failures in Indonesia." *New York Times*, February 11.

Schumpeter, Joseph. 1976 (5th Edition). *Capitalism, Socialism, and Democracy.* London: George Allen & Unwin Ltd.

Schwarz, Adam. 2000. *A Nation in Waiting: Indonesia's Search for Stability.* Boulder, CO: Westview Press.

Scott, James. 1998. *Seeing Like A State: How Certain Schemes to Improve the Human Condition Have Failed.* New Haven: Yale University Press.

Seeley, Jennifer. 2001. "A Political Analysis of Decentralization: Co-opting the Tuareg Threat in Mali." *Journal of Modern African Studies* 39 (3): pp. 499–525.

Sen, Amartya. 1989. "Food and Freedom." *World Development* 17 (6): pp. 769–781.

_____. 1997. "Human Rights and Asian Values." *The New Republic* (July 14, 1997): pp. 33–40.

Shapiro, Isaac. 2000. "Trends in U.S. Development Aid and the Current Budget Debate." Paper by the Center on Budget and Policy Priorities, May 9.

Shihata, Ibrahim. 1991a. *The World Bank in a Changing World* Volume I (1991). Based on a legal memorandum issued by the author on December 21.

_____. 1991b. "The World Bank and Governance Issues in its Borrowing Members." Chapter 2. *The World Bank in a Changing World: Selected Essays*, Volume I. Dordrecht, The Netherlands: Martinus Nijhoff Publishers.

_____. 1997. *Complementary Reform: Essays on Legal, Judicial and Other Institutional Reforms Supported by the World Bank.* Boston: Kluwer Law International.

Shuster, Mike. 2004. "Wahhabism is on the Decline in Saudi Arabia." *All Things Considered, National Public Radio,* March 18.

Siegle, Joseph. 2001. *Democratization and Economic Growth: The Contribution of Accountability Institutions,* Ph.D. dissertation for the School of Public Affairs, University of Maryland, College Park.

Smith, Elliot Blair. 1999. "Ecuador's Finances Unravel the Plan: Raise Taxes, Slash Outlays." *USA Today,* February 4.

Smith, Zeric Kay. 2001. "Mali's Decade of Democracy." *Journal of Democracy* 12 (3): pp. 73–79.

Snyder, Jack. 2000. *From Voting to Violence: Democratization and Nationalist Conflict.* New York: WW Norton & Company.

Sørensen, Georg. 1998. *Democracy and Democratization.* 2nd ed. Boulder, CO: Westview Press.

Sosnowski Saul and Roxana Patino (eds).1999. *Una Cultura para la Democracia en America Latina.* Mexico City: Fondo de Cultura Economica.

Starr, Harvey. 1991. "Democratic Dominoes: Diffusion Approaches to the Spread of Democracy in the International System." *The Journal of Conflict Resolution* 35 (2): p. 356.

Staub, Ervin. 2003. "Notes on Cultures of Violence, Cultures of Caring and Peace, and the Fulfillment of Basic Needs." *Political Psychology* 24 (1): pp. 1–21.

Stephen, Chris. 1991. "Bulgarians Savour Aroma of Victory: In a Sofia Coffee Shop, Chris Stephen finds Democrats Ready to Suffer for a Free Market." *The Guardian,* October 18.

Stiglitz, Joseph. 2000. "The Insider: What I Learned At the World Economic Crisis." *The New Republic,* April 17.

_____. 2002. *Globalization and Its Discontents.* New York: WW Norton & Company.

Tang, Kwong-leung. 1999. "Social Development in China: Progress and Problems." *Journal of Contemporary Asia* 29 (1): pp. 95–108.

This Day. 2002. "Sh!! . . . The Bank is Talking." *This Day,* December 11.

_____. 2002. "Nigeria for the Record." *This Day,* October 18.

Thompson, William and Richard Tucker. 1997. "A Tale of Two Democratic Peace Critiques." *The Journal of Conflict Resolution* 41 (3): pp. 428–454.

United Nations Development Program. 2002a. *Arab Human Development Report 2002: Creating Opportunities for Future Generations.* New York: United Nations Publications.

_____. 2002b. Human Development Report, 2002. New York: Oxford University Press.

United Nations AIDS. 2002. *Report on the Global HIV/AIDS Epidemic.* Geneva: UNAIDS.

U.S. Agency for International Development. 2001. "Remarks to Interaction Forum by USAID Administrator Andrew S. Natsios." Transcript of speech given June 5.

_____. 2002a. U.S. Overseas Loans and Grants and Assistance from International Organizations, Obligations and Loan Authorizations July1, 1945-September 30, 2000. (Statistical Annex I to the Annual Development Coordination Committee Report to Congress).

_____. 2002b. "Foreign Aid in the National Interest: Promoting Freedom, Security, and Opportunity." Washington, DC.

U.S. Committee for Refugees. 2003. *World Refugee Survey 2003: An Annual Assessment to Conditions Affecting Refugees, Asylum Seekers, and Internally Displaced Persons.* Washington, DC: U.S. Committee for Refugees (USCR), June.

U.S. Department of Defense Fiscal Year Series (as of September 30, 2000), published by Deputy for Financial Management Comptroller, D.O.D-Security Assistance Agency.

U.S. Department of State. 2001. "Background Note: Mali." U.S. Department of State, Africa Bureau, December.

van de Walle, Nicolas. 2003. "The International Community and the Poorest Economies." Paper prepared for the Center for Global Development.

Wagstyl, Stefan. 2001. "A Decade of Reform in Eastern Europe: The EBRD's problems are well documented but the Bank now has a valuable role" *Financial Times*, April 23.

Waldman, Peter and Jay Solomon. 1998. "Wasted Energy: How U.S. Companies and Soeharto's Circle Electrified Indonesia." *Wall Street Journal*, December 23.

Wallis, William. 2002a. "One Step Forward, Then One Step Back." *Financial Times*, April 9.

_____. 2002b. "I Know that We're Moving . . . That We're Improving: Interview with the President." *Financial Times*, April 9.

Watson, Peter. 2003. "The Fundamentalist Challenge." *International Herald Tribune*, May 1.

Weber, Steven. 1994. "Origins of the European Bank for Reconstruction and Development." *International Organizations* 48 (1): pp. 1–38.

Winters, Jeffrey. 1991. *Structural Power and Investor Mobility: Capital Control and State Policy in Indonesia, 1965–1990.* Doctoral Dissertation, Yale University, New Haven, CT.

_____. 1998. "World Bank Must Face the Corruption Music." *Jakarta Post*, September 23.

_____. 2002. "Some Comments on Soeharto's Wealth and Trying to Track It." *A Nation in Waiting: Indonesia's Search for Stability.* Edited by Adam Schwarz. Boulder, CO: Westview Press.

Wittman, Donald. 1989. "Why Democracies Produce Efficient Results." *Journal of Political Economy* 97 (6): pp. 1395–1424.

_____. 1995. *The Myth of Democratic Failure: Why Political Institutions are Efficient.* Chicago: University of Chicago Press.

World Bank. 1989. "Sub-Saharan Africa—From Crisis to Sustainable Growth: A Long Term Perspective Study." November.

_____. 1990. "Adjustment Policies for Sustainable Growth." *Policy and Research Series* 14 (1990).

_____. 1992. "Governance and Development." Washington, DC: World Bank.

_____. 1993a. *World Development Report 1993: Investing in Health.* New York: Oxford University Press, July.

_____. 1993b. *The East Asian Miracle: Economic Growth and Public Policy.* New York: Oxford University Press, December.

_____. 1997. *World Development Report 1997: The State in a Changing World.* New York: Oxford University Press, July.

_____. 1998a. "Addressing the Social Impact of the Crisis in Indonesia: A Background Note for the 1998 Consultative Group on Indonesia." July 29–30.

_____. 1998b. *World Development Report 1998/99: Knowledge for Development.* New York: Oxford University Press, October 1998.

_____. 1999a. "Indonesia, Country Assistance Strategy—Progress Report." The World Bank Group, Operations Evaluations Department, February 16.

_____. 1999b. "Memorandum to the Executive Directors and the President, Operations Evaluation Department, Indonesia: Country Assistance Note." The World Bank Group, March 29.

_____. 1999c. *World Development Report 1999/2000: Entering the 21st Century: The Changing Development Landscape.* New York: Oxford University Press, September.

_____. 2000a. "Bolivia: From Patronage to Professional State." Poverty Reduction and Economic Management, Latin America and the Caribbean Region, August 25.

_____. 2000b. *World Development Report 2000/2001: Attacking Poverty* New York: Oxford University Press, August.

_____. 2001. "Mali Qualifies for HIPC Debt Relief Totaling $870 Million." World Bank Press Release No. 2001/063/S.

_____. 2002a. "A User's Guide to Poverty and Social Impact Analysis," (Draft), World Bank Poverty Reduction Group (PRMPR) and Social Development Department (SDV), April 19.

_____. 2002b. "China 2020: Development Challenges in the New Century." Washington, DC: World Bank, September.

_____. 2002c. "Social Assessment: The Facts and Phases of Social Assessment." *Social Analysis Sourcebook*, Social Development Department, Working Draft v. 1.12, August 7.

_____. 2002d. *World Development Indicators, 2002*. Washington, D.C: World Bank.

_____. 2003a. "A User's Guide to Poverty and Social Impact Analysis." The World Bank Poverty Reduction Group (PRMPR) and Social Development Department (SDV), May 15.

_____. 2003b. *World Development Indicators 2003*. Washington, DC: World Bank.

_____. 2003c. "Social Assessment: The Facets and Phases of Social Assessment." Social Analysis Sourcebook, Social Analysis Thematic Group, Social Development Department.

World Health Organization. 1998. "Health Summary Measures: Russian Federation."

Woo, Wing Thye. 1999. "The Real Reasons for China's Growth." *The China Journal* 41: pp. 115–137.

Xinhua News Agency. 1999. "Indonesia's Capital Flight Reaches $32 Billion." October 30.

_____. 2002. "China: Major Improvements in Standard of Living in Past Five Years." February 27.

Young, Alwyn. 1994. "Lessons from the East Asian NICs: A Contrarian View." *European Economic Review* 38 (3/4): pp. 964–973.

_____. 2003. "Gold Into Base Metals: Productivity Growth in the People's Republic of China during the Reform Period." *Journal of Political Economy* 111 (6): pp. 1220–1260.

Zakaria, Fareed. 1997. "The Rise of Illiberal Democracy." *Foreign Affairs* 76 (6): pp. 22–43.

_____. 2003. *The Future of Freedom: Illiberal Democracy at Home and Abroad*. New York: WW Norton.

Zaman, Muhammad Qasim. 1998. "Sectarianism in Pakistan: The Radicalization of Shi'a and Sunni Identities." *Modern Asian Studies* 30 (3): pp. 689–716.

Zweifel, Thomas and Patricio Navia. 2000. "Democracy, Dictatorship, and Infant Mortality." *Journal of Democracy* 11(2): pp. 99–114.

Index

About the Authors

Morton H. Halperin is a Senior Vice President of the Center for American Progress. He is also the Director of the Open Society Policy Center. Dr. Halperin served in the Johnson and Nixon administrations, and in positions related to democracy promotion in the Clinton administration in the Defense and State Departments and the National Security Council, most recently as Director of the Policy Planning Staff at the Department of State (1998 to 2001). He taught at Harvard (1960 to 1966) and as a visitor at other universities including Columbia, George Washington, and Yale. He has been affiliated with a number of other think tanks including the Council on Foreign Relations, Carnegie Endowment for International Peace, the Century Foundation and the Brookings Institution. He is the author of numerous books and articles including *Bureaucratic Politics and Foreign Policy* and "Guaranteeing Democracy."

Joseph T. Siegle is an Associate Director at the Center for Institutional Reform and the Informal Sector (IRIS) at the University of Maryland. He researches and provides advisory guidance to countries undertaking political and economic reform. His current focus is on vital role a free press plays to economic development — and processes by which independent media can be established in previously closed societies. Research for this book was conducted while he was the Douglas Dillon Fellow at the Council on Foreign Relations. Prior to joining the Council, Dr. Siegle worked for 12 years on various development and humanitarian assistance programs in some 20 countries in Africa, Asia, and the Balkans. He was the country director for the international nongovernmental organization (NGO), World Vision, in Eritrea and a Peace Corps Volunteer in Liberia. He earned his Ph.D. from the University of Maryland's School of Public Policy, with a concentration in International Security and Economic Policy.

Michael M. Weinstein is Director of Programs for the Robin Hood Foundation. He holds a Ph.D. in economics from Massachusetts Institute of Technology (MIT) and served as chairman of the Department of Economics at Haverford College during the 1980s. He provided economics analysis and commentaries for National Public Radio before joining *The New York Times*, where he served on the editorial board and as the Times' economics columnist during the 1990s. In 2001, he became the first director of the Maurice R. Greenberg Center for Geoeconomic Studies at the Council on Foreign Relations, also holding the Paul A. Volcker Chair in international economics at the Council. Weinstein directs the Institutes for Journalists at the New York Times Company Foundation and is president and founder of WAD Financial Counseling, Inc., a nonprofit foundation that provides free financial counseling to poor families. He is editor of *Globalization: What's New* (Columbia University Press and the Council on Foreign Relations, forthcoming), author of *Recovery and Redistribution Under the N.I.R.A.* (Amsterdam, North Holland, 1980), journal articles, and about 1,500 columns, editorials, news analysis articles, and magazine pieces for *The New York Times* about welfare, inequality, poverty, health care, energy, social security, tax, budget, trade, environment, regulation, antitrust, telecommunications, education, banking, and many other public policy issues.